Introduction to Java Programming
(2nd Edition)

CADCIM Technologies
525 St. Andrews Drive
Schererville, IN 46375, USA
(www.cadcim.com)

Contributing Author
Prof. Sham Tickoo
Purdue University Northwest
Department of Mechanical Engineering Technology
Hammond, Indiana
USA

CADCIM Technologies

Introduction to Java Programming, 2ⁿᵈ Edition
Sham Tickoo

CADCIM Technologies
525 St Andrews Drive
Schererville, Indiana 46375, USA
www.cadcim.com

ISBN 9781-942689-85-0

NOTICE TO THE READER

DEDICATION

To teachers, who make it possible to disseminate knowledge
to enlighten the young and curious minds
of our future generations

To students, who are dedicated to learning new technologies
and making the world a better place to live in

THANKS

To employees of CADCIM Technologies for their valuable help

Online Training Program Offered by CADCIM Technologies

CADCIM Technologies provides effective and affordable virtual online training on various software packages including Computer Aided Design and Manufacturing and Engineering (CAD/CAM/CAE), computer programming languages, animation, architecture, and GIS. The training is delivered 'live' via Internet at any time, any place, and at any pace to individuals as well as the students of colleges, universities, and CAD/CAM/CAE training centers. The main features of this program are:

Training for Students and Companies in a Classroom Setting

Highly experienced instructors and qualified Engineers at CADCIM Technologies conduct the classes under the guidance of Prof. Sham Tickoo of Purdue University Northwest, USA. This team has authored several textbooks that are rated "one of the best" in their categories and are used in various colleges, universities, and training centers in North America, Europe, and in other parts of the world.

Training for Individuals

CADCIM Technologies with its cost effective and time saving initiative strives to deliver the training in the comfort of your home or work place, thereby relieving you from the hassles of traveling to training centers.

Training Offered on Software Packages

CADCIM Technologies provides basic and advanced training on the following software packages:

CAD/CAM/CAE: *CATIA, Pro/ENGINEER Wildfire, Creo Parametric, Creo Direct, SOLIDWORKS, Autodesk Inventor, Solid Edge, NX, AutoCAD, AutoCAD LT, AutoCAD Plant 3D, Customizing AutoCAD, SolidCAM, NX CAM, NX Mold, Creo Mold, Alias Design, Alias Automotive, Ansys Fluent and ANSYS*

Architecture and GIS: *Autodesk Revit (Architecture, Structure, MEP), AutoCAD Civil 3D, AutoCAD Map 3D, Navisworks, Primavera, Bentley STAAD Pro, MS Project, MX Road, ArcGIS, and Raster Design*

Animation and VFX: *Autodesk 3ds Max, Autodesk Maya, Blackmagic Design Fusion Studio, Adobe Premiere, Adobe Photoshop, Adobe Indesign, Adobe Illustrator, The Foundry NukeX, and MAXON CINEMA 4D*

Web & Programming: *C/C++, HTML5/CSS3, JavaScript, jQuery, Bootstrap, PHP, MySQL, Dreamweaver, VB.NET, Oracle, AJAX, and Java*

*For more information, please visit the following link: **www.cadcim.com***

Note
If you are a faculty member, you can register by clicking on the following link to access the teaching resources: ***www.cadcim.com/Registration.aspx***. The student resources are available at ***//www.cadcim.com***. We also provide **Live Virtual Online Training** on various software packages. For more information, write us at ***sales@cadcim.com***.

Table of Contents

Chapter 2: Fundamental Elements of Java

Chapter 3: Control Statements and Arrays

Chapter 4: Classes and Objects

Chapter 5: Inheritance

Chapter 6: Packages, Interfaces, and Inner Classes

Chapter 7: Exception Handling

Chapter 8: Multithreading

Chapter 9: String Handling

Chapter 10: Introduction to Applet and Event Handling

This page intentionally left blank

Preface

Java

Java is an object oriented, platform-independent, multithreaded programming language developed by Sun Microsystems. The basic concept of Java was taken from C and C++. The language provides choice, efficiency, and flexibility to the users. While providing the traditional ease-of-use, Java also allows optional use of new language features such as platform-independency, security, multithreading, and so on. Above all, it is portable and can run on any operating system. All these features make Java a powerful tool for learning object oriented programming.

Introduction to Java Programming is an example based textbook, written to cater the needs of beginners and intermediate users who wish to understand the basic concepts of Java. The textbook highlights Java as the easiest and most productive tool for creating programs, including Windows-based and Web-based programs.

The highlight of the textbook is that each concept introduced in it has been exemplified by a program to clarify and facilitate better understanding. Also, the line-by-line explanation of each program ensures that the users with no previous programming experience are able to understand the concepts and master the programming techniques and use them with flexibility while designing programs.

The main features of this textbook are as follows:

Programming Approach: This textbook introduces the key ideas of object oriented programming in an intuitive way. The concepts are illustrated through best programming examples.

Notes: Additional information is provided to the users in the form of notes.

Illustrations: There is an extensive use of examples, schematic representations, flowcharts, tables, screen capture images, and programming exercises.

Learning Objectives: The first page of every chapter summarizes the topics that are covered in it.

Self-Evaluation Test, Review Questions, and Exercises: Each chapter ends with Self-Evaluation Test so that the users can assess their knowledge. The answers of Self-Evaluation Test are given at the end of the chapter. Also, the Review Questions and Exercises are given at the end of each chapter that can be used by the instructor as test questions and exercises.

Free Companion Website

It has been our constant endeavor to provide you the best textbooks and services at affordable price. In this endeavor, we have come up with a Free Companion Website that will facilitate the process of teaching and learning of Java. If you purchase this textbook, you will get access to the files on the Companion website. The following resources are available for faculty and students in this website:

Faculty Resources

- **Technical Support**

  You can get online technical support by contacting *techsupport@cadcim.com*.

- **Instructor Guide**

  Solutions to all the review questions and exercises in the textbook are provided to help the faculty members test the skills of the students.

- **Example Files**

  The Java files used in examples are available for free download.

Student Resources

- **Technical Support**

  You can get online technical support by contacting *techsupport@cadcim.com*.

- **Example Files**

  The Java files used in examples are available for free download.

If you face any problem in accessing these files, please contact the publisher at ***sales@cadcim.com*** or the author at ***stickoo@pnw.edu*** or ***tickoo525@gmail.com***.

Stay Connected

You can now stay connected with us through Facebook and Twitter to get the latest information about our textbooks, videos, and teaching/learning resources. To stay informed of such updates, follow us on Facebook *(www.facebook.com/cadcim)* and Twitter *(@cadcimtech)*. You can also subscribe to our YouTube channel *(www.youtube.com/cadcimtech)* to get the information about our latest video tutorials.

Chapter 1

Introduction to Java

Learning Objectives

After completing this chapter, you will be able to:

* *Understand history, evolution, and features of Java*
* *Understand the concept of OOPS*
* *Understand Java complier and interpreter*
* *Install Java development kit*
* *Write, compile, set the path, and run your first Java program*
* *Install NetBeans IDE*
* *Write, build, and run Java program in NetBeans IDE*

INTRODUCTION

This chapter introduces you to Java programming language and allows you to write your first program in Java. In this chapter, you will get a brief idea about history, evolution, and features of the language. Also, you will learn how to install Java and Net Beans IDE (Integrated Development Environment) on your system and run Java programs. Moreover, you will gain knowledge about the concept of object oriented programming as well as its importance in developing Java programs.

 Note

1. An Integrated Development Environment (IDE) is a software application that provides comprehensive features to computer programmers for software development. It generally consists of a source code editor, build automation tools, and a debugger.

2. The examples in this book are tested on Windows platform which is itself written in Java.

HISTORY AND EVOLUTION OF JAVA

The first version of Java was developed by James Gosling at Sun Microsystems (which has since been acquired by Oracle Corporation) in USA, in the year 1991. Initially, it was named as Oak by James Gosling, but later in 1995, it was renamed to Java. The first version of the application was developed for the use of electronic devices and circuits, and the plan got successful. Later on, it was called the Green project that led to the invention of Java.

Apart from its general purpose use, it is considered as a leading web-based technology. When it was invented, nobody knew how popular it would be. It is the first object oriented programming language that is platform independent and can run on any platform. It allows the developers to follow "Write Once, Run Anywhere" (WORA) concept. Though the base syntax of Java has been taken from C and C++, still it is quite different from C or C++.

There are four primary version of Java available:

- Java Standard Edition (Java SE)
- Java Enterprise Edition (Java EE)
- Java Micro Edition (Java ME)
- JavaFX

The Java based applications used for computer software are developed on the Standard Edition of Java. Java based applications used for web servers are developed using the Enterprise Edition of Java. Applications for the multimedia platform are developed using JavaFX and the applications for mobile devices are developed on the Micro Edition of Java.

You can create two types of programs using the Java programming language: **applets** and **applications**. **Applets** are smaller pieces of programming codes intended for use on the web browsers. They are lighter applications, generally used to provide navigation enhancement or additional interactivity to the browser.

The other type of software you can create using Java is a **console application**. These applications are standalone programs meant to be run on your computer like any other program. IDEs like NetBeans comes with integrated console environment that you can use to run your Java programs.

Note

Unlike standalone applications, Java applets do not need any interpreter in order to execute.

FEATURES OF JAVA

Java became popular due to its advance features such as platform independency, simplicity, security, and so on. Some of the major features of Java are explained next.

Platform Independency

As you are already aware that Java is a platform independent language, implying that it can run on any operating system. For example, a Java application written on the Windows platform can run on Linux, Machintosh, and any other operating system. When Java runs on a system, it converts the source code into the byte code. This byte code is generated by Java compiler with the help of JVM(Java Virtual Machine) and can work independently on any system. You will learn more about JVM later in this chapter. Due to its portability, an application created in Java on one platform can be run on any other platform.

Simplicity

The syntax of Java language is very simple compared to other languages. It is very much similar to C or C++ language. Every keyword in Java is meaningful; as a result, you can easily identify the action of a keyword.

Double Stage System

Java offers you the facility to compile programs in two stage. In the first stage, the Java compiler converts the source code into the byte code and in the second stage, the Java interpreter converts that byte code into the machine code. Since a computer can understand the machine code, it executes the code and produces the output. This is called the Double Stage System.

Object Oriented

Java is completely an object oriented programming language because it treats everything as an object. The basic concept of Java was taken from C and C++ language. C is not an object oriented programming language, but a structure based programming language. However, C++, which is an extension of C, is an object oriented programming language. Java is more independent than C or C++. You will know more about similarities and differences between Java, C, and C++ later in this chapter.

Security

Security is one of the most important issues in any programming language. If your application is not secure, your data is also not secure. Java is security based language because Java does not support the pointers like C++ does, so, the code is not able to access the memory directly. The internal system of Java starts verifying the code that tries to access its memory.

Multithreading

Java supports multithreading, which means that Java can handle multiple tasks in a single process. This is one of the most important features of Java. Also, it supports thread synchronization, which helps multiple threads to work simultaneously in a synchronized way. You will learn more about multithreading in the later chapters.

Easy to Operate

Java is very user-friendly and easy to operate. It does not require any specific environment for writing a Java program. You can simply type the Java program in any text editor. For example, you can write a Java program in Notepad and after saving the program, you can execute it using the command window as you do in C or C++ programming language.

CONCEPT OF OBJECT ORIENTED PROGRAMMING

When talking about object oriented programming system, the name of Java comes first as it fulfills all requirements of a true object oriented programming system, such as it supports Data Abstraction, Encapsulation, Polymorphism, and Inheritance.

Classes, instances, and objects are integral part of a program, if it is created by using an object oriented programming language such as Java. A **class** can be defined as a template/ blueprint that describes the behavior/state of different objects. **Objects** are the specific elements that exhibit the properties and behaviors defined by its class. Objects of the same type are said to be of same type or same class. Once you derive an object from a class, it becomes an **instance**. The actions that an object can take are called **methods**. Methods in Java are called procedures, methods, functions, or subprograms in other languages.

To understand the concept of classes and objects, let's say Vehicles is a class. Under Vehicles class, you have different types of vehicles such as Cars, Buses, Trucks, and so on. Cars, Buses, and Trucks are the objects under the Vehicles class.

Features of Object-Oriented Programming

There are certain features that have made object-oriented programming very popular. These features are discussed next.

Data Abstraction

In terms of object oriented programming language, Data Abstraction means showing only functionality and hiding implementation details. It helps in hiding the complexities of multiple data. Real world example of data abstraction is sending E-mail, wherein a user only composes a mail and sends it to another user without knowing the internal process running in background.

Encapsulation

This is another feature of object oriented programming language. In encapsulation, methods and data are combined or wrapped together in a single unit. In other words, the method and data are encapsulated and they work as a single entity known as object, refer to Figure 1-1. This concept is also called data hiding. In this process, the data cannot be accessed by any external method or process, and only the methods that have been combined to work as a single entity can access it.

Figure 1-1 *Encapsulation of data and method*

Polymorphism

Polymorphism is a Greek word, wherein poly means many and morph means form. So, polymorphism is "one name many forms". In the object oriented concept, when a single operation plays multiple roles, it is called polymorphism.

The best example of polymorphism is method overloading. In method overloading, there can be more than one method with same name but having different number of arguments. For example, there can be a class called **calculate** with two methods **calculate_area(l, b)** and **calculate_area(s).** These methods have the same name **calculate_area** provided they have different number of arguments. So when two values are passed by the user, the method having two arguments **calculate_area(l, b)** will be invoked. But if the user passes single value, the method having single argument **calculate_area(s)** will be invoked.

Inheritance

Inheritance is a key feature of object oriented programming. It gives you the benefit of reusing methods and properties of a class and therefore, it reduces the lines of code in a Java program. When you create a class, you define some features in the form of properties and methods in it. Once the class is created, and later on you are required to create another class that has all features (properties and methods) of the existing class in addition to some new features (methods and properties). In that case, you do not need to create a separate class. You can do so by deriving a new class from the existing class and adding new features in the new class. By this way, you can avoid repeating same code.

Technically, inheritance is a technique of deriving new class from an existing class and reuse the features of the existing class in a new class. The derived class is also called sub-class or child class and the class from which you derive the new class is called super class or base class or parent class. Figure 1-2 will help you understand the concept of inheritance in a simple and easy way through an illustration.

As shown in Figure 1-2, **Vehicles** is a base class and it has two sub classes: **Two Wheeler** and **Four Wheeler**. These two subclasses, **Two Wheeler** and **Four Wheeler**, further have two more subclasses each **Honda** and **Suzuki**, and **Toyota** and **BMW** respectively. So, **Two Wheeler** and **Four Wheeler** will be the base classes for its subclasses and **Vehicles** will be the base class for all the subclasses.

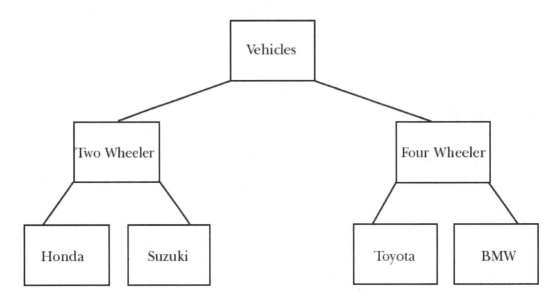

Figure 1-2 *The concept of inheritance*

Types of inheritance in Java
There are mainly three types of inheritance in java. These are as follows:

    a.   Single Inheritance
    b.   Multilevel Inheritance
    c.   Hierarchical Inheritance

Single Inheritance
When a single class is derived from single super class, it is called single inheritance. Figure 1-3 illustrates the concept of single inheritance, wherein **class B** inherits the properties of **class A**.

Multilevel Inheritance
When a class is derived from another derived class, it is called multilevel inheritance. Figure 1-4 shows multilevel inheritance, wherein the **class C** inherits the properties of the **class B**, which is a sub-class of **class A.**

Figure 1-3 *The concept of single inheritance*   **Figure 1-4** *The concept of multilevel inheritance*

Hierarchical Inheritance

When multiple classes are derived from a single base class, it is called hierarchical inheritance. Figure 1-5 illustrates the concept of hierarchical inheritance, wherein **class B** and **class C** inherit the properties of **class A**.

In object oriented programming, one more type of inheritance, called multiple inheritance is found. In multiple inheritance, a class is derived from more than one super class. The designers of Java considered multiple inheritance to be too complex and does not go well with the concept of keeping Java simple. Therefore, this type of inheritance is not implemented in Java. Figure 1-6 illustrates the concept of multiple inheritance.

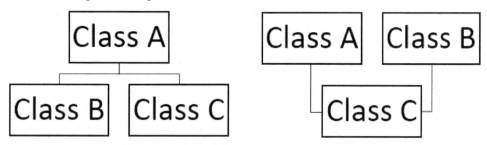

Figure 1-5 The concept of hierarchical inheritance   *Figure 1-6 The concept of multiple inheritance*

Java fulfills the requirement of multiple inheritance with the help of Interface. Interface is another important feature of object oriented programming and is discussed next.

Interface

An interface is a blueprint of a class. It is very much similar to the class but it contains only abstract method. An abstract method is a method that is declared but contains no implementation. The interface may also contain constants, method signatures, default methods, and static methods but it does not contain any constructor because it cannot be instantiated. Interfaces can only be implemented by classes or extended by other interfaces. A class inherits the abstract methods of an interface to implement it. You can use interfaces to achieve abstraction and multiple inheritance. You can also derive a class from any number of interfaces. Figure 1-7 illustrates the concept of interface, wherein **class C** inherits the properties of **interface A** and **interface B** as well as **class A**.

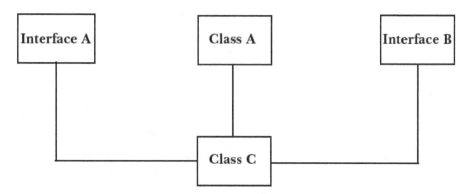

Figure 1-7 The concept of interface

JAVA COMPILER AND INTERPRETER

When you run a Java program, it passes through two stages: compilation and interpretation. During compilation, the source code is converted into an intermediate language by the compiler. Source code is a program written in Java and the intermediate code is a special type of code that is generated by the Java compiler. The intermediate code is known as Java byte-code or simple byte-code. As byte code is not a machine specific code, it needs to be converted into machine level code, and this task is performed by Java Interpreter. The Java interpreter reads the byte code line-by-line and converts it into the machine level code. Now, the computer executes the machine level code.

Note

1. Compiler is special purpose program that converts a high-level language (easy for people to write and to understand) such as Java program into a low-level language program (machine language).

2. Byte-code is a machine language for a virtual computer called Java Virtual Machine (JVM). Each computer platform has its own program to execute the byte-code instructions.

Java Virtual Machine

You know that in a Java program, the source code is converted into the byte-code, which is in turn converted to the machine code. Byte-code is not the machine language for any type of computer. In fact, it is a machine language for the fictitious computer called Java Virtual Machine or JVM. The term JVM is used to refer to the software that acts like a fictitious computer.

JVM has a very powerful architecture. Whenever you install JDK, it is automatically loaded into your computer memory and comes into action whenever you compile a Java program. The diagrammatic representation of converting a Java program into a machine specific code is shown in Figure 1-8.

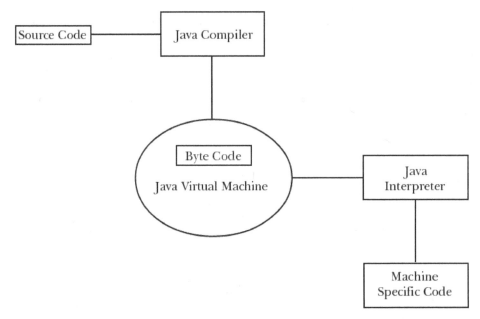

Figure 1-8 Converting Java program into machine specific code

INSTALLING JAVA DEVELOPMENT KIT

In this section, you will learn about the installation process of Java SE Development Kit (JDK) in your computer, as well as the procedure to run a Java program. Installing JDK is a very easy process, and it takes few minutes to install it. You can download the Windows version of JDK from the Oracle website to run it on the Windows platform. You can try the following link to download the latest version of JDK:

http://www.oracle.com/technetwork/java/javase/downloads/jdk8-downloads-2133151.html

Initially, you will be prompted to accept the license agreement, select the **Accept License Agreement** radio button and then click the jdk-8u111-windows-x64.exe corresponding to the Windows x64 entry. Save the file on your hard drive. If you have a 32-bit machine, click on the jdk-8u111-windows-i586.exe link corresponding to the Windows x86 entry. Once the file is downloaded completely, you need to run the setup on your system. During installation, leave the default settings of the setup intact. It will take a few minutes to complete the setup. Choose the **Finish** button to make sure that complete installation has been done. Now, you are ready to write and run Java programs.

Tools of JDK

The basic tools that will be installed when you install JDK on your system are discussed in the Table 1-1.

Table 1-1 List of JDK tools

Tool	Description
javac	This is the Java compiler, which converts the Java source code into byte code.
java	This is the Java interpreter, which converts the byte code into machine specific code.
javadoc	This tool is used to create HTML documentation.
appletviewer	This tool interprets Java applet classes.
javah	This tool is used to write native methods.
javap	This tool is used as a disassembler of class files.
jdb	This is a Java debugger tool and is used to debug a Java program.
jar	This tool is used to manage Java Archive(JAR) files.

JAVA STATEMENTS

Before writing and executing a Java program, you should know the basic keywords and syntax that are used in a simple Java program. Most of the keywords in Java are similar to C++. Some of the important keywords and syntax are discussed next.

Java API and Packages

Java API (Application Programming Interface) contains a number of classes and methods, which are grouped into different types of packages. Java API is used in various applications of Java. Packages can be of two types.

a. Built-in packages
b. User defined packages

Built-in Packages

Built-in packages are predefined in the Java library. There are a variety of built-in packages in Java that can be used in different ways. Every existing class in Java belongs to a package. Some important built-in packages that are widely used in Java programs are discussed next.

Java.lang

This is the most widely used package in Java, which provides the fundamental classes for programming. For example, **Integer**, **Float**, **Math**, **String**, **Thread**, and so on.

Java.IO

This package is used to handle input and output files of Java programs. It contains classes like **Reader**, **Writer**, **Stream**, and so on.

Java.util

It contains miscellaneous utility classes involving data structures, string manipulation, time and date, and so on.

Java.net

This package is used for Java network programming, socket programming, and so on.

Java.awt

This package provides classes for the GUI(Graphical User Interface) based applications.

User-defined Packages

You can also create your own package by using the **package** keyword with a valid name. Packages created in this way are called user-defined package. An example of a package is given below:

```
package book;
public class JavaBook
{
    public static void main(String[] args)
    {
            System.out.println("Hello Java");
    }
}
```

In this example, **package** is a keyword and **book** is the name of the package that contains a class with the name **JavaBook**. To import and use such type of packages in any other program, follow the syntax given next:

```
import book.*
```

The import Keyword

As the name suggests, this keyword is used to import packages, classes, or methods into your existing program. These packages or classes can be user-defined or in-built. For example, if you do not import a package into your existing program, you will not be able to access the features of all classes and methods of the package in your current program. To access the features of all classes and methods of the package, you need to import the package into your program.

For example:

```
import java.lang.Math;
```

It imports the **Math** class of the **lang** package. It is the in-built package of Java.

You can also import the package as follows:

```
import java.lang.*;
```

Here * means all the classes in the package. It imports all the classes of the **lang** package.

The class Keyword

The class is the base of object oriented programming language. It contains methods, objects, properties, variables, and many more. Any valid name of class can be used to define a class prefix by a **class** keyword.

For example:

```
class JavaBook
```

This line indicates a **class** with the name **JavaBook**.

System.out.println() Statement

This statement is used to print the output to the next line of the command prompt. Here **println** indicates the member of the **out** object, whereas **System** indicates **class**.

For example:

```
System.out.println("Hello Java");
```

This statement will print the string **Hello Java** to the next line of the command prompt.

Note
*Instead of keyword **println,** you can use keyword **print**. Both are same, but the only difference is, **println** shows the output in next line whereas **print** shows the output in the same line.*

Access Specifiers

Access specifiers are the keywords that can be used to declare a class or a method to make it accessible under different scopes within a class or a package. In Java, there are four types of access specifiers and they are explained next.

public

The **public** access specifier is declared when you want to make a method or any variable of a class accessible to any class in the Java program. These classes may be in the same package or in another package. The public access specifier achieves the widest scope of accessibility among all modifiers.

For example:

```
public class JavaBook
public Book() {...........}
```

default

If any modifier is not set, then it follows default accessibility. No specifier keyword is required for it. The **default** modifier is accessible only from within the package and not from outside it.

For example:

```
class JavaBook
Author() {...........}
```

protected

The **protected** access specifier is declared when you want to make the members of a class accessible in the class that defines them and also in other classes which inherit from that class.

For example:

```
protected class JavaBook
protected Author() {...........}
```

private

The **private** access specifier is declared when you want the members of a class to be accessed only by that particular class and not by other classes.

For example:

```
private class JavaBook
private Author() {...........}
```

Comments in Java

You can write comments in a Java program for your convenience. Java supports two types of comments that are also supported by C++. These are single line comment and multiple line comments.

Single Line Comment

A single line comment is used when you want to write a topic or a small comment in a Java program. It starts with two forward slashes (//).

For example:

```
//This is a single line comment.
```

Multiple Line Comment

A multiple line comment is used when you want to write a long description or a small documentation of the program. Multiple line comments are enclosed within /* and */. Anything between these marks is ignored by the compiler.

For example:

```
/*This is a multiple lines comment. Anything
  inside it is ignored by the compiler.*/
```

WRITING THE FIRST JAVA PROGRAM

There are many editors available in the market to write and run a Java program. You can either use an editor or simply use a Notepad editor to write a Java program. In this section, you will learn how to write Java programs in a Notepad editor, and to compile and run them in command prompt.

To write a Java program, first of all, open the Notepad editor from the **Start** menu and write the program in it and then save the program with the file name **FirstProgram.java**.

Example 1

The following example is a simple Java program. The program will print Hello Java on the screen.

```
// The program will print Hello Java
1    class FirstProgram
2    {
3            public static void main(String args[ ])
4            {
5                    System.out.println("Hello Java");
6            }
7    }
```

Explanation

The line-by-line explanation of the given program is as follows:

Line 1
class FirstProgram
This line indicates the creation of a class with the name **FirstProgram**.

Line 2
{
This line indicates the start of the definition of the **FirstProgram** class.

Line 3
public static void main(String arg[])
This statement is used in every Java program and is the main method of Java. This is the entry point of every program. The control will always reach to this statement.

public
This is an access specifier, any method with public access specifiers will be accessible throughout the program.

static
The **static** keyword allows the **main( )** method to be called without creating a particular instance of the class. This is necessary because the **main( )** method is called by the Java interpreter before any objects are created.

void
The **void** keyword indicates that the **main()** method will not return any value.

main(String args[ ])
The **args[ ]** is an array of objects of the **string** class which is the parameter of the **main()** method.

Line 4
{
This line indicates the start of the definition of the **main()** method.

Line 5
System.out.println("Hello Java");
This line will print Hello Java on the screen.

Line 6
}
This line indicates the end of the definition of the **main()** method.

Line 7
}
This line indicates the end of the definition of the **FirstProgram** class.

Note
The initial line in the program // ***The program will print Hello Java*** *is not a part of program. It is a single line comment and for reference only.*

Compiling and Running a Java Program

A Java program is easy to compile and run. You can compile a Java program in any command editor. Before compiling and running a Java program, you need to know the two keywords that are used to compile and run a Java program. These keywords are discussed next.

The javac Command

The **javac** command is used to compile a Java program. You can compile a Java program with the **javac** command in the following way:

```
javac Name_of_file with extension
```

Here, **javac** is a keyword and **Name_of_file** is the file name of the Java program with the extension **.java**.

The java Command

The **java** command runs the Java program after compilation and then displays the output to the command prompt.

You can run a Java program with the **java** command in the following way:

```
java Name_of_file
```

Here, **java** is a keyword and **Name_of_file** is the class file name of the Java program which is generated after compilation of program. Note that while executing the **java** command, you do not need to add extension of the Java file.

Note
*It is a good practice to save your java program with the class name which is in the program to avoid errors. For Example, Class name in the program is **FirstProgram** then file name must be saved as **FirstProgram.java**.*

SETTING THE PATH OF PROGRAM DIRECTORY

To compile and run a program, it is necessary to set a path (location) to locate JDK binaries such as "javac" and "java". The environment variable **path** is used to locate these JDK binaries.

There are two methods for setting the path directory. First, you can set the path on a temporary basis, which means you can use this path till the command editor is open. Once you exit the command editor, you cannot use it again. Secondly, you can set the path permanently, which means the path will not be lost even after you shut down your computer. Both these methods are discussed next in detail.

Setting the Path on a Temporary Basis

The following steps are required to set the path directory of your Java project on a temporary basis:

Step 1
Create a folder anywhere in your hard drive containing all Java programs and name them as per your convenience. For example, *Java Projects*.

Step 2

Open the command editor from the **Start** menu. Enter into the drive and directory, where you will save your file. For example, your root directory is *Ch01* which is inside *Java Projects* directory in the **D:** drive. You can do so by following the commands given in the Figure 1-9.

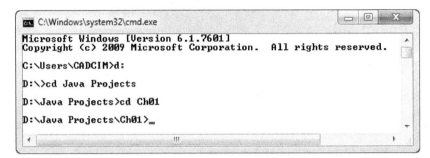

Figure 1-9 Commands to change the current drive and directory

Step 3

Write the following command at the command prompt:

```
path=The full path of bin directory of Java
```

Here, the **path** is a command. Write the full path of the bin directory of Java after the assignment operator and then press ENTER, as shown in Figure 1-10. The path will be set.

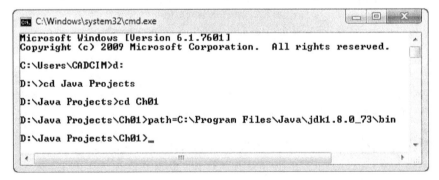

Figure 1-10 Setting the path of the bin directory on temporary basis

Step 4

Now, you can compile and run all your programs in your project directory. You can run Example 1 to test. Repeat the same process for compiling and running the program that you had learned earlier. The program will be executed without any errors.

The output of Example 1 after setting path on temporary basis is displayed in Figure 1-11.

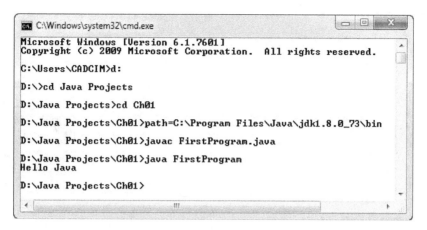

Figure 1-11 *The output of Example 1 after setting path on temporary basis*

Note

*To go back to previous directory, you can directly write **cd** in command prompt.*

Setting the Path Directory on a Permanent Basis

The following steps are required to set the path directory of your Java project on a permanent basis:

Step 1

Go to Control Panel from the Start menu. Next, click on the **System** icon; the **View basic information about your computer** window will be displayed, as shown in Figure 1-12. Alternatively, right-click on **Computer** from the **Start** menu and then choose **properties** to display the **View basic information about your computer** window.

Step 2

Next, choose **Advanced System Setting** option from the **View basic information about your computer** window; the **System Properties** dialog box will be displayed, as shown in Figure 1-13.

Step 3

In the **System Properties** dialog box, choose the **Advanced** tab and then choose the **Environment Variables** button; the **Environment Variables** dialog box will be displayed, as shown in Figure 1-14.

Step 4

Choose the **New** button in the **System variables** area of the **Environment Variables** dialog box; the **New System Variable** input box will be displayed.

Step 5

Enter **PATH** in the **Variable name** text box and enter complete path of the **bin** directory of your JDK in the **Variable value** text box and choose the **OK** button, as shown in Figure 1-15.

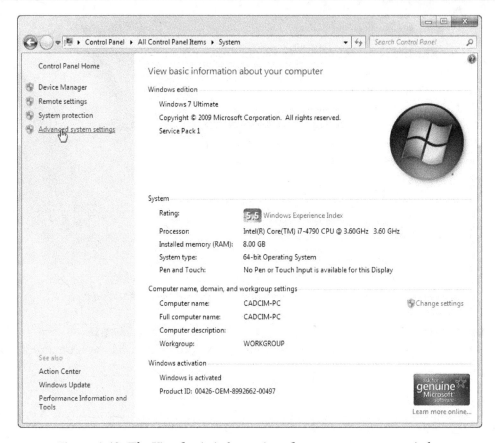

Figure 1-12 *The **View basic information about your computer** window*

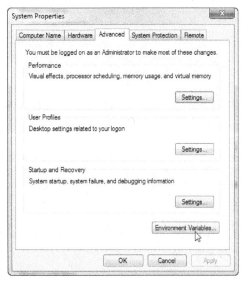

Figure 1-13 *The **System Properties** dialog box*

Figure 1-14 *The **Environment variables** dialog box*

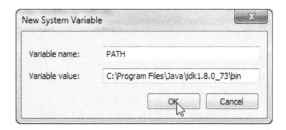

*Figure 1-15 The **New System Variable** input box*

Again, choose the **OK** button in the **Environment Variables** dialog box and then choose the **OK** button in the **System Properties** dialog box.

Now, the path directory is set permanently and you can compile and run the program anywhere in your hard drive using the command editor.

The output of Example 1 after setting path on permanent basis is displayed in Figure 1-16.

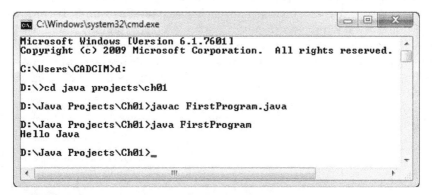

Figure 1-16 The output of Example 1 after setting path on permanent basis

INSTALLING NetBeans IDE

NetBeans is a popular free open source IDE for quickly and easily develop desktop, mobile, and web applications using Java, JavaScript, HTML5, PHP, C/C++, and much more. Most of the programmers use IDE because it eliminates the need for separate tools such as a text editor, a compiler, and a runner program.

An IDE integrates all these tools into a single toolset with a graphical user interface. There are many IDEs available on internet some of them have their own compilers and virtual machines.

To install NetBeans, navigate to *http://www.oracle.com/technetwork/java/javase/downloads/index.html* and then click on the **Download** button corresponding to the **NetBeans with JDK 8** entry, refer to Figure 1-17.

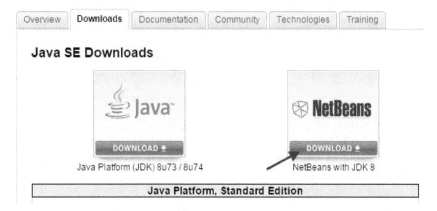

Figure 1-17 *NetBeans download link*

On the next page displayed, select the **Accept License Agreement** radio button and then click the **jdk-8u73-nb-8_1-windows-x64.exe** corresponding to the **Windows x64** entry. Save the file on your hard drive. If you have a 32-bit machine, click on the **jdk-8u73-nb-8_1-windows-i586.exe** link corresponding to the **Windows x86** entry. Double-click on the **jdk-8u73-nb-8_1-windows-x64** file; the installation process begins and you are prompted to accept the license agreement. Accept it and go ahead with the rest of installation process; the NetBeans shortcut icon will be placed on the desktop. Double-click on this icon; the NetBeans interface will be displayed, as shown in Figure 1-18.

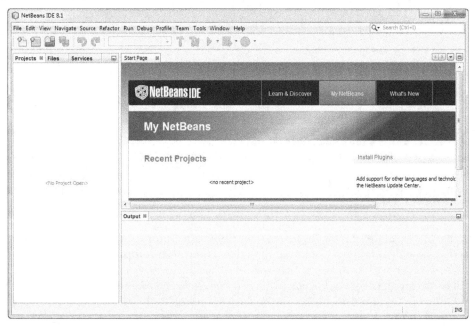

Figure 1-18 *The NetBeans Interface*

WRITING YOUR FIRST JAVA PROGRAM IN NETBEANS

The first step in writing the first Java program in netbeans is to create a new empty project in your preferred IDE, NetBeans in this case. To create a new project, choose **File > New Project** from the **NetBeans** menu bar to open the **New Project** dialog box, as shown in Figure 1-19.

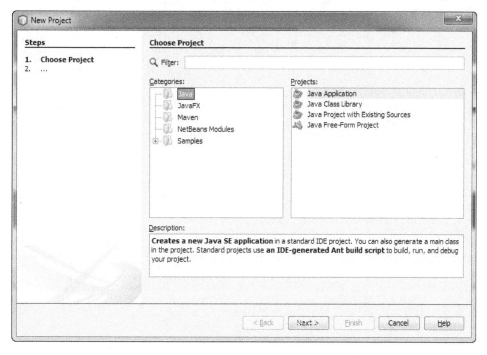

*Figure 1-19 The **New Project** dialog box*

In this dialog box, select **Java** in **categories** and **Java Application** from the **Project** list and then choose the **Next** button; the **New Java Application** dialog box will be displayed, as shown in Figure 1-20.

From the **Name and Location** area of the dialog box, enter the name of the project as **NetProgram** in the **Project Name** edit box. Choose the **Browse** button corresponding to the **Project Location** field if you want change the location of the projects and then choose the **Finish** button to close the dialog box and create the project.

The project is displayed in the Project window at the left in the interface, refer to Figure 1-21.

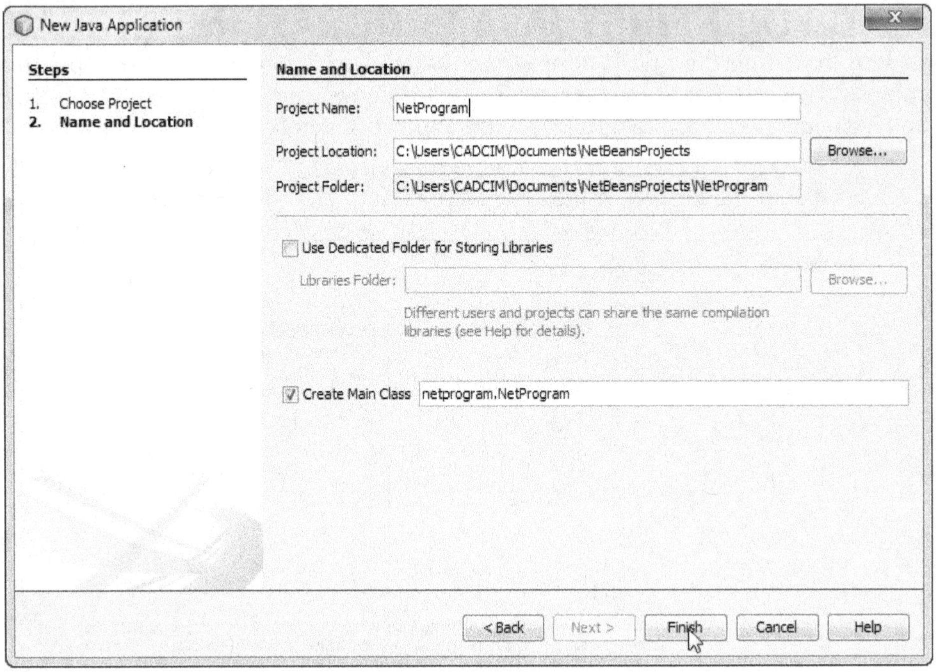

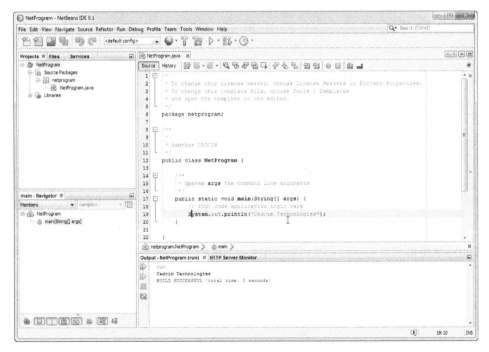

Figure 1-20 The **New Java Application** *dialog box of Netbeans*

Figure 1-21 Project **NetProgram** *displayed in the **Project** window*

The following code is displayed in the **NetProgram.java** tab of the editor.

```
1    /*
2    * To change this license header, choose License Headers in Project
     Properties.
3     * To change this template file, choose Tools | Templates
4     * and open the template in the editor.
5     */
6    package netprogram;

7    /**
8    *
9    * @author CADCIM
10   */
11   public class NetProgram {

12       /**
13       * @param args the command line arguments
14       */
15       public static void main(String[] args) {
16               // TODO code application logic here
17               System.out.println("Cadcim Technologies");
18       }
19   }
```

Explanation
The line-by-line explanation of the given program is as follows:

Line 1 to 5
/*
* To change this license header, choose License Headers in Project Properties.
* To change this template file, choose Tools | Templates
* and open the template in the editor.
*/
These lines are multiline comment. Anything between /* and */ is ignored by the compiler.

Line 6
package netprogram;
This line defines the package of the class where **package** is the keyword and **netprogram** is the name of the package.

Line 7 to 10
/**
*
* @author CADCIM
*/
Again, these lines are multiline comment which is ignored by the compiler.

Line 11
public class NetProgram {
In this line, **public** is an access specifier which is accessible throughout the program. **class** is a keyword and **NetProgram** is the name of the class and the curly bracket indicates the start of the definition of the class.

Line 12 to 14
/**
* @param args the command line arguments
*/
Again, these lines are multiline comment which is ignored by the compiler.

Line 15
public static void main(String[] args) {
This line contains the **main()** method which is treated as the starting point of every Java program. The curly bracket indicates the start of the definition of the **main()** method.

Line 16
// **TODO code application logic here**
This is a single line comment which is ignored by the compiler.

Line 17
System.out.println("Cadcim Technologies");
This line delivers the output **Cadcim Technologies** on the screen when Java program runs.

Line 18
}
This line indicates the end of the definition of the **main()** method.

Line 19
}
This line indicates the end of the definition of the **NetProgram** class.

To run the project, choose **Run > Run Project** from the menu bar or press **F6**. On successful run, the **BUILD SUCCESSFUL** message will be displayed in the **Output** window at the bottom of the interface. If there are any error(s) in the program, a window will be displayed with errors. You need to fix the error(s) and then rebuild the program.

The following output is shown in the Output window at the bottom of the interface.

Output
```
Cadcim Technologies
BUILD SUCCESSFUL (total time: 0 seconds)
```

Self-Evaluation Test

Answer the following questions and then compare them to those given at the end of this chapter:

1. What was the name initially given to Java ?

    (a) Aok   (b) Oak
    (c) Ako   (d) Oka

2. On which of the following platforms can Java run?

    (a) Linux   (b) Windows
    (c) Mac   (d) All of these

3. Which of the following inheritance is not supported by Java?

    (a) Multilevel Inheritance   (b) Multiple Inheritance
    (c) Single Inheritance   (d) Hierarchical Inheritance

4. Which of the following is supported by Java?

    (a) Data Abstraction   (b) Encapsulation
    (c) Polymorphism   (d) All of these

5. What do you call an inheritance, wherein multiple classes are derived from one super class?

    (a) Single Inheritance   (b) Multilevel Inheritance
    (c) Hierarchical Inheritance   (d) Multiple Inheritance

6. Which of the following commands is used to compile a Java program?

    (a) **java**   (b) **javap**
    (c) **javac**   (d) **jvm**

7. The term IDE stands for _____.

8. _____ helps in hiding the complexities of data.

9. In Encapsulation, methods and data are combined into a single unit. (T/F)

10. Java applets do not need any interpreter in order to execute. (T/F)

11. The **javac** command is used to interpret a Java program. (T/F)

12. While executing the **java** command, there is no need to add the extension file(*.java*). (T/F)

Review Questions

Answer the following questions:

1. What is byte code? How is it generated?

2. What is the use of **javac** and **java** commands?

3. What is JVM? How does JVM handle the byte-code?

4. What is the use of **import** keyword in java?

5. Check the syntax error in the following program and after correction, give the output of the program.

```
Class Hello
{
    Public static void main(String args[ ])
    {
            system.out.println("Hello")
            System.out.print('Welcome to the exciting world of Java');

    }
}
```

6. What is the difference between the following two statements?

```
System.out.print("Hello World!");
System.out.println("Hello World!");
```

EXERCISE

Exercise 1

Write a program to print the following statement on the screen:

Java is an interesting language.
It is easy to learn.

Answers to Self-Evaluation Test
1. b, **2.** d, **3.** b, **4.** d, **5.** c, **6.** c, **7.** Integrated Development Environment, **8.** Data Abstraction, **9.** T, **10.** T, **11.** F, **12.** T

Chapter 2

Fundamental
Elements
of Java

Learning Objectives

After completing this chapter, you will be able to:
- *Understand the concept of identifiers*
- *Understand the concept of keywords*
- *Understand the concept of data types*
- *Understand the escape sequences*
- *Understand the concept of variables*
- *Understand the concept of type conversion*
- *Understand the concept of operators*
- *Understand the concept of command-line arguments*

INTRODUCTION

In this chapter, you will learn about the fundamental elements of Java such as identifiers, keywords, literals, data types, variables, operators, and so on. Identifiers are the names of packages, classes, interfaces, methods, or variables. Literals are notations that represent a fixed value to be stored in variables. The data type of an element specifies the kind of data stored in it and the range of values that a data element can hold. A variable is a named storage location where the data can be stored. An operator is defined as a symbol that represents an operation. In this chapter, you will also learn about the concept of type conversion.

IDENTIFIERS

All components of Java require names. Therefore, identifiers are names of packages, classes, interfaces, methods, or variables. To name an identifier, you must follow certain rules. These rules are as follows:

a.   Identifier must start with an alphabet (A-Z, a-z) or an underscore(_) or dollar sign ($) but not with a digit.
b.   After the first character, an identifier can have any combination of characters which can be an alphabet or digit but no special character except underscore (_) and dollar sign ($).
c.   Java is case sensitive, so the uppercase and lowercase characters are considered individually by the compiler like Cadcim and CADCIM are two different identifiers.
d.   Java keywords cannot be used as identifiers.

The following variable names are valid in Java:

```
idname_6
id_name
_idname
```

The following variable names are invalid in Java:

```
6_idname   //Starting with a digit
idname#    //Using a special character (#) such as %, *, #, and so on
id name    //Using space
```

KEYWORDS

Java programming language has some reserved keywords that cannot be used as identifier names because they have special meaning for the compiler. Due to their specific functions in the language, the keywords are highlighted in a different color for easy identification in most integrated development environments of Java.

There are 50 keywords in Java which are listed as follows:

abstract	assert	boolean	break	byte
case	catch	char	class	const
continue	default	do	double	else
enum	extends	final	finally	float
for	goto	if	implements	import
instanceof	int	interface	long	native
new	package	private	protected	public
return	short	static	strictfp	super
switch	synchronized	this	throw	throws
transient	try	void	volatile	while

Some important points regarding Java keywords are given next:

a. **const** and **goto** are reserved keywords but not used.
b. All keywords are in lowercase.
c. **true**, **false**, and **null** are literals, not keywords.

DATA TYPES

Data type describes the size and type of values that can be stored in a variable. In any program, you need to store a particular type of data in the computer's memory. The compiler should know the amount of memory that has to be allocated to that particular data. For this purpose, the data types are used. The main role of a data type is to direct the compiler to allocate a specific amount of memory to a particular type of data. Java is a strongly typed language, which means each type of data is predefined as a part of the language. In Java, a data type is divided into three categories:

1. Primitive data types
2. Derived data types
3. User defined data types

Note
Variables will be discussed later in this chapter.

Primitive Data Types

The primitive data types are predefined by the Java programming language. These are the basic data types. They are declaration types and are used to represent single values but not multiple values. Java provides eight primitive data types that are as follows:

*   byte
*   short
*   int
*   long
*   float
*   double
*   char
*   boolean

These eight primitive data types are grouped into four different categories which are discussed next.

Note

In most of the programming languages such as C++, the amount of memory allocated to a particular data type depends upon the machine architecture. But in Java, the size of all data types is strictly defined and it does not depend upon the machine architecture.

Integers

The integer data type is used only for those numbers that do not contain any fractional part or decimal point. In other words, this data type is used only for signed whole numbers, either negative or positive. In Java, four integer types are defined, **byte**, **short**, **int**, and **long**. The main difference among them is the amount of memory allocated to each of them and the maximum range of values that can be stored using each data type. Table 2-1 shows the size and range of all integer data types.

Table 2-1 Integer types, their size and ranges

Name	Size (in bytes)	Ranges
byte	1	-128 to 127
short	2	-32,768 to 32,767
int	4	-2,147,483,648 to 2,147,483,647
long	8	-9,223,372,036,854,775,808 to 9,223,372,036,854,775,807

byte

The **byte** is the smallest integer type. The size of **byte** data type is 8-bits (1 byte is equal to 8 bits) and it ranges from -128 to 127. Here, range means that the **byte** data type can store -128 as the minimum value and 127 as the maximum value. This data type is very useful when working with files or streams in Java. It is used to save space in large arrays. You can create a variable of **byte** type by using the **byte** keyword with the variable name is given next:

```
byte var_name;
```

In this syntax, the variable **var_name** is declared as the **byte** data type.

short

The **short** data type is used rarely in Java. The size of **short** data type is 16-bits (2 bytes) and it ranges from -32,768 to 32,767. You can use it to save large space. You can create a variable of the **short** type as given next:

```
short var_name;
```

In this syntax, the variable **var_name** is declared as the **short** data type.

int

Among the integers, **int** is the most commonly used data type in Java. The size of **int** type is 32-bits (4 bytes) and it ranges from -2,147,483,648 to 2,147,483,647. It is generally used as the default data type for integer values unless there is a concern about memory. You can create a variable of the **int** type as given next:

```
int var_name;
```

In this syntax, the variable **var_name** is declared as the **int** data type.

long

Among the integers, **long** is the largest storage data type. This data type is required in those cases when the range of **int** type is not large enough to hold the resultant value. The size of the **long** type is 64-bits (8 bytes) and the range is large enough to hold the large whole numbers. You can create a variable of the **long** type as given next:

```
long var_name;
```

In this syntax, the variable **var_name** is declared as the **long** data type.

Floating-point Types

The floating-point data types are used only for those numbers that contain a decimal point or that have a fractional part. These types of numbers are also known as real numbers. In Java, two floating-point types are defined, **float** and **double**. Table 2-2 shows the size and range of these two data types.

Table 2-2 *Floating-Point types, their size and ranges*

Name	Size (in bytes)	Range(Approx.)
float	4	1.40e-45 to 3.40e+38
double	8	4.9e-324 to 1.8e+308

float

The **float** type is used for single-precision values (the values, which contain upto 8 digits after the decimal point). The size of **float** data type is 32-bits (4 bytes) and it ranges from 1.40e-45 to 3.40e+38. You can create a variable of **float** type as given next:

```
float var_name;
```

In this syntax, the variable **var_name** is declared as the **float** data type.

double

As the name implies, the **double** type is used for double precision values (the values, which contain upto 15 digits after the decimal point). This data type is mostly used in scientific operations where the end user wants accuracy in the resultant values. The size of **double** data type is 64-bits and it ranges from 4.9e-324 to 1.8e+308. You can create a variable of **double** type, as given next:

```
double var_name;
```

In this syntax, the variable **var_name** is declared as the **double** type.

Characters

The **char** type is included in this category. In Java, the **char** data type is used to hold the single character value that can be represented by alphabets, digits, and special symbols.

char

As already discussed, the **char** data type is used to hold the character values that belong to the Unicode character set. But the **char** type in Java is completely different from the **char** type in other programming languages such as C, C++, and so on. In C/C++, the size of **char** type is 8-bits (1 byte) and it can support only a few character sets such as English, German, and so on. In Java, the size of **char** type is 16-bits (2 bytes) and it is used to hold the values of Unicode character set. Unicode character set is a collection of those characters which exist in all human languages. The range of **char** type is from 0 (minimum) to 65,535 (maximum). You can create a variable of **char** type as given next:

```
char var_name;
```

In this syntax, the variable **var_name** is declared as the **char** data type.

Note

*A character that is assigned to a **char** variable should be enclosed in single quotes ' '.*

Boolean

The primitive data type **boolean** comes under this category. It can be used for storing true or false values.

boolean

This data type can hold only one value, either true or false. The size of **boolean** data type is 1-bit. This data type is used to hold only logical values. By default, it returns false. You can create a variable of **boolean** type, as given next:

```
boolean var_name;
```

In this syntax, the variable **var_name** is declared as the **boolean** data type.

Derived Data Types

Derived data types are the data types whose variables can hold more than one value of same type. They are not allowed to store multiple values of different types. They are made by using primitive data types. Example of derived data types are arrays and string.

For example:

```
int a[]={10, 20, 30};   //valid array
int b[]={10,10.5,'A'}; //invalid array
char carray[]={'c','a','d','c','i','m'};
```

User-defined Data types

User defined data types are the data types whose variables can store multiple values of either same type or different types. These data types are defined by programmers by making use of appropriate features of the language. Some user defined data types are classes and interfaces.

Note

You will learn about the arrays, strings, classes, and interfaces in the later chapters.

ESCAPE SEQUENCES

Escape sequence is a sequence of characters that are used to send a command to a device or a program. These characters are preceded by a backslash (\ ), which is called an escape character. These characters are not only used for text formatting but they also serve a special purpose. Table 2-3 shows the list of escape sequences used in Java.

Table 2-3 List of escape sequences

Escape Sequence	Description
\t	Insert a tab
\\	Insert a backslash
\'	Insert a single quote
\"	Insert a double quote
\r	Insert a carriage return
\n	Insert a new line
\b	Insert a backspace
\f	Insert a form feed

Example 1

The following program will display the use of escape sequence characters.

```
//Write a program to show the use of escape sequence characters
1    class Escape
2    {
3       public static void main(String[] args)
4       {
5          System.out.println("Linefeed          : \nLearning Java");
6          System.out.println("Single Quote      : \'Learning Java\'");
7          System.out.println("Double Quote      : \"Learning Java\"");
8          System.out.println("Backslash         : \\Learning Java\\");
9          System.out.println("Horizontal Tab    : Learning\tJava");
10         System.out.println("Backspace         : Learning\bJava");
11         System.out.println("Carriage Return   : Learning\rJava");
12      }
13   }
```

Explanation

Line 1

class Escape

In this line, the **class** keyword is used to define a new class and the identifier **Escape** is the name of the class.

Line 3

public static void main(String arg[])

This line contains the **main()** method which is treated as the starting point of every Java program. The execution of the program starts from this line.

Line 5

System.out.println("Linefeed   : \nLearning Java");

This line will display the following on the screen:

Linefeed   :

Learning Java

Line 6

System.out.println("Single Quote   : \'Learning Java\'");

This line will display the following on the screen:

Single Quote   : 'Learning Java'

Line 7

System.out.println("Double Quote   : \"Learning Java\"");

This line will display the following on the screen:

Double Quote   : "Learning Java"

Line 8

System.out.println("Backslash   : \\Learning Java\\");

This line will display the following on the screen:

Backslash   : \Learning Java\

Line 9

System.out.println("Horizontal Tab : Learning\tJava");

This line will display the following on the screen:

Horizontal Tab : Learning   Java

Line 10

System.out.println("Backspace   : Learning\bJava");

This line will display the following on the screen:

Backspace   : LearninJava

Line 11

System.out.println("Carriage Return: Learning\rJava");

This line will display the following on the screen:

Javaiage Return: Learning

The output of Example 1 is displayed in Figure 2-1.

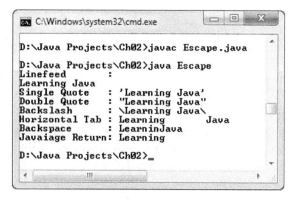

Figure 2-1 *The output of Example 1*

VARIABLES

A variable is a named location where the data can be stored. It is a location in the computer's memory with a specific address, where a value can be stored and retrieved, when required. The value of a variable can vary when the program is being executed.

Declaring a Variable

A variable must be declared before it is used in a program. The syntax for declaring a variable is as follows:

```
data_type var_name;
```

In this syntax, the declaration has two parts. The first part **data_type** represents a data type, which specifies the type of value to be stored in the variable and the amount of memory to be allocated. The second part **var_name** represents the variable name. To name a variable, you need to follow certain rules. As discussed earlier, identifier is the name used for variables, classes, and so on. The rules to name a variable are same as discussed earlier with identifiers.

For example, you can declare an integer type variable **age,** as follows:

```
int age;
```

When this statement executes, the compiler allocates 4 bytes (size of **int** data type is 4 bytes) of memory to the variable **age**. Now, the variable **age** is treated as a reference to the allocated memory location.

You can also declare multiple variables of the same type in a single statement. These variables are separated by commas. The syntax for declaring multiple variables is as follows:

```
data_type var1, var2, var3;
```

In this syntax, **var1**, **var2**, and **var3** are declared as the variables of the particular data type, which is represented by **data_type**. Here, all the three variables are of the same data type.

For example:

```
float highest_temp, lowest_temp;
```

In this example, the **highest_temp** and the **lowest_temp** are declared as the **float** type variables.

Initializing a Variable

Initialization means to assign an initial value to a variable. You can assign a value to a variable by using the assignment operator (**=**). The assignment operator will be discussed later in this chapter. The syntax for initializing a variable is as follows:

```
data_type var_name = value;
```

In this syntax, the **data_type** specifies the type of data, the **var_name** specifies the name of the variable, and the **value** specifies the initial value, which is assigned to the variable **var_name**.

For example:

```
char ch = 'y';
```

In this example, the character value **y** is assigned to the character variable **ch** as an initial value. Now, the character value **y** is stored at the memory location, which is referred by the variable **ch**.

Initializing a Variable Dynamically

In the previous section, you have learned that a variable is initialized at the time of its declaration. In Java, you can also initialize a variable dynamically (at the time of program execution).

For example:

```
int sum=a+b;
```

When this statement is executed, first the values of variables **a** and **b** are added with the help of the addition operator(+). Next, the resultant value is assigned to the integer variable **sum**.

Note
All the operators will be discussed later in this chapter.

Example 2

The following program illustrates the concept of dynamic initialization of a variable. The program will calculate the average of three numbers, assign the resultant value to another variable, and display it on the screen.

//Write a program to calculate the average of three numbers

```
1   class average
2   {
3       public static void main(String arg[])
4       {
5           int a=10, b=14, c=33;
6           float avg;
7           avg= (a+b+c)/3; //Dynamic initialization of variable avg
8           System.out.println("The average of three numbers is: " +avg);
9       }
10  }
```

Explanation

Line 5
int a=10, b=14, c=33;
In this line, a, b, and c are declared as integer type variables and the initial values **10**, **14**, and **33** are assigned to them, respectively with the help of the assignment operator(=).

Line 6
float avg;
In this line, avg is declared as a **float** type variable.

Line 7
avg=(a+b+c)/3;
This line represents the dynamic initialization of the variable **avg**. In this line, first the values 10, 14, and 33 of the variables **a**, **b**, and **c** are added. After that, the resultant value 57 is divided by 3. Next, the resultant value 19.0 is assigned to the variable **avg** at the execution time.

Line 8
System.out.println("The average of three numbers is:" +avg);
This line will display the following on the screen:
The average of three numbers is: 19.0

Note
*In line 8, the + sign is used to concatenate the value of the variable **avg** to the given string.*

The output of Example 2 is displayed in Figure 2-2.

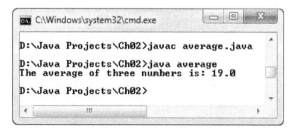

Figure 2-2 *The output of Example 2*

Types of Variables

There are four types of variables in Java as given next:

    a.   Local variables
    b.   Instance variables
    c.   Class/Static variables
    d.   Method Parameter variables

Local Variables

The variables that are declared inside a block of code or within the body of a method (or constructor) are known as local variables.

Constraints followed by local variables are:

- They have local scope; they cannot be accessed outside the block in which they are defined. These variables are accessible only within that particular block.
- Access modifiers cannot be used for local variables.
- There is no default value for the local variables. These variables should be declared and an initial value should be assigned to them before the first use.

For example:

```
int mul( )
{
    int a=10, b=10, c;
    c=a*b;
}
```

In this example, **mul( )** is a method and the variables **a, b**, and **c** are declared inside it. These variables are local to this method and can be accessed or manipulated within this method only. You will learn about the methods, constructor, or access modifiers in the later chapters.

Instance Variables

The variables that are declared inside a class but outside the method are known as instance variables. It is related to a single instance of a class. These variables can be used by different methods of the same class. They are also known as member variables and are not declared as static.

For example:

```
class Demo
{
    public static void main(String arg[])
    {
        int a, b;
        ----------;
    }
}
```

In this example, the variables **a** and **b** are declared inside the class definition but outside the methods. Therefore, they are treated as instance variables and they can be used by different methods of this class.

Class/Static Variables

Class variables are the same as the instance variables except that these variables are declared with the **static** keyword. These variables cannot be local. Regardless of the number of times a class has been instantiated, only one copy of static or class variable is created. You will learn about the **static** data in later chapters.

For example:

```
class Demo
{
    public static void main(String arg[])
    {
        static int a, b;
        ----------;
        ----------;
    }
}
```

In this example, the variables **a** and **b** are declared with the **static** keyword and treated as the class variables.

Method Parameter Variables

Method parameter variables are the variables that are declared in the method declaration signature. Whenever a java method is invoked, a variable is created with the same name as it is declared. Like local variables, it does not have any default value. So, an initial value should be assigned for it, otherwise compiler will give an error.

For example:

```
void demo_method( int a, int b)
{
    ----------;
    ----------;
}
```

In this example, **demo_method()** is a method and variables **a** and **b** are parameters to this method.

As you know that **public static void main(String[] arg)** is the main method which is the entry point of any program, the variable **arg** is the parameter to this method. The important thing to remember is that parameters are always classified as "variables" not "fields". This applies to other parameters (such as constructors and exception handlers) that you'll learn in later chapters.

Scope and Lifetime of Variables

The scope of a variable refers to that part of the program within which it can be accessed and manipulated. The scope also specifies when to allocate or deallocate memory to a variable. The lifetime specifies the life-span of a variable in the computer's memory. The four types of variables discussed earlier have different scopes and lifetime. The scope of a local variable is only limited to that block or method within which it is declared, and the lifetime of a local variable is only till the time when that particular block or method is being executed. Once that particular block or method is terminated, the variable gets deleted from the computer's memory.

TYPE CONVERSION

Type conversion means converting one data type into another, also known as Type Casting. For example, a data element of **byte** type can be converted into the **int** type with the help of type conversion. Java supports two following types of conversion:

    a.   Implicit conversion (Widening conversion)
    b.   Explicit conversion (Narrowing conversion)

Implicit Conversion (Widening Conversion)

The implicit conversion takes place when the destination data type is larger than the source data type and both the data types are compatible. It is also known as automatic conversion. For example, a data element of **short** type is converted into the **int** type. In such cases, Java performs implicit conversion because the **int** data type is larger than the **short** data type and both the data types are compatible. In implicit conversion, no information is lost during the conversion.

Example 3

The following program will convert a data element of **byte** type into the **int** type by using the concept of implicit type conversion and display the result on the screen.

```
//Write a program to convert a data element of byte type into the integer type
1    class Type_demo
2    {
3       public static void main(String arg[])
4       {
5            byte src=127;
6            int dest;
7            dest= src;
8            System.out.println("dest = " +dest);
9       }
10   }
```

Explanation
Line 5
byte src=127;
In this line, **src** is declared as a **byte** type variable and 127 is assigned as an initial value to it.

Line 6
int dest;
In this line, **dest** is declared as an integer type variable.

Line 7
dest= src;
In this line, the implicit conversion takes place and the value 127 of the variable **src** is assigned to the integer type variable **dest**.

Line 8
System.out.println("dest = " +dest);
This line will display the following on the screen:
dest = 127

The output of Example 3 is displayed in Figure 2-3.

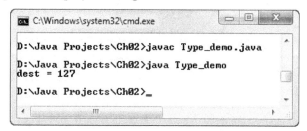

Figure 2-3 *The output of Example 3*

Explicit Conversion (Narrowing Conversion)

In the previous section, you learned about the type conversion in which the destination type was larger than the source type. But sometimes, you may need to convert a larger element type into a smaller one. For example, you may need to convert an **int** type into **byte** type. In such cases, explicit conversion is used. In explicit type of conversion, some information is always lost. Therefore, this type of conversion is also known as narrowing conversion. The syntax for explicit conversion is as follows:

```
(destination_data_type) value
```

In this syntax, the **destination_data_type** specifies the data type in which you want to convert the value, which is specified by **value**.

Tip
The thumb rule for explicit conversion is that the same data type should exist on both sides.

For example, you can convert a value of **int** type into the **byte** type, as given next:

```
byte b;
int i =300;
b = (byte) i;
```

In this example, **byte** in the parentheses directs the compiler to convert the value of the integer type **i** into the **byte** type. Now, the resultant value is assigned to the **byte** variable **b**.

Example 4

The following program will convert an **int** type into a **byte** type using the concept of explicit type conversion and display the resultant value on the screen:

//Write a program to convert an **int** type into a **byte** type

```
1    class Explicit_demo
2    {
3        public static void main(String arg[])
4        {
5            byte b;
6            int val = 300;
7            b = (byte) val;
8            System.out.println("After conversion, value of b is: " +b);
9        }
10   }
```

Explanation
Line 5
byte b;
In this line, variable **b** is declared as a **byte** data type.

Line 6
int val = 300;
In this line, **val** is declared as an integer type variable and **300** is assigned as an initial value to it.

Line 7
b = (byte) val;
In this line, the value of variable **val** is converted into **byte** because **byte** is the destination type and the resultant value will be assigned to the variable **b**.

Line 8
System.out.println("After conversion, value of b is: " +b);
This line will display the following on the screen:
After conversion, value of b is: 44

The output of Example 4 is displayed in Figure 2-4.

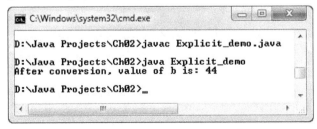

Figure 2-4 The output of Example 4

Note

A boolean value cannot be assigned to any other data type. Boolean is incompatible for conversion. Boolean value can be assigned only to another boolean.

OPERATORS

Operators are defined as the symbols that are used when an operation is performed on the variables or constants. Java provides with a rich variety of operators and these operators are divided into different categories, which are as follows:

a. Unary operator
b. Arithmetic operators
c. Bitwise operators
d. Relational operators
e. Logical operators
f. Assignment operators
g. Miscellaneous operators

Unary Operators

Operators that require only one operand are known as unary operators. Table 2-4 lists all unary operators that are used in Java.

Table 2-4 Unary operators with their syntax

Operator	Description	Syntax
+	Unary plus operator; indicates positive value (numbers are positive without this)	var1=+var2
-	Unary minus operator; negates an expression	var1=-var2
++	Increment operator; increments a value by 1	var1=var2++, var1=++var2
--	Decrement operator; decrements a value by 1	var1=var2--, var1=--var2
!	Unary Compliment operator; inverts the value of a boolean	!var1

Increment (++) and Decrement (--) Operators

The **++** operator is used to increase the value of its operand by one and the **--** operator is used to decrease the value of its operand by one; refer to syntax shown in Table 2-4.

You can use these operators in two notations, which are as follows:

a. Postfix notation
b. Prefix notation

The Postfix notation

In postfix notation, the increment or decrement operator is used after the operand. The syntax for using the postfix operator is as follows:

```
var1++;        //increment
var1--;        //decrement
```

In this syntax, the increment and decrement operators (++ and --) are used after the operand **var1**. It will increase and decrease the value of the variable **var1** by one.

If the postfix notation is used in an expression, then first the value of an operand is assigned to the variable at the left and then the value of the operand will be incremented or decremented by one.

For example:

```
y = x--;
```

In this example, first the value of the variable **x** is assigned to the variable **y** and then it is decreased by one.

The following two statements produce the same result as produced by the **y = x--** statement given in the previous example.

```
y = x;
x = x-1;
```

The Prefix notation

In prefix notation, the increment or decrement operator is used before the operand. The syntax for using the prefix operator is as follows:

```
++var1;
--var1;
```

In these syntaxes, the increment and decrement operator (++ and --) is used before the operand **var1**. It will increase or decrease the value of the variable **var1** by one.

If the prefix notation is used in an expression, then first the value of an operand is incremented or decremented by one and then it will assign to the variable at the left.

For example:

```
y = --x;
```

In this example, first the value of the variable **x** is decreased by one and then it is assigned to the variable **y**.

The following two statements produce the same result as was produced by the **y = --x** statement given in the previous example.

```
x = x-1;
y = x;
```

Example 5

The following program will perform all the unary operations and display the resultant values on the screen.

```
//Write a program to perform various unary operations
1    class UnaryOp_Demo
2    {
3       public static void main(String[] arg)
4       {
5            int result,res=+10;
6            System.out.println("Unary plus Operator result is " +res);
7            res = -res;
8            System.out.println("Unary Minus Operator result is " +res);
9            result=res++;
10           System.out.println("Post-increment result is " +result);
11           result=++res;
12           System.out.println("Pre-increment result is " +result);
13           result=res--;
14           System.out.println("Post-decrement result is " +result);
15           result=--res;
16           System.out.println("Pre-decrement result is " +result);
17           boolean success = false;
18           System.out.println("Result without compliment operator is "
                 +success);
19           System.out.println("Result with compliment operator is "+!success);
20       }
21   }
```

Explanation
Line 5
int result,res=+10;
In this line, **result** and **res** are declared as an integer type variables and **+10** is assigned as the initial value to variable **res**. **+** is an unary operator which indicates positive value. If you do not use unary plus operator, still it indicates the positive value.

Line 6
System.out.println("Unary plus Operator result is " +res);
This line will display the following on the screen:
Unary plus Operator result is 10

Line 7
res = -res;
In this line, **res** is the variable and its value is updated to negative value by using **unary minus operator (-).**

Line 8
System.out.println("Unary Minus Operator result is " +res);
This line will display the following on the screen:
Unary Minus Operator result is -10

Line 9
result=res++;
In this line, first the value (-10) of the variable **res** is assigned to the variable **result**. Next, the value of the variable **res** is incremented by 1.

Line 10
System.out.println("Post-increment result is " +result);
This line will display the following on the screen:
Post-increment result is -10

Line 11
result=++res;
In this line, first the value (-9) of the variable **res** is incremented by 1. Next, it is assigned to the variable **result**.

 Note
*In Line 10, the output is -10. But in Line 11, the initial value of **res** variable is -9 because in post increment, first the value is assigned to the variable then incremented by 1. So, Line 10 shows the assigned value as output and incremented value (-9) is stored in the memory.*

Line 12
System.out.println("Pre-increment result is " +result);
This line will display the following on the screen:
Pre-increment result is -8

Line 13
result=res--;
In this line, first the value (-8) of the variable **res** is assigned to the variable **result**. Next, it is decremented by 1.

Line 14
System.out.println("Post-decrement result is " +result);
This line will display the following on the screen:
Post-decrement result is -8

Line 15
result=--res;
In this line, first the value (-9) of the variable **res** is decremented by 1. Next, it is assigned to the variable **result**.

Line 16
System.out.println("Pre-decrement result is " +result);
This line will display the following on the screen:
Pre-decrement result is -10

Line 17
boolean success = false;
In this line, success is declared as a boolean type variable and **false** is assigned as an initial value to it.

Line 18
System.out.println("Result without compliment operator is " +success);
This line will display the following on the screen:
Result without compliment operator is false

Line 19
System.out.println("Result with compliment operator is " +!success);
This line will display the following on the screen:
Result with compliment operator is true

The output of Example 5 is displayed in Figure 2-5.

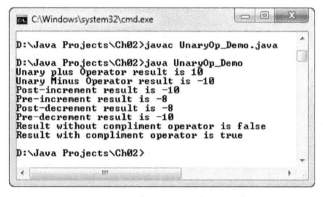

Figure 2-5 *The output of Example 5*

Arithmetic Operators

Operators that are used in mathematical expressions are known as arithmetic operators. Table 2-5 lists all arithmetic operators that are used in Java.

Table 2-5 *Arithmetic Operators with their syntax*

Operator	Description	Syntax
+	Addition	var1=var2 + var3
-	Subtraction	var1=var2 - var3
*	Multiplication	var1=var2 * var3
/	Division	var1=var2 / var3
%	Modulus Operator; gives remainder	var1=var2 % var3

Example 6

The following program will perform addition, subtraction, multiplication, division and modulus operations on two numbers using arithmetic operators and display the resultant values on the screen.

/* Write a program to perform various arithmetic operations on two numbers using the arithmetic operators: */

```
1   class Arith_operators
2   {
3       public static void main(String arg[])
4       {
5           int val1=30, val2=10;
6           int sum= val1+val2;
7           int sub= val1-val2;
8           int mul= val1*2;
9           int div= val1/val2;
10          int mod=mul%7;
11          System.out.println("Value 1 = " +val1);
12          System.out.println("Value 2 = " +val2);
13          System.out.println("Addition = " +sum);
14          System.out.println("Subtraction = " +sub);
15          System.out.println("Multiplication = " +mul);
16          System.out.println("Division  = " +div);
17          System.out.println("Modulus = " +mod);
18      }
19  }
```

Explanation

Line 5

int val1=30, val2=10;

In this line, **val1** and **val2** are declared as integer type variables and their initial values are assigned as 30 and 10, respectively.

Line 6
int sum= val1+val2;
In this line, the value (30) of the variable **val1** is added to the value (10) of the variable **val2** and the resultant value (40) is assigned to the integer variable **sum**.

Line 7
int sub= val1-val2;
In this line, the value (10) of the variable **val2** is subtracted from the value (30) of the variable **val1** and the resultant value (20) is assigned to the integer variable **sub**.

Line 8
int mul= val1*2;
In this line, the value (30) of the variable **val1** is multiplied by 2 and the resultant value (60) is assigned to the integer variable **mul**.

Line 9
int div= val1/val2;
In this line, the value (30) of the variable **val1** is divided by the value (10) of the variable **val2** and the resultant value (3), which represents the quotient, is assigned to the integer variable **div**.

Line 10
int mod=mul%7;
In this line, the value (60) of the variable **mul** is divided by 7 and the resultant value (4), which represents the remainder is assigned to the integer variable **mod**. Therefore, **mul%7** returns the remainder value 4.

Line 11
System.out.println("Value 1 =" +val1);
This line will display the following on the screen:
Value 1=30

The working of lines 12 to 17 is similar to that of line 11.

The output of Example 6 is displayed in Figure 2-6.

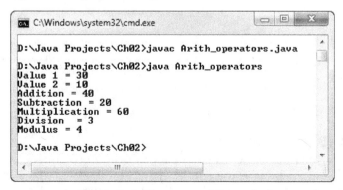

Figure 2-6 *The output of Example 6*

The Bitwise Operators

The data is stored in the computer's memory in the form of 0's and 1's, and these are known as bits. For example, a **byte** value 3 is stored in the computer's memory as 00000011. To operate or manipulate these bits individually, Java provides some operators that are known as bitwise operators. The bitwise operators are used to operate on the single bits of an operand. These operators are mostly applied on the integer types such as **byte**, **short**, **int**, and **long**. They can also be applied on the **char** type. Table 2-6 shows a list of bitwise operators.

Table 2-6 Bitwise Operators

Operator	Operation
~	Bitwise Compliment
&	Bitwise AND
|	Bitwise OR
^	Bitwise XOR
>>	Right Shift
<<	Left Shift
>>>	Zero Fill Right Shift

These operators are the least commonly used operators. Some of the bitwise operators are categorized under bitwise logical operators and these are discussed next.

The Bitwise Compliment (~) Operator

The bitwise Compliment (~) operator comes under the category of bitwise logical operators. The ~ operator inverts all bits of its operand; for example, 0 becomes 1 and 1 becomes 0. This operator is also known as the bitwise unary NOT operator. The syntax for using the compliment (~) operator is as follows:

```
~ value or expression;
```

For example:

```
int a = 3;
int b = ~a;
```

In this example, 3 is assigned to the integer variable **a** as an initial value, which is stored in the computer's memory as 00000011. In the next statement, ~ operator is used with the integer variable **a**. This operator inverts all the bits 00000011 of the value 3 into 11111100. Then, the resultant value is assigned to the integer variable **b**.

The Bitwise AND (&) Operator

The bitwise AND (&) operator also comes under the category of bitwise logical operators. If both the operands consist of the value 1, then the & operator will produce bit 1 as the result. But, if one or both the operands consist of the value 0, then the & operator will produce 0 as the result.

The syntax for using the **&** operator is as follows:

```
operand1 & operand2;
```

For example, you can use the AND (**&**) operator with two operands: 23 and 15, as given next:

```
  00010111        //Bits representing the value 23
& 00001111        //Bits representing the value 15
  --------
  00000111        //Bits representing the value 7
```

The Bitwise OR (|) Operator

The bitwise OR (|) operator also comes under the category of bitwise logical operators. If one or both the operands consist of the value 1, then the | operator will produce bit 1 as the result. But, if both the operands contain 0, then the | operator will produce 0 as the result. The syntax for using the | operator is as follows:

```
operand1 | operand2;
```

For example, you can use the OR (|) operator with two operands: 23 and 15, as follows:

```
  00010111        //Bits representing the value 23
| 00001111        //Bits representing the value 15
  --------
  00011111        //Bits representing the value 31
```

The Bitwise exclusive OR (^) Operator

The bitwise exclusive OR (^) or XOR operator also comes under the category of bitwise logical operators. The ^ operator produces bit 1 as the result, if only one of the operands consists of the value 1. Otherwise, it produces bit 0 as the result. The syntax for using the ^ operator is as follows:

```
operand1 ^ operand2;
```

For example, you can use the XOR (^) operator with two operands: 23 and 15, as follows:

```
  00010111        //Bits representing the value 23
^ 00001111        //Bits representing the value 15
  --------
  00011000        //Bits representing the value 24
```

Table 2-7 represents all (~, &, |, and ^) bitwise logical operators.

Table 2-7 *Bitwise Logical Operators*

X	Y	X&Y	X|Y	X^Y	~X
0	0	0	0	0	1
0	1	0	1	1	1
1	0	0	1	1	0
1	1	1	1	0	0

Other than the bitwise logical operators, the following operators are also available:

The Right Shift (>>) Operator

The right shift (**>>**) operator is used to move all the bits of an operand to the right direction. The **>>** operator operates on the bits for a specified number of times. The syntax for using the right shift operator is as follows:

```
value or expression >> num
```

In this syntax, the **num** specifies the total number of times you want to perform the right shift operation on all the bits of a value, which is specified by **value** or **expression**.

For example:

```
int a = 17;
int b = a>>2;
```

This example operates in the following way:

```
00010001   //Bits representing the value 17
```

When the **>>** operator operates on the given bits for the first time, the right most bit, bit 1, is lost and all other bits shifts to the right. The bit pattern, which is produced after the first step is as follows:

```
00001000   //Bits representing the value 8
```

In the second step, the same process is repeated as in the first step and the bit pattern, which is produced after the second step is as follows:

```
00000100   //Bits representing the value 4
```

The Left Shift (<<) Operator

The left shift (**<<**) operator is used to move all the bits of an operand to the left direction. The **<<** operator operates on the bits for a specified number of times. The syntax for using the left shift operator is as follows:

```
value or expression << num
```

In this syntax, the **num** specifies the total number of times you want to perform the left shift operation on all bits of a **value** or **expression**.

For example:

```
int a = 17;
int b = a<<2;
```

This example operates in the following way:

00010001   //Bits representing the value 17

When the **<<** operator operates on the given bits for the first time, the leftmost bit, bit 0 is lost and all other bits shifts to the left. The bit pattern that is produced after the first step is as follows:

00100010   //Bits representing the value 34

In the second step, the same process is repeated as in the first step and the bit pattern, which is produced after the second step is as follows:

01000100   //Bits representing the value 68

The Zero Fill Right Shift (>>>) Operator

The zero fill right shift (**>>>**) operator is used to move all the bits of an operand to the right direction and shifted values are filled up with zeros. It is also known as Unsigned right shift operator. The **>>>** operator operates on the bits for a specified number of times. The syntax for using the right shift operator is as follows:

```
value or expression >>> num
```

In this syntax, the num specifies the total number of times you want to perform the right shift operation on all the bits of a value, which is specified by value or expression.

For example:

```
int a = 10;
int b = a>>>2;
```

This example operates in the following way:

00001010   //Bits representing the value 10

When the **>>>** operator operates on the given bits for the first time, the rightmost bit (bit 1), is lost and all other bits shift to the right by filling the left most bit with zero. The bit pattern which is produced after the first step is as follows:

00000101   //Bits representing the value 8

In the second step, the same process is repeated as in the first step and the bit pattern which is produced after the second step is as follows:

00000010   //Bits representing the value 4

Note

Difference between the right shift (>>) and the zero fill right shift (>>>) operator is the sign extension. The zero fill right shift operator ">>>" shifts a zero into the leftmost position, whereas in right shift (>>), the leftmost position depends on sign extension.

Example 7

The following program will perform all the bitwise operations and display the resultant values on the screen.

```
//Write a program to perform various bitwise operations
1    class BitwiseOp_demo
2    {
3       public static void main(String args[])
4       {
5          int a = 15, b = 10, c = 0;
6          c = a & b;          /* 10 = 0000 1010 */
7          System.out.println("a & b = " + c );
8          c = a | b;          /* 15 = 0000 1111 */
9          System.out.println("a | b = " + c );
10         c = a ^ b;          /* 5 = 0000 0101 */
11         System.out.println("a ^ b = " + c );
12         c = ~a;             /*-16 = 1111 0000 */
13         System.out.println("~a = " + c );
14         c = a << 2;         /* 60 = 0011 1100 */
15         System.out.println("a << 2 = " + c );
16         c = a >> 2;         /* 3 = 0000 0011 */
17         System.out.println("a >> 2  = " + c );
18         c = a >>> 2;        /* 3 = 0000 1111 */
19         System.out.println("a >>> 2 = " + c );
20      }
21   }
```

Explanation
Line 5
int a = 15, b = 10, c = 0;
In this line, **a**, **b** and **c** are declared as integer type variables and 15, 10 and 0 are assigned as initial value to them.

Line 6
c = a & b;
In this line, **&** is the bitwise AND operator between **a** and **b** variables which is performing the bitwise AND operation and the resultant value is assigned to the variable **c.**

Line 7
System.out.println("a & b = " + c);
This line will display the following on the screen:
a & b = 10

Line 8
c = a | b;
In this line, | is the bitwise OR operator between **a** and **b** variables which is performing the bitwise OR operation and the resultant value is assigned to the variable **c**.

Line 9
System.out.println("a | b = " + c);
This line will display the following on the screen:
a | b = 15

Line 10
c = a ^ b;
In this line, ^ is the bitwise XOR operator between **a** and **b** variables which is performing the bitwise XOR operation and the resultant value is assigned to the variable **c**.

Line 11
System.out.println("a ^ b = " + c);
This line will display the following on the screen:
a ^ b = 5

Line 12
c = ~a;
In this line, ~ is the bitwise compliment operator which is performing compliment of variable **a** and the resultant value is assigned to the variable **c**.

Line 13
System.out.println("~a = " + c);
This line will display the following on the screen:
~a = -16

Line 14
c = a << 2;
In this line, << is the bitwise left shift operator which moves all the bits of variable **a** to the left direction by 2 bits. In this process, the leftmost bits are lost and the resultant value is assigned to the variable **c**.

Line 15
System.out.println("a << 2 = " + c);
This line will display the following on the screen:
a << 2 = 60

Line 16
c = a >> 2;
In this line, **>>** is the bitwise right shift operator which moves all the bits of variable **a** to the right direction by 2 bits. In this process, the right most bits are lost, and the resultant value is assigned to the variable **c**.

Line 17
System.out.println("a >> 2 = " + c);
This line will display the following on the screen:
a >> 2 = 3

Line 18
c = a >>> 2;
In this line, **>>>** is the bitwise zero fill right shift operator which moves all the bits of variable **a** to the right direction by 2 bits. The shifted values are filled by zero and the resultant value is assigned to the variable **c**.

Line 19
System.out.println("a >>> 2 = " + c);
This line will display the following on the screen:
a >>> 2 = 3

The output of Example 7 is displayed in Figure 2-7.

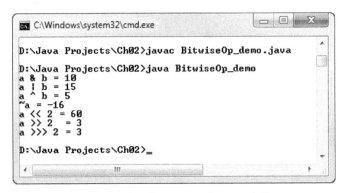

Figure 2-7 *The output of Example 7*

The Relational Operators

The relational operators are used to determine the relationship between two expressions. These operators are basically used to compare two values and the outcome of these operators is a **boolean** value, either **true** or **false**. Table 2-8 shows the list of relational operators and their syntax.

Table 2-8 Relational operators and their syntax

Operator	Operation	Syntax
==	Equal to	var1==var2
!=	Not equal to	var1!=var2
>	Greater than	var1>var2
<	Less than	var1<var2
>=	Greater than equal to	var1>=var2
<=	Less than equal to	var1<=var2

In the syntax shown in Table 2-8, the relational operators are used to check the relation between the two variables, **var1** and **var2**. If the values of variable **var1** and **var2** satisfy the condition then the outcome of this operation is true. Otherwise, it is false.

You will learn more about the working of the relational operators in the next chapter as these operators are mostly used in the control flow statements.

The Logical Operators

In the previous section, you learned about the relational operators, which are used to compare two expressions or which operate on a single condition. But sometimes, you may need to compare two or more conditions in a single statement. For this purpose, Java provides another set of operators, known as the logical operators. The logical operators are used to compare two or more relational expressions (statements that contain a relational operator) at a time and the outcome of these operators is a **boolean** value, either true or false. Table 2-9 shows the list of logical operators.

Table 2-9 The Logical Operators

Operator	Operation
&&	Logical Short-circuiting AND Operator
||	Logical Short-circuiting OR Operator
!	Logical NOT Operator

Among these operators, the working of Logical NOT (!) operator is the same as the unary Compliment Operator which is used for inverting a **boolean** value from **false** to **true** and vice-versa.

For example:

```
! (x == y)
```

In this example, the **==** (equal to) operator is used to check the equality between the two variables, **x** and **y**. If the outcome of the relational expression (x == y) is true then this outcome is inverted by logical not operator. Therefore, the final outcome is false.

Logical Short-Circuit AND (&&) and OR (||) Operators

The short-circuit **&&** and **||** operators are mostly used in control flow statements, in which the final outcome is based on the outcome of two or more than two conditions. The **&&** operator returns **true**, if the outcome of all operands is **true.** Otherwise, **false**. However, the **||** operator returns **true**, if the outcome of any one of the operands is **true**. Otherwise, it is **false**. Table 2-10 shows the working of short-circuit **&&** and **||** operators.

Table 2-10 *Logical Operators*

X	Y	X && Y	X||Y
False	False	False	False
False	True	False	True
True	False	False	True
True	True	True	True

In Table 2-10, you can observe that the **&&** operator returns **true,** only when both the operands are **true**. Otherwise, it returns **false**. Whereas, the **||** operator returns **true**, even if any one or both the operands are **true**. These operators are also known as the short-circuit operators because when these operators are used, only the left-hand operand is evaluated. Based on the result of that single operand, the final outcome will be produced. You will learn more about the working of these operators in the next chapter.

The Assignment (=) Operators

Assignment operators are used to assign value to a variable. These operators can be categorized as follows:

a.   Simple assignment operator
b.   Compound assignment operator

Simple Assignment Operator

Simple assignment operator is denoted by the single equal (**=**) symbol and is used to assign a value to a variable. The = operator has already been discussed in the previous examples of this chapter. The syntax for using the assignment operator is as follows:

```
variable_name = value;
```

In this syntax, the **value** on the right of the assignment operator (**=**) is assigned to the variable **variable_name** on the left. You need to assign a variable on the left side and the value to be assigned to this variable is always placed on the right side of the operator. The value assigned on the right can be a variable, a constant, or the result of an operation.

You can also use the assignment operator (**=**) for multiple assignments. Its syntax is as follows:

```
var1 = var2 = var3 = value;
```

In this syntax, the same value represented by **value** is assigned to all the three variables **var1**, **var2**, and **var3**. The assignment operator is evaluated from right to left; therefore **var1 = var2 = var3 = 0;** would assign 0 to var3, then var3 to var2, then var2 to var1.

Compound Assignment Operators

Compound assignment operators are a combination of two operators: first that specifies the operation to be performed and the second is the assignment operator. Compound assignment operators are also known as Short hand assignment operators. Table 2-11 shows the list of compound assignment operators with their syntax.

Table 2-11 *Compound assignment operators and their syntax*

Operator	Description	Syntax	Equivalent Expression
+=	It adds right operand to the left operand and assigns the result to the left operand.	var1+=var2;	var1=var1+var2;
-=	It subtracts right operand from the left operand and assigns the result to the left operand.	var1-=var2;	var1=var1-var2;
*=	It multiplies right operand to the left operand and assigns the result to the left operand.	var1*=var2;	var1=var1*var2;
/=	It divides left operand with the right operand and assigns the result to the left operand.	var1/=var2;	var1=var1/var2;
%=	It takes modulus using left operand and right operand, and assigns the result to the left operand.	var1%=var2;	var1=var1%var2;
&=	Bitwise AND assignment operator	var1&=var2;	var1=var1&var2;
|=	Bitwise OR assignment operator	var1|=var2;	var1=var1|var2;
^=	Bitwise XOR assignment operator	var1^=var2;	var1=var1^var2;
<<=	Bitwise left shift assignment operator	var1<<=2;	var1=var1<<2;
>>=	Bitwise right shift assignment operator	var1>>=2;	var1=var1>>2;
>>>=	Bitwise zero right shift assignment operator	var1>>>=2;	var1=var1>>>2;

In the syntax as shown in Table 2-11, first the given operation is performed on the variable **var1** and **var2**. Next, the resultant value is assigned back to **var1**.

For example, to add the value 4 to the value of the variable **a**, and again assign the resultant value to **a**, use the following statement:

```
a+=4;
```

You can also perform the same operation in the following way:

```
a = a + 4 ;
```

Example 8

The following program will apply the compound assignment operations on the given values and also display the resultant values on the screen.

//Write a program to perform assignment operations
```
1   class Assign_demo
2   {
3       public static void main(String args[])
4       {
5           int var = 10, result = 0;
6           result += var ;//10
7           System.out.println("result += var : " + result );
8           result *= var ;//100
9           System.out.println("result *= var : " + result );
10          result -= var ;//90
11          System.out.println("result -= var : " + result );
12          result /= var ;//9
13          System.out.println("result /= var : " + result );
14          result %= var ;//9
15          System.out.println("result %= var : " + result );
16          result ^= var ;//3
17          System.out.println("result ^= var = " + result );
18          result |= var ;//11
19          System.out.println("result |= var = " + result );
20          result &= var;//10
21          System.out.println("result &= var = " + result );
22          result <<= 2 ;//40
23          System.out.println("result <<= 2 = " + result );
24          result >>= 2 ;//10
25          System.out.println("result >>= 2 = " + result );
26          result >>>= 3 ;//1
27          System.out.println("result >>>= 3 = " + result );
28      }
29  }
```

Explanation

Line 5

int var = 10, result = 0;

In this line, **var** and **result** are declared as integer type variables and 10 and 0 are assigned as initial value to them.

Line 6

result += var ;

In this line, first the value (0) of the variable **result** is added to the value (10) of the variable **var**. Next, the resultant value is assigned back to the variable **result**.

Line 7

System.out.println("result += var : " + result);

This line will display the following on the screen:

result += var : 10

Line 8

result *= var ;

In this line, first the value (10) of the variable **result** is multiplied to the value (10) of the variable **var**. Next, the resultant value is assigned back to the variable **result**.

Line 9

System.out.println("result *= var : " + result);

This line will display the following on the screen:

result *= var : 100

Line 10

result -= var ;

In this line, first the value (10) of the variable **var** is subtracted from the value (100) of the variable **result**. Next, the resultant value is assigned back to the variable **result**.

Line 11

System.out.println("result -= var : " + result);

This line will display the following on the screen:

result -= var : 90

Line 12

result /= var ;

In this line, first the value (90) of the variable **result** is divided by the value (10) of the variable **var**. Next, the resultant (quotient) value is assigned back to the variable **result**.

Line 13

System.out.println("result /= var : " + result);

This line will display the following on the screen:

result /= var : 9

Line 14
result %= var ;
In this line, first the value (9) of the variable **result** is divided by the value (10) of the variable **var**. Next, the remainder value is assigned back to the variable **result**.

Line 15
System.out.println("result %= var : " + result);
This line will display the following on the screen:
result %= var : 9

Line 16
result ^ = var ;
In this line, first the bitwise XOR operation is performed between the variables **result** and **var** whose values are 9 and 10, respectively. Next, the resultant value is assigned back to the variable **result**.

Line 17
System.out.println("result ^ = var : " + result);
This line will display the following on the screen:
result ^ = var : 3

Line 18
result |= var ;
In this line, first the bitwise OR operation is done between the variables **result** and **var** whose values are 3 and 10, respectively. Next, the resultant value is assigned back to the variable **result**.

Line 19
System.out.println("result |= var : " + result);
This line will display the following on the screen:
result |= var : 11

Line 20
result &= var ;
In this line, first the bitwise AND operation is done between the variables **result** and **var** whose values are 3 and 10, respectively. Next, the resultant value is assigned back to the variable **result**.

Line 21
System.out.println("result &= var : " + result);
This line will display the following on the screen:
result &= var : 10

Line 22
result <<= 2 ;
In this line, first the bitwise left shift operation is performed on the variable **result** whose value is 10. It moves all the bits of variable **result** to the left direction by 2 bits and the left most bits are lost. Next, the resultant value is assigned back to the variable **result**.

Line 23
System.out.println("result <<= 2 : " + result);
This line will display the following on the screen:
result <<= 2 : 40

Line 24
result >>= 2 ;
In this line, first the bitwise right shift operation is performed on the variable **result** whose value is 40. It moves all the bits of variable **result** to the right direction by 2 bits and the right most bits are lost. Next, the resultant value is assigned back to the variable **result**.

Line 25
System.out.println("result >>= 2 : " + result);
This line will display the following on the screen:
result >>= 2 : 10

Line 26
result >>>= 2 ;
In this line, first the bitwise zero fill right shift operation is performed on the variable **result** whose value is 10. It moves all the bits of variable **result** to the right direction by 2 bits and the shifted values are filled by zero. Next, the resultant value is assigned back to the variable **result**.

Line 27
System.out.println("result >>>= 2 : " + result);
This line will display the following on the screen:
result >>>= 2 : 1

The output of Example 8 is displayed in Figure 2-8.

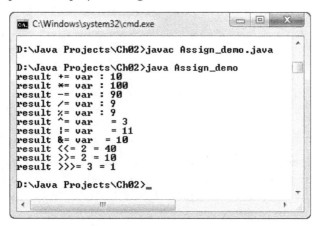

Figure 2-8 The output of Example 8

The ? : Operator

The **?** : operator is also known as the ternary operator because it works on three operands. The first operand is a boolean expression. If the expression is true then it returns second operand, else it returns third operand. It is a conditional operator that provides a shorter syntax for the **if-else** statement (discussed in the later chapters). The syntax for using the **?** : operator is as follows:

```
conditional_expression ? statement 1 : statement 2
```

In this syntax, if the condition specified by **conditional_expression** results in true, the **statement 1** is executed. Otherwise, the **statement 2** is executed.

For example:

```
int c = a!=0 ? a : b;
```

In this example, first the conditional expression **a!=0** (value of the variable **a** is not equal to 0) is evaluated. If it results in **true**, the value of the variable **a** will be assigned to the integer variable **c**. Otherwise, the value of the variable **b** will be assigned to the integer variable **c**.

Example 9

The following program will find the greater of the two given numbers using ternary operator, assign the resultant value to another variable, and also display the resultant value on the screen.

```
//Write a program to find the greater number
1    class Ternary_demo
2    {
3          public static void main(String arg[])
4          {
5                int a=20, b=11, c;
6                c= a>b ? a : b;
7                System.out.println("The greater value is: " +c);
8          }
9    }
```

Explanation
Line 6
c= a>b ? a : b;
In this line, the **?** : operator is used. First, the conditional expression **a>b** is evaluated. The expression results in **true** because the value 20 of the variable **a** is greater than the value 11 of the variable **b**. Now, the resultant value 20 of the variable **a** is assigned to the integer variable **c**.

Line 7
System.out.println("The greater value is: " +c);
This line will display the following on the screen:
The greater value is: 20

The output of Example 9 is displayed in Figure 2-9.

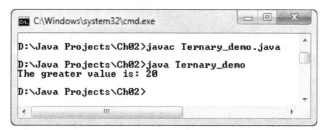

Figure 2-9 *The output of Example 9*

The instanceof Operator

The **instanceof** operator is used to check whether the object is an instance of the specified type (class or subclass or interface) at runtime. It is also known as type comparison operator because it compares the instance with type. If object is of the specified type, then the **instanceof** operator evaluates to true. Otherwise, the result is false. If you apply the **instanceof** operator with any variable that has a null value, it returns false.

The syntax for the **instanceof** operator is as follows:

```
object_name instanceof class_name
```

Example 10

The following program will check whether the object is an instance of the class by using the **instanceof** operator and display the resultant value on the screen.

```
//Write a program to check whether the object is an instance of the class
1   class Instanceof_demo
2   {
3       public static void main(String args[])
4       {
5           Instanceof_demo id=new Instanceof_demo();
6           boolean i=id instanceof Instanceof_demo;
7           System.out.println( "value:" +i);
8       }
9   }
```

Explanation

Line 5
Instanceof_demo id=new Instanceof_demo();
In this line, an **id** object of **instanceof_demo** class is created.

Line 6
boolean i=id instanceof Instanceof_demo;
In this line, **instanceof** operator is used to check whether the **id** object is instance of **Instanceof_demo** class.

Line 7
System.out.println("value:" +i);
This line will display the following on the screen:
value: true

The output of Example 10 is displayed in Figure 2-10.

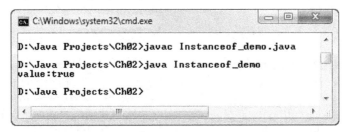

Figure 2-10 *The output of Example 10*

Operator Precedence

The operator precedence determines the order of execution of operators by the compiler. An operator with a high precedence is executed before an operator with a low precedence.
All binary operators except the assignment operators are evaluated from left to right. When operators of equal precedence appear in the same expression then they are evaluated from left to right whereas assignment operators are evaluated from right to left.

A list of Java operators arranged from the highest to the lowest precedence is given in the Table 2-12.

Note
In the operator precedence table, the highest precedence is represented by 1 and the lowest precedence is represented by 14. And, the operators given in the same line have the same precedence.

For example:

```
x=a+b*c
```

The multiplication operator (*****) has a higher precedence than the addition (**+**) and the assignment operators (**=**). Therefore, in the given example, first the value of the variable **b** is multiplied by the value of the variable **c**, and then the resultant value is added to the variable **a** (because the addition operator has a higher precedence than the assignment operator). Next, the resultant value of the expression **a+b*c** is assigned to the variable **x**.

Table 2-12 *Operator Precedence*

Precedence	Operators
1	() [] .
2	++var --var +var -var ~var !var
3	* / %
4	+ -
5	<< >> >>>
6	> < <= >= instanceof
7	== !=
8	&
9	^
10	|
11	&&
12	||
13	?:
14	= += -= *= /= %= &= ^= |= <<= >>= >>>=

COMMAND-LINE ARGUMENTS

You must have noted that in all examples explained in this book, no information was passed to the program during the time of its execution. But sometimes, you need to pass some information to a program during the time of its execution. This can be done by using the command-line arguments. You can simply pass these arguments by appending them after the name of the program during the time of its execution. The command-line arguments that are passed during the execution time are stored in the String type array **arg[ ]** of the **main( )** method.

For example:

```
D:\Java Projects\Ch02>java demo How are you
```

In this example, **demo** is the program name and **How are you** are the command-line arguments. Here, the first argument **How** is stored at **arg[0]**, **are** is stored at **arg[1]**, and so on.

Example 11

The following program illustrates the use of the command-line arguments. The program will display all the command-line arguments entered by a user.

//Write a program to display the command-line arguments

```
1   class Commandline_demo
2   {
3       public static void main(String arg[])
4       {
5           System.out.println("First argument is: " +arg[0]);
6           System.out.println("Second argument is: " +arg[1]);
7       }
8   }
```

Explanation

In this example, the arguments are passed by the user during the time of program's execution at 0th and 1st position of array **arg[]**.

Now, execute the program using the following statement:

```
java Commandline_demo Hello User
```

The output of Example 11 is displayed in Figure 2-11.

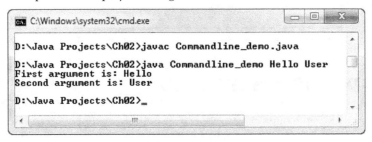

Figure 2-11 The output of Example 11

As you know, you can pass only string type array through command line arguments because array **arg[]** is of string type. If you want to pass values other than string then you will have to convert it into other types. You can use different ways for these conversions which are discussed next.

String to int

We can convert **String** to **int** in Java by using **Integer.parseInt()** method. Whenever users want to do any mathematical operation, they need numbers. But when they pass numbers, JVM treats them as **String** type. In such cases, users have to convert these values from **String** to **int**. To do so, they will use **Integer.parseInt()** method.

For example:

```
int x=Integer.parseInt(arg[0]);
```

In this example, **parseInt** is the method of the **Integer** class and is used to read numeric values from the command-line arguments. Next, the resultant value will be assigned to the integer type variable **x**.

String to long

We can convert **String** to **long** in Java by using the **Long.parseLong()** method. Whenever users want to do any mathematical operations on long numbers, they need to convert **String** to **long** by using **Long.parseLong()** method.

For example:

```
long y=Long.parseLong(arg[0]);
```

In this example, **parseLong** is the method of the **Long** class and is used to read long numeric values from the command-line arguments. Next, the resultant value will be assigned to the long type variable **y**.

String to float

We can convert **String** to **float** in Java by using **Float.parseFloat()** method. Whenever users want to do any mathematical operations on float numbers, they need to convert **String** to **float** by using the **Float.parseFloat()** method.

For example:

```
float z=Float.parseFloat(arg[0]);
```

In this example, **parseFloat** is the method of the **Float** class and is used to read float numeric values from the command-line arguments. Next, the resultant value will be assigned to the float type variable **z**.

Example 12

The following program illustrates the use of **String** to **int** conversion through command-line arguments. The program will calculate the sum of two integer values entered by the user and display the resultant value on the screen.

//Write a program to calculate the sum of two integer numbers entered by user.

```
1   class Command_demo
2   {
3       public static void main(String arg[])
4       {
5           int a,b,c;
6           a= Integer.parseInt(arg[0]);
7           b= Integer.parseInt(arg[1]);
8           c=a+b;
9           System.out.println("Addition = " +c);
10      }
11  }
```

Explanation

Lines 6 and 7
int a = Integer.parseInt(arg[0]);
int b = Integer.parseInt(arg[1]);

In these lines, **parseInt** is the method of the **Integer** class and is used to read numeric values from the command-line arguments. Next, the resultant values will be assigned to the integer type variables **a** and **b**, respectively.

The output of Example 12 is displayed in Figure 2-12.

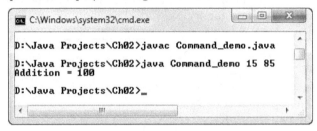

Figure 2-12 *The output of Example 12*

Self-Evaluation Test

Answer the following questions and then compare them to those given at the end of this chapter:

1. A _____ is a named storage location, where the data can be stored.

2. Variables declared inside a class but outside the method are known as the _____ variables.

3. The _____ conversion is used to convert a larger data type into a smaller one.

4. A _____ operator returns the remainder after the division of two numbers.

5. The _____ operator is used to increase the value of its operand by one.

6. In Java, the size of all primitive data types is clearly defined. (T/F)

7. A variable can start with a digit. (T/F)

8. In Java, the **+** sign is used for concatenation. (T/F)

9. In Java, a class variable is declared with **static** keyword. (T/F)

10. The **%** operator returns the quotient after the division of two numbers. (T/F)

Review Questions

Answer the following questions:

1. Differentiate between the local and instance variables.

2. Explain explicit type conversion with the help of a suitable example.

3. Explain the working of the % operator with the help of a suitable example.

4. Explain the working of the prefix increment operator with the help of a suitable example.

5. Explain ? : operator with a suitable example.

6. Explain **instanceof** operator.

7. Differentiate between primitive and user defined data types.

8. Find errors in the following program statements:

(a)
```
class Demo
{
    public static main void(String args[])
    {
        System.out.println("Hello Java");
    }
}
```

(b)
```
class Variable_demo
{
    public static void main(String args[])
    {
        int a =10, b=19;
        c=a+b;
        System.out.println(c);
    }
}
```

(c)
```
class Type_convert
{
    public static void main(String args[])
    {
        byte a;
        int b = 200;
        a = b;
        ----------;
        ----------;
    }
}
```

(d) ```
Class Syntax
{
    public static void main(String args[])
    {
        System.out.println("Error");
    }
}
```

(e) ```
class Ternary
{
    public static void main(String args[])
    {
        int x= 10, y=10, c;
        c= x==y ? x : y;
        ----------;
        ----------;
    }
}
```

EXERCISES

Exercise 1

Write a program to shift the value 200 to the right by two positions using the (shift right) **> >** operator.

Exercise 2

Write a program to calculate the area of a circle whose radius is entered by the user.

Answers to Self-Evaluation Test
1. variable, **2.** instance, **3.** explicit, **4.** %, **5.** ++, **6.** T, **7.** F, **8.** T, **9.** T, **10.** F

Chapter 3

Control Statements and Arrays

Learning Objectives

After completing this chapter, you will be able to:
- *Understand the if statement*
- *Understand the if-else statement*
- *Understand the if-else-if statement*
- *Understand the nested if statement*
- *Understand the switch statement*
- *Understand the while loop*
- *Understand the do-while loop*
- *Understand the for loop*
- *Understand the jump statements*
- *Understand the concept of arrays*
- *Understand the foreach loop*

INTRODUCTION

In the earlier chapters, you observed that the program statements were executed sequentially. But in certain cases, you need to skip some statements or execute some statements based on a particular condition. For this purpose, Java provides control statements. The control statements are used to alter the flow of execution of a program. In this chapter, you will learn about the control statements and their usage. Also, you will become familiar with the concept of flowcharts, as well as arrays, relational, and logical operators.

Before learning about the control statements, you need to learn about the flow charts.

FLOWCHARTS

A flowchart is a graphical representation of steps that constitute a program. It shows how the control moves in a program. A flowchart is drawn using some special symbols, which are as follows:

Oval

The oval symbol, as shown in Figure 3-1, represents the start and end of the program.

Rectangle

The rectangle symbol, as shown in Figure 3-2, represents the process box in which certain actions such as calculations are performed.

Diamond

The diamond symbol, as shown in Figure 3-3, represents the decision box in which a particular condition is checked and on the basis of the result, a path is selected from multiple paths.

Figure 3-1 An oval symbol   *Figure 3-2* An rectangle symbol   *Figure 3-3* A diamond symbol

Arrow

The arrow symbols, as shown in Figure 3-4, represent the path through which the control passes from one symbol to another symbol. In a flowchart, the control is passed from left to right or from up to down.

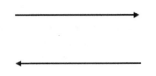

Figure 3-4 The arrow symbols

Parallelogram

The parallelogram symbol, as shown in Figure 3-5, represents the input or the output box.

Figure 3-5 A parallelogram symbol

CONTROL STATEMENTS

The control statements are used to alter the flow of execution in a program based on a particular condition. Note that in Java, the control statements are divided into the following three categories:

a. Selection Statements
b. Iteration Statements
c. Jump Statements

Selection Statements

A selection statement contains one or more conditional expressions and based on its result, the block of code associated with it will be executed or skipped. It is also known as decision making statement. If conditional expression is found to be true then next block of the statements will be executed. Else, this statement will be skipped and the next statement after the block will be executed. Note that in selection statements, the associated code is executed only once. Java supports various statements that are as follows:

a. if statement
b. if else statement
c. if else if statement
d. nested if statement
e. switch statement

The if Statement

The **if** statement is a single path statement, which means it will execute a statement or a block of statements only if the condition given in it returns true. The **if** statement is also known as the conditional branching statement. The syntax for the **if** statement is given next:

```
if(conditional expression)
statement1;
```

In this syntax, **if** is a keyword. The **conditional expression** represents a condition that returns a **boolean** value: either true or false. If the **conditional expression** returns true, the **statement1** will be executed. Otherwise, the control will be transferred to the next statement after the **if** block, as shown in Figure 3-6.

For example:

```
if(a>b)
System.out.println("a is greater");
System.out.println("Bye");
```

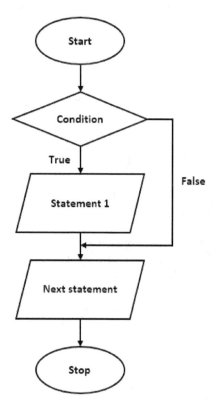

Figure 3-6 *Flow chart of the **if** statement*

In this example, the condition **a>b** will be checked. If the condition returns true, then both the next statements will be executed. But if the condition returns false then the statement **System.out.println("a is greater")** will be skipped and the control will be transferred to the next statement and the statement **System.out.println("Bye")** will be executed.

Note
If there are more than one statements associated with an if statement, the statements should be enclosed in the curly braces {} to make a block.

Example 1

The following example will illustrate the use of the **if** statement. The program will assess the performance of a sales executive, calculate his salary by adding incentives into the current salary, and display the current salary on the screen.

//Write a program to assess the performance of a sales executive and calculate his salary

```
1   class if_demo
2   {
3       public static void main(String arg[])
4       {
5           double salary = 25000;
6           double incentives = 1000;
7           int sales = 10000;
8           int target = 15000;
9           if( sales>=target)
10          {
11              System.out.println("You have achieved the target");
12              salary = salary+incentives;
13          }
14          System.out.println("Salary = " +salary);
15      }
16  }
```

Explanation
Line 9
if(sales>=target)
In this line, first the conditional expression is checked, whether the value 10000 of the **sales** variable is greater than or equal to the value 15000 of the **target** variable. Here, this condition will return false. The control will be transferred to the next statement (line 14) immediately after the **if** block. But if the conditional expression **sales>=target** returns true, the control will be transferred inside the **if** block and all statements (lines 11 and 12) associated with the **if** statement will be executed.

Line 10
{
This line indicates the start of the **if** block.

Line 11
System.out.println("You have achieved the target");
This line will display the following on the screen:
You have achieved the target

Line 12
salary = salary+incentives;
In this line, the value 25000 of the **salary** variable will be added to the value 1000 of the **incentives** variable and the resultant value 26000 will be assigned back to the **salary** variable.

Line 13
}
This line indicates the end of the **if** block.

Line 14
System.out.println("Salary = " +salary);
This line will display the following on the screen:
Salary = 25000.0

The output of Example 1 is displayed in Figure 3-7.

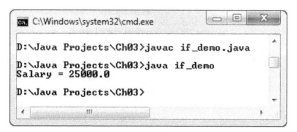

Figure 3-7 *The output of Example 1*

The if-else Statement

The **if-else** statement is a dual path statement, which routes the flow of execution in two different paths. The path selection is based on the result of a particular condition. The **if-else** statement works in such a way that if the condition given within the **if** statement is true, the statements associated with the **if** block will be executed. Otherwise, the **if** block will be skipped and the statements associated with the **else** block will be executed. The syntax for the **if-else** statement is as follows:

```
if(conditional_expression)
{
    statement 1;
    statement 2;
}
else
{
    statement 3;
    statement 4;
}
```

In this syntax, if the given **conditional_expression** is true, the **statements 1** and **2,** which are associated with the **if** block, will be executed and the **else** block will be skipped. Otherwise, the **if** block will be skipped and the **statements 3** and **4,** which are associated with the **else** block, will be executed, refer to Figure 3-8 for if-else flowchart.

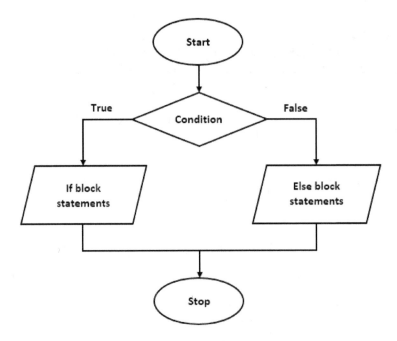

Figure 3-8 *Flow chart of the **if-else** statement*

For example:

```
if (a>b)
{
    System.out.println("a is greater");
    System.out.println("b is smaller");
}
else
{
    System.out.println("b is greater");
    System.out.println("a is smaller");
}
```

In this example, if the value of the **a** variable is greater than the value of the **b** variable, the statements: **System.out.println("a is greater");** and **System.out.println("b is smaller");** associated with the **if** block will be executed. Otherwise, the **if** block will be skipped and the statements: **System.out.println("b is greater");** and **System.out.println("a is smaller");** associated with the **else** block will be executed.

Example 2

The following example will illustrate the use of the **if-else** statement. The program will assess the performance of a sales executive, calculate his salary by adding incentives into the current salary, and display the current salary on the screen.

//Write a program to assess the performance of a sales executive and calculate his salary

```
1   class if_else_demo
2   {
3      public static void main(String arg[])
4      {
5         double salary = 25000;
6         double incentives = 1000;
7         int sales = 20000;
8         int target = 15000;
9         if( sales>=target)
10        {
11           System.out.println("You have achieved the target");
12           salary = salary+incentives;
13           System.out.println("Salary = " +salary);
14        }
15        else
16        {
17           System.out.println("You did not achieve the target");
18           incentives =0;
19           System.out.println("Salary = " +salary);
20        }
21     }
22  }
```

Explanation
Line 9
if(sales>=target)
In this line, first the conditional expression is checked, whether the value of the **sales** variable is greater than or equal to the value of the **target** variable. Here, this condition will return **true**. The control will be transferred inside the **if** block and the statements (from lines 10 to 14) associated with it will be executed.

Line 11
System.out.println("You have achieved the target");
This line will display the following on the screen:
You have achieved the target

Line 12
salary = salary+incentives;
In this line, the value 25000 of the **salary** variable is added to the value 1000 of the **incentives** variable and the resultant value 26000 is returned to the **salary** variable.

Line 13
System.out.println("Salary = " +salary);
This line will display the following on the screen:
Salary = 26000.0

Line 15
else
The control will be transferred to this line when the condition given in the **if** statement becomes
false. When the control transfers to this line, the statements (from line 16 to 20) associated with
the **else** block will be executed.

Line 17
System.out.println("You did not achieve the target");
This line will display the following on the screen:
You did not achieve the target

Line 18
incentives =0;
In this line, the value 0 is assigned to the **incentives** variable.

Line 19
System.out.println("Salary = " +salary);
This line will display the following on the screen:
Salary = 25000.0

The output of Example 2 is displayed in Figure 3-9.

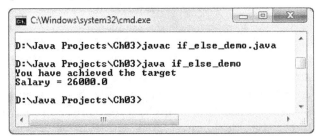

Figure 3-9 *The output of Example 2*

The if-else-if Statement

The **if-else-if** is also a conditional statement and it is used to verify more than one condition. The
syntax for the **if-else-if** statement is as follows:

```
if(conditional_expression1)
{
    statements;
}
else if(conditional_expression2)
{
    statements;
}
```

```
else if(conditional_expression3)
{
    statements;
}
else
{
    statements;
}
```

The **if-else-if** statement works in such a way that the **conditional_expression1** will be evaluated. In case it returns true, the statements associated with the **if** statement will be executed. Otherwise, the control will be transferred to the next **else if** statement and the **conditional_expression2** will be evaluated. Again, if it returns true, the statements associated with the **else if** statement will be executed. Otherwise, the control will be transferred to the next **else if** statement. This process will continue until a conditional expression evaluates to true. If each and every conditional expression evaluates to false, then the **else** block will be executed (if it exists). Otherwise, the control will be transferred to the next statement immediately after the **if-else-if** statement, refer to Figure 3-10.

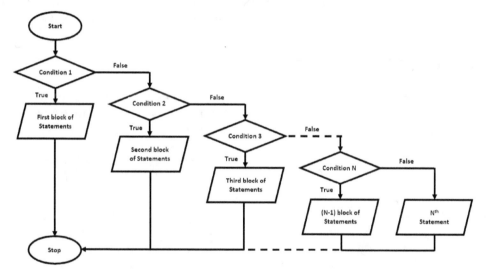

Figure 3-10 *Flow chart of the* ***if-else-if*** *statement*

For example:

```
if(sales>target)
{
        System.out.println("Excellent Performance");
        ----------;
        ----------;
}
else if(sales==target)
{
        System.out.println("Good Performance");
        ----------;
        ----------;
```

```
        }
    else if(sales<target)
    {
            System.out.println("Bad Performance");
            ----------;
            ----------;
    }
    else
    {
            System.out.println("Terminated");
            ----------;
            ----------;
    }
```

In this example, if the conditional expression **sales>target** evaluates to true, the statements associated with the **if** statement will be executed. Otherwise, the next conditional expression **sales==target** will be evaluated. If it evaluates to true, the statement associated with the **else if** statement will be executed. Otherwise, the control will be transferred to the next **else if** statement and the conditional expression **sales<target** will be evaluated. If none of the conditions evaluates to true, the control will be transferred to the **else** statement and the statements associated with it will be executed.

Example 3

The following example illustrates the use of the **if-else-if** statement. The program will calculate the grade according to the points scored by a student in the examination and display the result on the screen.

/* Write a program to calculate the grade of a student according to the points scored by him in the examination */

```
1    class if_else_if_demo
2    {
3        public static void main(String arg[])
4        {
5            int total_points = 75;
6            if(total_points>=90)
7            {
8                System.out.println("Grade A");
9                System.out.println("Excellent Performance");
10           }
11           else if(total_points>=80)
12           {
13               System.out.println("Grade B");
14               System.out.println("Good Performance");
15           }
16           else if(total_points>=70)
17           {
18               System.out.println("Grade C");
19               System.out.println("Average Performance");
20           }
```

```
21          else
22          {
23              System.out.println("Bad Performance");
24          }
25      }
26 }
```

Explanation

Line 5

int total_points = 75;

In this line, **total_points** is declared as an integer type variable and 75 is assigned as an initial value to it.

Line 6

if(total_points>=90)

In this line, first the conditional expression **total_points>=90** will be evaluated. This conditional expression returns false because 75 is less than 90. Now, the **if** block (from lines 7 to 10) will be skipped and the control will be transferred to the **else if** statement (line 11).

Line 11

else if(total_points>=80)

In this line, the conditional expression **total_points>=80** will be evaluated. This conditional expression will return false because 75 is less than 80. Now, the **else if** block (from lines 12 to 15) will be skipped and the control will be transferred to the next **else if** statement (line 16).

Line 16

else if(total_points>=70)

In this line, the conditional expression **total_points>=70** will be evaluated. This conditional expression will return true because 75 is greater than 70. Now, the statements associated with this **else if** block will be executed.

Line 18

System.out.println("Grade C");

This line will display the following on the screen:
Grade C

Line 19

System.out.println("Average Performance");

This line will display the following on the screen:
Average Performance

Line 21

else

If none of the conditional expressions evaluates to true, then the control will be transferred to this **else** statement.

The output of Example 3 is displayed in Figure 3-11.

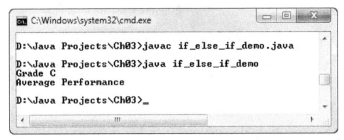

Figure 3-11 The output of Example 3

The Nested if Statement

When an **if** statement is used within another **if** statement, the resulting statement is known as the nested **if** statement. In the nested **if** structure, the last **else** statement is always associated with the preceding **if** block. The syntax for the nested **if** statement is as follows:

```
if(conditional_expression1)
{
    if(conditional_expression2)
    {
        statement1;
    }
    else
    {
        statement2;
    }
}
```

The nested **if** statement works in such a way that the **conditional_expression1** will be evaluated. In case, it returns true, the control will go to the next **if** statement where it will check the **conditional_expression2**. If the **conditional_expression2** returns true, the control will go to its block (**statement1**). If it returns false, the control will be passed to **else** block (**statement2**). And if the **conditional_expression1** returns false, the block associated with the **conditional_expression2** will be skipped and the control will be transferred to the next statement or **else** block (if it exists), refer to Figure 3-12.

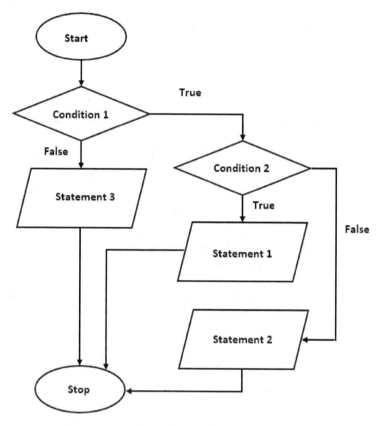

Figure 3-12 *Flow chart of the nested **if** statement*

For example:

```
if(a>b)           //External
{
   if(a>c)              //Internal
   {
      System.out.println("a is greater than b and c");
   }
   else          //Internal
   {
      System.out.println("c is greater than a and b");
   }
}
else              //External
{
   if(c>b)
   {
      System.out.println("c is greater than a and b");
   }
```

```
        else
        {
           System.out.println("b is greater than a and c");
        }
   }
```

In this example, first the conditional expression **a>b** (a is greater than b) will be checked. If it returns true, the control will go to the next **if** statement. Otherwise, the **if** block will be skipped and the control will be transferred to the **else** block. Now, the statement **System.out.println("b is greater than a and c");** associated with it will be executed. The working of the internal **if** statement is the same as the external **if** statement.

Example 4

The following example illustrates the use of nested **if** statement. The program will select a candidate based on the points scored by him in the technical and HR rounds of interview, using the nested **if** statement and display the output on the screen.

/* Write a program to select a candidate based on the points scored in the technical and HR rounds of interview, using the nested **if** statement */

```
1    class nested_if_demo
2    {
3        public static void main(String arg[])
4        {
5            int tech_score = 8;
6            int hr_score = 5;
7            if(tech_score>=10)
8            {
9                System.out.println("You are eligible for the HR round");
10               if(hr_score>=6)
11               {
12                   System.out.println("You are selected");
13               }
14               else
15               {
16                   System.out.println("You are not selected");
17               }
18           }
19           else
20           {
21               System.out.println("You are not eligible");
22           }
23       }
24   }
```

Explanation

Line 7

if(tech_score>=10)

In this line, the value of the **tech_score** variable is checked whether it is greater than or equal to 10 or not. If the conditional expression **tech_score>=10** returns true, the control will be transferred to the next statement (line 9) inside the **if** block. Otherwise, the control will be transferred to the **else** block (line 19).

Line 9

System.out.println("You are eligible for the HR round");

This line will display the following on the screen:

You are eligible for the HR round

Line 10

if(hr_score>=6)

In this line, the value of the **hr_score** variable is checked whether it is greater than or equal to 6 or not. If the conditional expression **hr_score>=6** returns true, the control will be transferred to the next statement (line 12) inside the **if** block. Otherwise, the control will be transferred to the **else** block (line 14).

Line 12

System.out.println("You are selected");

This line will display the following on the screen:

You are selected

Line 14

else

This **else** block is associated with the **if** statement given in line 10. When the conditional expression **hr_score>=6** given in the **if** statement (line 10) returns false, the control will be transferred to this **else** block and the statements associated with it will be executed. Otherwise, this **else** block (from line 14 to 17) will be skipped.

Line 16

System.out.println("You are not selected");

This line will display the following on the screen:

You are not selected

Line 19

else

This **else** block is associated with the **if** statement given in line 8. When the conditional expression **tech_score>=10** given in the **if** statement (line 8) returns false, the control will be transferred to this **else** block and the statements associated with it will be executed. Otherwise, this **else** block will be skipped.

Line 21

System.out.println("You are not eligible");

This line will display the following on the screen:

You are not eligible

The output of Example 4 is displayed in Figure 3-13.

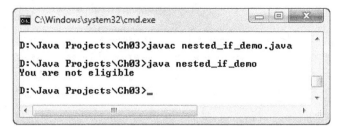

Figure 3-13 *The output of Example 4*

The switch Statement

The **switch** statement is a multiway selection or case control statement. The **switch** statement makes it possible for the compiler to transfer the control to different statements within the **switch** body depending on the value of a variable or expression. In a **switch** statement, the flow of execution is controlled by the value of a variable or an expression. This variable or expression is known as the control variable. The syntax for using the **switch** statement is as follows:

```
switch(value or expression)
{
    case 1:
          statement1;
          break;
    case 2:
          statement2;
          break;
    ----------;
    ----------;
    case N:
          statement3;
          break;
    default:
          statement;
}
```

In this syntax, the **value** or **expression** given in the **switch** statement represents a control variable. This variable should be of **byte**, **short**, **int**, or **char** type, and the type of case constant values should be compatible to the type of control variable. The **switch** statement works in such a way that the value of the control variable is matched with all values in the case constant statements, one by one. If match is found, the statement associated with that particular case will be executed. If no match is found, the statements associated with the **default** case will be executed (if it exists). The **break** statement, which is used inside the **switch** body, is a jump statement. When a **break** statement is encountered inside a **switch** body, it transfers the control to the statement that is immediately after the **switch** body, refer to Figure 3-14. You will learn more about the jump statements later in this chapter.

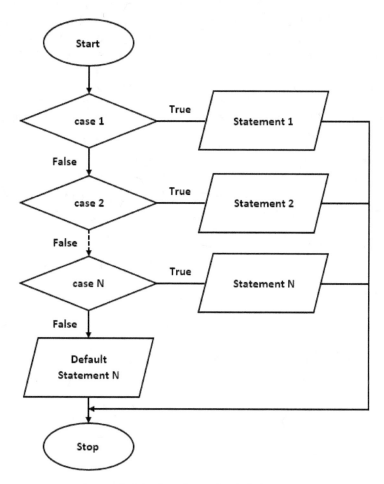

Figure 3-14 *Flow chart of switch Statement*

For example:

```
int mon=12;
switch(mon)
{
        case 1:
        System.out.println("January");
        break;
        case 2:
        System.out.println("February");
        break;
        ----------;
        ----------;
        case 12:
        System.out.println("December");
        break;
        default:
        System.out.println("Invalid choice");
}
```

In this example, **mon** variable is treated as a control variable and value 12 is assigned as an initial value to it. In the first step, the value of the control variable **mon** is compared with the first case with literal value 1. Here, no match is found. Now, the control is transferred to the next case statement and again the value of the control variable **mon** is compared with the second case with literal value 2. This process is repeated until no match or the default case is found. While repeating this process, a match is found and the statement associated with it, **System. out.println("December");** is executed. Next, the control is transferred to the statement, which is immediately after the **switch** body.

Example 5

The following example illustrates the use of the **switch** statement. The program will display the day of a week based on the value given in the program.

```
//Write a program to display the day of a week
1   class Switch_demo
2   {
3       public static void main(String arg[])
4       {
5           int day = 5;
6           switch (day)
7           {
8               case 1:
9                   System.out.println("Monday");
10                  break;
11              case 2:
12                  System.out.println("Tuesday");
13                  break;
14              case 3:
15                  System.out.println("Wednesday");
16                  break;
17              case 4:
18                  System.out.println("Thursday");
19                  break;
20              case 5:
21                  System.out.println("Friday");
22                  break;
23              case 6:
24                  System.out.println("Saturday");
25                  break;
26              case 7:
27                  System.out.println("Sunday");
28                  break;
29              default:
30                  System.out.println("Invalid choice");
31          }
32      }
33  }
```

Explanation

Line 5
int day = 5;
In this line, **day** is declared as an integer type variable and 5 is assigned as an initial value to it.

Line 6
switch (day)
In this line, the value of the **day** variable is passed in the parentheses with the **switch** keyword. Here, the **day** variable is treated as a control variable and its value will be compared with all cases.

Line 8
case 1:
In this line, first the value of the control variable **day** will be compared with the case with literal value 1. If match is found, the control will be transferred to the next line (line 9). But in this case, as no match is found, the control will be transferred to the next case statement (line 11).

Line 9
System.out.println("Monday");
This line will display the following on the screen:
Monday

Line 10
break;
The **break** statement is a jump statement, which transfers the control outside the **switch** body. If this statement is not used in the **switch** body, all cases from the matched statements including the default one will be executed.

The working of lines 11 to 19 is the same as the working of lines from 8 to 10.

Line 20
case 5:
Again in this line, the value of the control variable **day** will be compared with the case with literal value 5. Here, match is found and the control will be transferred to the next line (line 21).

Line 21
System.out.println("Friday");
This line will display the following on the screen:
Friday

Lines 29 and 30
default:
System.out.println("Invalid choice");
These lines contain the default case. This case will be executed only when no match is found in all other cases.

The output of Example 5 is displayed in Figure 3-15.

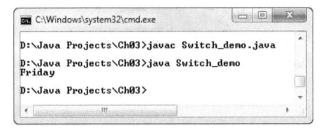

Figure 3-15 *The output of Example 5*

Iteration Statements

Iteration means to repeat something for a specified number of times. In Java, the iteration statements are used to repeat a particular set of instructions until the termination condition is met. These statements are also known as loops. The iteration statements consist of three expressions: initialization, condition, and increment or decrement. These expressions are discussed next.

Initialization Expression

The initialization expression gets executed only once at the start of the loop. It is used to set the initial value of the loop control variable such as **int x=1**.

Condition Expression

The condition expression gets evaluated every time before the execution of the body of the loop. The execution of the body of the loop depends on the condition whether it is true or false. If the condition is true, the body of the loop will be executed. Otherwise, it will skip and the control will be transferred to the next instruction after the loop.

Increment or Decrement Expression

The increment or decrement expression updates the variables that control the condition statement. It is used to increase or decrease the value of the loop control variable by 1. This expression is always executed after the statements in the body of the loop have been executed.

Java provides three types of iteration or loop statements and these are as follows:

    a.   while loop
    b.   do-while loop
    c.   for loop

The while Loop

The **while** loop is an entry controlled loop where the condition is evaluated at the start and the statements associated with it will continue executing and repeating until the condition becomes false. The syntax for using the **while** loop is as follows:

```
initialization;
while(condition)
{
    statements;
    increment/decrement;
}
```

In this syntax, the **initialization** part of the loop is executed. It sets the value of the loop control variable which acts as a counter that controls the loop. Next, **while** is a keyword and the condition given in the **while** statement is evaluated. It evaluates to either true or false. Till the condition evaluates to true, the statements in the **while** block will be executed repeatedly. Otherwise, the loop terminates. After executing the statements in the **while** block, the control will be transferred to the **increment** or **decrement** part. It will increment or decrement the value of the control variable by 1. Next, again the conditional expression will be evaluated. This process will be repeated until the conditional expression evaluates to false, refer to Figure 3-16.

For example:

```
int count =1;
while (count <=5)
{
     ----------;//These lines

     ----------;//indicate the body
     ----------;//of the loop
     count++;
}
```

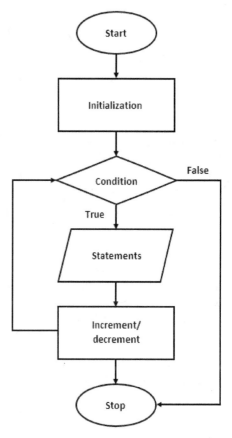

Figure 3-16 *Flow chart of* ***while*** *loop*

In this example, the **count** variable is treated as a loop control variable and 1 is assigned as an initial value to it. This variable acts as a counter and controls the entire loop. Next, the conditional expression **count<=5** will be evaluated. If it evaluates to true, the body of the loop will be executed. Otherwise, the body of the loop will be skipped. After executing the statements in the **while** block, the control will be transferred to the increment part **count++**, which will increment the value of the control variable by 1. Next, again the condition will be evaluated. This process will be repeated until the value of the **count** variable becomes less than or equal to the value 5.

Example 6

The following example illustrates the use of the **while** statement. The program will compare two variables and continue displaying the values of both the variables until they are equal.

```
//Write a program to compare two variables using the while loop
1  class while_demo
2  {
3      public static void main(String arg[])
4      {
5          int a = 5, b=1;
```

```
6            while(a>b)
7            {
8                System.out.println("a = " +a+ ", b = " +b);
9                b++;
10           }
11           System.out.println("a and b are equal");
12    }
13  }
```

Explanation

Line 5

int a = 5, b=1;

In this line, **a** and **b** are declared as the integer type variables and they are assigned the initial values 5 and 1, respectively.

Line 6

while(a>b)

In this line, the conditional expression **a>b** will be evaluated repeatedly until it evaluates to false. When the conditional expression evaluates to true, the body of the loop (lines 8 and 9) will be executed. Otherwise, the control will be transferred to the next statement (line 11), which is immediately after the body of the loop.

Line 8

System.out.println("a = " +a+ ", b = " +b);

This line will display the following on the screen:

a= 5, b= 1

 Note

*In line 8, while the body of the loop executes repeatedly, the value of the variable **b** keeps on changing.*

Line 9

b++;

In this line, the **++** (postfix increment) operator is used. This operator will increment the value of the **b** variable while the body of the loop executes repeatedly. After the execution of each loop, the value of the **b** variable will be incremented by one.

Line 11

System.out.println("a and b are equal");

When the conditional expression given in the **while** statement evaluates to false, the control will be transferred to this line and it will display the following on the screen:

a and b are equal

The output of Example 6 is displayed in Figure 3-17.

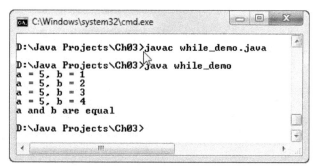

Figure 3-17 The output of Example 6

The do-while loop

In the **while** loop, first the conditional expression is evaluated and if it evaluates to true, only then the body of the loop will be executed. Otherwise, the body of the loop will be skipped. But sometimes it is required that the body of the loop must be executed at least once and then the conditional expression should be evaluated. For this, Java provides a loop statement which is known as the **do-while** loop. In the **do-while** loop, the body of the loop will be executed at least once, and then the conditional expression will be evaluated. It is also known as exit control loop. The syntax for using the **do-while** loop is as follows:

```
initialization;
do
{
    statements;
    increment/decrement;
}
while (condition);
```

In this syntax, the **initialization** part of the loop is executed. It sets the value of the loop control variable which acts as a counter that controls the loop. Next **do** is a keyword and statements in the **do** block execute at least once. After executing the statements in the **do** block, the control will be transferred to the **increment** or **decrement** part. It will increment or decrement the value of the control variable by 1. Next, **while** is again a keyword and the **condition** given in the **while** statement is evaluated. If it evaluates to true, the **do** block will execute again. Otherwise, the loop will terminate and the control will be transferred to the next statement which is immediately after the **do-while** loop, refer to Figure 3-18.

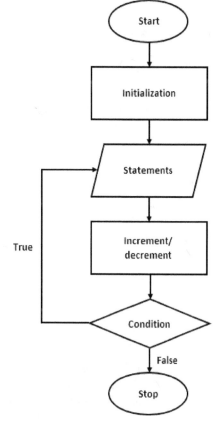

Figure 3-18 Flow chart of the do-while loop

Note

In the do-while loop, the while statement should be terminated with a semicolon (;).

For example:

```
int count =1;
do
{
        ----------;   //These lines indicate
        ----------;   //the body of the loop
        count++;
}
while (count <=5);
```

In this example, the **count** variable is treated as a loop control variable and 1 is assigned as an initial value to it. This variable acts as a counter and controls the entire loop. Next, the statements in the **do** block will be executed at least once. After executing the statements in the **do** block, the control will be transferred to the increment part **count++** which will inturn increment the value of the control variable by one. Next, the condition given in the **while** statement, **count<=5** will be evaluated. If it evaluates to true, the body of the loop will be executed again. Otherwise, the body of the loop will be skipped. This process will be repeated until the value of the **count** variable becomes less than or equal to the value 5.

Example 7

The following example illustrates the use of the **do-while** statement. The program will compare two variables and display the values of both the variables until they are equal.

//Write a program to compare two variables using the **do-while** loop

```
1   class dowhile_demo
2   {
3       public static void main(String arg[])
4       {
5           int a=5, b=1;
6           do
7           {
8               System.out.println("a = " +a+ ", b = " +b);
9               b++;
10          }
11          while(a>b);
12          System.out.println("a and b are equal");
13      }
14  }
```

Explanation

The working of this program is the same as the previous programming example except that here the body of the loop (lines 8 and 9) must be executed at least once. Next, the condition **a>b** given in the **while** statement will be evaluated. If the condition evaluates to true, the body of the loop will be executed again. Otherwise, the loop will be terminated.

The output of Example 7 is displayed in Figure 3-19.

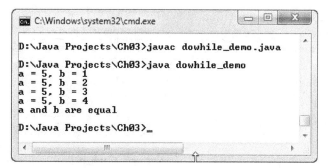

Figure 3-19 *The output of Example 7*

The for loop

The **for** loop is an iteration statement, which is used to execute a particular block of code for a specific number of times. The **for** loop is mostly used when you know the number of times the body of the loop will be executed. The **for** loop is easy to understand because all control elements (initialization, condition, and increment or decrement) are placed together.

The syntax for using the **for** loop is as follows:

```
for(initialization; condition; increment or decrement)
```

In this syntax, **for** is a keyword and **initialization**, **condition**, and **increment or decrement** are the control expressions. **Initialization** is the first statement inside the **for** loop parentheses. In the **initialization** part, counter variable is assigned by an initial value. It is the control variable of the loop. Next, **condition** is the second expression inside the **for** loop parentheses. It is an expression that should evaluate to either true or false. If it evaluates to true, the **for** loop is evaluated one more time. If it evaluates to false, the **for** loop is not executed anymore, and execution jumps to the first statement after the body of the **for** loop. The third expression in the **for** loop is the **increment** or **decrement**. It executes after each iteration of the **for** loop. It will increment or decrement the value of the variable by 1, refer to Figure 3-20. These three expressions must be separated by a **semicolon (;)**. For example:

```
for(i=0; i<5; i++)
{
    body of the loop;
}
```

In this example, the variable **i** is treated as a loop control variable and **0** is assigned as an initial value to it. This variable acts as a counter and controls the entire

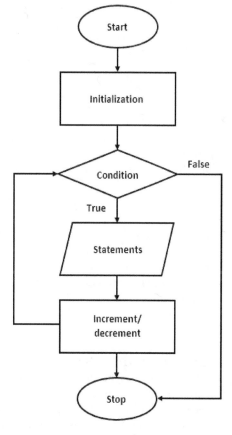

Figure 3-20 *Flow chart of the **for** loop*

loop. This initialization part is executed only once. Next, the conditional expression **i<5** will be evaluated. If it evaluates to **true**, the body of the loop will be executed. Otherwise, the body of the loop will be skipped. After executing the body of the loop, the control will be transferred to the increment part **i++**, which will inturn increment the value of the control variable **i** by 1. Next, again the conditional expression will be evaluated. This process will be repeated until the value of **i** variable becomes less than 5. It will be evaluated 5 times.

Example 8

The following example illustrates the use of the **for** loop. The program will calculate the multiples of a given number and display them on the screen.

//Write a program that displays the multiples of a number
```
1   class for_demo
2   {
3       public static void main(String arg[])
4       {
5           int num = 7;
6           int mul;
7           System.out.println("The multiples of " +num+ ":");
8           for(int i=1; i<=10; i++)
9           {
10              mul = num*i;
11              System.out.println(num+ " * " +i+ " = " +mul);
12          }
13      }
14  }
```

Explanation
Line 5
int num = 7;
In this line, **num** is declared as an integer type variable and 7 is assigned as an initial value to it.

Line 6
int mul;
In this line, mul is declared as an integer type variable.

Line 7
System.out.println("The multiples of " +num+ ":");
This line will display the following on the screen:
The multiples of 7 are as follows:

Line 8
for(int i=1; i<=10; i++)
This line contains the **for** loop. In this line, the **i** variable (loop control variable) is initialized to 1 and the condition **i<=10** will be checked. If the condition is true, the body of the loop will be executed and the control will be transferred to line 11. This process will be repeated till the condition is true. When the condition becomes false, the loop will terminate.

Line 10
mul = num*i;
In this line, the value of the **num** variable is multiplied by the value of **i** variable and the resultant value will be assigned to the **mul** variable.

Line 11
System.out.println(num+ " * " +i+ " = " +mul);
This line will display the following on the screen:
7 * 1 = 7

Note
In line 11, the value of the variable i will be increased by 1 in each iteration.

The output of Example 8 is displayed in Figure 3-21.

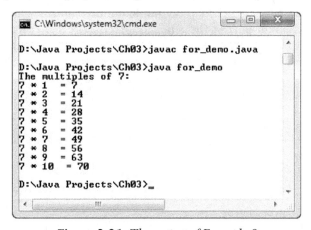

Figure 3-21 The output of Example 8

Multiple Statements Using Comma

You can also include multiple statements in the initialization and the increment/decrement part by using the comma (,) separator. But only one conditional expression can be included in this type of **for** loop.

For example:

```
for(a=50, b=1; a>b; a--, b++)
{
    body of the loop;
}
```

In the initialization part, the **a** and **b** variables are initialized with 50 and 1, respectively. In the increment/decrement part, the **a** variable is decremented by 1 and the **b** variable is incremented by 1. But in this case, only one conditional expression **a>b** is included. Therefore, body of the loop will be executed until the given condition becomes **false**.

Nested for Loop

When a **for** loop is used within another **for** loop, it is known as the nested **for** loop. In the nested **for** loop, the outer **for** loop takes control over the inner **for** loop. The syntax for using the nested **for** loop is as follows:

```
for(initialization; condition; increment/decrement)        //Outer Loop
{
    for(initialization; condition; increment/decrement) //Inner Loop
    {
        body of the loop;
    }
}
```

In a nested loop, when the execution begins, the compiler first encounters the outer loop. If the condition in the outer loop is true, the control will be transferred to the inner loop. When the execution of the inner loop is completed, the control will be transferred back to the increment/decrement part of the outer loop. This process is repeated until the outer loop finishes or the condition in the outer loop becomes false. Note that for every execution of the outer **for** loop, the inner **for** loop will also execute.

Example 9

The following example illustrates the use of the nested **for** loop. The program will display the right-angled triangle of digits on the screen.

```
//Write a program to display a right-angled triangle of digits
1   class nestedfor_demo
2   {
3       public static void main(String arg[])
4       {
5           int i, j;
6           for(i=0; i<5; i++)   //Outer loop
7           {
8               for(j=0; j<=i; j++)       //Inner loop
9               {
10                  System.out.print((j+1) + " ");
11              }
12              System.out.println("");
13          }
14      }
15  }
```

Explanation

Line 6

for(i=0; i<5; i++)

The outer **for** loop begins with this line. In this line, the **i** variable will be initialized to 0. Next, the condition **i<5** will be evaluated. If the condition evaluates to true, the control will be transferred to the inner loop (line 8). After the execution of the inner loop, the control will be transferred back to the increment/decrement part of the outer loop. This process will be repeated until the given condition is satisfied. If the condition evaluates to false, the body of the outer loop will be skipped and the loop will terminate.

Line 8
for(j=0; j<=i; j++)
The inner **for** loop begins from this line. This loop is controlled by the outer loop. If the condition in the outer loop evaluates to true, only then the control will be transferred to this loop. Otherwise, this loop will be skipped. If the condition given in the inner loop evaluates to true, the body of the inner loop will be executed and the control will directly be transferred to line 10. Otherwise, the body of the inner loop will be skipped and the control will be transferred back to the increment/decrement part of the outer loop.

The output of Example 9 is displayed in Figure 3-22.

Figure 3-22 *The output of Example 9*

The Jump Statements

The jump statements are used to skip a part of the loop and transfer the control for certain conditions. When a jump statement is encountered within a block, it transfers the control outside the existing block. Java supports the following three jump statements:

1. break
2. continue
3. return

break

The **break** statement is used to skip the nearest enclosing statement such as **switch** or loop such as **for, while, do-while**, and so on. Whenever a break statement is encountered within the body of the loop, the loop terminates and the control is transferred to the next immediate statement after the loop.

Example 10

The following example illustrates the use of the **break** statement. The program will create the Fibonacci series and also display the resultant series on the screen.

//Write a program to create a Fibonacci series of digits

```
1    class break_demo
2    {
3        public static void main(String args[])
4        {
5            int a=0, b=1, c=0, i=0;
6            while(c<=200)
7            {
8                System.out.println(c);
9                c=a+b;
10               a=b;
11               b=c;
12               i++;
13               if(i==10)
14               break;
15           }
16           System.out.println("Exit from the loop");
17       }
18   }
```

Explanation

Line 5
int a=0, b=1, c=0, i=0;
In this line, **a, b, c,** and **i** variables are declared as integer type variables and the values 0, 1, 0, and 0 are assigned as initial values to them, respectively.

Line 6
while(c<=200)
This line contains the **while** statement. In this line, first the conditional expression **c<=200** will be evaluated. If it evaluates to true, the statements (from lines 8 to 14) associated with the **while** loop will be executed. Otherwise, the loop will terminate and the control will be transferred to line 16, which is immediately after the **while** loop.

Line 8
System.out.println(c);
This line will display the value of the **c** variable on the screen.

Line 9
c=a+b;
In this line, the value of the **a** variable will be added to the value of the **b** variable. Next, the resultant value will be assigned to the **c** variable.

Line 10
a=b;
In this line, the value of the **b** variable will be assigned to the **a** variable.

Line 11
b=c;
In this line, the value of the **c** variable will be assigned to the **b** variable.

Line 12
i++;
The **i** variable is treated as a counter variable, which is increased by 1 every time the body of the loop is executed. In this line, the value of the **i** variable will be increased by 1.

Line 13
if(i==10)
In this line, the conditional expression **i==10** will be evaluated. If it evaluates to true, the control will be transferred to line 14. Otherwise, line 14 will be skipped.

Line 14
break;
This line will be executed when the conditional expression given in line 13 evaluates to true. When this statement is executed, it will transfer the control outside the **while** loop. As a result, now the control will be transferred to line 16.

The output of Example 10 is displayed in Figure 3-23.

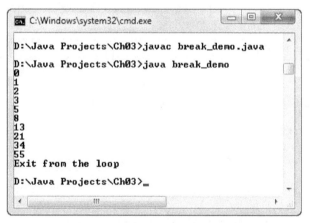

Figure 3-23 *The output of Example 10*

In the previous section, you learned that the **break** statement is used to jump outside the loop or to exit from the loop. You can also use the **break** statement in another form and this form is known as labeled **break** statement. The syntax for using the labeled **break** statement is given next:

```
break label;
```

In this syntax, the **label** is a valid identifier, which represents a name that points to a particular block of code. When the given statement is executed, the control will be transferred outside that particular block. To name a block, put a label followed by a colon at the beginning of the block.

For example:

```
greater:
{
    ----------;
    ----------;
    if(conditional expression)
            break greater;
    ----------;
    ----------;
}
```

In this example, **greater** represents a label. The curly braces {} indicate the start and the end of the named block. In this block, if the given conditional expression evaluates to **true**, the control will be transferred to the next statement, which is a labeled **break** statement.

Example 11

The following example illustrates the use of a labeled **break** statement. The program will illustrate the working of the labeled **break** statement.

```
//Write a program to illustrate the working of a labeled break statement
1    class labeled_break_demo
2    {
3        public static void main(String args[])
4        {
5            outer:
6            for(int i=0; i<3; i++)
7            {
8                inner:
9                for(int j=0; j<4; j++)
10               {
11                   System.out.println("Value of i is: " +i);
12                   System.out.println("Value of j is: " +j);
13                   if(j<i)
14                       break inner;
15               }
16               System.out.println("Outside the inner block");
17           }
18       }
19   }
```

Explanation
In this program, **outer** and **inner** represent labels. Here, the **for** loops will work in the same way as described earlier in this chapter. When the condition **j<i** given in the **if** statement (line 13) evaluates to true, the labeled **break** statement will be executed. Here, the label given with the **break** keyword is **inner**. So, the control will exit from the block named **inner** and will be transferred to the next statement (line 16) immediately after the **inner** block.

The output of Example 11 is displayed in Figure 3-24.

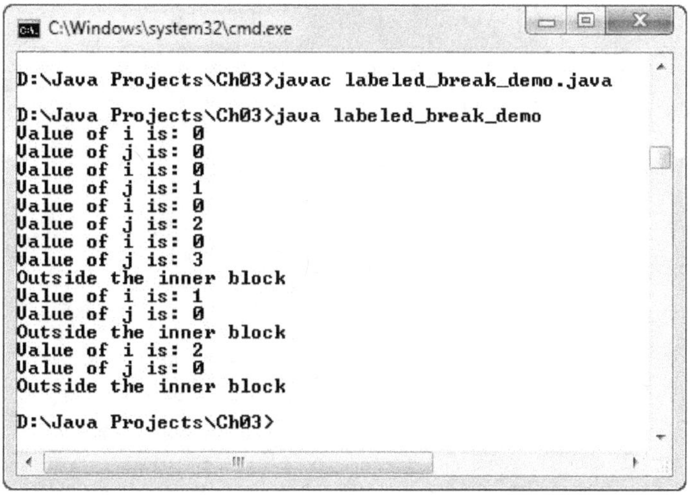

Figure 3-24 *The output of Example 11*

continue

The **continue** statement is similar to the break statement except that instead of exiting from the loop, the **continue** statement transfers the control back to the top of the loop for the next iteration. The **continue** statement is used in those cases, where you want an early iteration of the loop. When the **continue** statement is encountered inside the block of code, it will skip the remaining part (statements, which are immediately after the **continue** statement) of that particular block. The syntax for using the **continue** statement is as follows:

```
continue;
```

For example:

```
for(i=0;i<=10;i++)
{
    statement 1;
    if(i==5)
            continue;
    statement 2;
}
```

In this example, when the value of the **i** variable is equal to 5, the **continue** statement will be executed. Next, the control will be transferred to the increment part (i++) of the **for** loop and the remaining part (statement 2) will be skipped.

Example 12

The following example illustrates the use of the **continue** statement. The program will display all odd numbers from 1 to 20.

//Write a program to find the odd numbers from 1 to 20

```
1   class continue_demo
2   {
3       public static void main(String args[])
4       {
5           System.out.println("Odd numbers from 1 to 20:");
6           for(int i=1; i<=20; i++)
7           {
8               if(i%2==0)
9               continue;
10              System.out.println(i);
11          }
12      }
13  }
```

Explanation
Line 8
if(i%2==0)
In this line, the % (modulus) operator returns the remainder after dividing the value of the **i** variable with the value **2**. If the remainder value is equal to **0**, the control will be transferred to the next line (line 9). Otherwise, the control will be transferred to line 10.

Line 9
continue;
This line will execute when the condition given in the **if** statement evaluates to true. When the **continue** statement is executed, the control will be transferred to the increment part of the loop and the next iteration will continue.

Line 10
System.out.println(i);
This line will display the value of the **i** variable on the screen when the condition given in the **if** statement evaluates to false.

The output of Example 12 is displayed in Figure 3-25.

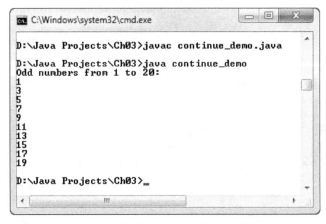

Figure 3-25 *The output of Example 12*

return

The **return** statement is another type of **jump** statement that terminates the execution of the method and returns a value given in the expression. The syntax for using the **return** statement is as follows:

```
return expression;
```

In this statement, the expression represents some values that will be returned by the **return** statement.

You will learn more about the working of the **return** statement in the later chapters.

ARRAYS

An array is a collection of data elements of the same type. These elements are referred by a common name and are stored in contiguous memory locations. You can refer to a particular data element by using the index value. The index starts from the lowest address **(0)** and ends at the highest address **n-1** (here, **n** specifies the total number of elements). Various types of arrays are discussed next.

One-Dimensional Arrays

The one-dimensional arrays are those arrays, which contain only one subscript and the elements in them are stored in a list form. The syntax for declaring one-dimensional array is as follows:

```
datatype arr_name[ ];
```

In this syntax, the **datatype** specifies the type of data that can be stored in the array specified by **arr_name**.

For example, you can declare an integer type array named **even_numbers** by using the following source code:

```
int even_numbers[ ];
```

In Java, no memory space is allocated to a newly declared array. Therefore, in this example, no memory space is allocated to the array **even_numbers** and its value is set to **null**. In such a case, to provide memory space to an array, the array needs to be defined with the **new** operator. The **new** operator is a special operator, which is used to allocate memory. The syntax for using the **new** operator is as follows:

```
arr_name = new datatype[size];
```

In this syntax, the **arr_name** specifies the name of an array. The **new** operator is used to allocate the required memory space. The **datatype** specifies the type of data that the array can hold. The **size** in the square brackets specifies the maximum number of elements that the array can hold.

For example:

```
even_numbers = new int[5];
```

In this example, the **new** operator provides contiguous memory space of 20 bytes for five integer elements. By default, all these integer elements are initialized to 0.

After allocating the memory to an array, you can access any of its elements by using the index value. The syntax for accessing an element of an array is as follows:

```
arr_name[index value];
```

In this syntax, the **arr_name** specifies the array and the **index value** specifies a value, which can be from 0 to n-1 (here, n specifies the total number of elements in the array).

For example:

```
even_numbers[4];
```

In this example, the value stored at the index value **4** is accessed by the compiler.

Example 13

The following example illustrates the use of a one-dimensional array. The program will create a one-dimensional array, initialize each of its elements, access the element at index 3, and display the resultant value on the screen.

```
//Write a program to create a one-dimensional array
1    class one_dim_demo
2    {
3        public static void main(String arg[])
4        {
5            int odd_num[];
6            odd_num = new int[5];
7            odd_num[0] = 1;
8            odd_num[1] = 3;
9            odd_num[2] = 5;
10           odd_num[3] = 7;
11           odd_num[4] = 9;
12           System.out.println("Value at index 3 : " +odd_num[3]);
13       }
14   }
```

Explanation
Line 5
int odd_num[];
In this line, the integer type array **odd_num** is declared.

Line 6

odd_num = new int[5];

In this line, the **new** operator is used that will allocate 20 bytes of contiguous memory space for the storage of 5 integer elements. Each of these 5 integer elements will be initialized to 0 by default.

Line 7

odd_num[0] = 1;

In this line, the value 1 will be assigned to the integer element at the 0th index, as an initial value.

The working of the lines from 8 to 11 is the same as the line 7.

Line 12

System.out.println("Value at index 3 : " +odd_num[3]);

This line will display the following on the screen:

Value at index 3 : 7

The output of Example 13 is displayed in Figure 3-26.

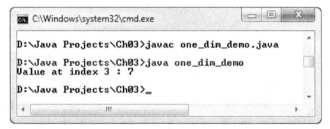

Figure 3-26 The output of Example 13

In the previous program, all elements were initialized after the allocation of memory space by the **new** operator. In some programs, you can also initialize an array without using the **new** operator. In such cases, there is no need to use the **new** operator and also no need to define the size of an array. Moreover, the maximum size of an array is specified by the number of elements specified in the array initializer, as given next:

```
int odd_numbers[ ] = {1, 3, 5, 7, 9, 11, 13, 15, 17, 19};
```

When this code is executed by the Java compiler, the maximum size of the array **odd_numbers** will be set to 10. The values given in the array initializer will be assigned to all elements of the array such as 1 is assigned to the 0th element, 3 is assigned to the 1st element and so on.

Example 14

The following example illustrates the use of one-dimensional array without using the **new** operator. The program will calculate the average of three numbers and display the resultant value on the screen.

//Write a program to calculate the average of three numbers.

```
1   class one_dim_array
2   {
3       public static void main(String arg[])
4       {
5.          int numbers[ ] = {52, 56, 82};
6           int avrg = 0;
7           for (int i=0; i<3; i++)
8           avrg= avrg + numbers[i];
9           avrg = avrg/3;
10          System.out.println("Average is: " +avrg);
11      }
12  }
```

Explanation

Line 5

int numbers[ ] = {52, 56, 82};

In this line, an integer type array **numbers** is declared and three values 52, 56, and 82 are passed to the array initializer. These values will be assigned to the three elements of the array such as 52 to element 0, 56 to element 1, and so on.

Line 6

int avrg = 0;

In this line, **avrg** is declared as an integer type variable and 0 is assigned as an initial value to it.

Line 7

for (int i=0; i<3; i++)

This line contains the **for** loop. In this loop, the **i** variable is treated as a loop control variable. This loop works in such a way that the loop control variable **i** is declared as an integer type and 0 is assigned as an initial value to it. Next, the condition **i<3** will be evaluated. If it evaluates to true, the control will be transferred to the next line (line 8). Otherwise, the control will be transferred to the next line (line 9) immediately after the **for** loop.

Line 8

avrg= avrg + numbers[i];

In this line, the value of the **avrg** variable will be added to the index value of array **numbers**. Next, the resultant value will be assigned back to the **avrg** variable.

Line 9

avrg = avrg/3;

In this line, the value of the **avrg** variable will be divided by the integer value 3. Next, the resultant value will be assigned to the **avrg** variable.

Line 10

System.out.println("Average is: " +avrg);

This line will display the following on the screen:

Average is: 63

The output of Example 14 is displayed in Figure 3-27.

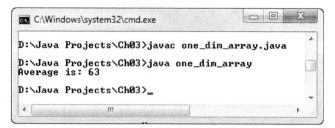

Figure 3-27 *The output of Example 14*

Multidimensional Arrays

A multidimensional array is also known as an array of arrays. The multidimensional array can have more than one dimension such as 2, 3, 4, upto n. A two-dimensional array is the simplest type of multidimensional array. The syntax for declaring a two-dimensional array is as follows:

```
data_type arr_name [ ] [ ] = new data_type[size] [size];
```

This syntax contains two square brackets, which represent that this is a two-dimensional array. The **size** given in the first square bracket specifies the number of rows in an array and the **size** given in the second square bracket specifies the number of columns in an array.

For example, to create a two-dimensional array of an integer type that has four rows and three columns in each row, the code will be as follows:

```
int matrix[ ] [ ] = new int [4][3];
```

The number of bytes occupied by a two-dimensional array can be calculated as follows:

Total number of bytes= number of rows * number of columns * size of data type

For example, the two-dimensional array **matrix** occupies 48 bytes (4*3*4).

In a two-dimensional array, the index value consists of two values. One value specifies the row number and the other value specifies the column number in that particular row. For example, you may want to access the data element, which is stored in the second column of first row in the array **matrix[ ] [ ]**. You can access the given element by specifying the following index value:

```
matrix[1] [2];
```

Figure 3-28 represents a two-dimensional array, which contains 4 rows and 3 columns.

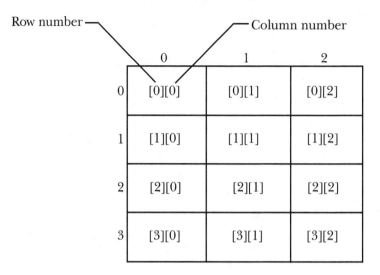

Figure 3-28 *Representation of a two-dimensional array*

Example 15

The following program illustrates the use of a two-dimensional array. The program will create a two-dimensional array, initialize all array elements, and display the resultant array on the screen.

```
//Write a program to create a two-dimensional array
1   class two_dim_demo
2   {
3       public static void main(String arg[])
4       {
5           int matrix[ ][ ]= new int[4][3];
6           int i, j, count =20;
7           for(i=0;i<4; i++)//loop for rows
8           {
9               for(j=0;j<3;j++)//loop for columns
10              {
11                  matrix[i][j] = count++;
12              }
13          }
14          for(i=0;i<4;i++)//loop for rows
15          {
16              for(j=0;j<3;j++)//loop for columns
17              {
18                  System.out.print(matrix[i][j] + " ");
19              }
20              System.out.println();
21          }
22      }
23  }
```

Explanation

Line 5

int matrix[ ][ ]= new int[4][3];

In this line, **matrix** is declared as an integer type of two-dimensional array, which contains 4 rows and 3 columns.

Line 7

for(i=0;i<4; i++)

In this line, the **for** loop is used to check iterations of rows of the array **matrix[ ] [ ]**. The number of iterations of this loop are equal to the number of rows. In this program, the number of rows are 4. So, this loop will be executed 4 times. In each iteration, it will initialize the elements of each row. In the first iteration, it will initialize the elements of row 0, in the second iteration of row 1, in the third iteration of row 2, and in the end of row 4.

Line 9

for(j=0;j<3;j++)

When the condition given in line 7 is **true**, the control will be transferred to this line. This loop is used for columns and is repeated thrice because the number of columns in a row is 3. In each iteration, it will initialize one element in each column.

Line 11

matrix[i][j] = count++;

When the condition given in line 9 is true, the control will be transferred to this line. In this line, the value of the **count** variable will be assigned to the array **matrix[i][j]**. As a result, the value of the **count** variable will be incremented by one. For example, in the first iteration of the loop (line 9), this statement will initialize one element with value 20 at the location **a[0][0]**, in the second iteration it will initialize another element with value 21 at **a[0][1]**, and so on.

The **for** loops given in lines 14 and 16 are used to display the values stored in the array at different locations.

The output of Example 15 displayed in Figure 3-29.

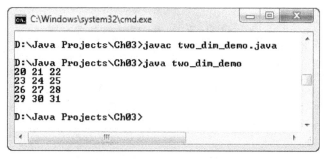

Figure 3-29 The output of Example 15

THE foreach LOOP

The **foreach** loop is a basic **for** loop which is defined in a special way. The **foreach** loop is used to make iteration over a collection of objects such as arrays and so on. It is also known as the **advanced for loop** or **enhanced for loop**. The syntax for using the **foreach** statement is given next:

```
for(datatype var_name : collection)
```

In this syntax, the **datatype** specifies the type of data and the **var_name** represents a variable that is used to receive elements from a collection or an array one by one from the beginning to the end. The **collection** represents a collection of objects such as an array and so on. The **foreach** loop works in such a way that in each iteration, one element is retrieved from the collection and it is stored in the iteration variable, which is represented by **var_name**. This process is repeated until all elements in the collection are retrieved.

For example:

```
int numbers[ ] = {10, 20, 30};
mul = 1;
for(int itr_var: numbers)
    mul*=itr_var;
    ----------;
    ----------;
```

In this example, when the **foreach** statement is executed, the value (10) of the first element of the array **numbers[ ]** will be assigned to the iteration variable **itr_var**. The value of the **itr_var** variable will be multiplied by the value of the **mul** variable and the resultant value will be assigned back to the **mul** variable. In the next step, the value 20 of the next element will be assigned to the **itr_var** variable. This process is repeated until all the three elements of the array **numbers[ ]** are retrieved.

The working of the **foreach** statement used in the previous example is the same as the **for** loop given next:

```
for(int itr_var =0; itr_var<3; itr_var++)
    mul*=numbers[i];
    ----------;
    ----------;
```

You have already learned the use of **foreach** statement in one-dimensional array. In this section, you will learn how to use this statement on two-dimensional arrays. As you already know that the two-dimensional arrays are also known as the array of arrays, therefore when a **foreach** statement is iterated over the two-dimensional array, a complete array is returned to the iteration variable in place of a single variable.

For example:

```
int numbers[ ] [ ] = new int[4][5];
for(int i=0; i<4; i++)
{
    for(j=0; j<5;j++)
    {
            ----------;
    }
}
```

These **for** statements can be replaced by the **foreach** statements given next:

```
for(int a[ ]: numbers)  //Outer foreach statement
{
    for(int b: a)//Inner foreach statement
    {
            ----------;
            ----------;
    }
}
```

In this statements, first the outer **foreach** statement executes and it obtains a single-dimension array from the two-dimensional array **numbers[ ] [ ]**. The resultant array is assigned to the iteration array **a[ ]**. Next, the control is transferred to the inner **foreach** statement. The working of the inner **foreach** statement is the same as that of a single-dimensional array.

Example 16

The following program illustrates the use of **foreach** loop. The program will calculate the sum of all 2-D array elements, and will also display the array and sum on the screen.

```
//Write a program to calculate the sum of 2-D array elements
 1   class ForEach_demo
 2   {
 3      public static void main(String args[])
 4      {
 5          int sum=0;
 6          int arr[][]={{10,20},{30,40}};
 7          for(int i[]:arr)
 8          {
 9              for(int j:i)
10              {
11                  System.out.print(j +" ");
12                  sum+=j;
13              }
14              System.out.println();
15          }
16          System.out.println("Sum of array elements :  " +sum);
17      }
18   }
```

Explanation

Line 6

int arr[][]={{10,20},{30,40}};

In this line, an integer type two dimensional (2-D) array **arr** is declared and four values 10, 20, 30, and 40 are passed to the array initializer where each subset represents the row. Here, subset {10, 20} and {30, 40} represent two rows. These values will be assigned to the four elements of the array such as 10 to element [0][0], 20 to element [0][1], and so on.

Line 7

for(int i[]:arr)

This line represents the outer **foreach** loop. When this loop is executed, it obtains a single-dimensional integer type array **i** from the two-dimensional integer type array **arr[ ] [ ]**.

Line 9

for(int j:i)

This line represents the inner **foreach** loop. When this loop is executed, the value (**10**) of the first element of the array **i[ ]** will be assigned to the iteration variable **j**. This process is repeated until all the elements of the array **i[ ]** are retrieved.

The output of Example 16 is displayed in Figure 3-30.

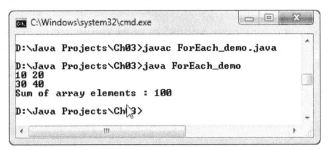

Figure 3-30 *The output of Example 16*

Self-Evaluation Test

Answer the following questions and then compare them to those given at the end of this chapter:

1. A _____ is a graphical representation of the steps that constitute a program.

2. The _____ statement is a single path statement.

3. The _____ statement routes the path in two different directions.

4. The _____ statement is used to verify more than one condition.

5. The statement used for multiway selection is known as the _____ statement.

6. The **for** loop is used when you know the number of times the body of a loop will be executed. (T/F)

7. You can skip some or all parts of the **for** loop. (T/F)

8. In a nested **for** loop, the outer **for** loop takes control over the inner **for** loop. (T/F)

9. The **break** statement transfers the control back to the start of a loop. (T/F)

10. The **continue** statement is used to terminate a loop. (T/F)

Review Questions

Answer the following questions:

1. Define control statements.

2. Differentiate between the selection and iteration statements.

3. Explain the working of the nested **if** statement with the help of a suitable example.

4. Explain the working of the **for** loop with the help of a suitable example.

5. Differentiate between the **break** and **continue** statements.

6. Find the errors in the following source codes:

(a)
```
class if_demo
{
    public static main void(String args[])
    {
        int i=10, j=20;
        if(i<=j);
        {
            System.out.println("Value of i is: " +i);
            System.out.println("Value of j is: " +j);
        }
    }
}
```

(b)
```
class switch_demo
{
    public static void main(String args[ ])
    {
        int a=10,b=20,result;
        Switch(i)
        {
          case 1:
              result=a+b;
              System.out.println("Addition: " +result);
              break;
          Case 2:
              result=b-a;
              System.out.println("Subtraction: " +result);
              break
          case 3:
              result=a*b;
              System.out.println("Multiplication: " +result);
              Break;
          case 4:
              result=b/a;
              System.out.println("Division: " +result);
              break;
          default:
              System.out.println("invalid Choice");
        }
    }
}
```

(c)
```
class do_while_demo
{
    public static main void(String args[])
    {
        int i=1;
        do
        {
            System.out.println("Value of i is: " +i);
            i++;
        }
        while(i<=10)
    }
}
```

(d)
```
class for_demo
{
    public static void main(String args[ ])
    {
        for(int i=0, i<=10, i++)
        System.out.println("Value of i is: " +i);
    }
}
```

```
(e) class labeled_break_demo
    {
        public static void main(String args[ ])
        {
            label1;
            for(int i=0; i<=10; i++)
            {
                if(i==5);
                break label1;
            }
        }
    }
```

EXERCISES

Exercise 1

Write a program to check whether a character is consonant or vowel.

Exercise 2

Write a program to calculate the square of the first ten odd numbers by using the **do-while** loop.

Exercise 3

Write a program to produce the following output:

```
* * * *
* * *
* *
*
```

Exercise 4

Write a program to create a two-dimensional array of [5][4] and assign the following values to all array elements. Also, display these values on the screen.

```
0  1  2  3
4  5  6  7
8  9  10  11
12  13  14  15
16  17  18  19
```

Answers to Self-Evaluation Test
1. flowchart, 2. if, 3. if-else, 4. if-else-if, 5. switch, 6. T, 7. T, 8. T, 9. F, 10. F

Chapter 4

Classes and Objects

Learning Objectives

After completing this chapter, you will be able to:

- *Understand the concept of classes*
- *Understand the concept of objects*
- *Understand the concept of methods*
- *Understand the concept of passing parameters to methods*
- *Understand the concept of passing objects to methods*
- *Understand the concept of passing arrays to methods*
- *Understand the concept of method overloading*
- *Understand the concept of constructors*
- *Understand the concept of constructor overloading*
- *Understand the concept of garbage collection*
- *Understand the concept of finalize( ) method*
- *Understand the concept of this keyword*
- *Understand the concept of static data members and methods*
- *Understand the concept of recursion*

INTRODUCTION

Java is purely an object oriented programming language. Object-oriented programming (OOP) is developed to overcome the limitations of the procedure-oriented programming and is an improved technique for developing the programs. In case of OOP, the data is treated as the most critical element and the primary focus is on the data and not on the procedures. In this technique, the data is grouped together with the functions that operate on it. A problem is divided into entities known as objects. Each object maintains its own copy of data and functions. The data cannot be accessed directly by the other objects of the program. It can only be accessed through a proper interface such as functions. In this chapter, you will learn more about classes, objects, methods, constructors, garbage collection, and so on.

CLASSES

A class is a user-defined data type. It can be used to create objects of the specified data type. The objects thus created are known as the instances of a class. A class is a collection of data and methods and it acts as a blueprint or prototype in the creation of objects. The data specifies the nature of a class, whereas the methods are used to operate on the data inside a class. Both the data and methods are known as the members of a class. The motive behind using a class is to encapsulate the data and methods into a single unit so that the data members can be accessed only through a well-defined interface. This process is known as data hiding.

Defining a Class

A class is defined by using the **class** keyword with the class name. The class name should be a valid identifier. The class definition consists of data members and methods. The syntax for defining a class is as follows:

```
class class_name
{
    datatype variable1;
    datatype variable2;
    datatype method_name1(List of arguments)
    {
        body of the method;
    }
    datatype method_name2(List of arguments)
    {
        body of the method;
    }
}
```

In this syntax, the declaration begins with the **class** keyword followed by the **class_name**, which is an identifier given by the programmer to specify the name of the class. The **variable1** and **variable2** variables that are defined inside a class are known as the instance variables. In most of the cases, these instance variables can only be accessed by the methods of the same class. The body of the methods contains statements that are used to operate on the data.

For example:

```
class Rectangle
{
    double length;
    double breadth;
}
```

In this example, the **Rectangle** class is defined. In the class definition, two instance variables **length** and **breadth** are defined. This class also defines a new data type that is called **Rectangle**. Now, this new data type **Rectangle** can be used to declare objects of its type.

OBJECTS

An object is defined as an instance or a physical instantiation of a class. It is also known as a living entity within a program. When an object is created within a class, it maintains its own copy of instance variables that are defined inside the class. A class provides certain attributes and each object can have different values for those attributes. Therefore, each object of a class is uniquely identified.

Creating an Object

Whenever a new class is defined, a new data type is created. You can use this data type to create objects of that particular type. You can create an object of a class by using the following two steps:

1. In the first step, you need to declare a variable of the class type. This variable will be used as a reference to the object of that particular class.

2. In the second step, a physical copy of the object is acquired and assigned to the variable, which is already declared in the first step with the help of the **new** operator. The **new** operator allocates memory to the object at run-time and returns the memory address of the object. Now, this memory address is assigned to the variable as a reference.

For example, you can create an object of the **Rectangle** class as follows:

```
Rectangle obj1;            //Step 1
obj1= new Rectangle( );    //Step 2
```

In the first step, obj1 is declared as a reference to an object of the type Rectangle. When this line is executed, the value NULL is assigned to the **obj1** variable. Now, the **obj1** variable contains NULL value and it does not refer to any actual object. In the second step, the required memory (16 bytes) is reserved with the help of the **new** operator. Next, the **new** operator returns the reference of the reserved memory space, which is assigned to the **obj1** variable. Now, the **obj1** variable holds the memory address of the real **Rectangle** object, as shown in Figure 4-1.

Note

*In the given example, **Rectangle( )** is a constructor, and it is used to initialize the objects of the class **Rectangle**. You will learn more about constructors later in this chapter.*

You can also create an **obj1** object of the **Rectangle** class by using the following statement:

```
Rectangle obj1 = new Rectangle( );
```

The above statement is a combination of the two statements, which were discussed before.

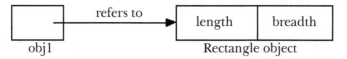

Figure 4-1 Representation of step 2

Assigning Initial Values to Instance Variables

As you know that whenever an object of a class is created, it maintains its own copy of instance variables, which are defined inside that particular class. For example, if you create ten objects of the **Rectangle** class, each object will maintain its own copy of instance variables, **length** and **breadth**. You can assign an initial value to an instance variable of the object of a class with the help of the dot (.) operator. The syntax for assigning an initial value to an instance variable is as follows:

```
obj_name.var_name = value or expression;
```

In this syntax, the **obj_name** represents an object, whereas the **var_name** represents the instance variable of a class, and the **value or expression** represents an initial value.

Accessing Instance Variables

As already discussed, each object maintains its own copy of instance variables and it can access its own copy of instance variables by using the dot (.) operator. The syntax for accessing an instance variable is as follows:

```
obj_name.var_name;
```

In this syntax, **obj_name** represents an object, and the **var_name** represents the instance variable of a class.

For example, to access the **breadth** instance variable of the **obj1** object, you need to use the following statement:

```
obj1.breadth;
```

Example 1

The following example illustrates the concept of class and its object. The program will calculate the area of a rectangle with the given dimensions, and then display the resultant value on the screen.

//Write a program to calculate the area of a rectangle

```
1    class Rectangle
2    {
3         double length;
4         double breadth;
5    }
6    class Rectangle_demo
7    {
8         public static void main(String arg[ ])
9         {
10            Rectangle obj1 = new Rectangle( );
11            double area;
12            obj1.length = 85;
13            obj1.breadth = 73;
14            area= obj1.length * obj1.breadth;
15            System.out.println("Area is: " +area);
16        }
17   }
```

Explanation

Lines 1 to 5
class Rectangle
{
        double length;
        double breadth;
}
In these lines, the **Rectangle** class is defined. The curly braces {} indicate the start and end of the **Rectangle** class. The **length** and **breadth** are declared as the **double** type variables inside the class definition. These variables are known as instance variables.

Line 6
class Rectangle_demo
In this line, the **Rectangle_demo** class is defined.

Line 10
Rectangle obj1 = new Rectangle( );
After the execution of this line, **obj1** is treated as an instance of the **Rectangle** class.

Line 11
double area;
In this line, **area** is declared as a variable of **double** type.

Line 12
obj1.length = 85;
In this line, 85 is assigned as an initial value to the **length** instance variable of the **obj1** object.

Line 13
obj1.breadth = 73;
In this line, 73 is assigned as an initial value to the **breadth** instance variable of the **obj1** object.

Line 14
area = obj1.length * obj1.breadth;
In this line, first the values, 85 and 73, of the **length** and **breadth** instance variables of the **obj1** object is multiplied. Next, the resultant value 6205.0 is assigned to the **area** variable.

Line 15
System.out.println("Area is: " +area);
This line will display the following on the screen:
Area is: 6205.0

The output of Example 1 is displayed in Figure 4-2.

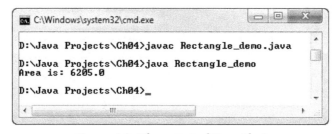

Figure 4-2 The output of Example 1

Note
*You need to save Example 1 with the name **Rectangle_demo.java** because the **main( )** method resides inside the class **Rectangle_demo**, not in the class **Rectangle**.*

In Example 1, you have observed that only one object was created and it maintained copy of all its instance variables. However, if more than one object is created, then you need to understand the link of these objects with the copies of their instance variables. Also, you need to know that if an object makes a change in its instance variable, then whether it affects other objects or not. In Example 2, you will understand all these concepts.

Example 2

The following example illustrates the concept of class and its multiple objects. The program will calculate the volume of a cylinder with the given dimensions and then display the resultant values on the screen.

```
//Write a program to calculate the volume of a cylinder
1    class Cylinder
2    {
3        double radius;
4        double height;
5    }
6    class Cylinder_demo
7    {
8        public static void main(String arg[ ])
9        {
10           double pi = 3.14;
11           double volume;
```

```
12          Cylinder obj1 = new Cylinder( );
13          Cylinder obj2 = new Cylinder( );
14          obj1.radius = 13.5;
15          obj1.height = 30;
16          obj2.radius = 15.5;
17          obj2.height = 40;
18          volume = pi * (obj1.radius*obj1.radius) * obj1.height;
19          System.out.println("Volume is: " +volume);
20          volume = pi * (obj2.radius*obj2.radius) * obj2.height;
21          System.out.println("Volume is: " +volume);
22      }
23  }
```

Explanation

Line 12
Cylinder obj1 = new Cylinder( );
In this line, **obj1** is created as an object of the type **Cylinder**.

Line 13
Cylinder obj2 = new Cylinder( );
In this line, **obj2** is created as another object of the type **Cylinder**.

Line 14
obj1.radius = 13.5;
In this line, 13.5 is assigned as an initial value to the **radius** instance variable of the **obj1** object.

Line 15
obj1.height = 30;
In this line, 30 is assigned as an initial value to the **height** instance variable of the **obj1** object.

Line 16
obj2.radius = 15.5;
In this line, 15.5 is assigned as an initial value to the **radius** instance variable of the **obj2** object.

Line17
obj2.radius = 40;
In this line, 40 is assigned as an initial value to the **radius** instance variable of the **obj2** object.

Line 18
volume = pi * (obj1.radius*obj1.radius) * obj1.height;
In this line, first the expression given in the parentheses, **obj1.radius*obj1.radius** is solved. Then, the resultant value 182.25 is multiplied with the value of **pi** variable (3.14) and **obj1.height** (30). Next, the resultant value 17167.95 is assigned to the **volume** variable.

Line 19
System.out.println("Volume is: " +volume);
This line will display the following on the screen:
Volume is: 17167.95

The working of lines 20 and 21 is the same as lines 18 and 19, respectively.

The output of Example 2 is displayed in Figure 4-3.

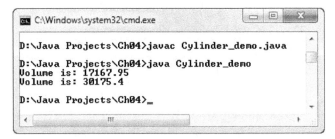

Figure 4-3 The output of Example 2

Assigning Object Reference Variables

In the previous example, you may have noticed that two objects of the **Cylinder** class were created and both maintained the copies of their instance variables. Moreover, if any change is made in the copy of instance variables of an object, it does not affect other objects. But, if you want both objects to share the same copy of instance variables, you can do so by assigning an object reference variable to another variable. The syntax for assigning an object reference variable to another variable is as follows:

```
class_name var_name = obj_ref_var;
```

In this syntax, the **class_name** represents a class. The **obj_ref_var** represents an object reference variable, which is already referred to the object of the class represented by **class_name**. The **obj_ref_var** assigns the reference to the variable that is specified by **var_name** with the help of the assignment (**=**) operator.

For example:

```
Rectangle obj1 = new Rectangle( );
Rectangle obj2 = obj1;
```

In this example, both the **obj1** and **obj2** objects of **Rectangle** class share the same copy of the **length** and **breadth** instance variables, as shown in Figure 4-4. If either of the objects make any change in the value of its instance variable, the other object also gets affected.

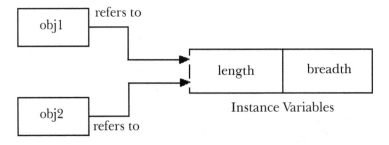

Figure 4-4 Representation of the example

Example 3

The following example illustrates the concept of assigning an object reference variable. The program will calculate the volume of a cylinder with the given dimensions and then display the resultant values on the screen.

```
//Write a program to calculate the volume of a cylinder
1    class Cylinder_Vol
2    {
3        double radius;
4        double height;
5    }
6    class Cylinder_Vol_demo
7    {
8        public static void main(String arg[ ])
9        {
10           double pi = 3.14;
11           double volume;
12           Cylinder_Vol obj1 = new Cylinder_Vol( );
13           obj1.radius = 13.5;
14           obj1.height = 30;
15           Cylinder_Vol obj2 = obj1;
16           volume = pi * (obj1.radius*obj1.radius) * obj1.height;
17           System.out.println("Volume is: " +volume);
18           volume = pi * (obj2.radius*obj2.radius) * obj2.height;
19           System.out.println("Volume is: " +volume);
20           obj2.radius = 15;
21           obj2.height = 32.5;
22           volume = pi * (obj1.radius*obj1.radius) * obj1.height;
23           System.out.println("Volume is: " +volume);
24           volume = pi * (obj2.radius*obj2.radius) * obj2.height;
25           System.out.println("Volume is: " +volume);
26       }
27   }
```

Explanation
Line 13
obj1.radius = 13.5;
In this line, 13.5 is assigned as an initial value to the **radius** instance variable of **obj1**.

Line 14
obj1.height = 30;
In this line, 30 is assigned as an initial value to the **height** instance variable of **obj1**.

Line 15
Cylinder1 obj2 = obj1;
In this line, the **obj1** object reference variable is assigned to **obj2**, which means that both the **obj1** and **obj2** are referred to the same object. Also, they will share the same copy of instance variables.

The working of lines 16 to 19 is the same as explained in the previous example.

Line 20
obj2.radius = 15;
In this line, 15 is assigned as an initial value to the **radius** instance variable of **obj2**. Therefore in this line, the value 13.5, assigned earlier by **obj1**, is overwritten by **obj2**. In this way, both **obj1** and **obj2** objects affect each other.

Line 21
obj2.height = 32.5;
In this line, 32.5 is assigned as an initial value to the **height** instance variable of **obj2**. Therefore in this line the value 30, assigned earlier by **obj1**, is overwritten by **obj2**.

The working of lines 22 to 25 is the same as explained in the previous example.

The output of Example 3 is displayed in Figure 4-5.

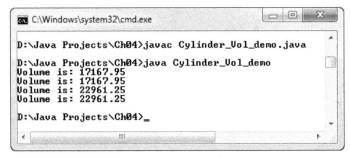

Figure 4-5 The output of Example 3

METHODS

In this chapter, you have already learned that class definition contains instance variables and methods. Now, in this section, you will learn more about methods. A method is a group of statements that are used to perform a particular task. A method operates on the data and it defines the behavior of a class.

Defining a Method

The syntax for defining a method is as follows:

```
access_specifier return_type method_name(list of arguments)
{
    body of the method;
    return value;
}
```

In this syntax, the **access_specifier** represents an access specifier that can be **public**, **private**, or **protected**. The **return_type** specifies the type of data, which is returned by a method. If a method does not return any value, then the **return_type** should be **void**. The **method_name** specifies the name of the method. The name of a method should be a valid identifier. The **list of arguments** inside the parentheses represents the list of identifiers and their types, separated by commas. These arguments will be used when some values are passed to the method at the time of a method call. The curly braces {} indicate the start and end of the body of the method that contains the statements, which need to be executed when a call is made to that particular method. Note that whenever a call is made to a particular method, it will perform the same task repeatedly. The next statement within the body of a method is a **return** statement. The **value** represents the value returned by the method. This statement is used only in those methods, which have some return type. The methods, which have a **void** return type, do not use the **return** statement inside their bodies.

For example:

```
public void cylinder_volume( )
{
    double volume = pi * (obj1.radius*obj1.radius) * obj1.height;
    System.out.println("Volume is: " +volume);
}
```

In this example, the return type of the **cylinder_volume( )** method is **void**, which means it does not return any value when a call is made. The parentheses is also empty because no value is passed when a call is made to it.

Calling a Method

The syntax for calling a method is as follows:

```
obj_name.method_name(list of values);
```

In this syntax, **method_name** specifies the method which is invoked by a relative object, represented by **obj_name**. The **list of values** represents the values that are passed to the identifiers in the list of arguments of the method definition.

For example:

```
obj1.cylinder_volume( );
```

In this example, the **cylinder_volume( )** method is called by the **obj1** object.

Example 4

The following example illustrates the concept of defining and calling a method. The program will calculate the volume of a cylinder with the given dimensions and display the resultant values on the screen.

```
//Write a program to calculate the volume of a cylinder
1   class Cylinder1
2   {
3       double radius;
4       double height;
5       public void cylinder_volume( )
6       {
7           double volume, pi = 3.14;
```

```
8              volume = pi * (radius*radius) * height;
9              System.out.println("Volume is: " +volume);
10     }
11  }
12  class Cylinder1_demo
13  {
14      public static void main(String arg[ ])
15      {
16          Cylinder1 obj1 = new Cylinder1( );
17          Cylinder1 obj2 = new Cylinder1( );
18          obj1.radius = 13.5;
19          obj1.height = 30;
20          obj1.cylinder_volume( );
21          obj2.radius = 15.5;
22          obj2.height = 10.5;
23          obj2.cylinder_volume( );
24      }
25  }
```

Explanation

Line 5

public void cylinder_volume( )

In this line, **void** is a return type, which indicates that the method will not return any value. The **cylinder_volume( )** is the name of the method.

Line 7

double volume, pi = 3.14;

In this line, **volume** and **pi** are declared as double type variables and 3.14 is assigned to **pi** as an initial value.

Line 8

volume = pi * (radius*radius) * height;

In this line, the **radius** and **height** variables will use the values of the instance variables of that object with which the **cylinder_volume( )** method will be called.

Line 20

obj1.cylinder_volume( );

In this line, a call is made to the **cylinder_volume( )** method with the **obj1** object. Now, the control is transferred to the method definition and the statements associated with it are executed.

Line 23

obj2.cylinder_volume( );

In this line, a call is made to the **cylinder_volume( )** method with the **obj2** object. Now, the control is transferred to the function definition and the statements associated with it are executed.

The output of Example 4 is displayed in Figure 4-6.

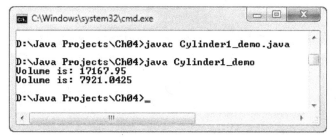

Figure 4-6 *The output of Example 4*

Methods that Return a Value

In the previous example, all operations were performed inside the definition of the **cylinder_volume( )** method and it did not return any value to the caller. In such a case, you use another way of calling a method. In this process, the **cylinder_volume( )** method will compute the volume inside its definition and then return the resultant value to the caller.

For example:

```
public double cylinder_volume( )
{
    return pi * (radius*radius) * height;
}
```

In this example, first the volume is calculated inside the method definition. Next, the resultant value is returned to the caller with the help of the **return** statement.

Note

In these types of methods, the return type of method should be compatible to the type of data returned by the method. Also, the type of variable that receives the value returned by the method should be compatible to the return type specified for the method.

Example 5

The following example illustrates the working of methods that return a value. The program will calculate the volume of a cylinder with the given dimensions and then display the resultant values on the screen.

//Write a program to calculate the volume of a cylinder

```
1   class Cylinder2
2   {
3       double radius;
4       double height;
5       double pi =3.14;
6       public double cylinder_volume( )
7       {
8           return pi * (radius*radius) * height;
9       }
10  }
```

```
11  class Cylinder2_demo
12  {
13      public static void main(String arg[ ])
14      {
15          Cylinder2 obj1 = new Cylinder2( );
16          Cylinder2 obj2 = new Cylinder2( );
17          double volume;
18          obj1.radius = 13.5;
19          obj1.height = 30;
20          volume = obj1.cylinder_volume( );
21          System.out.println("Volume is: " +volume);
22          obj2.radius = 15.5;
23          obj2.height = 10.5;
24          volume = obj2.cylinder_volume( );
25          System.out.println("Volume is: " +volume);
26      }
27  }
```

Explanation

Lines 6 to 9
public double cylinder_volume( )
{

   return pi * (radius*radius) * height;

}

These lines contain the definition of the **cylinder_volume( )** method. Here, the return type of the method is **double** that means the value returned by this method is of **double** type. Inside the definition, first the volume of the cylinder is computed and then the resultant value is returned to the caller.

Line 20
volume = obj1.cylinder_volume( );
In this line, a call is made to the **cylinder_volume( )** method with the **obj1** object. Next, the control is transferred to the method definition (from lines 6 to 9). Inside the function definition, the volume is computed with the values (13.5 and 30) of the **obj1**. The method returns the resultant value (17167.95) with the help of the **return** statement. Next, the resultant value is assigned to the **double** type variable **volume**.

The working of line 24 is the same as explained in Line 20. A call is made to the **cylinder_volume( )** method with the **obj2** object.

The output of Example 5 is displayed in Figure 4-7.

Figure 4-7 *The output of Example 5*

Passing Parameters to Methods

You can also pass some values to a method when a call is made to that particular method. To do so, a parameter list can be specified while defining a method. The syntax for defining a method that takes parameters is as follows:

```
access_specifier ret_type method_name( type par_name1, type par_name2,...)
{
    body of the method;
}
```

In this syntax, a parameter list separated by commas is specified inside the parentheses. In this list, the **type** specifies the data type of parameters and the **par_name1**, **par_name2** represent the variables.

For example:

```
int sum(int a, int b)
{
    int c = a+b;
    ----------;
    ----------;
}
```

In this example, two integer type parameters **a** and **b** are specified within the parentheses. These parameters take the values, which are passed to the **sum( )** method when a call is made to it with an object of a class, as given next:

```
obj1.sum(10,20);
```

In this statement, a call is made to the **sum( )** method with the **obj1** object and two integer values, 10 and 20 are passed. These values are assigned to the two parameters **int a** and **int b**, respectively.

Example 6

The following program illustrates the concept of passing parameters to methods. The program will perform the addition, subtraction, multiplication, and division operations on the given values using different methods and then display the resultant values on the screen.

/* Write a program to perform addition, subtraction, multiplication, and division operations on the given values. */

```
1    class Calculator
2    {
3        int sum(int i, int j)
4        {
5            int result = i+j;
6            return result;
7        }
8        int subtract(int i, int j)
9        {
10           int result = i-j;
11           return result;
12       }
13       int multi(int i, int j)
14       {
15           int result = i*j;
16           return result;
17       }
18       double div(int i, int j)
19       {
20           double result = i/j;
21           return result;
22       }
23   }
24   class Calculator_demo
25   {
26       public static void main(String arg[])
27       {
28           Calculator obj1 = new Calculator( );
29           int add = obj1.sum(210,15);
30           System.out.println("Sum is: " +add);
31           int sub = obj1.subtract(210,15);
32           System.out.println("Subtraction is: " +sub);
33           int mul = obj1.multi(210,15);
34           System.out.println("Multiplication is: " +mul);
35           double div = obj1.div(210,15);
36           System.out.println("Division is: " +div);
37       }
38   }
```

Explanation

Line 28

Calculator obj1 = new Calculator( );

In this line, **obj1** is declared as an instance of the **Calculator** class.

Line 29

int add = obj1.sum(210,15);

In this line, first a call is made to the **sum()** method and two integer values 210 and 15 is passed as parameters. Now, the control is transferred to the definition of the **sum()** method (lines 3 to 7). The values 210 and 15 is assigned to the two integer variables **i** and **j**, respectively. Next, the addition operation is performed inside the method body and the resultant value (225) is returned. Now, the control is transferred back to the line 29. Next, the resultant value is assigned back to the integer type variable **add**.

Line 30
System.out.println("Sum is: " +add);
This line will display the following on the screen:
Sum is: 225

Line 31
int sub = obj1.subtract(210,15);
In this line, first a call is made to the **subtract()** method and two integer values 210 and 15 are passed as parameters. Now, the control is transferred to the definition of the **subtract**() method (lines 8 to 12). The values 210 and 15 is assigned to the two integer variables **i** and **j**, respectively. Next, inside the method body, the subtraction operation is performed and the resultant value (195) is returned. Now, the control is transferred back to the line 31. Next, the resultant value is assigned back to the integer type variable **sub**.

Line 32
System.out.println("Subtraction is: " +sub);
This line will display the following on the screen:
Subtraction is: 195

The working of lines 33 to 36 is the same as lines 29 to 32.

The output of Example 6 is displayed in Figure 4-8.

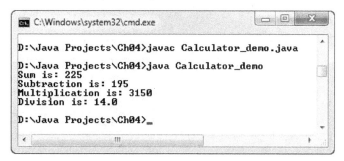

Figure 4-8 The output of Example 6

Passing Objects to Methods

In the earlier section of this chapter, you have already learned about passing parameters to methods, wherein, when you pass a simple data item to a method, Java passes only a copy of the data, not the original data item. This process is called **pass by value**. In the **pass by value**, you can only make changes in the copy of the data item without affecting the original data item. Similarly, you can also pass an object to a method, but this process is different from passing parameters. Java passes the object reference 'by value'. When an object is passed as argument to a method, actually the reference to that object is passed. Therefore, if you make any change in the passed object, it will affect the original object.

For example:

```
class Demo
{
    -----------;
    int area(Rect obj1, Rect obj2)
    {
        ----------;
        ----------;
    }
}
```

In this example, the **area( )** method of the **Demo** class contains two parameters. Both the parameters, **obj1** and **obj2**, are represented as the objects of the **Rect** class. So, whenever a call is made to the **area( )** method, the two objects of the **Rect** class are passed as arguments.

Example 7

The following example illustrates the use of passing objects to a method. The program will calculate the area of a rectangle using the concept of passing objects to methods and then display the resultant value on the screen.

//Write a program to calculate the area of a rectangle
```
1   class Rectangle
2   {
3       double length, width;
4       void getvalues(double l, double w)
5       {
6           length = l;
7           width = w;
8       }
9       void area(Rectangle obj)
10      {
11          double result;
12          result = obj.length * obj.width;
13          System.out.println("Area is: " +result);
14      }
15  }
16  class PassingObj
17  {
18      public static void main(String arg[])
19      {
20          Rectangle obj1 = new Rectangle( );
21          obj1.getvalues(14.2, 12.5);
22          obj1.area(obj1);
23      }
24  }
```

Explanation

Lines 20

Rectangle obj1 = new Rectangle( );

In these lines, **obj1** is created as object of the **Rectangle** class.

Line 21

obj1.getvalues(14.2, 12.5);

In this line, a call is made to the **getvalues( )** method of the **Rectangle** class and two values, 14.2 and 12.5 are passed as arguments to it. These values are assigned to the parameters, **l** and **w** inside the method definition. Next, the values of the **l** and **w** variables are assigned to the **length** and **width** instance variables of the **obj1** object, respectively.

Line 22

obj1.area(obj1);

In this line, a call is made to the **area( )** method with the **obj1** object, and the **obj1** object is passed as an argument to it. Now, the reference of the **obj1** object is assigned to the **obj** object in the method definition. Next, all statements inside the definition of the method is executed.

The output of Example 7 is displayed in Figure 4-9.

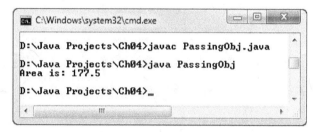

Figure 4-9 *The output of Example 7*

Returning Objects from Methods

In the previous examples of this chapter, you have observed that the methods only returned the variables of the simple data types such as **int**, **double**, and so on. In this section, you will learn how a method can return to objects of a class with the help of the **return** statement.

For example:

```
Demo sum( )
{
    Demo obj = new Demo( );
    return obj;
}
```

In this example, the return type of the **sum( )** method is of class type **Demo**. Whenever a call is made to the **sum( )** method, it returns the **obj** object of the **Demo** class, as given next:

```
obj2 = obj1.sum( );
```

When this statement is executed, the **sum( )** method returns the reference of the **obj1** object. Now, the resultant reference is assigned to another **obj2** object of the **Demo** class.

Example 8

The following example illustrates the concept of returning objects from methods. The program will calculate the square of first ten natural numbers and then display the resultant values on the screen.

//Write a program to calculate the square of first ten natural numbers
```
1   class Test
2   {
3       int x;
4       void getvalue(int j)
5       {
6           x = j;
7       }
8       Test square( )
9       {
10          Test temp = new Test( );
11          temp.x = x * x;
12          return temp;
13      }
14  }
15  class ReturnObj
16  {
17      public static void main(String arg[])
18      {
19          Test obj1 = new Test( );
20          Test obj2;
21          for(int i=1; i<=10; i++)
22          {
23              obj1.getvalue(i);
24              obj2 = obj1.square();
25              System.out.println("Square of " +obj1.x+ "  is: " +obj2.x);
26          }
27      }
28  }
```

Explanation
Line 19
Test obj1 = new Test( );
In this line, **obj1** is created as an object of the **Test** class.

Line 20
Test obj2;
In this line, **obj2** is declared as an object of the **Test** class. Here, the **obj2** object is not initialized.

Line 21

for(int i=1; i<=10; i++)

In this line, the **for** loop is used. Inside this loop, first the loop control variable **i** is initialized. Next, the condition **i<=10** is evaluated. If the condition evaluates to **true**, the control is transferred to the body of the **for** loop. After the execution of all statements associated with the **for** loop, the control is transferred back to the increment portion **i++** of the loop.

Line 23

obj1.getvalue(i);

In this line, a call is made to the **getvalue( )** method of the **Test** class and the value of the **i** variable is passed as an argument. Now, this value is assigned to the **j** variable in line 4. Next, the value of the **j** variable is assigned to the **x** instance variable of the **obj1** object.

Line 24

obj2 = obj1.square( );

In this line, a call is made to the **square( )** method with the **obj1** object. Now, the control is transferred to line 8 (definition of the method). Inside the method definition, first **temp** is created as an object of the **Test** class. Next, the square is calculated and the resultant value is assigned to the **x** instance variable of the **temp** object. Then, the reference of the **temp** object is returned by the **square( )** method. The resultant reference of the **temp** object is assigned to the **obj2** object in line 24.

The output of Example 8 is displayed in Figure 4-10.

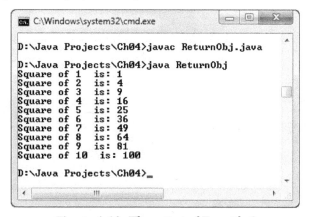

Figure 4-10 *The output of Example 8*

Passing Arrays to Methods

Like variables and objects, you can also pass an array to a method as an argument. In this case, only the reference of the array is passed. If any changes are made to the passed array inside the body of the method, the original array also gets affected. You can pass an array by simply passing its name inside the parentheses of a method.

For example:

```
int arr[ ] = {10, 20, 30, 40};
Demo obj1 = new Demo ( );
obj1.sum(arr);
```

In this example, the integer type array **arr[ ]** is passed as an argument to the method **sum( )** by writing its name within the parentheses of the method.

Example 9

The following example illustrates the concept of passing arrays to methods. The program will calculate the square of first five odd numbers and then display the resultant values on the screen.

```
//Write a program to calculate the square of first five odd numbers
1   class Square
2   {
3       int result;
4       void sqr(int a[])
5       {
6           for(int i=0; i<a.length; i++)
7           {
8               result = a[i]*a[i];
9               System.out.println("Square of " +a[i]+ " is: "+result);
10          }
11      }
12  }
13  class PassArray
14  {
15      public static void main(String arg[])
16      {
17          int i;
18          int numbers[ ] = {1, 3, 5, 7, 9};
19          Square obj1 = new Square( );
20          obj1.sqr(numbers);
21      }
22  }
```

Explanation
Line 6
for(int i=0; i<a.length; i++)
This line contains the **for** loop. In this line, the **i** variable (loop control variable) is initialized to 0 and the condition **i<a.length** is checked. This condition is evaluated to be true until the **i** variable is less than the length of array **a**. If the condition is true then the control will be transferred to the statements inside the loop. When the condition is evaluated to be false, the loop will be terminated.

Line 8
result = a[i]*a[i];
In this line, the value of the array **a** at the **i**th index is multiplied to itself and the resultant value is assigned to the **result** variable.

Line 18
int numbers[ ] = {1, 3, 5, 7, 9};
In this line, **numbers** is declared as an array of integers and the values (1, 3, 5, 7, and 9) are assigned to its elements.

Line 19
Square obj1 = new Square( );
In this line, **obj1** is declared as an object of the **Square** class.

Line 20
obj1.sqr(numbers);
In this line, a call is made to the **sqr( )** method and the array of integers **numbers** is passed as an argument to it. Now, the control is transferred to line 4. Next, the reference of the array **numbers** is assigned to the array of integers **a[ ]** and the statement associated with the **sqr( )** method is executed.

The output of Example 9 is displayed in Figure 4-11.

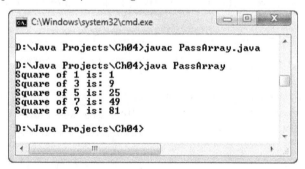

Figure 4-11 *The output of Example 9*

Method Overloading

Inside a class, when you define two or more than two methods with the same name but different parameter lists, you are overloading the methods. Method overloading is a way to achieve polymorphism in Java. In method overloading, all overloaded methods must contain different number or different types of parameters. So, whenever a call is made to an overloaded method, the compiler differentiates that particular method from its type and /or number of parameters. Whenever the exact match is found, the compiler executes the body of that particular method.

For example:

```
class Demo
{
    int i, j;
    void setvalues( )
    {
        i=0;
        j=0;
    }
    void setvalues(int x, int y)
    {
        i =x;
        j =y;
    }
    ----------;
    ----------;
}
```

In this example, two methods are defined within the **Demo** class and both share the common name **setvalues**. But, both methods contain different parameter lists. The parameter list of the first method **void setvalues( )** is empty and the other method **void setvalues(int x, int y)** contains two parameters. Now, whenever a call is made to the overloaded method **setvalues**, the compiler differentiates between them on the basis of the number and / or type of parameters, as given next:

```
obj1.setvalues( );
obj2.setvalues(10, 20);
```

When these statements are executed, the compiler first executes the method that contains no parameter, and then it will execute the another method that contains two integer type variables inside the parameter list.

Example 10

The following example illustrates the concept of method overloading. The program will calculate the square of the given values and then display the resultant values on the screen.

//Write a program to calculate the square of the given values
```
1   class Overload
2   {
3       void square( )
4       {
5           System.out.println("No parameters");
6       }
7       void square(int x)
8       {
9           int result;
10          result = x*x;
11          System.out.println("Square of " +x+ " is: " +result);
12      }
```

```
13    void square(double x)
14    {
15        double result;
16        result = x*x;
17        System.out.println("Square of " +x+ " is: " +result);
18    }
19  }
20  class Overload_demo
21  {
22      public static void main(String arg[])
23      {
24          Overload obj1 = new Overload( );
25          Overload obj2 = new Overload( );
26          Overload obj3 = new Overload( );
27          obj1.square( );
28          obj2.square(10);
29          obj3.square(14.5);
30      }
31  }
```

Explanation

Lines 24 to 26

Overload obj1 = new Overload( );
Overload obj2 = new Overload( );
Overload obj3 = new Overload( );

In these lines, **obj1**, **obj2**, and **obj3** are created as the objects of the **Overload** class.

Line 27

obj1.square( );

In this line, a call is made to the overloaded method **square( )** and no parameter is passed. Next, the compiler compares the return type, number and /or type of parameters with all overloaded methods. It finds a match at line 3 and the statement associated with that particular method is executed.

Line 28

obj2.square(10);

In this line, a call is made to the overloaded method **square( )** and an integer value 10 is passed as an argument. Next, the compiler again searches for a match, which is found at line 7. Now, the statements associated with that particular method are executed.

Line 29

obj3.square(14.5);

Similar to line 27 and 28, the compiler again searches for a match, which is found at line 13 and the statements associated with that particular method is executed.

The output of Example 10 is displayed in Figure 4-12.

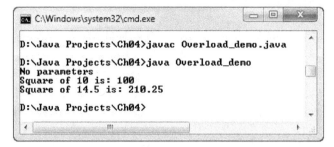

Figure 4-12 The output of Example 10

CONSTRUCTORS

A constructor is a special method of a class that is used to initialize an object when it is created. It is called a special member of a class because it shares its name with the class name. Whenever an object of the class is created, a call is made to the constructor of that particular class. The main property of a constructor is that it does not contain any return type, not even **void**. The syntax for defining a constructor is given next:

```
class_name (list of parameters)
{
    body of the constructor;
}
```

In this syntax, **class_name** is the name of the constructor which can have list of parameters.

There are three types of constructors in Java. They are as follows:

1. Default Constructor
2. Parameterized Constructor
3. Copy Constructor

Default Constructor

Constructor which has no parameter is known as default constructor. It is used to provide default values to variables like 0, null, and so on, depending upon the type of data. It is also known as no-argument constructor.

For example:

```
class Demo
{
    int i, j;
    Demo ( )
    {
        i = 0;
        j = 0;
    }
    ----------;
    ----------;
}
```

In this example, both the class and constructor have the same name, **Demo**. The parameter list is empty. Now, whenever an object of the **Demo** class will be created, a call will be made to the **Demo( )** constructor, as given next:

```
Demo obj1 = new Demo( );
```

In this statement, **obj1** is declared as an object of the **Demo** class. Here, a call is made to the **Demo( )** constructor and the **i** and **j** instance variables of the **obj1** object are initialized to zero.

Note

If no constructor is defined inside a class, the default constructor is created by the compiler automatically.

Example 11

The following example illustrates the use of the constructors. The program will perform the addition, subtraction, multiplication, and division operations on the given values and display the resultant values on the screen.

```
/* Write a program to perform addition, subtraction, multiplication, and division operations
on the given values */
1   class Construct
2   {
3       int x, y;
4       Construct()//Constructor
5       {
6           x=210;
7           y=15;
8       }
9       int sum( )
10      {
11          int result = x+y;
12          return result;
13      }
14      int subtract( )
15      {
16          int result = x-y;
17          return result;
18      }
19      int multi( )
20      {
21          int result = x*y;
22          return result;
23      }
24      double div( )
25      {
26          double result = x/y;
27          return result;
28      }
29  }
```

```
30  class Construct_demo
31  {
32      public static void main(String arg[])
33      {
34          Construct obj1 = new Construct( );
35          int add = obj1.sum( );
36          System.out.println("Sum is:  " +add);
37          int sub = obj1.subtract( );
38          System.out.println("Subtraction is:  " +sub);
39          int mul = obj1.multi( );
40          System.out.println("Multiplication is:  " +mul);
41          double div = obj1.div( );
42          System.out.println("Division is:  " +div);
43      }
44  }
```

Explanation

Line 3

int x, y;

In this line, **x** and **y** are declared as the member variables of the **Construct** class.

Lines 4 to 8

Construct( )//Constructor

{

> **x=210;**
> **y=15;**

}

These lines contain the definition of the constructor of the **Construct** class. Whenever an object of the **Construct** class is created, the body of the constructor is executed. Inside the body, the **x** and **y** instance variables are initialized with the values 210 and 15, respectively.

Line 34

Construct obj1 = new Construct( );

In this line, **obj1** is created as an object of the **Construct** class. Here, a call is made to the **Construct( )** constructor and it assigns the initial values (210 and 15) to the copy of the instance variables (x and y) of **obj1** object.

Line 35

int add = obj1.sum( );

In this line, a call is made to the **sum( )** method with the **obj1** object of the **Construct** class. Now, the control is transferred to the definition of the **sum( )** method (from lines 9 to 13). Next, the addition operation is performed inside the definition and the resultant value 225 is transferred back to this line (line 35). And, the resultant value is assigned to the integer variable **add**.

Line 36

System.out.println("Sum is: " +add);

This line will display the following on the screen:

Sum is: 225

The working of lines 37 through 42 is the same as lines 35 and 36.

The output of Example 11 is displayed in Figure 4-13.

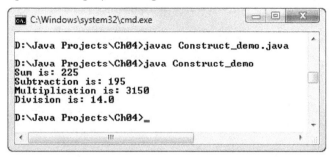

Figure 4-13 The output of Example 11

Parameterized Constructor

In the previous example, when the **obj1** object was created, the **Construct( )** constructor initialized the **x** and **y** instance variables with the values 210 and 15, respectively. Similarly, whenever you create different objects of the **Construct** class, the instance variables of different objects will be initialized with the same values 210 and 15. But, in practice, when these objects are created, you may need to initialize the instance variables of different objects with different values. In such cases, you can use the parameterized constructor. In these type of constructors, you can pass the parameters at the time of object creation.

For example:

```
class Demo
{
    int i, j;
    Demo(int x, int y)   //Parameterized Constructor
    {
        i = x;
        j = y;
    }
    ----------;
    ----------;
}
```

In this example, the **Demo(int x, int y)** constructor represents a parameterized constructor. Now, whenever an object of the **Demo** class will be created, you need to pass two integer values as parameters, as given next:

```
Demo obj1 = new Demo(10,20);
```

In this statement, two integer values 10 and 20 are passed as parameters to the **Demo( )** constructor. Now, these values are assigned to the two integer variables **x** and **y** inside the constructor definition.

Example 12

The following example illustrates the use of parameterized constructors. The program will calculate the area of a rectangle with different dimensions and display the resultant values on the screen.

//Write a program to calculate the area of a rectangle
```
1   class Rect
2   {
3       double length, width;
4       Rect(double l, double w)
5       {
6           length = l;
7           width = w;
8       }
9       double area( )
10      {
11          return length * width;
12      }
13  }
14  class Rect_demo
15  {
16      public static void main(String arg[])
17      {
18          double result;
19          Rect obj1 = new Rect(12.6, 14.8);
20          Rect obj2 = new Rect(13.6, 12.7);
21          result = obj1.area( );
22          System.out.println("Area is: " +result);
23          result = obj2.area( );
24          System.out.println("Area is: " +result);
25      }
26  }
```

Explanation

Line 19

Rect obj1 = new Rect(12.6, 14.8);

In this line, **obj1** is created as an object of the **Rect** class. Here, a call is made to the **Rect( )** constructor and two **double** values **12.6** and **14.8** are passed. Now, these values are assigned respectively to two **double** variables l and **w** inside the definition of the **Rect( )** constructor (line 4). Next, the values (12.6, 14.8) of the l and **w** variables are assigned to the copy of the instance variables, **length** and **width** of the **obj1**.

Line 20

Rect obj2 = new Rect(13.6, 12.7);

In this line, **obj2** is created as an object of the **Rect** class. Here, a call is made to the **Rect( )** constructor and two double values **13.6** and **12.7** is passed. Now, these values is assigned respectively to two **double** variables l and **w** inside the definition of the **Rect( )** constructor (line 4). Next, the values (**13.6, 12.7**) of the l and **w** variables is assigned to the copy of the **length** and **width** instance variables of the **obj2**.

Line 21
result = obj1.area( );
In this line, a call is made to the **area( )** method with the **obj1** object. Now, the control is transferred to the body of the method (lines 9 to 12). Inside the body of the method, the area is calculated on the basis of **12.6** and **14.8** value of the **length** and **width** instance variables of the **obj1** object, respectively. Next, the **return** statement returns the resultant value **186.48**, which is assigned to the **result** variable.

Line 22
System.out.println("Area is: " +result);
This line will display the following on the screen:
Area is: 186.48

The working of lines 23 and 24 is the same as lines 21 and 22.

The output of Example 12 is displayed in Figure 4-14.

Figure 4-14 *The output of Example 12*

Copy Constructor

When the value of one object is copied to another object then it is known as copy constructor. A constructor takes only one argument which is of the class type in which it is implemented. It is widely used for creating duplicates of objects known as cloned objects. A duplicate object is the object that has same characteristics as that of the original object from which it is created.

For example:

```
class Demo
{
    int i, j;
    Demo(Demo ob) //Copy Constructor
    {
        i = ob.i;
        j = ob.j;
    }
}
```

In this example, the **Demo(Demo ob)** constructor represents a copy constructor. Now, whenever an object of the **Demo** class will be created, you need to pass an object as parameter whose value you want to copy in this object, as given next:

```
Demo obj2 = new Demo(obj1);
```

In this statement, an **obj1** object is passed as parameter to the **Demo( )** constructor. Now, the values of **obj1** are assigned to the values of **obj2** inside the constructor definition.

Example 13

The following example illustrates the use of copy constructor. The program will calculate the area of a rectangle using the concept of passing object to the constructor and then display the resultant value on the screen.

```
//Write a program to calculate the area of a rectangle
1   class Rectangle
2   {
3       int x, y;
4       Rectangle (int i, int j)
5       {
6           x=i;
7           y=j;
8       }
9       Rectangle(Rectangle r)
10      {
11          x = r.x;
12          y = r.y;
13      }
14      void Area()
15      {
16          int area=x*y;
17          System.out.println("Area of rectangle : " +area);
18      }
19  }
20  class Copy_demo
21  {
22      public static void main(String args[])
23      {
24          Rectangle r1 = new Rectangle(15,30);
25          Rectangle r2 = new Rectangle(r1);
26          r1.Area();
27          r2.Area();
28      }
29  }
```

Explanation
Line 24
Rectangle r1 = new Rectangle(15, 30);
In this line, **r1** is created as an object of the **Rectangle** class. Here, a call is made to the **Rectangle( )** constructor and two integer values **15** and **30** are passed. Now, these values are assigned respectively to two integer variables **i** and **j** inside the definition of the **Rectangle()** constructor (line 4). Next, the values (**15, 30**) of the **i** and **j** variables are assigned to the copy of the **x** and **y** instance variables of the **r1** object.

Line 25
Rectangle r2 = new Rectangle(r1);
In this line, **r2** is created as an object of the **Rectangle** class. Here, a call is made to the **Rectangle( )** constructor and another **r1** object is passed. Now, the values of **r1** object are assigned to the copy of the instance object **r2** in the definition of **Rectangle( )** constructor (line 9). Next, the values (**15**, **30**) of the **r1** object are assigned to the **x** and **y** variables of the **r2** object.

Line 26
r1.Area();
In this line, a call is made to the **Area( )** method with the **r1** object. Now, the control is transferred to the body of the method (lines 14 to 19). Inside the body of the method, the area is calculated on the basis of **15** and **30** value of the **x** and **y** instance variables of the **r1** object, respectively. Next, the resultant value **450** is assigned to the **area** variable of the integer type.

Line 26
r2.Area();
In this line, a call is made to the **Area( )** method with the **r2** object. Now, the control is transferred to the body of the method (lines 14 to 19). Inside the body of the method, the area is calculated on the basis of **15** and **30** values of the **x** and **y** instance variables of the **r1** object, respectively. Next, the resultant value **450** is assigned to the **area** variable of the integer type.

The output of Example 13 is displayed in Figure 4-15.

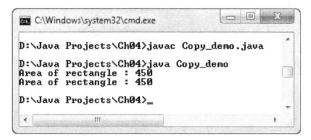

Figure 4-15 *The output of Example 13*

Constructor Overloading
Constructor overloading means defining more than one constructor within the same class. These constructors are differentiated by number and/or types of parameters. The overloaded constructors work in the same way as the overloaded methods. The overloaded constructors are used to initialize instance variables with different values.

For example:

```
class Demo
{
    int i, j;
    Demo ( )
    {
        i = 0;
        j = 0;
    }
```

```
Demo(int x)
{
    i = j =x;
}
Demo(int x, int y)
{
    i = x;
    j = y;
}
----------;
----------;
}
```

In this example, the **Demo( )** constructor is overloaded thrice. These three constructors are differentiated on the basis of the number of parameters. The first constructor contains no parameter, the second constructor contains only one parameter, and the third constructor contains two parameters. The compiler will execute the body of a constructor on the basis of the number of parameters passed during the time of creation of an object, as given next:

```
Demo obj1 = new Demo(10);
```

In this statement, only one integer type parameter is passed. So, the compiler executes the second constructor.

Example 14

The following example illustrates the use of overloading constructors. The program will add two numbers and display the resultant values on the screen.

```
//Write a program to add two numbers
1   class Sum
2   {
3       int val1, val2;
4       Sum( )
5       {
6           val1 = 0;
7           val2 = 0;
8       }
9       Sum(int x)
10      {
11          val1 = val2 = x;
12      }
13      Sum(int x, int y)
14      {
15          val1 = x;
16          val2 = y;
17      }
18      int add( )
19      {
20          return val1+val2;
21      }
```

```
22  }
23  class OverloadConst
24  {
25      public static void main(String arg[])
26      {
27          int result;
28          Sum obj1 = new Sum();
29          Sum obj2 = new Sum(10);
30          Sum obj3 = new Sum(10,20);
31          result = obj1.add( );
32          System.out.println("Result with no parameter : " +result);
33          result = obj2.add( );
34          System.out.println("Result with 1 parameter : " +result);
35          result = obj3.add( );
36          System.out.println("Result with 2 parameters : " +result);
37      }
38  }
```

Explanation

Line 28

Sum obj1 = new Sum();

In this line, **obj1** is created as an object of the **Sum** class. Here, a call is made to the **Sum( )** constructor and no value is passed. Now, the compiler automatically executes the first constructor (lines 4 to 8) and set the value of both **val1** and **val2** instance variables of the **obj1** object to zero.

Line 29

Sum obj2 = new Sum(10);

In this line, **obj2** is created as an object of the **Sum** class. Here, a call is made to the **Sum( )** constructor and only a single value 10 is passed. Now, the compiler automatically executes the second constructor (lines 9 to 12) and set the value of both **val1** and **val2** instance variables of the **obj2** object to 10.

Line 30

Sum obj3 = new Sum(10,20);

In this line, **obj3** is created as an object of the **Sum** class. Here, a call is made to the **Sum( )** constructor and two values 10, and 20 are passed. Now, the compiler automatically executes the third constructor (lines 13 to 17) and set the value of the **val1** and **val2** instance variables of the **obj3** object to 10 and 20, respectively.

Line 31

result = obj1.add( );

In this line, a call is made to the **add( )** method with **obj1**. Now, the control is transferred to the definition of the **add( )** method (line 18). Inside the definition of the method, the addition operation is performed and the resultant value is returned to its caller (line 31). Next, the resultant value (0) is assigned to the integer type variable, **result**.

Line 32

System.out.println("Result with no parameter : " +result);

This line will display the following on the screen:

Result with no parameter : 0

The working of the lines 33 to 36 is the same as lines 31 and 32.

The output of Example 14 is displayed in Figure 4-16

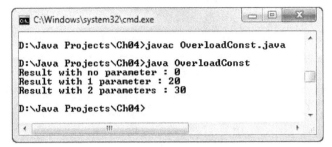

Figure 4-16 *The output of Example 14*

GARBAGE COLLECTION

In some object-oriented programming languages such as C++, you need to reclaim the memory space that is no longer in use. This can be done manually using some operators such as **delete** and so on. But, Java provides a mechanism that reclaims the memory automatically. It is known as garbage collection. The mechanism of garbage collection is handled by Java's runtime environment. In garbage collection, when it determines that an object is no longer required, the garbage collector reclaims the memory space used by that particular object. An object becomes eligible for garbage collection when there are no more references to that particular object. During the program execution, the garbage collector runs automatically by the Java runtime environment after a particular interval of time. You can also use this mechanism manually by using a **gc( )** method of the **System** class.

THE finalize( ) METHOD

As discussed before, in garbage collection, the objects that are no longer in use are destroyed. But sometimes, you want to perform certain operations before the destruction of an object. For this purpose, Java provides a method known as **finalize( )**. In the **finalize( )** method, you need to specify those actions that must be performed before an object is destroyed. The main purpose of using the **finalize( )** method is to release some non-Java resources used by an object before the destruction of that particular object. The **finalize( )** method is also known as the cleanup method. The syntax for using the **finalize( )** method is given next:

```
protected void finalize( )
{
    //finalization code
}
```

In this syntax, the **protected** keyword is an access specifier. The use of the **void** keyword represents that the method does not return any value. And, the finalization code represents those actions that should be performed before an object is destroyed.

THE this KEYWORD

In Java, the **this** keyword is used to refer to the current object of a class. The **this** keyword is used when a method or a constructor of a class needs the reference of the object that invokes it. You can also refer to any instance variable of current object within a method or a constructor by using the **this** keyword.

For example:

```
Rectangle(double l, double w)
{
    this.length = l;
    this.width = w;
}

Rectangle  obj1 = new Rectangle(10.2, 12.5);
```

In this example, the **this** keyword refers to the invoking **obj1** object.

Example 15

The following example illustrates the use of the **this** keyword. The program will calculate the area of a rectangle and display the resultant values on the screen.

//Write a program to calculate the area of a rectangle
```
1   class Rectangle
2   {
3       double length, width;
4       Rectangle(double l, double w)
5       {
6           this.length = l;
7           this.width = w;
8       }
9       double area()
10      {
11          return this.length * this.width;
12      }
13  }
14  class this_demo
15  {
16      public static void main(String arg[ ])
17      {
18          double result;
19          Rectangle obj1 = new Rectangle(10.5, 12.2);
20          Rectangle obj2 = new Rectangle(12.5, 15.2);
21          result = obj1.area();
22          System.out.println("Area is: " +result);
23          result = obj2.area();
24          System.out.println("Area is: " +result);
25      }
26  }
```

Explanation

The working of this example is same as the Example 12 with the only difference that in this example the **this** operator is used. When the **obj1** object is created, the **this** keyword refers to it. Similarly, when the **obj2** object is created, the **this** keyword refers to it. In line 21, when a call is made to the **area( )** method with the **obj1** object, the **this.length** and the **this.width** are referred to the **length** and **width** instance variables of **obj1**, respectively. This example makes it clear that the **this** keyword refers only to a current object of a class.

The output of Example 15 is displayed in Figure 4-17.

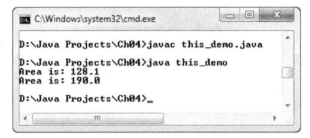

Figure 4-17 The output of Example 15

STATIC DATA MEMBERS AND METHODS

In all previous examples, you observed that each object of a class maintained its own copy of the instance variables. But sometimes, you need to define a variable whose copy is shared by all objects of a class. For this purpose, Java provides the **static** data member. Only a single copy of the **static** variable exists in a class, which is shared by all the objects. The syntax for declaring the **static** data members is given next:

```
static data_type var_name;
```

In this syntax, the **static** keyword directs the compiler that only one copy of the variable that is specified by **var_name** exists in a class.

For example:

```
static int a;
```

In this example, **a** is declared as an integer type **static** variable.

The main property of a **static** variable is that you can use it without creating an object of a class. In Java, these variables are treated in the same way as the global variables in the other object-oriented languages.

Like **static** variables, you can also create **static** methods. The main difference between a normal method of a class and a **static** method is that a **static** method can only access the **static** data members and **static** methods of a class. But they cannot use **this** keyword. You can use these methods without creating an object of its class. The most common example of a **static** method is the **main( )** method. In all the previous examples, the **main( )** method was declared as a **static** method.

Example 16

The following example illustrates the use of the **static** data members and methods. The program will add two numbers and also display the resultant value on the screen.

//Write a program to add two numbers
```
1   class static_demo
2   {
3       static int a = 110, b, c;
4       static int sum(int var)
5       {
6           b = var;
7           c = a+b;
8           return c;
9       }
10      public static void main(String arg[ ])
11      {
12          int result = sum(102);
13          System.out.println("The result is: "  +result);
14      }
15  }
```

Explanation

In this program, first the value 110 is assigned to the **static** integer variable **a**. Next, a call is made to the **main( )** method. Inside the **main( )** method, a call is made to the **sum( )** method. Then, the value 102 is passed as an argument. Now, this value is assigned to the **static** integer variable **b**. Next, the addition operation is performed and the resultant value is assigned to the integer variable **result**.

The output of Example 16 is displayed in Figure 4-18.

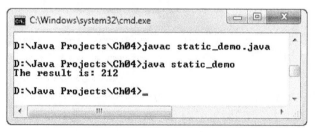

Figure 4-18 *The output of Example 16*

RECURSION

Recursion is a process in which a method calls itself repeatedly to perform successive steps, wherein each step uses the output of the preceding step.

For example:

```
long fib(long n)
{
    if(n==0||n==1)
    {
        return n;
    }
    else
    {
        return fib(n-1) + fib(n-2);
    }
}
```

In the given example, the **fib( )** method is said to be recursive because it is called repeatedly to return the final output of the statement given inside the **else** block.

Example 17

The following example illustrates the use of recursion. The program will calculate the factorial of a number and also display the resultant value on the screen.

//Write a program to calculate the factorial of a given number
```
1   class Factorial
2   {
3       int fact(int n)
4       {
5           if(n==1)
6           {
7               return n;
8           }
9           else
10          {
11              return n* fact(n-1);
12          }
13      }
14  }
15  class Recursion_demo
16  {
17      public static void main(String arg[])
18      {
19          int result;
20          Factorial obj1 = new Factorial( );
21          result = obj1.fact(5);
22          System.out.println("Factorial of 5 is: " +result);
23          result = obj1.fact(6);
```

```
24              System.out.println("Factorial of 6 is: "  +result);
25              result = obj1.fact(7);
26              System.out.println("Factorial of 7 is: "  +result);
27       }
28  }
```

Explanation

Line 20

Factorial obj1 = new Factorial( );

In this line, **obj1** is declared as an object of the class **Factorial**.

Line 21

result = obj1.fact(5);

In this line, first call will be made to the method **fact( )** and the value 5 will be passed as an argument to it. Then, control will be transferred to the definition of the method (line 3). Now, the value 5 will be assigned to the integer type variable **n**. Next, the condition given inside the **if** statement will be evaluated. Here, the condition **n==1** will produce the result false because the value stored in the **n** variable is 5. Now, the control will be transferred to the **else** block. In the **else** block, when the factorial of the given value will be computed, it will result in the second call to the method **fact( )** with an argument 4. The second call will result the third call to the method **fact( )** with an argument 3. This process will continue till the value of the variable **n** is equal to 1. When the value of the **n** variable will be equal to 1, the method **fact( )** will return 1. This value will be multiplied by 2 (the value of the **n** variable in the second last invocation). Now, the resultant value 2 will be multiplied by 3. Next, the resultant value 6 will be multiplied by 4. Now, the resultant value 24 will be multiplied by 5 and the resultant value 120 will be returned to the caller. This statement works as follows:

```
5 * fact(4)   //Step 1
4 * fact(3)   //Step 2
3 * fact(2)   //Step 3
2* fact(1)    //Step 4 returns 2
```

The given statements will work as follows:

```
5*4*3*2*1 = 120
```

Line 22

System.out.println("Factorial of 5 is: " +result);

This line will display the following on the screen:

Factorial of 5 is: 120

The working of lines 23 to 26 is the same as lines 20 and 21.

The output of Example 17 is displayed in Figure 4-19.

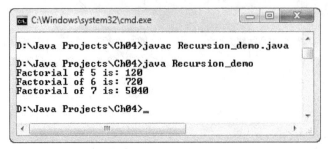

Figure 4-19 *The output of Example 17*

Self-Evaluation Test

Answer the following questions and then compare them to those given at the end of this chapter:

1. A _____ is a user-defined data type.

2. A variable defined inside a class is known as _____ variable.

3. An object is defined as the _____ of a class.

4. The operator, which is used for the memory allocation to an object at runtime is the _____ operator.

5. A _____ is a group of statements and is used to perform a particular task.

6. _____ is a technique in which you can define two or more than two methods with the same name but with different parameter lists.

7. The _____ is a special method that is used to initialize an object at the time of its creation.

8. The mechanism that is used to reclaim the memory automatically is known as _____.

9. The _____ keyword is used to refer to the current object of a class.

10. When a method calls itself repeatedly to perform successive steps, wherein each step uses the output of the preceding step. It is called _____.

Review Questions

Answer the following questions:

1. Define a class.

2. Define an object. Explain the steps that are used to create an object with the help of a suitable example.

3. Define the term overloading. Explain method overloading with the help of a suitable example.

4. Define constructors with the help of a suitable example.

5. Explain the **static** data members and methods with the help of a suitable example.

6. What is Recursion? Explain with the help of a suitable example.

7. Find errors in the following source codes:

(a)
```
class Rectangle
{
    double length;
    double breadth;
    Rectangle(double l, double w)
    {
        length = l;
        width = w;
    }
}
class Rectangle_demo
{
    public static void main(String arg[ ])
    {
        Rectangle obj1 = new Rectangle( );
    }
}
```

(b)
```
class static_demo
{
    static int a = 110, b;
    int c;
    static int sum(int var)
    {
        b = var;
        c = a+b;
        return c;
    }
```

```
    public static void main(String arg[ ])
    {
        int result = sum(102);
        System.out.println("The result is: " +result);
    }
}
```

(c)
```
class Rectangle
{
    double length, width;
    void getvalues(double l, double w)
    {
        length = l;
        width = w;
    }
    void area(Rectangle obj)
    {
        double result;
        result = obj.length * obj.width;
        System.out.println("Area is: " +result);
    }
}
class PassingObj
{
    public static void main(String arg[])
    {
        Rectangle obj1 = new Rectangle( );
        Rectangle obj2 = new Rectangle( );
        obj1.getvalues( )
        obj2.area(14.2, 12.5);
    }
}
```

(d)
```
class Cylinder1
{
    double radius;
    double height;
}
class Cylinder1_demo
{
    public static void main(String arg[ ])
    {
        double pi = 3.14;
        int volume;
        Cylinder1 obj1 = new Cylinder1( );
        volume = pi * (obj1.radius*obj1.radius) * obj1.height;
    }
}
```

```
(e) class Cylinder2
    {
        double radius;
        double height;
        public void cylinder_volume( )
        {
            double volume, pi = 3.14;
            volume = pi * (radius*radius) * height;
            System.out.println("Volume is: " +volume);
        }
    }
    class Cylinder2_d
    {
        public static void main(String arg[ ])
        {
            Cylinder2 obj1 = new Cylinder2( );
            Cylinder2 obj2 = new Cylinder2( );
            obj1.radius = 13.5;
            obj1.height = 30;
            obj1.cylinder_volume( );
            obj2.radius = 15.5;
            obj2.height = 10.5;
            obj2.cylinder_volume( );
        }
    }
```

EXERCISES

Exercise 1

Write a program to calculate the volume of a cube with different dimensions using constructor overloading.

Exercise 2

Write a program to calculate the Fibonacci series using recursion.

Answers to Self-Evaluation Test

1. class, **2.** instance, **3.** physical instantiations, **4. new**, **5.** method, **6.** Method overloading, **7.** constructor, **8.** garbage collection, **9.** this, **10.** recursion

Chapter 5

Inheritance

Learning Objectives

After completing this chapter, you will be able to:

- *Understand the fundamentals of inheritance*
- *Understand the concept of access specifiers*
- *Understand the concept of super keyword*
- *Understand the concept of overriding methods*
- *Understand the concept of dynamic method dispatch*
- *Understand the concept of abstract classes*
- *Understand the concept of final keyword*

INTRODUCTION

In the previous chapter, you have already learned about some features of the object oriented programming such as classes, objects, and so on. In this chapter, you will learn about another important feature of the object oriented programming known as inheritance. This feature enables you to create a new class by using some or all characteristics (instance variables and methods) of an existing class.

INHERITANCE FUNDAMENTALS

The process of creating a new class by using the characteristic and implementation of another class is known as inheritance. The class that inherits the characteristics of another class is known as subclass and the class whose characteristics are inherited is known as superclass. The main advantage of using inheritance is the reusability of code that enables you to use the predefined methods and/or instance variables of a class to create a new class. In this way, you do not need to write the same code repeatedly. Moreover, when a subclass is created, it adds some of its functionalities to the characteristics inherited from the superclass. Therefore, this subclass can be used as a superclass for further subclasses. A common example of inheritance is the parent and child relationship. A child inherits most of the characteristics of his parents and also adds some of his own characteristics.

In inheritance, a superclass acts as a general class and it contains only common characteristics. But, the classes derived from a particular superclass are defined as specialized classes, as each subclass add its own specific characteristics with the characteristics inherited from a superclass.

Inheritance can be well defined with the help of hierarchy of classes. In Java, every class is inherited from a particular class named as **Object** (the **Object** class comes under the default package **java.lang**). So, in the hierarchy of classes, the **Object** class is on the top of the hierarchy. In this hierarchy, a superclass can be a direct or an indirect superclass. The direct superclass is the class from which a subclass is explicitly inherited. The indirect superclass is the class from which a subclass is not explicitly inherited, but it is two or more than two levels up in the class hierarchy, as shown in Figure 5-1.

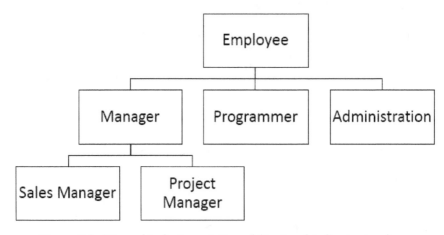

Figure 5-1 *Hierarchical representation of direct and indirect superclasses*

In Figure 5-1, three classes **Manager**, **Programmer**, and **Administration** explicitly inherit the properties of the **Employee** class. Therefore, the **Employee** class is known as the direct superclass of the given three subclasses. Here, the **Manager** subclass is acting as the superclass for the **Sales Manager** and **Project Manager** classes. Therefore, the **Manager** class is treated as the direct superclass and the **Employee** class is treated as an indirect superclass for the **Sales Manager** and **Project Manager** classes.

In Java, a new class can inherit some or all characteristics of a superclass by using the **extends** keyword. Inheritance is categorized into five types which are as follows:

1. Single inheritance
2. Multilevel inheritance
3. Hierarchical inheritance
4. Multiple inheritance
5. Hybrid inheritance

Single Inheritance
When a single class is inherited from a single base class, it is called single inheritance.

For example:

```
class A
{
    int a, b;
    int sum( )
    {
        ----------;
        ----------;
    }
}
class B extends A
{
    ----------;
    ----------;
}
```

In this example, **A** class is inherited by **B** class. Now, **B** class can use the characteristics (instance variables **a** and **b**, instance method **sum( )**) of the **A** class and also add some new characteristic of its own.

Example 1

The following example illustrates the concept of inheritance. The program will calculate the volume of a box with the given dimensions and also display the resultant value on the screen.

//Write a program to calculate the volume of a box

```
1   class Box
2   {
3       double length, width, height;
4       void display( )
5       {
6           System.out.println("Length is: " +length);
7           System.out.println("Width is: " +width);
8           System.out.println("Height is: " +height);
9       }
10  }
11  class Volume extends Box
12  {
13      double result;
14      void volume( )
15      {
16          result = length*width*height;
17          System.out.println("Volume is: " +result);
18      }
19      public static void main(String arg[])
20      {
21          Volume obj1= new Volume( );
22          obj1.length=10.5;
23          obj1.width=12;
24          obj1.height=26.7;
25          obj1.display( );
26          obj1.volume( );
27      }
28  }
```

Explanation
Line 1
class Box
In this line, **Box** is defined as a class and no access specifier (Private, Public, or Protected) is used. So, the default access specifier (no modifier) is assigned to the **Box** class. Now, during inheritance, the instance variables and methods of the **Box** class can be inherited by a subclass.

Line 3
double length, width, height;
In this line, **length**, **width**, and **height** are declared as **double** type variables. These variables are treated as the instance variables of the **Box** class.

Lines 4 to 9
void display( )
{
       System.out.println("Length is: " +length);
       System.out.println("Width is: " +width);
       System.out.println("Height is: " +height);
}

These lines contain the definition of the **display( )** method. This method is the member of the **Box** class and is used to display the dimensions of a box.

Line 11
class Volume extends Box
In this line, the **extends** keyword is used. The **extends** keyword specifies that the **Volume** class inherits the characteristics of the **Box** class.

Line 13
double result;
In this line, result is declared as a **double** type variable.

Lines 14 to 18
void volume( )
{

   result = length*width*height;
   System.out.println("Volume is: " +result);
}
These lines contain the definition of the **volume( )** method. This method is the member of the **Volume** class. The **length**, **width**, and **height** variables of the **Box** class are inherited and their values are multiplied. Now, the resultant value is assigned to the **result** variable and it will be displayed on the screen.

Line 21
Volume obj1 = new Volume( );
In this line, **obj1** is declared as an object of the **Volume** class.

Lines 22 to 24
obj1.length=10.5;
obj1.width=12;
obj1.height=26.7;

In these lines, three instance variables **length**, **width**, and **height** of the **Box** class are accessed by the **obj1** object of the **Volume** class and **10.5**, **12**, and **26.7** are assigned to them as their initial values, respectively.

Line 25
obj1.display( );
In this line, the member **display( )** method of the **Box** class is inherited by the **obj1** object of the **Volume** class. Now, the control is transferred to the definition of the method at line 5.

Line 26
obj1.volume( );
In this line, a call is made to the **volume( )** method of the **Volume** class with the **obj1** object. Now, the control is transferred to the definition of the method at line 14.

The output of Example 1 is displayed in Figure 5-2.

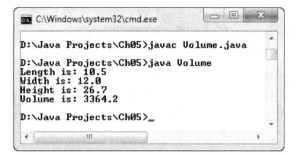

Figure 5-2 *The output of Example 1*

Multilevel Inheritance

In all earlier examples of this chapter, you might have observed the simple type of class hierarchy that consists of a superclass and a subclass. But, in this section, you will learn about multilevel hierarchy of inheritance which is known as multilevel inheritance. In multilevel inheritance, a subclass is used as a superclass for another class.

For example:

```
class A
{
    ----------;
    ----------;
}
class B extends A
{
    ----------;
    ----------;
}
class C extends B
{
    ----------;
    ----------;
}
```

In this example, the **B** class acts as a subclass of the **A** class and the **C** class acts as a subclass of the **B** class. Here, the **B** subclass acts as a superclass for the **C** class. Therefore, the **B** class inherits all or some of the characteristics of **A** superclass and the **C** class inherits all or some of the characteristics of both the classes **A** and **B**.

Example 2

The following example illustrates the use of multilevel inheritance. The program will calculate the points scored by a student in all subjects and displays the resultant value on the screen.

//Write a program to calculate the result of a student

```
1   class Rollnumber
2   {
3       int roll_num;
4       void get_rollnum(int x)
5       {
6           roll_num = x;
7       }
8       void show_rollnum()
9       {
10          System.out.println("Roll Number is: "+roll_num);
11      }
12  }
13  class Marks extends Rollnumber
14  {
15      double math, physics, chemistry;
16      void get_marks(int a, int b, int c)
17      {
18          math = a;
19          physics = b;
20          chemistry = c;
21      }
22      void show_marks()
23      {
24          System.out.println("Marks in Mathematics are: " +math);
25          System.out.println("Marks in Physics are: " +physics);
26          System.out.println("Marks in Chemistry are: " +chemistry);
27      }
28  }
29  class Result extends Marks
30  {
31      double res;
32      void calculate_result()
33      {
34          res = ((math+physics+chemistry)*100)/300;
35      }
36      void show_result()
37      {
38          System.out.println("Total is: " +res+ "%");
39      }
40      public static void main(String[] args)
41      {
42          Result obj1 = new Result();
43          obj1.get_rollnum(101);
44          obj1.get_marks(74, 90, 91);
45          obj1.calculate_result();
46          obj1.show_rollnum();
47          obj1.show_marks();
48          obj1.show_result();
49      }
50  }
```

Explanation

In this example, the **Marks** class inherits the characteristics of the **Rollnumber** superclass. Now, the **Marks** subclass acts as a superclass for the **Result** class. So, the **Result** class inherits the characteristics of both the classes **Rollnumber** and **Marks**.

The output of Example 2 is displayed in Figure 5-3.

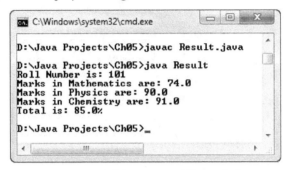

Figure 5-3 *The output of Example 2*

Hierarchical Inheritance

When multiple subclasses inherit the characteristics from one superclass, then it is known as hierarchical inheritance. There is only one superclass and multiple subclasses in this type of inheritance.

For example:

```
class A
{
     ------------;
     ------------;
}
class B extends A
{
     -----------;
     -----------;
}
class C extends A
{
     -----------;
     -----------;
}
```

In this example, **A** class is inherited by **B** class and **C** class. Therefore, both the subclasses **B** and **C** will inherit all or some of the characteristics of its superclass **A**.

Example 3

The following example illustrates the use of hierarchical inheritance. The program will calculate the square and cube of a number and display the resultant values on the screen.

//Write a program to calculate the square and cube of a number

```
1    class Number
2    {
3        int num;
4        void getNumber(int x)
5        {
6            num = x;
7        }
8        void showNumber()
9        {
10           System.out.println("Number is: " +num);
11       }
12   }
13   class Square extends Number
14   {
15       int sqr;
16       void show_Square()
17       {
18           sqr=num*num;
19           System.out.println(" Square of Number is: " +sqr +"\n");
20       }
21   }
22   class Cube extends Number
23   {
24       int cube;
25       void show_Cube()
26       {
27           cube=num*num*num;
28           System.out.println(" Cube of Number is: " +cube);
29       }
30   }
31   class Hierarchical_demo
32   {
33       public static void main(String arg[])
34       {
35           Square s = new Square();
36           s.getNumber(30);
37           s.showNumber();
38           s.show_Square();
39           Cube c = new Cube();
40           c.getNumber(15);
41           c.showNumber();
42           c.show_Cube();
43       }
44   }
```

Explanation

In this example, **Number** is a superclass and **Square** and **Cube** are its subclasses. Both **Square** and **Cube** classes inherit the characteristics of their superclass.

The output of Example 3 is displayed in Figure 5-4.

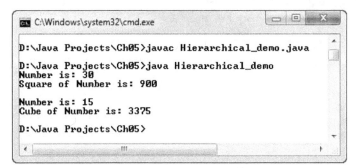

Figure 5-4 *The output of Example 3*

Multiple Inheritance
When one single class inherits the characteristics of multiple superclasses then it is known as multiple inheritance. Java does not support multiple inheritance. For achieving multiple inheritance in Java, interfaces can be used.

Why Java does not support multiple inheritance
If multiple inheritance is used in Java, it can lead to ambiguity. If a method with the same name exists in multiple superclasses, then on calling that method the compiler will not be able to determine as to which of the methods in the superclasses is to be called, leading to error or incorrect result.

Hybrid Inheritance
When one or more types of inheritance are combined together, it is known as Hybrid Inheritance. If one of the combinations in a hybrid inheritance is multiple inheritance then that hybrid inheritance is not supported by Java.

For example, if you combine hierarchical and multilevel inheritance together then this becomes hybrid inheritance and Java supports it. But if you combine multiple inheritance with some other type of inheritance then it is not supported by Java.

ACCESS SPECIFIERS AND INHERITANCE
In the previous example, you must have noticed that no access specifier was used with the instance variables **length**, **width**, and **height** and also with the **display( )** method. So, the default access specifier was assigned to them. The main purpose of using an access specifier with an instance variable, a method, or a class is to define its visibility to the other parts of a class and also to the other classes. The syntax for using the access specifiers with instance variables, methods, and classes is as follows:

```
access_specifier class class_name
{
    access_specifier datatype var1;
    ----------;
    access_specifier datatype varN;
    access_specifier return_type name(parameters list)
```

```
    {
        //body of the method;
    }
}
```

In this syntax, the **access_specifier** represents a specifier, which can be one of the following:

Private

If a class member, either an instance variable or a method, is declared as **private**, it will be visible or can be accessed only within that particular class in which it is specified. It cannot be accessed from outside the class in which it is declared or defined. Also, if a class is declared as **private**, it cannot be used as a superclass, which means that you cannot inherit that particular class, its members, or methods.

For example:

```
class Demo
{
    private double age;
    private double income;
    ----------;
}
```

In this example, **age** and **income** are declared as **double** type variables. These variables can only be used in the **Demo** class because they are declared as **private**. The subclasses of the **Demo** class cannot access these variables directly. Like variables, if a method is declared as **private** inside the **Demo** class, it cannot be accessed or used outside the **Demo** class.

Public

When a class member, either an instance variable or a method, is declared as **public**, it will be visible or can be accessed from anywhere in your program. You can access a **public** member of a class within or outside the class, in which it is declared. Therefore, this access specifier can be used when you want complete data to be visible or accessed from everywhere in a program.

For example:

```
class Demo
{
    public double age;
    public double income;
    ----------;
}
```

In this example, **age** and **income** are declared as **double** type variables. These variables can be used or accessed in the **Demo** class and also outside the classes other than **Demo** because they are declared as **public**. Like variables, if a method is declared as **public** inside the **Demo** class, it can be accessed or used from outside the **Demo** class.

Protected

When a class member, either an instance variable or a method, is declared as **protected**, it can be used or accessed within the same class in which it is declared or defined and also, within the subclasses of that particular class. It can also be accessed by the classes that are in the same package. You will learn more about packages in the later chapters.

For example:

```
class Demo
{
    protected double age;
    protected double income;
    ----------;
}
class Sub extends Demo
{
    ----------;
}
```

In this example, the **Demo** class is inherited by the **Sub** class. Here, the **Sub** class can directly access the protected data members **age** and **income** of the **Demo** class.

Default

If you do not specify any specifier with the members of a class, the default specifier is assigned to those members. The default specifier is mostly used while working with packages.

Note

While defining a class, it is recommended to declare all instance variables as private and the methods as public.

Example 4

The following example illustrates the use of access specifiers. The program will calculate the average of points scored by a student in three subjects and also display the resultant value on the screen.

//Write a program to calculate the average of points scored in three subjects

```
1   class student
2   {
3       private int roll_num;
4       protected void get_rollnum(int x)
5       {
6           roll_num = x;
7       }
8       void show_rollnum( )
9       {
10          System.out.println("Roll Number is: " +roll_num);
11      }
12  }
```

```
13  class Points extends student
14  {
15      private double sub1, sub2, sub3;
16      public void get_points(double a, double b, double c)
17      {
18          sub1 = a;
19          sub2 = b;
20          sub3 = c;
21      }
22      public void show_points( )
23      {
24          System.out.println("Points scored in Subject1 are: " +sub1);
25          System.out.println("Points scored in Subject2 are: " +sub2);
26          System.out.println("Points scored in Subject3 are: " +sub3);
27      }
28      public double avrg( )
29      {
30          return (sub1+sub2+sub3)/3;
31      }
32  }
33  class Average
34  {
35      public static void main(String arg[])
36      {
37          double result;
38          Points obj1 = new Points( );
39          obj1.get_rollnum(101);
40          obj1.get_points(66,78.5,89.5);
41          result = obj1.avrg( );
42          obj1.show_rollnum( );
43          obj1.show_points( );
44          System.out.println("Average is: " +result);
45      }
46  }
```

Explanation

Line 3

private int roll_num;

In this line, **roll_num** is declared as an integer type variable and a **private** instance variable of the **student** class. So, it can only be accessed by other members of the **student** class.

Lines 4 to 7

protected void get_rollnum(int x)

{

        roll_num = x;

}

These lines contain the definition of the **get_rollnum( )** method of the **student** class. This method is declared as **protected**. So, it can be accessed by other members as well as the subclasses of the **student** class. Inside this method, the value which is passed during the method call is assigned to the instance variable **roll_num**.

Lines 8 to 11
void show_rollnum( )
{

        System.out.println("Roll Number is: " +roll_num);

}

These lines contain the definition of the **show_rollnum( )** method of the **student** class. No access specifier is used with this method. So, the default specifier is automatically assigned to it by the Java environment. This method is used to display the value of the **roll_num** variable on the screen.

Line 13
class Points extends student
In this line, the **extends** keyword is used and it specifies that the **Points** class inherits the characteristics of the **student** class. Now, the **student** class is treated as the superclass for the **Points** class.

Line 15
private double sub1, sub2, sub3;
In this line, **sub1**, **sub2**, and **sub3** are declared as **double** type variables. These variables are also declared as **private** instance variables of the **Points** class.

Lines 16 to 21
public void get_points(double a, double b, double c)
{

        sub1 = a;
        sub2 = b;
        sub3 = c;

}

These lines contain the definition of the **get_points( )** method of the **Points** class. The **public** access specifier is used with this method. So, it can be accessed from anywhere in the program. Inside this method, three values are passed during the method call and then they are assigned to the instance variables **sub1**, **sub2**, and **sub3**, respectively.

Lines 22 to 27
public void show_points( )
{

        System.out.println("Points scored in Subject1 is: " +sub1);
        System.out.println("Points scored in Subject2 is: " +sub2);
        System.out.println("Points scored in Subject3 is: " +sub3);

}

These lines contain the definition of the **show_points( )** method. This method is used to display the values of the instance variables **sub1**, **sub2**, and **sub3** on the screen.

Lines 28 to 31
public double avrg( )
{

        return (sub1+sub2+sub3)/3;

}

These lines contain the definition of the **avrg( )** method. Inside this method, the average of the points scored in three subjects is calculated. Next, the resultant value is returned to its caller.

Line 37
double result;
In this line, **result** is declared as a **double** type variable.

Line 38
Points obj1 = new Points( );
In this line, **obj1** is declared as an object of the **Points** class.

Line 39
obj1.get_rollnum(101);
In this line, a call is made to the **get_rollnum( )** method of the **student** class with the **obj1** object of the **Points** class and the value 101 is passed as an argument. Now, the control is transferred to line 4 and value 101 is assigned to the **x** variable.

Line 40
obj1.get_points(66,78.5,89.5);
In this line, a call is made to the **get_points( )** method with the **obj1** object of the **Points** class and the values 66, 78.5, and 89.5 are passed as arguments. Now, the control is transferred to line 16 and values 66, 78.5, and 89.5 are assigned to the **a**, **b**, and **c** variables, respectively.

Line 41
result = obj1.avrg( );
In this line, a call is made to the **avrg( )** method with the **obj1** object of the **Points** class. Now, the control is transferred to line 28. Inside the method body, the average is calculated and the resultant value (78) is returned to the caller with the help of the **return** statement. Next, the resultant value is assigned to the **result** variable.

Line 42
obj1.show_rollnum( );
In this line, a call is made to the **show_rollnum( )** method of the **student** class with the **obj1** object of the **Points** class. Now, the control is transferred to line 8 and the value, 101 of the **roll_num** variable is displayed on the screen.

Line 43
obj1.show_points( );
In this line, a call is made to the **show_points( )** method with the **obj1** object of the **Points** class. Now, the control is transferred to line 22 and the values of the **sub1**, **sub2**, and **sub3** variables are displayed on the screen.

Line 44
System.out.println("Average is: " +result);
This line will display the following on the screen:
Average is: 78

The output of Example 4 is displayed in Figure 5-5.

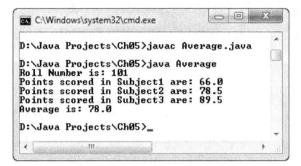

Figure 5-5 The output of Example 4

THE super KEYWORD

Whenever a derived class is inherited from the base class, some features of the derived class might be similar to the features of the base class. Such cases cause ambiguity for JVM and therefore need to be differentiated to avoid it. To differentiate base class features and derived class features, the '**super**' keyword is used. By using the **super** keyword, a subclass can easily refer to its immediate superclass. The **super** keyword is used mainly for the following two purposes:

   a.   To call the superclass constructor.
   b.   To access same members of superclass and subclass.

Note

Only public and protected members of a superclass are accessed by super keyword. Private members of superclass cannot be accessed by it.

Calling Superclass Constructors

A subclass can make a call to a constructor, which is defined by its superclass using the **super** keyword, as given next:

```
super(arg1, arg2, ........, argN);
```

In this statement, **arg1** to **argN** specifies the list of arguments that are needed by the constructor of a superclass.

For example:

```
class A
{
    A(int a, int b)
    {
        ----------;
        ----------;
    }
        ----------;
        ----------;
}
```

```
class B extends A
{
   B( int x, int y, int z)
   {
      super(x, y);
      ----------;
      ----------;
   }
      ----------;
      ----------;

}
```

In this example, the **B** class inherits the characteristics of the **A** class. Inside the constructor of the **B** subclass, a call is made to the constructor of the **A** superclass using the **super** keyword and the values of the two integer type variables **x** and **y** are passed as arguments. Now, these values are assigned to the **a** and **b** variables inside the parameter list of the superclass constructor.

 Note

*Inside the subclass constructor, the **super( )** statement should be the first statement to be executed otherwise you will get the compilation error message: "Constructor call must be the first statement in a constructor".*

Example 5

The following example illustrates the concept of calling a constructor of a superclass. The program will calculate the volume of cylinders and also display the resultant values on the screen.

//Write a program to calculate the volume of a cylinder
```
1   class Cylinder
2   {
3      double radius;
4      Cylinder(double r)
5      {
6         radius = r;
7      }
8   }
9   class Cylinderheight extends Cylinder
10  {
11     double height;
12     double pi = 3.14;
13     Cylinderheight(double rad, double hgt)
14     {
15        super(rad);
16        height = hgt;
17     }
18     double volume()
19     {
20        return pi*(radius*radius)*height;
21     }
22  }
```

```
23  class Volume
24  {
25     public static void main(String[] args)
26     {
27         double result;
28         Cylinderheight obj1 = new Cylinderheight(10.5,20.2);
29         result = obj1.volume();
30         System.out.println("Volume of first cylinder is: " +result);
31         Cylinderheight obj2 = new Cylinderheight(8.5,12);
32         result = obj2.volume();
33         System.out.println("Volume of second cylinder is: " +result);
34     }
35  }
```

Explanation

Lines 4 to 7
Cylinder(double r)
{

      radius = r;

}

These lines contain the definition of the constructor of the **Cylinder** class. The parameter list contains the **double** type variable **r**. Whenever a call is made to this constructor, a **double** type value or variable is passed as an argument. Inside the body of the constructor, the instance variable **radius** is initialized with the value that is passed to it during its call.

Line 9
class Cylinderheight extends Cylinder
This line represents that the **Cylinderheight** class can inherit the characteristics of the **Cylinder** class. Here, the **Cylinder** class acts as the superclass for the **Cylinderheight** class.

Lines 13 to 17
Cylinderheight(double rad, double hgt)
{

      super(rad);
      height = hgt;

}

These lines contain the definition of constructor of the **Cylinderheight** class. The parameter list contains two **double** type variables **rad** and **hgt**. Whenever a call is made to this constructor, two **double** type values or variables is passed as arguments. Inside the body of the constructor, a call is made to the constructor of the **Cylinder** superclass using the **super** keyword and one double type variable **rad** is passed as an argument. Now, the control is transferred to line 4 and the value of the **rad** variable is assigned to the **r** variable in line 4. Inside the body of the constructor, the value of the **hgt** variable is assigned to the **height** variable.

Line 28
Cylinderheight obj1 = new Cylinderheight(10.5,20.2);
In this line, **obj1** is declared as an object of the **Cylinderheight** class. Here, a call is made to the constructor and two double type values, 10.5 and 20.2 are passed as arguments. Now, the control is transferred to line 13 and the values 10.5 and 20.2 are assigned to the **double** type variables **rad** and **hgt**, respectively.

The output of Example 5 is displayed in Figure 5-6.

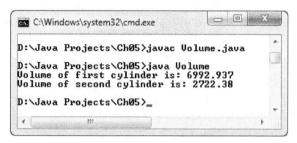

Figure 5-6 *The output of Example 5*

Using the super Keyword for Accessing the Members

A subclass can access or initialize the members of superclass by adding the **super** keyword before the member name. If **super** keyword is not used before the member name then it will access the member of subclass. In this section, you will learn how to use the **super** keyword to access the members of superclass which are common in both the classes, superclass and subclass. In such a case, the syntax for using the **super** keyword is as follows:

```
super.member_name;
```

In this syntax, **member_name** represents either an instance variable or a method of a superclass.

For example:

```
class A
{
    int x;
    ---------;
    ---------;
}
class B extends A
{
    int x;
    ---------;
    ---------;
    super.x = a;
    x = b;
    ---------;
}
```

In this example, the instance variable **x** is same in both the classes, **A** superclass and **B** subclass. Therefore, **x** variable of the **A** superclass is accessed with the help of the **super** keyword inside the **B** subclass.

Example 6

The following example illustrates the use of the **super** keyword for accessing the members of a superclass. The program will display the values of a superclass and its subclass on the screen.

/* Write a program to display the values of the instance variables of a superclass and its subclass */

```
1   class Super
2   {
3       int v1, v2;
4   }
5   class Sub extends Super
6   {
7       int v1, v2;
8       Sub(int a, int b, int c, int d)
9       {
10          super.v1 = a;
11          super.v2 = b;
12          v1 = c;
13          v2 = d;
14      }
15      void display()
16      {
17          System.out.println("Instance variables of superclass are "
                +super.v1 + " and " + super.v2);
18          System.out.println("Instance variables of subclass are " + v1
                + " and " + v2);
19      }
20  }
21  class Super_demo
22  {
23      public static void main(String[] args)
24      {
25          Sub obj1 = new Sub(10, 20, 30, 40);
26          obj1.display();
27      }
28  }
```

Explanation
Line 3
int v1, v2;
In this line, **v1** and **v2** are declared as the instance variables of the **Super** class.

Line 7
int var1, v2;
In this line, **v1** and **v2** are declared as the instance variables of the class **Sub**. Here, the instance variables of the **Sub** subclass are hiding the instance variables of its **Super** superclass.

Lines 10 and 11
super.v1 = a;
super.v2 = b;
In these lines, the instance variables **v1** and **v2** of the **Super** class are accessed with the help of the **super** keyword and the values of the **a** and **b** variables are assigned to the **v1** and **v2**, respectively.

Line 25
Sub obj1 = new Sub(10, 20, 30, 40);
In this line, **obj1** is declared as an object of the **Sub** class. Here, a call is made to the constructor **Sub( )** of the **Sub** subclass and the values 10, 20, 30, and 40 are passed as arguments. Now, the control is transferred to line 8 and the values 10, 20, 30, and 40 are assigned to the **a**, **b**, **c**, and **d** variables, respectively.

The output of Example 6 is displayed in Figure 5-7

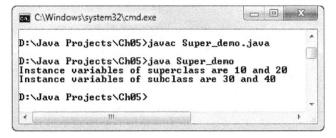

Figure 5-7 *The output of Example 6*

OVERRIDING METHODS

In a subclass, if you define a method that has the same name, same type, and same number of parameters as the method defined inside its superclass, the new method definition will hide the old method definition. This process is known as overriding. In method overriding, both the subclass and its superclass contain a method with the same signature.

For example:

```
class A
{
    void show(int x)
    {
        ----------;
    }
}
class B extends A
{
```

```
void show(int y)
{
    super.show(20);
    //Making a call to show() method of the A superclass
    ----------;
}
```
}

In this example, **B** class inherits the characteristics of **A** class. Here, **B** class contains the **show( )** method that has the has name, return type, type, and number of parameters same as the **show( )** method of **A** superclass. So, the **super** keyword is used to make a call to the **show( )** method of **A** superclass.

Example 7

The following example illustrates the use of overriding method. The program will calculate the volume of a rectangle and a cuboid, and display the resultant values on the screen.

//Write a program to calculate the volume of a rectangle and a cuboid

```
1   class Rectangle
2   {
3       double l, w;
4       Rectangle(double length, double width)
5       {
6           l = length;
7           w = width;
8       }
9       double area( )
10      {
11          return l * w;
12      }
13  }
14  class Cuboid extends Rectangle
15  {
16      double h;
17      Cuboid(double a, double b, double c)
18      {
19          super(a, b);
20          h = c;
21      }
22      double area( )    //overridden method
23      {
24          return 2*((l*w) + (w*h) + (h*l));
25      }
26      void show_message()
27      {
28          double result;
29          result = super.area();
30          System.out.println("Area of the rectangle is " +result);
31          result = area();
32          System.out.println("Area of the cuboid is " +result);
33      }
```

```
34     public static void main(String[] args)
35     {
36          Rectangle r = new Rectangle(10.5, 20);
37          Cuboid c = new Cuboid(10, 20.5, 30.7);
38          c.show_message();
39     }
40  }
```

Explanation

Lines 9 to 12
double area( )
{
      return l * w;
}
These lines contain the definition of the **area( )** method of the **Rectangle** class. Inside the method body, the values of the **l** and **w** variables are multiplied. Next, the resultant value is returned to the caller with the help of the **return** statement.

Lines 22 to 25
double area( )   //overridden method
{
      return 2*((l*w) + (w*h) + (h*l));
}
These lines contain the definition of the **area( )** method of the **Cuboid** class. This is an overridden method. This method has the name, return type, and an empty parameters list same as defined in the **Rectangle** superclass. Inside the method body, the values of the **l**, **w**, and **h** variables are evaluated. Next, the resultant value is returned to the caller with the help of the **return** statement.

Lines 26 to 33
void show_message()
{
      double result;
      result = super.area();
      System.out.println("\n Area of the rectangle is " +result);
      result = area();
      System.out.println(" Area of the cuboid is " +result);
}
These lines contain the definition of the **show_message( )** method of the **Cuboid** class. Inside the method body, the **super** keyword is used to access the overridden **area()** method of the superclass and the control is transferred to line 9. The resultant value is assigned to the **result** variable and displayed on screen using **System.out.println("\n Area of the rectangle is " +result);** In the next line, the overridden **area()** method of the **Cuboid** subclass is accessed and the control is transferred to line 22. Again, the resultant value is assigned to the **result** variable and displayed on screen using **System.out.println(" Area of the cuboid is " +result);**.

Line 36
Rectangle r = new Rectangle(10.5, 20);
In this line, **r** is declared as an object of the **Rectangle** class and the values 10.5, and 20 are assigned to the **length**, and **width** variables, respectively, in line 4.

Line 37
Cuboid c = new Cuboid(10, 20.5, 30.7);
In this line, **c** is declared as an object of the **Cuboid** class and the values 10, 20.5, and 30.7 are assigned to the **a**, **b**, and **c** variables, respectively, in line 17.

Line 38
c.show_message();
In this line, a call is made to the **show_message( )** method with the help of the **c** object of the class Cuboid. Now, the control is transferred to line 26.

The output of Example 7 is displayed in Figure 5-8.

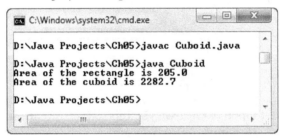

Figure 5-8 *The output of Example 7*

DYNAMIC METHOD DISPATCH

The dynamic method dispatch is a unique feature of Java. It is also known as runtime polymorphism. Dynamic method dispatch is a process by which a superclass reference variable can store the reference of subclass object. When a call is made to an overridden method, the dynamic method dispatch decides the sequence based on the object being referred by the reference variable. When superclass reference variable refers to subclass object then it is known as upcasting.

Note
Subclass reference variable cannot refer to a superclass object.

Example 8

The following example illustrates the use of dynamic method dispatch. The following program to display a message on the screen by using overriding methods.

//Write a program to display a message on the screen

```
1    class Super1
2    {
3       void display( )
4       {
5            System.out.println("Method of the class Super1");
6       }
7    }
8    class Sub1 extends Super1
9    {
10      void display( )
11      {
12           System.out.println("Method of the class Sub1");
13      }
14   }
15   class Sub2 extends Super1
16   {
17      void display( )
18      {
19           System.out.println("Method of the class Sub2");
20      }
21   }
22   public class Dynamic_demo
23   {
24      public static void main(String arg[])
25      {
26           Super1 sup1 = new Super1( );
27           Sub1 sub1 = new Sub1( );
28           Sub2 sub2 = new Sub2( );
29           Super1 s;
30           s = sup1;
31           s.display( );
32           s = sub1;
33           s.display( );
34           s = sub2;
35           s.display( );
36      }
37   }
```

Explanation
Line 29
Super1 s;
In this line, **s** is declared as a reference of the type **Super1**.

Line 30
s = sup1;
In this line, a reference to the **sup1** object of the **Super1** class is assigned to **s**.

Line 31
s.display( );
In this line, a call is made to the **display( )** method of the **Super1** class because **s** contains the reference of the **sup1** object.

The working of the lines 32 to 35 is the same as lines 30 and 31.

The output of Example 8 is displayed in Figure 5-9.

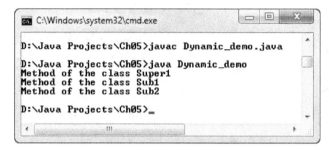

Figure 5-9 *The output of Example 8*

  Note

*In this example, a call will be made to the method **display( )** of the class whose reference is available in the variables.*

ABSTRACT CLASSES

As you already know that a superclass contains characteristics, which are common to all its subclasses. Sometimes it is required that a superclass must provide only structure, not the entire implementation. In such cases, a superclass must be declared as an abstract class with the help of the **abstract** keyword. The syntax for defining an abstract class is as follows:

```
access_specifier abstract class class_name
{
     ----------;
     ----------;
}
```

When a class is defined as an abstract class, it cannot be instantiated (cannot create an object) but only be inherited by its subclasses.

For example:

```
abstract class Demo
{
     ----------;
     ----------;
}
```

```
class Sub1 extends Demo
{
    ----------;
    ----------;
}
```

In this example, the **Demo** class is defined as an abstract class. Here, it is inherited by the **Sub1** class.

Like abstract classes, Java also provides abstract methods. The abstract methods are those methods that contain only the declaration part, not the implementation part. These type of methods are declared without curly braces and terminated with a semicolon. The syntax for declaring an abstract method is as follows:

```
abstract return_type method_name(parameter list);
```

An abstract class may or may not contain abstract methods. But if a class contains an abstract method, then that particular class must be declared as an abstract class. Otherwise, during the compilation time, an error will be generated by the compiler.

Example 9

The following example illustrates the use of abstract classes and abstract methods. The program will calculate the area of a rectangle and also display the resultant value on the screen.

```
//Write a program to calculate the area of a rectangle
1   abstract class Shape
2   {
3       abstract double area( );
4   }
5   class Rect extends Shape
6   {
7       double length, width;
8       Rect(double l, double w)
9       {
10          length = l;
11          width = w;
12      }
13      double area( )
14      {
15          return length * width;
16      }
17  }
```

```
18  class Abstract_demo
19  {
20     public static void main(String arg[])
21     {
22        double result;
23        Rect r1 = new Rect(10.5, 12.3);
24        result = r1.area( );
25        System.out.println("Area of the rectangle is: " +result);
26     }
27  }
```

Explanation

Line 1
abstract class Shape
In this line, **Shape** is declared as an abstract class with the help of the **abstract** keyword. Here, the abstract class **Shape** is used to provide only the structure not the implementation to its subclasses.

Line 3
abstract double area( );
In this line, **area** is declared as an abstract method and its return type is **double**. Here, this method contains only the declaration part, not the implementation or the definition part. Whenever a class inherits the **Shape** class then that particular subclass defines this method according to its requirement.

Line 5
class Rect extends Shape
In this line, the **Rect** class inherits the abstract class **Shape**.

Lines 13 to 16
double area( )
{
        return length * width;
}
In these lines, the abstract **area( )** method of the **Shape** class is defined inside the definition of its **Rect** subclass. Inside the method body, the values of the **length** and **width** variables are multiplied. Next, the resultant value is transferred to the caller of this method.

The output of Example 9 is displayed in Figure 5-10.

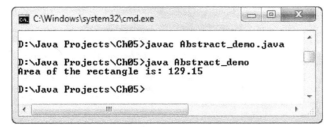

Figure 5-10 *The output of Example 9*

THE final KEYWORD

In Java, the **final** is a reserved keyword. It is used to restrict the user. It is used for three purposes that are as follows:

    a.   To declare a variable as a constant
    b.   To prevent overriding
    c.   To prevent inheritance

To Declare a Variable as a Constant

The **final** keyword is used to declare a variable as a constant. You can assign a value to the **final** variable only once and that value cannot be changed throughout the program. In Java, the final variable is treated the same as the constant variable in other programming languages. The syntax for declaring a final variable is as follows:

```
final datatype var_name = value;
```

For example:

```
final int i = 10;
```

In this example, the integer type variable **i** is declared as the **final** variable with the help of the **final** keyword. Next, the value 10 is assigned as an initial value to it and this value will be retained throughout the program.

To Prevent Overriding

In this chapter, you have already learned about overriding methods. Sometimes, you need to prevent a method from being overridden by its subclass. In such cases, you can declare the given method by using the **final** keyword. The syntax for declaring the final method is as follows:

```
final returntype method_name(parameters list)
{
    //body of the method;
}
```

For example:

```
class A
{
    ----------;
    final double area( )
    {
            ----------;
            ----------;
    }
}
```

```
class B extends A
{
     ----------;
     ----------;
}
```

In this example, the **area( )** method of the **A** class is declared with the **final** keyword and it cannot be overridden by the **B** subclass. If the **B** subclass tries to override the method **area( )** inside its definition, an error will be generated by the compiler.

To Prevent Inheritance

In inheritance, a class is inherited by another class to reuse its code or characteristics. But in some cases, you need to prevent a class from being inherited by any other class. In such cases, you must declare the class using the **final** keyword. When a class is declared as final, the methods inside it are also declared as **final**. The syntax for declaring a final class is as follows:

```
final class classname
{
    //body of the class;
}
```

For example:

```
final class A
{
    ----------;
    void area( )
    {
         ----------;
    }
}
```

In this example, the **A** class is declared as the **final** class. Therefore, **area( )** method in this class is also implicitly declared as the final method. Now, the **A** class cannot be inherited by any other class.

Self-Evaluation Test

Answer the following questions and then compare them to those given at the end of this chapter:

1. The mechanism of deriving a class from the existing one is known as _____.

2. The main advantage of using inheritance is the _____ of code.

3. In Java, every class is inherited from a particular class known as the _____ class.

4. _____ are used to define the visibility of data members, methods, or a class to the other parts of the class and also to the outside classes.

5. A superclass is the class from which a subclass is explicitly inherited. (T/F)

6. When an instance variable is declared as **protected**, it can be accessed by the methods of the same class as well as the methods of the subclasses of that particular class. (T/F)

7. In Java, the default access specifier is **protected**. (T/F)

8. You cannot use the **super** keyword to access the hidden members of a superclass. (T/F)

9. The Dynamic method dispatch is used in Java to implement the run-time polymorphism. (T/F)

10. Constant variable can be declared by using **const** keyword in Java. (T/F)

Review Questions

Answer the following questions:

1. Define inheritance with the help of a suitable example.

2. Explain the uses of the **super** keyword.

3. Explain multilevel inheritance with the help of a suitable example.

4. Why does Java not support multiple inheritance?

5. What do you mean by method overriding? Explain.

6. What is an abstract class?

7. Find errors in the following source codes:

(a)
```
class final_demo
{
    public static void main(String arg[])
    {
        final int i =10;
        i = 11;
        System.out.println("Value of i is: " +i);
    }
}
```

(b)
```java
private class demo
{
    int a, b;
    demo(int var1, int var2)
    {
        a = var1;
        b = var2;
    }
    void display( )
    {
        System.out.println("a = " +a);
        System.out.println("b = " +b);
    }
}
class sub extends demo
{
    int c;
    void sum( )
    {
        c = a+b;
        System.out.println("Sum = " +c);
    }
}
class Error_demo
{
    public static void main(String arg[])
    {
        demo d1 = new demo(10, 20);
        d1.display( );
        sub obj1 = new sub( );
        sub.sum( );
    }
}
```

(c)
```java
final class A
{
    void display( )
    {
        System.out.println("Class A");
    }
}
class B extends A
{
    void display( )
    {
        System.out.println("Class B");
    }
}
```

```
     class C
     {
        public static void main(String arg[])
        {
           A a1 = new A( );
           a1.display( );
           B b1 = new B( );
           b1.display( );
        }
     }


(d)  class Cylinder
     {
        double radius;
        Cylinder(int r)
        {
           radius = r;
        }
     }
     class Cylinderheight extends Cylinder
     {
        double height;
        double pi = 3.14;
        Cylinderheight(double rad, int hgt)
        {
           super(rad);
           height = hgt;
        }
        double volume()
        {
           return pi*(radius*radius)*height;
        }
     }
     class Volume
     {
        public static void main(String[] args)
        {
           double result;

           Cylinderheight obj1 = new Cylinderheight(10.5,20.2);
           result = obj1.volume();
           System.out.println("Volume of first cylinder is: " +result);
           Cylinderheight obj2 = new Cylinderheight(8.5,12);
           result = obj2.volume();
           System.out.println("Volume of second cylinder is: " +result);
        }
     }
```

EXERCISE

Exercise 1

Write a program to create a **Student** superclass that will be used to get the personal details of a student such as his name, class, roll number, and so on. Next, create its **Points** subclass that will be used to get the points scored by the student in every subject. Finally, calculate the percentage and display the resultant value on the screen.

Answers to Self-Evaluation Test
1. inheritance, **2.** reusability, **3.** Object, **4.** Access specifiers, **5.** T, **6.** T, **7.** F, **8.** F, **9.** T, **10.** F

Chapter 6

Packages, Interfaces, and Inner Classes

Learning Objectives

After completing this chapter, you will be able to:
- *Understand the concept of object class*
- *Understand the concept of packages*
- *Understand the concept of interfaces*
- *Understand the concept of nested classes*

INTRODUCTION

In the previous chapter, you learned about the concepts of super classes and subclasses. In this chapter, you will learn about the **Object** class which is the superclass of each class created in Java. Also, you will learn about packages, interfaces and inner classes. A class defined inside the body of another class is known as inner class. Packages are treated as containers for classes. Also, they are used to provide access protection and name space management.

THE Object CLASS

In Java, each class, whether it is a super class or a subclass, is automatically derived from the **Object** class. The **Object** class remains at the top in the class hierarchy. Therefore, this class is treated as the super class of all classes that are defined using Java. The **Object** class provides certain methods that can be used for specific purposes such as comparing the contents of two objects, creating a new object from an existing one, and so on. These methods along with their brief descriptions are given in Table 6-1.

Table 6-1 *Methods of* *object* *class*

Method	Description
protected object clone( )	Used to create a new object from an existing object
boolean equals(Object obj)	Used to compare the contents of two objects
protected void finalize( )	Garbage collector calls this method whenever an object is about to dispose
Class getclass( )	Returns the class of an object during run-time
int hashCode( )	Returns the hashcode value of the invoking object
void notify( )	Wakes up a single thread, which is waiting on the invoking object
void notifyAll( )	Wakes up all threads that are waiting on the invoking object
String toString( )	Returns a string that represents an object textually
void wait( ) void wait(long time) void wait(long time, int nanosecond)	Causes current thread to wait

Some methods of the **Object** class such as **getclass( )**, **notify( )**, **notifyall( )**, and **wait( )** are declared as **final**, therefore, they cannot be overridden inside other classes. However, you can override the remaining methods.

PACKAGES

You must have noticed that in earlier chapters, the programs were declared using different names. It was done to avoid the collision of names as all classes in these programs used the same namespace. To solve this problem, Java provides the mechanism of packages. A package is defined as a container of classes. It provides both naming and access protection control mechanism. You can not only define classes inside a package but also their visibility to other parts of the same package. Visibility can also be defined to other packages. There are two types of packages:

Built-in packages

The packages which are already defined in the Java library such as java.io.*, java.lang.*, and so on are known as built-in packages.

User defined packages

The packages which can be created by user are known as user defined packages.

Defining a Package

You can define or create a package by making a **package** statement as the first statement in the Java program. The syntax for defining a package is as follows:

```
package pack_name;
```

In this statement, **package** is a keyword and **pack_name** defines the package name.

When a class is declared inside a package, it only belongs to that particular package. But, if no package is defined while declaring a class, that particular class will be included inside the default package **java.lang**. In Java, you can include only one **package** statement in each program file and the same **package** statement can be included in more than one program file.

For example:

```
package demo;

class A
{
    ----------;
    ----------;
}
```

In this example, a package statement **package demo** is included as the first statement in the source file and the **A** class is declared inside the **demo** package. Now, the **A** class belongs to the **demo** package.

Whenever a package is created, Java uses the file system directories to store that package. All classes defined inside that package are stored under the file system directories. The name of the directory, where you store the package, should be the same as the name of the package.

Accessing a Package

As you know that when a package is created, Java stores it into the file system directories. By default, Java creates a subdirectory inside the current working directory to store the newly created package. For example, if the current directory is bin, Java creates a subdirectory with the same name as the name of the package inside the bin directory.

Example 1

The following example illustrates the use of a package. The program will calculate the average of points scored by a student in three subjects and displays the resultant value on the screen.

```
//Write a program to calculate the average of points scored in three subjects
 1   package Student;
 2   class Avg_demo
 3   {
 4       double sub1, sub2, sub3, result;
 5       void get_points(double s1, double s2, double s3)
 6       {
 7           sub1 = s1;
 8           sub2 = s2;
 9           sub3 = s3;
10       }
11       void average( )
12       {
13           result = (sub1+sub2+sub3)/3;
14           System.out.println("Average is: " +result);
15       }
16       public static void main(String arg[])
17       {
18           Avg_demo avg = new Avg_demo( );
19           avg.get_points(75.5, 89.5, 78);
20           avg.average( );
21       }
22   }
```

Explanation

Line 1

package Student;

In this line, **Student** is defined as a package with the help of the **package** keyword. Here, the package statement is included as the first statement in the Java source file. So, the classes defined inside this source file will be stored inside the **Student** package.

Line 2

class Avg_demo

In this line, **Avg_demo** is declared as a class inside the **Student** package. So, it will be stored inside the **Student** package.

Note

You can compile and execute the given source code by using the following statements:

D:\Java Projects\Ch06>javac -d . Avg_demo.java
D:\Java Projects\Ch06>java Student.Avg_demo

In the given statement, -d switch specifies the destination to put the generated class file. Dot signifies that you can keep the package within the same directory.

*Alternatively, you can create a new folder with the name **Student** in the current working directory (in this case, the folder name is Ch06) and save the program in this folder as **Avg_demo.java**.*

You can compile and execute the given source code by using the following statements:

D:\Java Projects\Ch06\Student>javac Avg_demo.java
D:\Java Projects\Ch06>java Student.Avg_demo

The output of Example 1 is displayed in Figure 6-1.

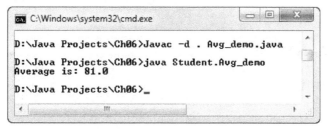

Figure 6-1 The output of Example 1

Accessing Protection in Packages

In the previous section, you learned that the mechanism of package is used for the namespace management and visibility control. In this section, you will learn how to implement the visibility control or access protection in packages. As you already know that a class is a collection of data members and methods. A package acts as a container of classes. Therefore, a package can control the access of the data members of a class from another class of the same package or different packages. The Java package provides the following four types of visibility controls for the class members:

1. Whether or not subclasses of a class in the same package can access the data members.
2. Whether or not non-subclasses of a class in the same package can access the data members.
3. Whether or not subclasses of a class in a different package can access the data members.
4. Whether or not non-subclasses of a different package can access the data members.

These visibility controls can be applied in different modes using different access specifiers, as described in Table 6-2.

Table 6-2 *Visibility controls*

Classes and Packages	Public	Private	Protected	Default
Same class	Yes	Yes	Yes	Yes
Subclasses in same package	Yes	No	Yes	Yes
Non-subclasses in same package	Yes	No	Yes	Yes
Subclasses in different packages	Yes	No	Yes	No
Non-subclasses in different packages	Yes	No	No	No

As shown in Table 6-2, when the data members of a class are declared as **public** data members, they can be accessed not only by the subclasses and non-subclasses of the same package, but also by the subclasses and non-subclasses of different packages. When the data members of a class are declared as **private** data members, they can only be accessed by the members of the same class. When the data members of a class are declared as **protected** data members, they can be accessed by the subclasses and non-subclasses of the same package, and also by the subclasses of different packages. When no access specifier is used with the data members of a class, they are declared as default data members. Therefore, they can be accessed by the subclasses and non-subclasses of the same package.

Importing Packages

In case you want to use any one or all classes of the **pack** package in another program, you need to use the import statement. The import statement helps you import a specific member of a package into another source file. For example, if you want to access only the **Package_data** class of the **pack** package, you can do so with the help of the following statement:

```
import pack.Package_data;
```

You can also use the **import** statement to access the entire package, as shown in the following statement:

```
import pack.*;
```

In this statement, the asterisk (*) symbol has been used to represent all members of the **pack** package. Now, the current source file can access all classes of the **pack** package.

 Note
*When an asterisk (*) symbol is used in a program, its compilation time increases as compared to when a class is explicitly specified in the **import** statement. Therefore, it is better to specify each class explicitly, especially when you use many import statements in a source file.*

When a source file imports a complete package with the help of the **import** statement, the visibility of the members of the package depends upon the access specifiers used by them, as described in Table 6-2.

Example 2

The following example illustrates the use of the **import** statement. The program will display details of an employee on the screen.

//Write a program to display details of an employee

```
1   //The below program is for Details.java
2   package Employee;
3   public class Details
4   {
5       String name;
6       int emp_id;
7       long salary;
8       public Details(String n, int id, long sal)
9       {
10          name = n;
11          emp_id = id;
12          salary = sal;
13      }
14      public void display( )
15      {
16          System.out.println("Name: " +name);
17          System.out.println("Employee ID is: " +emp_id);
18          System.out.println("Salary: " +salary);
19      }
20  }
```

```
1   //The below program file is for Emp_demo.java
2   import Employee.Details;
3   class Emp_demo
4   {
5       public static void main(String arg[])
6       {
7           Details obj1 = new Details("Smith", 102, 5000);
8           obj1.display( );
9       }
10  }
```

Explanation (Details.java)

Line 2

package Employee;

This statement defines the **Employee** package. Now, the classes defined under this statement will be included inside the **Employee** package.

Line 3

public class Details

This line contains the declaration part of the **Details** class. The **Details** class is defined under the **Employee** package. Here, the **Details** class is declared with the access specifier **public**. This means the **Details** class can be accessed by any class outside the **Employee** package.

Lines 8 to 13
public Details(String n, int id, long sal)
{

   name = n;
   emp_id = id;
   salary = sal;

}

These lines define the public constructor **Details( )** of the **Details** class. The parameters list contains three parameters: **String n**, **int id**, and **long sal**. Now, whenever a call is made to this constructor, three values will be passed to it as arguments. Next, the passed arguments will be assigned to the **n**, **id**, and **sal** variables. Inside the body of the constructor, the values of the **n**, **id**, and **sal** variables will be assigned to the **name**, **emp_id**, and **salary** variables, respectively.

> **Note**
> *In this program, the **Details** class, the **Details( )** constructor, and the **display( )** method are declared as **public** which enables any class outside the package **Employee** to access them.*

Explanation (Emp_demo.java)

Line 1
import Employee.Details;
In this line, the **import** statement is used to access the **Details** class of the **Employee** package. Now, the **Details** class can be used by the current **Emp_demo** class.

Line 7
Details obj1 = new Details("Smith", 102, 5000);
In this line, **obj1** is declared as an object of the **Details** class. Also, a call will be made to the **Details( )** constructor and three values: **Smith**, **102**, **5000** will be passed to **Details obj1** as arguments.

Line 8
obj1.display( );
In this line, a call will be made to the **display( )** method with the **obj1** object of the **Details** class.

The output of Example 2 is displayed in Figure 6-2.

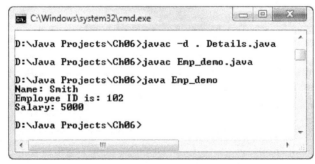

Figure 6-2 *The output of Example 2*

Note

*You can use alternate method to compile and run the source files: **Details.java** and **Emp_demo.java** by saving them separately in different directories. Save the class **Details.java** in the directory **Employee** and the **Emp_demo.java** class in the current directory.*

INTERFACES

Some object-oriented languages such as C++ provide multiple inheritances. In multiple inheritance, a single class can inherit the characteristics of more than one class. But, Java does not support multiple inheritance. Instead, it provides a new feature known as interface. An interface is similar to an abstract class in which no method is implemented, and only the declaration parts are given. In other words, an interface defines the task to be performed by the class but it does not specify the procedure to perform it. Interfaces are same as classes, but they do not contain any instance variable (except **static** and **final** type) or any type of code. A single interface can be implemented by any number of classes and vice-versa. This means a class can implement multiple interfaces.

Defining an Interface

You can define an interface in the same way as you define a class except that you need to use the **interface** keyword in the definition statement, as shown in the following syntax:

```
access_specifier interface interface_name
{
    return_type method_name1 (parameters list);
    return_type method_name2 (parameters list);
    final data_type var_name = value;
    return_type method_name3 (parameters list);
}
```

In this syntax, **access_specifier** represents an access specifier that can be **public**, **private**, **protected**, or **default**. An access specifier represents the visibility of an interface. For example, if you define an interface with the access specifier **public**, then it can be used by any other source code. The **interface** in the syntax represents a keyword and **interface_name** represents the name of an interface and it should be a valid identifier. The methods inside an interface end with a semicolon and contain no implementation. Variables that are declared inside the interface body are of either **final** or **static** type, and the values of these variables cannot be changed in any classes.

For example:

```
public interface demo
{
    void show( );
    int sqr( );
    final int num =10;
}
```

In this example, the **demo** interface contains two methods with their signatures but the method body is not defined. Here, **num** is declared as an integer type variable using **final** keyword and value 10 is assigned as an initial value to it which cannot be changed throughout the program.

Implementing an Interface

Once an interface has been defined, other classes can implement that interface by using the **implements** keyword in the class definition statement. The syntax for implementing an interface is as follows:

```
access_specifier class class_name [extends superclass] implements
interface_name
{
    //Body of the class
}
```

In this syntax, the class represented by **class_name** implements the interface that is represented by **interface_name**. If a class implements an interface, all methods declared inside the interface should be implemented by the class.

A class can also implement more than one interface by using the comma to separate the list of interfaces. The syntax for implementing more than one interface is as follows:

```
access_specifier class class_name implements interface1, interface2,
interfaceN
{
    //Body of the class
}
```

Example 3

The following example illustrates the use of an interface. The program will calculate the factorial and square of the given numbers and displays the resultant values on the screen.

//Write a program to calculate the factorial and square of the given numbers

```
1    interface Calculate
2    {
3        long fact(int num);
4        long sqr(int n);
5    }
6    class interface_demo implements Calculate
7    {
8        public long fact(int num)
9        {
10           int a = 1;
11           while(num>0)
12           {
13               a = num*a;
14               num--;
15           }
16           return a;
17       }
```

```
18     public long sqr(int n)
19     {
20         return n*n;
21     }
22     public static void main(String arg[])
23     {
24         long fac, sq;
25         interface_demo obj1 = new interface_demo();
26         fac = obj1.fact(10);
27         sq = obj1.sqr(23);
28         System.out.println("Factorial of 10 is: " +fac);
29         System.out.println("Square of 23 is: " +sq);
30     }
31 }
```

Explanation

Lines 1 to 5
interface Calculate
{
      long fact(int num);
      long sqr(int n);
}

These lines contain the definition of the **Calculate** interface. Inside the body of the interface, **fact( )** and **sqr( )** methods are declared and both the methods take integer parameters.

Line 6
class interface_demo implements Calculate
In this line, **interface_demo** is declared as a class and the **Calculate** interface is implemented by the class with the help of the **implements** keyword. Now, the **interface_demo** class must implement all those methods that have already been declared inside the **Calculate** interface.

Lines 8 to 17
public long fact(int num)
{
      int a = 1;
      while(num>0)
      {
            a = num*a;
            num--;
      }
      return a;
}

These lines contain the implementation of the **fact( )** method of the **Calculate** interface. This method is declared as **public** because it is an interface method.

Lines 18 to 21
public long sqr(int n)
{

       return n*n;

}

These lines contain the implementation of the **sqr( )** method of the **Calculate** interface.

Line 25
interface_demo obj1 = new interface_demo( );
In this line, **obj1** is declared as an object of the **interface_demo** class.

Line 26
fac = obj1.fact(10);
In this line, the **fact( )** method is called and the value 10 is passed to it as an argument. Now, the control will be transferred to the method body (from lines 8 to 17) and the factorial of the value 10 will be calculated. Next, the resultant value 3628800 will be returned to this line and assigned to the **fac** variable.

Line 27
sq = obj1.sqr(23);
In this line, a call is made to the **sqr( )** method and the value 23 is passed as an argument. Now, the control will be transferred to the method body (from lines 18 to 21) and the square of the value 23 will be calculated. Next, the resultant value 529 will be returned to this line and assigned to the sq variable.

The output of Example 3 is displayed in Figure 6-3.

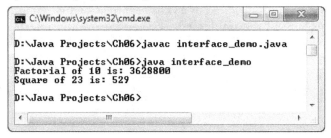

Figure 6-3 *The output of Example 3*

Interface Variables
Once an interface is defined, you cannot use the operator **new** to create an object of the interface in the same way as you did in the case of classes. But, you can create interface variables that must refer to an object of a class, which implements the interface. The syntax for declaring an interface variable is as follows:

```
interface_name var_name;
```

In this syntax, **interface_name** represents an interface and **var_name** is a valid identifier.

For example:

```
class Test
{
    public static void main(String arg[])
    {
        long fac, sqr;
        calculate obj = new interface_demo( );
        obj.fact(10);
        obj.squr(23);
        ----------;
        ----------;
    }
}
```

In Example 3, you must have noticed that the **interface_demo** class was implemented on the **calculate** interface. Moreover, first **obj1** object of the **interface_demo** class was created inside the body of the **main()** method and then it was used to call the **fact( )** and **sqr( )** methods. But in this example, **obj** is declared as a variable of the **calculate** interface and it refers to an object of the **interface_demo** class that implements the interface. Now, the interface variable **obj** is used to make a call to the **fact( )** and **sqr( )** methods, which are implemented inside the **interface_demo** class.

Extending an Interface

In the previous chapter, you have learned about inheritance. A class inherits the characteristics of another class. In the same way, the concept of inheritance can be applied on interfaces also. An interface can inherit the characteristics of another interface using the **extends** keyword. When an interface is implemented by a class and the interface inherits another interface, the class must provide the implementation for all methods of all interfaces that are inherited.

For example:

```
interface A
{
    void getdata( );
}
interface B extends A
{
    void showdata( );
}
class demo implements B
{
    public void getdata( )
    {
        ----------;
        ----------;
    }
```

```
        public void showdata( )
        {
            ----------;
            ----------;
        }
    }
```

In this example, the **A** interface contains only one **getdata( )** method and the **B** interface contains only one **showdata( )** method. Here, the **B** interface inherits the characteristics of the **A** interface by using the **extends** keyword and the **demo** class implements it. In this way, inside the **demo** class, both the methods, **getdata( )** and **showdata( )**, of the **A** and **B** interfaces are defined.

Example 4

The following example illustrates the use of extended interfaces. The program will perform certain mathematical operations on the given values and displays the resultant values on the screen.

```
//Write a program to perform certain mathematical operations
1    interface mathematical
2    {
3        int sum(int a, int b);
4        long mul(int num1, int num2);
5    }
6    interface remainder extends mathematical
7    {
8        int remdr(int a, int b);
9    }
10   class Extend_interface implements remainder
11   {
12       public int sum(int a, int b)
13       {
14           return a+b;
15       }
16       public long mul(int num1, int num2)
17       {
18           return num1*num2;
19       }
20       public int remdr(int a, int b)
21       {
22            return a%b;
23       }
24       public static void main(String arg[])
25       {
26           int total, rem;
27           long result;
28           Extend_interface obj1 = new Extend_interface( );
29           total = obj1.sum(105, 63);
30           result = obj1.mul(105, 63);
31           rem = obj1.remdr(105, 63);
```

```
32              System.out.println("The sum is: " +total);
33              System.out.println("The multiplication is: " +result);
34              System.out.println("The remainder is: " +rem);
35      }
36  }
```

Explanation

Line 1
interface mathematical
In this line, **mathematical** is defined as an interface using the **interface** keyword.

Lines 3 and 4
int sum(int a, int b);
long mul(int num1, int num2);

These lines contain the declaration part of the two methods **sum( )** and **mul( )**. These methods are declared inside the **mathematical** interface. The implementation part of the methods will be defined by the class that implements the **mathematical** interface.

Line 6
interface remainder extends mathematical
In this line, **remainder** is defined as an interface by using the **interface** keyword. Also, it inherits another **mathematical** interface.

Line 8
int remdr(int a, int b);
This line contains the declaration part of the **remdr( )** method. This method is declared inside the **remainder** interface. So, it must be implemented by the class that implements the **remainder** interface.

Line 10
class Extend_interface implements remainder
In this line, the **Extend_interface** class implements the **remainder** interface by using the **implements** keyword. This class can implement all methods of both the interfaces, **remainder** and **mathematical**.

Lines 12 to 15
public int sum(int a, int b)
{
        return a+b;
}
These lines contain the implementation of the **sum( )** method of the **mathematical** interface. Inside the method body, the values of the **a** and **b** variables will be added and the resultant value will be returned to the caller.

Lines 16 to 19
public long mul(int num1, int num2)
{
   return num1*num2;
}
These lines contain the implementation of the **mul( )** method of the **mathematical** interface. Inside the method body, the values of the **num1** and **num2** variables will be multiplied and the resultant value will be returned to the caller.

Lines 20 to 23
public int remdr(int a, int b)
{
   return a%b;
}
These lines contain the implementation of the **remdr( )** method of the **remainder** interface. Inside the method body, the value of the **a** variable will be divided by the value of the **b** variable and the remainder value will be returned to the caller.

Line 28
Extend_interface obj1 = new Extend_interface( );
In this line, **obj1** is declared as an object of the **Extend_interface** class.

Line 29
total = obj1.sum(105, 63);
In this line, a call is made to the **sum( )** method and the values 105 and 63 are passed as arguments. These values will be assigned to two parameters **a** and **b** in line 12. After execution of the body of the **sum( )** method, the resultant value will be returned and assigned to the **total** variable.

The working of lines 30 and 31 is same as that of line 29.

The output of Example 4 is displayed in Figure 6-4.

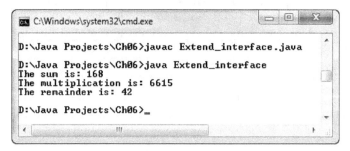

Figure 6-4 The output of Example 4

Nested Interfaces

When an interface is declared inside a class or another interface, then it is known as a member or a nested interface. You can declare a member or a nested interface by using any one of the access specifiers such as **public**, **private**, or **protected**.

For example:

```
public interface Outer
{
    //Body of the interface
    public interface Inner
    {
        //Body of the interface
    }
}
```

In this example, the **Inner** interface is declared inside another **Outer** interface. So, it is known as a nested interface. Now, a class can implement the **Inner** nested interface by using the following statements:

```
class Demo implements Outer.Inner
{
    //Body of the class
}
```

In these statements, **Outer** represents the interface in which the **Inner** interface is a member.

The following example illustrates a member interface:

```
class Demo
{
    //Body of the class
    public interface Inner
    {
        //Body of the interface
    }
}
```

In this example, the **Inner** interface is declared inside the **Demo** class. So, it is known as a member interface. Now, a class can implement the **Inner** member interface by using the following statements:

```
class A implements Demo.Inner
{
    //Body of the class
}
```

In these statements, **Demo** represents the class in which the **Inner** interface is a member.

Example 5

The following example illustrates the use of the nested interface. The program will calculate the square of a number and displays the result on the screen.

//Write a program to calculate the square of a number

```
 1  class Outer
 2  {
 3      public interface member
 4      {
 5          void getdata(int n);
 6          void sqr( );
 7          void showdata( );
 8      }
 9  }
10  class Nested_demo implements Outer.member
11  {
12      int num, result;
13      public void getdata(int n)
14      {
15          num = n;
16      }
17      public void sqr( )
18      {
19          result = num*num;
20      }
21      public void showdata( )
22      {
23          System.out.println("The square of " +num+ " is: " +result);
24      }
25      public static void main(String arg[])
26      {
27          Nested_demo obj1 = new Nested_demo( );
28          obj1.getdata(56);
29          obj1.sqr( );
30          obj1.showdata( );
31      }
32  }
```

Explanation
Line 1
class Outer
In this line, **Outer** is declared as a class using the **class** keyword.

Line 3
public interface member
This line represents the declaration part of the **member** interface. This interface is declared inside the **Outer** class. So, it will be treated as a member of the **Outer** class.

Lines 4 to 8
{
         void getdata(int n);
         void sqr( );
         void showdata( );
}

These lines contain the body of the **member** interface. Here, the curly braces {} represent the start and end of the interface body. Inside the body, three methods **getdata( )**, **sqr( )**, and **showdata( )** are declared. Whenever a class implements the **member** interface, the class will provide the implementation of all these three methods.

Line 10
class Nested_demo implements Outer.member
In this line, the **Nested_demo** class implements the **member** interface by using the **implements** keyword.

Lines 13 to 16
public void getdata(int n)
{
        num = n;
}
These lines contain the implementation of the **getdata( )** method of the **member** interface. The parameters list of the **getdata( )** method contains one integer type parameter, which indicates that an integer value must be passed whenever a call is made to the method. This integer value will be assigned to the **n** variable. Inside the method body, the value of the **n** variable will be assigned to the **num** variable.

Lines 17 to 20
public void sqr( )
{
        result = num*num;
}
These lines contain the implementation of the **sqr( )** method of the **member** interface. Inside the body of the method, the value of the **num** variable will be multiplied by itself and the resultant value will be assigned to the **result** variable.

Lines 21 to 24
public void showdata( )
{
        System.out.println("The square of " +num+ " is: " +result);
}
These lines contain the implementation of the **showdata( )** method of the **member** interface.

Line 27
Nested_demo obj1 = new Nested_demo( );
In this line, **obj1** is declared as an object of the **Nested_demo** class.

Line 28
obj1.getdata(56);
In this line, the **getdata( )** method is called and the value 56 is passed as an argument.

The working of lines 29 and 30 is the same as that of line 28.

The output of Example 5 is displayed in Figure 6-5.

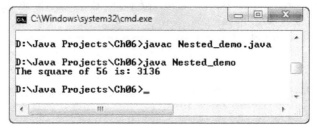

Figure 6-5 *The output of Example 5*

Note

If a class implements an interface and provides implementation only for some methods, the class should be declared as an abstract class.

NESTED CLASSES

A class that is defined inside the body of another class is known as a nested class. It enhances the security mechanism and readability and maintainability of code. Nested classes are divided into two categories:

1. Static nested classes
2. Non-static nested classes

Static Nested Classes

The static nested classes are the static members of the outer class and are declared with the **static** keyword. They can access only the static members of the outer class and not the instance members of the outer class, such as static members. Therefore, the static nested classes are used rarely. The example of static nested class is as follows:

```
class outer
{
    static class static_nested
    {
        ---------;
        ---------;
    }
}
```

In this example, **outer** represents the outer class and the **static_nested** class is defined inside the **outer** class followed by the **static** keyword.

You can create an object of static nested class by prefixing the outer class name.

For example:

```
outer.static_nested obj = new outer.static_nested();
```

In this example, **obj** represents an object of static nested class **static_nested** which is created by prefixing the **outer** class.

Example 6

The following example illustrates the use of static nested class. The program will calculate the area of rectangle and display the resultant value on the screen.

//Write a program to calculate the area of rectangle

```
1    class Static_demo
2    {
3        static int area,l,b;
4        static class Inner
5        {
6            Inner(int x, int y)
7            {
8                l=x;
9                b=y;
10           }
11           void Calculate()
12           {
13               area=l*b;
14               System.out.println("Area of rectangle is " +area);
15           }
16       }
17       public static void main(String args[])
18       {
19           Static_demo.Inner obj=new Static_demo.Inner(85, 63);
20           obj.Calculate();
21       }
22   }
```

Explanation

Line 1
class Static_demo
In this line, **Static_demo** is declared as an outer class using the **class** keyword.

Line 3
static int area, l, b;
In this line, **area**, **l**, and **b** variables are declared as static integer type using **static** as the keyword.

Line 4 to 16
static class Inner
{
      Inner(int x, int y)
      {
        l=x;
        b=y;
      }

```
      void Calculate()
      {
        area=l*b;
        System.out.println("Area of rectangle is " +area);
      }
}
```

These lines contain the definition of **Inner** class which is declared as static using the **static** keyword inside the **Static_demo** class. It has an **Inner** constructor and a **Calculate()** method which act as static members of **Inner** class and can also access static members of **Static_demo** outer class.

Line 19
Static_demo.Inner obj=new Static_demo.Inner(85, 63);
In this line, **obj** is declared as the object of **Inner** class prefixing by the **Static_demo** class. Here, a call will be made to the **Inner( )** constructor and two integer values 85 and 63 will be passed to the **x** and **y** variables in line 6. Now, these values will be assigned respectively to integer variables **x** and **y** inside the definition of the **Inner** constructor. Next, the values (85, 63) of the **x** and **y** variables will be assigned to the copy of the static variables **l** and **b**.

Line 20
obj.Calculate();
In this line, a call will be made to the **Calculate( )** method and the control will be transferred to line 11.

The output of Example 6 is displayed in Figure 6-6.

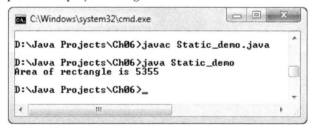

Figure 6-6 The output of Example 6

Non-static Nested Classes
The non-static nested classes are used frequently. These are also known as inner classes. A class cannot be declared as private, but inside an outer class, an inner class can be declared as private and can be hidden from the outside world. Now, the inner class can directly access all the instance members of the outer class including the private members, but outer class still cannot access the members of inner class directly. There are three types of non-static nested classes in java:

1. Member inner class
2. Local inner class
3. Anonymous inner class

Member Inner Class

When a non-static class is declared inside another class but outside a method, it is known as member inner class. The example of member inner class is as follows:

```
class outer
{
    --------;
    --------;
    class member_inner
    {
        --------;
        --------;
    }
}
```

In this example, **member_inner** represents the inner class which acts as a member of enclosing **outer** class. The scope of the **member_inner** class is bounded by the **outer** class and the **member_inner** class can directly access any member (also private members) of the **outer** class.

To create an object of inner class, you need to create the object of outer class first. The inner class object is declared using the reference of both outer and inner classes. To initialize the inner class object, **new** keyword is prefixed by the outer class object.

For example:

```
outer obj = new outer();
outer.member_inner in_obj = obj.new member_inner();
```

In this example, the **obj** object of the **outer** class is created and **in_obj** is the object of inner class which is declared using the reference of both the **outer** and **member_inner** classes. To initialize the **in_obj**, the **new** keyword is prefixed by the **obj** which is the object of the outer class.

Example 7

The following example illustrates the use of member inner class. The program will perform the addition of two numbers and display the resultant value on the screen.

```
//Write a program to add two numbers
1    class member_demo
2    {
3        int result;
4        class Inner
5        {
6            int i, j;
7            Inner(int x, int y)
8            {
9                    i = x;
10                   j = y;
11           }
```

```
12          void add( )
13          {
14              result = i+j;
15              System.out.println("The result of addition is: " +result);
16          }
17      }
18      public static void main(String arg[])
19      {
20          member_demo obj1 = new member_demo( );
21          member_demo.Inner obj = obj1.new Inner(10, 20);
22          obj.add( );
23      }
24  }
```

Explanation

Line 1

class member_demo

In this line, **member_demo** is declared as an outer class using the **class** keyword.

Line 4

class Inner

In this line, the **Inner** class is declared inside another class called **member_demo**. So, the **Inner** class is treated as an inner class of the **member_demo** class. Now, the **Inner** class can directly access the members of its enclosing **member_demo** class.

Line 6

int i, j;

In this line, **i** and **j** are declared as the integer type variables. These variables are the instance variables of the **Inner** class and cannot be accessed directly by the **member_demo** class.

Line 20

member_demo obj1 = new member_demo( );

In this line, **obj1** is declared as an object of the **member_demo** class.

Line 21

member_demo.Inner obj = obj1.new Inner(10, 20);

In this line, **obj** is declared as an object of the **Inner** class using the reference of enclosing **member_demo** class and the values 10 and 20 will be passed as arguments. Next, these values will be assigned to the **x** and **y** variables in line 7.

Line 22

obj.add( );

In this line, a call will be made to the **add( )** method and the control will be transferred to line 12.

The output of Example 7 is displayed in Figure 6-7

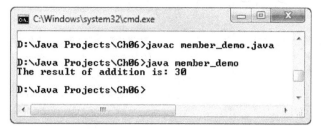

Figure 6-7 *The output of Example 7*

Local Inner Class

When a non-static class is declared inside the method of another class, it is known as local inner class. This local inner class will be having limited scope inside the method hence it cannot have any access specifier. If you want to invoke the methods of local inner class, you must create object for this class inside the method. The example of local inner class is as follows:

```
class Outer
{
    ---------;
    void declare()
    {
        class local_inner
        {
            ---------;
            ---------;
        }
        local_inner L = new local_inner();    //creating object
    }
}
```

In this example, **local_inner** is the inner class inside the **declare()** method of **Outer** class. It is not a member of **Outer** class as the scope of the **local_inner** class is bounded within the **declare()** method. **L** is an object of **local_inner** class which must be declared inside the method.

Example 8

The following example illustrates the use of local inner classes. Here, the program will calculate cube of a number and display the resultant value on the screen.

```
//Write a program to calculate the cube of a number
1    class Local_demo
2    {
3        int cube, num;
4        void show()
5        {
6            class Inner
7            {
```

```
8                  Inner(int x)
9                  {
10                     num = x;
11                 }
12                 void Cube( )
13                 {
14                     cube= num*num*num;
15                     System.out.println("Cube of " + num + " is " +cube);
16                 }
17             }
18          Inner ob = new Inner(19);
19          ob.Cube();
20      }
21      public static void main(String arg[])
22      {
23          Local_demo obj = new Local_demo( );
24          obj.show();
25      }
26 }
```

Explanation

Line 1

class Local_demo

In this line, **Local_demo** is declared as an outer class using the **class** keyword.

Line 4

void show()

This line contains the declaration of **show()** method of **Local_demo** class.

Line 6

class Inner

In this line, the **Inner** class is declared inside the **show()** method of **Local_demo** class. **Inner** class is not a member of **Local_demo** class as its scope is bounded within the **show()** method.

Line 8 to 11

Inner(int x)

{

    num = x;

}

These lines contain the definition of **Inner** constructor of inner class. The parameters list of the **Inner( )** constructor contains one integer type parameter which indicates that an integer value must be passed whenever object is created. This integer value will be assigned to the **x** variable. Inside the constructor body, the value of the **x** variable will be assigned to the **num** variable.

Lines 12 to 16

void Cube( )
{

       cube= num*num*num;
       System.out.println("Cube of " + num + " is " +cube);

}

These lines contain the implementation of the **Cube( )** method of the **Inner** class. Inside the body of the method, the value of the **num** variable will be multiplied 3 times by itself and the resultant value will be assigned to the **cube** variable.

Line 18

Inner ob = new Inner(19);
In this line, **ob** is declared as an object of the **Inner** class inside the **show()** method of **Local_demo** class and value 19 is passed as argument to the constructor in line 8.

Line 23

Local_demo obj = new Local_demo( );
In this line, **obj** is declared as an object of the **Local_demo** class.

Line 24

obj.show( );
In this line, a call will be made to the **show( )** method and the control will be transferred to line 4.

The output of Example 8 is displayed in Figure 6-8.

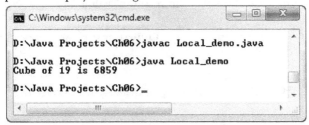

Figure 6-8 The output of Example 8

Anonymous Inner Class

When an inner class is declared without a class name, it is known as anonymous inner class. It is declared and instantiated at the same time. It can be used to override method of another class. The example of anonymous class is as follows:

```
class outer
{
    -----------;
    -----------;
    public static void main(String arg[])
    {
        Anonymous_demo a = new Anonymous_demo()
            //declaring and instantiating an anonymous class
        {
```

```
            void demo()
            {

                -----------;
                -----------;

            }
    };
    a.demo();  //method calling of anonymous class
  }
}
class Anonymous_demo
{
    void demo()
    {
    }
}
```

In this example, **Anonymous_demo** is anonymous inner class which is declared at the time of instantiation and **a** is instance of anonymous class. When a call is made to the **demo()** method using the instance **a, demo()** method of **Anonymous_demo** class will be overridden by the method of the anonymous inner class. If a call is made to the method which is not a member of the anonymous class using the instance of the anonymous class then an error will be generated.

Example 9

The following example illustrates the use of anonymous inner classes. Here the program will calculate square of a number and display the resultant value on the screen.

```
//Write a program to calculate the square of a number
1    class anonymous_demo
2    {
3        int num=15, sqr;
4        public static void main(String[] args)
5        {
6            anonymous_demo ad = new anonymous_demo();
7            Square s = new Square()
8            {
9                void calculate()
10               {
11                   ad.sqr=ad.num*ad.num;
12                   System.out.println("Square of " +ad.num +" is " +ad.sqr);
13               }
14           };
15           s.calculate();
16       }
17   }
```

```
18  class Square
19  {
20      void calculate()
21      {
22      }
23  }
```

Explanation

Line 6
anonymous_demo ad = new anonymous_demo();
In this line, **ad** object of enclosing **Anonymous_demo** class is created.

Line 7 to 14
Square s = new Square()
{

      void calculate()
      {

            ad.sqr=ad.num*ad.num;
            System.out.println("Square of " +ad.num +" is " +ad.sqr);

      }

};

These lines contain the definition of the anonymous inner class **Square**. In line 7, anonymous class **Square** is declared and instantiated. The definition of anonymous class contains the **calculate()** method which overrides the **calculate()** method (in line 20) of another **Square** class. The square of **num** variable will be performed using the object reference of the enclosing **Anonymous_demo** class. Next, the resultant value will be assigned to the **sqr** variable and the value of the **sqr** variable will be displayed.

The output of Example 9 is displayed in Figure 6-9.

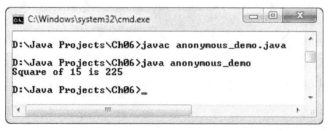

Figure 6-9 The output of Example 9

Self-Evaluation Test

Answer the following questions and then compare them to those given at the end of this chapter:

1. In Java, all classes are derived from the _____ class.

2. A _____ is known as a container of classes.

3. You can use the classes of a package by using the _____ statement.

4. The two types of nested classes are _____ and _____.

5. The class, declared as **protected** inside a package, can be accessed by a non subclass which is defined inside another package. (T/F)

6. When an interface is defined, you can create its object by using the operator **new**. (T/F)

7. Local inner class is declared inside a method. (T/F)

8. A static nested class can directly access the members of its enclosing class. (T/F)

Review Questions

Answer the following questions:

1. Define a package with a suitable example.

2. What is an interface? Explain it with a suitable example.

3. How can you import a complete package into a Java program file? Explain it with the help of a suitable example.

4. Differentiate between a static and a non-static nested class.

5. Define member inner class and explain it with a suitable example.

6. Find errors in the following source codes:

    ```
    (a) class A
        {
              interface demo
              {
                    void get(int n);
                    void show( );
              }
        }
    ```

```
      class B implements demo
      {
            int num;
            void get(int n)
            {
                  num = n;
            }
      }
```

(b)
```
   package demo
   class A
   {
         int data;
         void getdata(double n)
         {
               data = n;
         }
         void showdata( )
         {
               System.out.println("Value is: ", +data);
         }
   }
```

(c)
```
   interface A
   {
         void get(int n);
         void show( );
   }
   abstract class implements A
   {
         int num;
         public void get(int n)
         {
               num = n;
         }
         public void show( )
         {
               System.out.println("Value is: " +num);
         }
   }
```

(d)
```
   interface A
   {
         void sum(int a, int b);
         void mul(int x, int y);
   }
   interface B
   {
         int rmndr(int var1, int var2)
   }
```

```
interface C extends A, B
{
        //Body of the interface
}
```

EXERCISES

Exercise 1

Write a program to create a **employee** package that contains the **details** class. Inside the class, define the methods that will be used to obtain and display details of an employee.

Exercise 2

Write a program to create an **demo** interface that contains the following methods:

　　void getnum(int a) - To get the value
　　void evodd( ) - To check whether the given number is even or odd
　　void show( ) - To display the result on the screen

Chapter 7

Exception Handling

Learning Objectives

After completing this chapter, you will be able to:

- *Understand the exception classes*
- *Understand the types of exceptions*
- *Understand the use of try block*
- *Understand the use of catch block*
- *Understand throw statement*
- *Understand the concept of throws keyword*
- *Understand the concept of finally clause*
- *Define your own exception subclasses*

INTRODUCTION

Sometimes while executing a program, its normal flow is disrupted due to the occurrence of certain abnormal conditions. These conditions are known as exceptions or run-time errors. In some programming languages, these exceptions are handled manually that makes the programming process very tedious. However, in Java, you can handle such exceptions easily with the help of a mechanism called as exception handling.

EXCEPTION HANDLING MECHANISM

Whenever a run-time error occurs during the execution of a method or a piece of code, an object is created. This object represents the error and is called an exception. This exception is thrown to the method that caused the error. Now, the method has two ways to deal with the exception, either it can handle the exception by itself or pass it to other methods for handling. In both cases, Java run-time environment searches for a particular block of code that can be used for handling the exception. When the code is found, the exception passes to it and handles by itself. This code is known as handler and the process is known as exception handling.

Exception Classes

As you know that whenever an exception is raised, an object of that exception is created and thrown to the method. But, this is true only for the objects of those classes that are the subclasses of the **Throwable** class. The **Throwable** class remains at the top of the hierarchy of exception classes, as shown in Figure 7-1.

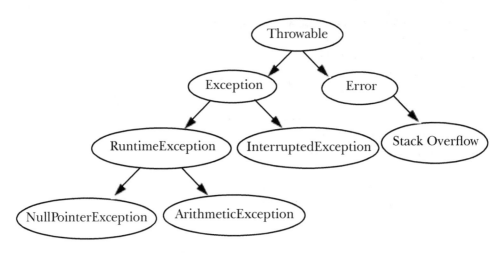

Figure 7-1 *Partial representation of hierarchy of the **Throwable** class*

The **Throwable** class has two direct subclasses: **Exception** and **Error**, refer to Figure 7-1. The **Exception** class is used for abnormal conditions that can be easily caught and handled inside the program. It also has certain direct subclasses such as **RuntimeException**, **InterruptedException**, and so on. The **Error** class, on the other hand, defines those types of exceptions that a simple Java program cannot handle.

Types of Exceptions

In Java, there are two types of exceptions that are discussed next.

1. Checked exceptions
2. Unchecked exceptions

Checked Exceptions

The checked exceptions are checked during the compile time of a program. For example, **EOFException** is a checked exception. The parent class of these types of exceptions is **java.lang.Exception**.

Unchecked Exceptions

The unchecked exceptions occur during the run-time of a program. These exceptions are handled by Java itself. **NullPointerException** and **IndexOutOfBoundsException** are two examples of unchecked exceptions.

Blocks Used in Exception-Handling Mechanism

In Java, five types of blocks are used in exception-handling mechanism. These are as follows:

1. try
2. catch
3. throw
4. throws
5. finally

The try Block

The **try** block contains the statements that are monitored for an abnormal condition or an exception. The syntax for using the **try** block is as follows:

```
try
{
    //Statements that are monitored for errors or exceptions
}
```

In this syntax, **try** is a keyword and curly braces {} represent the start and end of the **try** block. The body of the **try** block contains the statements that monitor the exceptions or errors.

For example:

```
try
{
    int result = 10/0;
}
```

In this example, the **try** block contains a single statement that is monitored for an exception.

The catch Block

The **catch** block catches the exception generated by the **try** block. The **catch** block acts as an exception handler and contains the statements that are executed to handle the exception. The syntax for using the **catch** block is as follows:

```
catch(Exception Type obj)
{
    //Statements to be executed
}
```

In this syntax, **catch** is the keyword, **Exception Type** represents the type of exception and **obj** represents the object of the exception type generated by the **try** block. The body of the **catch** block contains the statements that are used to handle the exception.

For example:

```
try
{
    result = 10/0;
}
catch(ArithmeticException e)
{
    System.out.println("Divide by zero");
}
```

In this example, the **try** block generates the exception **java.lang.ArithmeticException: / by zero**. Next, an object representing this exception is generated and thrown. The **catch** block catches this object and the statement "Divide by zero" is displayed inside the **catch** block.If the **try** and **catch** blocks were not used, the program would have terminated abnormally.

Note

*Either the **catch** or the **finally** block should be associated with the **try** block. Moreover in the **catch** block, instead of using a particular exception type, you can use an object of the **Exception** class.*

Example 1

The following example illustrates the use of the **try** and **catch** statements. The program will access all elements of an array and display them on the screen.

```
//Write a program to display all elements of an array
1   class Exception_demo
2   {
3       public static void main(String[] args)
4       {
5           int i[ ] = {10, 20, 30, 40, 50};
6           int len = i.length;
7           try
8           {
9               for(int j=0; j<=len; j++)
10              {
```

```
11                    System.out.println(i[j]);
12              }
13          }
14      catch(IndexOutOfBoundsException e)
15          {
16                    System.out.println("Out of index");
17          }
18      }
19  }
```

Explanation

Line 5

int i[ ] = {10, 20, 30, 40, 50};

In this line, **i** is declared as an array of integers and values 10, 20, 30, 40, and 50 are assigned to its elements; for example, 10 is assigned to the element at i[0] position, 20 to i[1], and so on.

Line 6

int len = i.length;

In this line, the parameter **length** will return the total number of elements contained in the array **i**. Next, the resultant value (5) will be assigned to the integer type variable **len**.

Lines 7 to 13

try

{

       for(int j=0; j<=len; j++)

       {

              System.out.println(i[j]);

       }

}

These lines contain the definition of the **try** block. Inside the block, the **for** loop is used to display the elements of the array **i**. Inside the **for** loop, first the loop control variable **j** will be initialized to zero and then the condition **j<=len** will be evaluated. In this case, the condition will return **true** and the statement associated with the **for** loop will be executed that will display the value (10) of the element **i[0]**. This process will also be repeated for the values 1, 2, 3, and 4 of the loop control variable **j**. Now when the **for** loop starts execution for the value 5 of **j** variable, an exception **IndexOutOfBoundsException** will occur and an object of that exception will be created and thrown.

Lines 14 to 17

catch(IndexOutOfBoundsException e)

{

       System.out.println("Out of index");

}

These lines contain the definition of the **catch** block. This block will catch and handle the object (exception) thrown by the **try** block.

The output of Example 1 is displayed in Figure 7-2.

Figure 7-2 *The output of Example 1*

In this program, if the **try** and **catch** blocks would have not been used, then the program would have produced the following output:

10
20
30
40
50

Exception in thread "main" java.lang.ArrayIndexOutOfBoundsException: 5
        at exceptiondemo.main(exceptiondemo.java:11)

Multiple catch Blocks

In the previous example, the code inside the **try** block generated only one type of exception that was handled by a single **catch** block. But sometimes, the code generates multiple exceptions. In such cases, you need to define multiple **catch** blocks to handle multiple exceptions such that these blocks are associated with a single **try** block. The syntax for using multiple **catch** blocks is as follows:

```
try
{
        //Statements to be monitored
}
catch(ExceptionType1 obj)
{
        //Statements to handle an exception
}
catch(ExceptionType2 obj)
{
        //Statements to handle an exception
}
----------;
----------;
catch(ExceptionTypeN obj)
{
        //Statements to handle an exception
}
```

In this syntax, first the exception generated in the **try** block is thrown and then this exception is matched with exceptions of all the **catch** blocks one by one. When a match is found, statements associated with that particular **catch** block are executed to handle the exception. After the execution of the matched **catch** block, the remaining **catch** blocks are skipped and the control is transferred to the next immediate statement after the **try/catch** block.

Example 2

The following example illustrates the implementation of multiple **catch** blocks The program will divide a number and display the elements of an array on the screen.

//Write a program to illustrate the implementation of multiple catch blocks

```
1    class multi_catch_demo
2    {
3        public static void main(String arg[])
4        {
5            int num=10;
6            int a = arg.length;
7            int ar[ ] = {12, 23, 35, 46, 78};
8            try
9            {
10               int result = num/a;
11               System.out.println("After division, the result is: "
                 +result);
12               for(int i=0; i<=5; i++)
13               {
14                   System.out.println("Value at ar["+i+"] is: "+ar[i]);
15               }
16           }
17           catch(ArrayIndexOutOfBoundsException e)
18           {
19               System.out.println("An exception " +e+ " occurred");
20           }
21           catch(ArithmeticException e)
22           {
23               System.out.println("An exception " +e+ " occurred");
24           }
25       }
26   }
```

Explanation
Line 6
int a = arg.length;
In this line, the **length** method will return the number of arguments that will be passed during the execution of the program. Next, the resultant value will be assigned to the integer type variable **a**.

Line 7
int ar[ ] = {12, 23, 35, 46, 78};
In this line, **ar** is declared as an integer type array. The values 12, 23, 35, 46, and 78 will be assigned to the elements of the array **ar[ ]**; for example, value 12 will be assigned to **ar[0]**, 23 to **ar[1]**, and so on.

Lines 8 to 16
try
{
       int result = num/a;
       System.out.println("After division, the result is: " +result);
       for(int i=0; i<=5; i++)
       {
              System.out.println("Value at ar["+i+"] is: "+ar[i]);
       }
}
These lines contain the definition of the **try** block. Inside the **try** block, the value of **num** variable will be divided by the value of **a** variable and the resultant value will be assigned to the integer type variable **result**. If the value of **a** variable will be 0, the arithmetic exception / **by zero** will be generated and the remaining part of the **try** block will be skipped. Otherwise, the value of **result** variable will be displayed. Moreover, inside the body of the **for** loop, the values stored in the elements of the array **ar[ ]** will be displayed. Here, the **for** loop will generate the exception **ArrayIndexOutOfBoundsException** because an attempt will be made to access the sixth element which does not exist in the array **ar[ ]**.

Lines 17 to 20
catch(ArrayIndexOutOfBoundsException e)
{
       System.out.println("An exception " +e+ " occurred");
}
These lines contain the definition of the **catch** block that will be used to handle the exception of the type **ArrayIndexOutOfBoundsException** with the help of the **e** object. When the exception occurs, the statement given inside the **catch** block is executed and the following result is displayed:

An exception java.lang.ArrayIndexOutOfBoundsException: 5 occurred

Next, the remaining **catch** block will be skipped and the control will be transferred to the statement that is immediately after the **try/catch** block.

Lines 21 to 24
catch(ArithmeticException e)
{
       System.out.println("An exception " +e+ " occurred");
}

These lines contain the definition of the **catch** block that will be used to handle the exception of the type **ArithmeticException** with the help of the **e** object. When the exception occurs, the statement given inside the **catch** block will be executed and the following output will be displayed on the screen:

An exception java.lang.ArithmeticException: / by zero occurred

The output of Example 2 is displayed in Figure 7-3.

Figure 7-3 *The output of Example 2*

If you pass a single command line argument during the time of execution as follows:

D:\Java Projects\Ch07 >java multi_catch_demo first

The output will be displayed as shown in Figure 7-4.

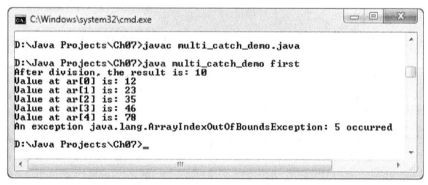

Figure 7-4 *The output of Example 2 using single command line argument*

As you have already learned that all exception classes such as **ArithmeticException**, **ArrayIndexOutOfBoundsException**, **NullPointerException**, and so on are subclasses of the **Exception** class. Sometimes, in multiple **catch** blocks, the **Exception** superclass is used before its subclasses. In such cases, the control does not reach to subclasses and an error occurs.

For example:

```
try
{
    int result = num/a;
    System.out.println("After division, the result is: " +result);
    for(int i=0; i<=5; i++)
    {
        System.out.println("Value at ar[" +i+ "] is: " +ar[i]);
    }
}
catch(Exception e)
{
    System.out.println(e);
}
catch(ArrayIndexOutOfBoundsException e)
{
    System.out.println("An exception " +e+ " occurred");
}
catch(ArithmeticException e)
{
    System.out.println("An exception " +e+ " occurred");
}
```

In this example, the **Exception** superclass is used before its subclasses
ArrayIndexOutOfBoundsException and **ArithmeticException**. If the code is compiled, it
will produce the following errors:

multi_catch_demo.java:23: exception java.lang.ArrayIndexOutOfBoundsException has already
been caught
                    catch(ArrayIndexOutOfBoundsException e)

multi_catch_demo.java:27: exception java.lang.ArithmeticException has already been caught

                    catch(ArithmeticException e)

The code produced two errors that you can rectify by using the **Exception** superclass after its
subclasses, as shown in the following example.

For example:

```
try
{
    int result = num/a;
    System.out.println("After division, the result is: " result);
    for(int i=0; i<=5; i++)
    {
        System.out.println("Value at ar[" +i+ "] is: " +ar[i]);
    }
}
```

```
catch(ArrayIndexOutOfBoundsException e)
{
    System.out.println("An exception " +e+ " occurred");
}
catch(ArithmeticException e)
{
    System.out.println("An exception " +e+ " occurred");
}
catch(Exception e)
{
    System.out.println(e);
}
```

Here, this code does not produce any error and executes normally.

Nested try Statement

When the **try** statement is used inside the body of another **try** statement, it is known as the nested **try** statement. The syntax for using the nested **try** statement is as follows:

```
try         //Outer try statement
{
    //statements
    try     //Inner try statement
    {
        //statements
    }
    catch(ExceptionType obj)
    {
        //statements
    }
}
catch(ExceptionType obj)
{
    //statements
}
```

In this syntax, if the inner **try** statement generates an exception and the **catch** block associated with the statement does not handle that exception, the next **catch** block, associated with the next **try** block is checked, and this process is repeated until a suitable match is found or until all the nested **try** blocks have been used. If no match is found inside the nested **try/catch** blocks, the outer **catch** block is checked. If that particular exception is not handled even by the outer **catch** block, the Java run-time environment handles the exception.

Example 3

The following example illustrates the use of the nested **try** statements. The program will handle the **ArithmeticException** and **ArrayIndexOut OfBoundsException** exceptions and display a message.

//Write a program to handle exceptions using nested **try** statements

```
1    class nested_try_demo
2    {
3        public static void main(String arg[])
4        {
5            int num=10, val=0;
6            int a = arg.length;
7            int ar[ ] = {12, 23, 35, 46, 78};
8            try
9            {
10               int result = num/a;
11               System.out.println("After division, the result is: "
                 +result);
12               try
13               {
14                   for(int i=0; i<=5; i++)
15                   {
16                       System.out.println("Value at ar["+i+"] is: "
                         +ar[i]);
17                   }
18               }
19               catch(ArrayIndexOutOfBoundsException e)
20               {
21                   System.out.println("An exception " +e+ " occurred");
22               }
23           }
24           catch(ArithmeticException e)
25           {
26               System.out.println("An exception " +e+ " occurred");
27           }
28       }
29   }
```

Explanation
The working of this program is similar to the previous example. In this program, when no argument is passed during the time of execution, the exception **ArithmeticException / by zero** will be generated and it will be handled by the outer **catch** block. Otherwise, the other exception **ArrayIndexOutOfBoundsException** will be generated by the nested **try** block and handled by the inner **catch** block.

The output of Example 3 is displayed in Figure 7-5.

Figure 7-5 The output of Example 3

If you pass the single command line argument during the execution time as follows:

> *D:\Java Projects\Ch07>java nested_try_demo first*

The output will be displayed as shown in Figure 7-6.

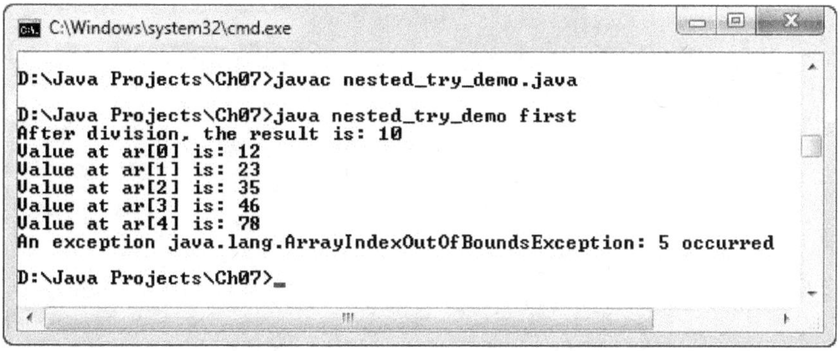

```
C:\Windows\system32\cmd.exe

D:\Java Projects\Ch07>javac nested_try_demo.java

D:\Java Projects\Ch07>java nested_try_demo first
After division, the result is: 10
Value at ar[0] is: 12
Value at ar[1] is: 23
Value at ar[2] is: 35
Value at ar[3] is: 46
Value at ar[4] is: 78
An exception java.lang.ArrayIndexOutOfBoundsException: 5 occurred

D:\Java Projects\Ch07>_
```

Figure 7-6 *The output of Example 3 using single command line argument*

The throw Statement

In the examples given so far, the **catch** block handled only those exceptions that were thrown by the Java run-time environment. But, a program can also throw an exception explicitly using the **throw** statement. The syntax for using the **throw** statement is as follows:

```
throw ThrowableObject;
```

In this syntax, **throw** is the keyword and **ThrowableObject** represents an object of any of the subclasses of the **Throwable** class.

Using the **throw** keyword, you can only throw an object either of the **Throwable** class or its subclasses. If you try to throw an object of any class other than the **Throwable** class or its subclasses, the compiler will compile your program and display an error message.

When the **throw** statement is encountered in a program, then after the execution of that statement, the program will display an error message. In this case, all subsequent statements are skipped and the control is transferred to the nearest **try/catch** block to check whether the **catch** block can handle the exception type that is thrown with the help of the **throw** statement or not. If no match is found, the next **try/catch** block is checked, and this process is repeated until all **catch** blocks get exhausted. If none of the **catch** blocks is able to handle the exception, the default exception handler handles the exception by halting the program.

Example 4

The following example illustrates the use of the **throw** statement. The program will handle the arithmetic exception thrown by using the **throw** statement and display a message on the screen.

//Write a program to handle the arithmetic exception

```
1   class throw_demo
2   {
3       public static void main(String arg[ ])
4       {
5           int a = Integer.parseInt(arg[0]);
6           int b = Integer.parseInt(arg[1]);
7           try
8           {
9               if(b==0)
10              {
11                  throw new ArithmeticException("demo");
12              }
13              else
14              {
15                  int result = a%b;
16                  System.out.println("After division, the remainder is: "
                    +result);
17              }
18          }
19          catch(ArithmeticException e)
20          {
21              System.out.println("Thrown exception caught " +e);
22          }
23      }
24  }
```

Explanation
Lines 5 and 6
int a = Integer.parseInt(arg[0]);
int b = Integer.parseInt(arg[1]);
In these lines, **parseInt** is the method of the **Integer** class and is used to read numeric values from the command-line arguments. Next, the resultant values will be assigned to the integer type variables **a** and **b**, respectively.

Lines 9 to 12
if(b==0)
{
        throw new ArithmeticException("demo");
}
In these lines, first the value of the **b** variable will be checked to find out whether it is equal to zero or not. If it is equal to zero, the control will be transferred to the **throw** statement. The **throw** statement will create a new object of the **ArithmeticException** class with the help of the **new** operator, and **demo** name will be given to it. Next, this object will be thrown by the **throw** statement. After the execution of the **throw** statement, the subsequent statements will be skipped and the control will be transferred to the **catch** statement (line 19).

Lines 13 to 17
else
{

      int result = a%b;
      System.out.println("After division, the remainder is: " +result);

}
If the value of the **b** variable is not equal to 0, the control will be transferred to the **else** statement. Inside the **else** block, the value of the **a** variable will be divided by the value of the **b** variable and the remainder value will be assigned to the integer variable **result**.

Lines 19 to 22
catch(ArithmeticException e)
{

      System.out.println("Thrown exception caught " +e);

}
These lines contain the definition of the **catch** block. The parameter list of the **catch** statement contains the **e** object of the **ArithmeticException** . The **catch** block will handle the exception that is thrown by the **throw** statement and then the output will be displayed.

The output of Example 4 is displayed in Figure 7-7.

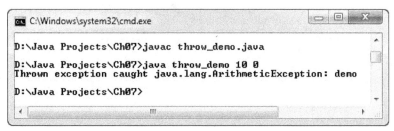

Figure 7-7 *The output of Example 4*

The throws Keyword
Sometimes, the method of a program generates an exception but is not able to handle it. In such cases, the method should specify other parts of the program or callers so that they can be protected against exception. For this purpose, the method should use the **throws** keyword in the method's declaration statement. Using the **throws** keyword, you can specify the type of exceptions that the method will throw. The syntax for using the **throws** keyword is as follows:

```
returntype method_name(parameter list) throws exception1, exception2,.....,
exceptionN
{
    //Body of the method
}
```

In this syntax, **exception1** to **exceptionN** represent the type of exceptions that this method can throw.

For example:

```
static void demo(int a, int b) throws IllegalAccessException
{
    ----------;
    throw new IllegalAccessException("trial");
}
```

In this example, the **demo()** method can throw the exception of the type **IllegalAccessException**, but cannot handle it.

Example 5

The following example illustrates the use of the **throws** block. The program will handle the checked exception **NoSuchMethodException** and display a message on the screen.

```
//Write a program to handle a checked exception
1    class throws_demo
2    {
3        static void demo( ) throws NoSuchMethodException
4        {
5            System.out.println("Inside demo method");
6            throw new NoSuchMethodException("Trial");
7        }
8        public static void main(String arg[ ])
9        {
10           try
11           {
12               demo( );
13           }
14           catch(NoSuchMethodException e)
15           {
16               System.out.println("Exception caught " +e);
17           }
18       }
19   }
```

Explanation
Line 3
static void demo( ) throws NoSuchMethodException
This line is the declaration statement of the **demo( )** method. In this line, the exception of type **NoSuchMethodException** is specified with the **throws** keyword, which indicates that the **demo()** method can throw an object of this exception type, but cannot handle it.

Line 6
throw new NoSuchMethodException("Trial");
This line is given inside the body of the **demo()** method. In this line, an object of the **NoSuchMethodException** class will be created with the help of the **new** operator and thrown with the help of the **throw** keyword.

Line 12
demo( );
In this line, a call will be made to the **demo( )** method. Next, the control will be transferred to the definition part of the **demo()** method (from lines 3 to 7).

Lines 15 to 18
catch(NoSuchMethodException e)
{
    System.out.println("Exception caught " +e);
}
In this line, the object of the exception, which is thrown inside the body of the **demo()** method, will be caught and handled by the **catch** block. Consequently, the statement given inside the body of the **catch** statement will display a message on the screen.

The output of Example 5 is displayed in Figure 7-8.

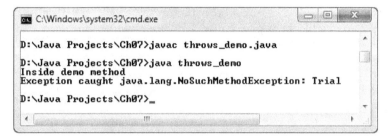

Figure 7-8 *The output of Example 5*

The finally Clause

When an exception occurs in the **try** block, the normal flow of execution of the program changes and some of the statements given inside the **try** block are skipped. In such a cases, some resources such as files, database connections, and so on are not properly closed. As a result, these resources cannot be used further in other programs or in any other part of the same program. So to avoid this problem, Java uses the **finally** clause. This clause contains code to release resources that are acquired by some of the statements of its enclosing **try** block. Note that the **finally** clause is used in a program only if the **try** block exists in it.

If the **finally** clause exists in a program, it will be executed after the **try/catch** block, but before the statements that follow the **try/catch** block. The main advantage of using this clause is that the code given inside it gets executed irrespective of occurrence of an exception. The syntax for using the **finally** clause is as follows:

```
finally
{
    //Statements to be executed
}
```

The **finally** clause is optional and if it is used with the **try** block, it will be placed after the last **catch** block that is associated with that particular **try** block, as shown in the following code:

```
try
{
    //Statements
}
catch(ExceptionType obj)
{
    //Statements
}
 catch(ExceptionType obj)
{
    //Statements
}
finally
{
    //Statements
}
```

But, if there is no **catch** block associated with the **try** block, the **finally** clause is placed immediately after the **try** block, as given next:

```
try
{
    //Statements
}
finally( )
{
    //Statements
}
```

Example 6

The following example illustrates the use of the **finally** clause. The program will calculate the square of a number that will be passed as a command-line argument by the user. Also, this program will handle the exception using the **try-catch-finally** mechanism and display a message on the screen.

//Write a program to calculate the square of a number and also to handle an exception

```
1    class finally_demo
2    {
3        public static int sqr(int n)
4        {
5            try
6            {
7                int result = n*n;
8                if(result ==0)
9                {
10                    throw new ArithmeticException("demo");
11                }
```

```
12                 else
13                 {
14                     return result;
15                 }
16             }
17         finally
18         {
19                 System.out.println("Inside the finally block");
20         }
21     }
22     public static void main(String arg[ ])
23     {
24         int sq;
25         int val = Integer.parseInt(arg[0]);
26         try
27         {
28             sq = sqr(val);
29             System.out.println("The square of " +val+ " is: " +sq);
30         }
31         catch(ArithmeticException e)
32         {
33             System.out.println("Exception caught " +e);
34         }
35     }
36 }
```

Explanation

Line 3

public static int sqr(int n)

This line contains the declaration part of the **sqr( )** method. The parameter list of the method contains one integer type parameter **n**. Whenever a call is made to this parameter, an integer value will be passed that is assigned to the integer variable **n**.

Lines 5 to 16

try
{

      int result = n*n;
      if(result ==0)
      {

            throw new ArithmeticException("demo");

      }
      else
      {

            return result;

      }

}

These lines contain the definition of the **try** block. Inside the **try** block, first the value of the **n** variable will be multiplied by itself and the resultant value will be assigned to the integer type variable **result**. Next, the condition given inside the **if** statement will be evaluated. If it evaluates to **true**, an object of the **ArithmeticException** exception will be thrown. Otherwise, the **return** statement associated with the **else** block will be executed. But, immediately before the execution of the **return** statement, the control will be transferred to the **finally** block.

Lines 17 to 20
finally
{
        System.out.println("Inside the finally block");
}
These lines represent the **finally** block. The statement associated with it will display the following message on the screen:

Inside the finally block

After the execution of the **finally** block, the **return** statement will be executed.

Line 25
int val = Integer.parseInt(arg[0]);
In this line, the value that is passed as a command line argument will be read and assigned to the integer type variable **val**.

Lines 27 to 31
try
{
        sq = sqr(val);
        System.out.println("The square of " +val+ " is: " +sq);
}
These lines contain the definition of the **try** block that is defined inside the **main( )** method. Inside the **try** block, a call will be made to the **sqr( )** method and the value of the **val** variable will be passed as an argument to the **sqr()** method, which is then assigned to the **n** variable in line 3.

Lines 31 to 34
catch(ArithmeticException e)
{
        System.out.println("Exception caught " +e);
}
When the value 0 is passed as a command-line argument, the **throw** statement given in line 11 will throw an object of the **ArithmeticException** class. This object will be caught and handled by the **catch** block.

If you pass 0 as a command line argument during the time of execution as follows:

        D:\Java Projects\Ch07>java finally_demo 0

The output will be displayed as shown in Figure 7-9.

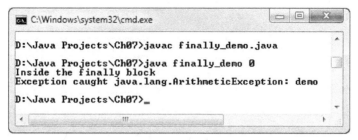

Figure 7-9 *The output of Example 6*

If you pass 10 as a command line argument during the time of execution as follows:

D:\Java Projects\ Ch07>java finally_demo 10

The output will be displayed as shown in Figure 7-10.

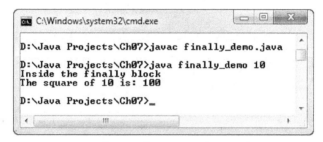

Figure 7-10 *The output of Example 6*

Defining Your Own Exception Subclasses

In the previous sections of this chapter, you might have observed that all programs were used to handle Java's in-built exceptions. But, if you want to create your own exceptions and handle them as per your need and requirement, you can do so by defining a subclass of the **Exception** class. The syntax for using a new subclass in the **Exception** class is as follows:

```
class class_name extends Exception
{
    //Body of the class
}
```

When a subclass of the **Exception** class is defined, the class basically inherits all methods of the **Throwable** class because the **Exception** class does not define any method of its own; all methods available to it are of the **Throwable** class.

Example 7

The following example illustrates the method of defining a subclass of the **Exception** class. The program will create a new exception type **NewException** by extending the **Exception** class and display some messages on the screen.

```
//Write a program to create a new exception type
1    class NewException extends Exception
2    {
3        public String getLocalizedMessage( )
4        {
5            return "Exception occurs";
6        }
7    }
8    class New_demo
9    {
10       static void demo(int age) throws NewException
11       {
12           if(age<=0)
13                   throw new NewException( );
14           else
15           {
16                   System.out.println("No exception occured");
17                   System.out.println("Your age is: " +age+ " Years");
18           }
19       }
20       public static void main(String arg[])
21       {
22           try
23           {
24               demo(10);
25               demo(0);
26           }
27           catch(NewException e)
28           {
29               System.out.println("Caught " +e);
30           }
31       }
32   }
```

Explanation

Line 1

class NewException extends Exception

In this line, the **NewException** class is defined as a subclass of the **Exception** class.

Lines 3 to 6

public String getLocalizedMessage( )

{

       return "Exception occurs";

}

These lines contain the definition of the **getLocalizedMessage( )** method. This method is basically defined inside the **Throwable** class, but in this case, it is overridden inside the new exception type **NewException**.

Line 24
demo(10);
In this line, a call will be made to the **demo( )** method of the **New_demo** class and the value 10 will be passed as an argument to this method. Next, the control will be transferred to the method definition and the value 10 will be assigned to the integer variable **age**.

Lines 27 to 30
catch(NewException e)
{
       System.out.println("Caught " +e);
}
In these lines, the **catch** block will catch and handle the exception of the **NewException** type. As a result, the statement associated with it will display the following message on the screen:

Caught NewException: Exception occurs

The output of Example 7 is displayed in Figure 7-11.

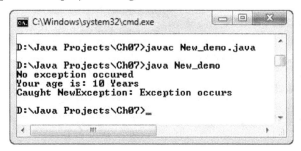

Figure 7-11 *The output of Example 7*

Self-Evaluation Test

Answer the following questions and then compare them to those given at the end of this chapter:

1. The _____ class remains at top of the hierarchy of the exception classes.

2. The _____ and _____ are the direct subclasses of the **Throwable** class.

3. The _____ class is used for abnormal conditions that can be caught and handled inside a program.

4. Exceptions that are checked during the compile time of a program are known as _____ exceptions.

5. The _____ block contains the statement or statements which are monitored for an exception.

6. The block that acts as an exception handler is known as the _____ block.

7. A program can also throw an exception explicitly by using the _____ statement.

8. The _____ clause will be executed even if an exception occurs or not.

9. You can create your own exception type by defining a subclass of the _____ class.

10. The **ArithmeticException** exception is a subclass of the _____ class.

Review Questions

Answer the following questions:

1. Define an exception.

2. Explain the types of exceptions.

3. List the keywords that are used in the exception handling mechanism.

4. Explain the function of the **throw** statement.

5. Explain the **finally** clause.

6. Find errors in the following source codes:

(a)
```
class demo
{
    public static void main(String arg[ ])
    {
        int a = 10, b = 0, c;
        c = a/b;
        System.out.println("After division, the result is: " +c);
    }
}
```

(b)
```
class throwdemo
{
    static void demo( )
    {
        throw new NullPointerException("trial");
    }
    public static void main(String arg[ ])
    {
        demo( );
    }
}
```

(c)
```
class arraydemo
{
    public static void main(String arg[ ])
    {
        int ar[ ] = {10, 20, 30, 40, 50};
        int len = ar.length;
        try
        {
            for (i=0; i<=len; i++)
            {
                System.out.println(ar[i]);
            }
        }
    }
}
```

(d)
```
class throwdemo
{
    static void demo( )
    {
        try
        {
            throw new IllegalArgumentException("demo");
        }
        catch(IllegalArgumentException e)
        {
            System.out.println("Exception caught");
            throw e;
        }
    }
    public static void main(String arg[ ])
    {
        demo( );
    }
}
```

(e)
```
class throwsdemo
{
    static void demo( ) throws NullPointerException
    {
        throw new NullPointerException("trial");
    }
    public static void main(String arg[ ])
    {
        demo( );
    }
}
```

EXERCISES

Exercise 1

Write a program to illustrate the function of the nested **try** statements.

Exercise 2

Write a program to handle an arithmetic exception by using the **throws** statement.

Answers to Self-Evaluation Test
1. Throwable, 2. Exception, Error, 3. Exception, 4. Checked, 5. try, 6. catch, 7. throw,
8. finally, 9. Exception, 10. RuntimeException

Chapter 8

Multithreading

Learning Objectives

After completing this chapter, you will be able to:

- *Understand the concept of multithreading*
- *Understand the thread model*
- *Understand the concept of main thread*
- *Understand the procedure of creating a new thread*
- *Understand the procedure of creating multiple threads*
- *Understand the concept of isAlive( ) and join( ) methods*
- *Set the thread priorities*
- *Understand the concept of synchronization*
- *Understand the concept of deadlock*

INTRODUCTION

In this chapter, you will learn about another special feature of Java that is known as multithreading. Before learning the concept of multithreading, you should know about the thread. A thread is a part of a program or a sequence of instructions being executed. The path of execution of each thread is different from all other threads of a program, but these threads can directly share their data with each other. Therefore, besides learning the concepts of multithreading and thread synchronization, you will learn to create multiple threads in this chapter.

MULTITHREADING

Multithreading means execution of two or more threads or parts of a program concurrently. It is a special form of multitasking. It provides you with the facility to write programs that help in maximize the CPU usage and minimize the CPU idle time. The process of multitasking is divided into two categories, process-based and thread-based multitasking. These types are discussed next.

1. In process-based multitasking, two or more programs can run concurrently. In this type of multitasking, each program is treated as a process. This process is also known as heavyweight process. The main drawbacks of the process-based multitasking are that each process in it requires its own separate address space and the context switching time from one process to another is considerably high.

2. In thread-based multitasking, two or more than two parts of a program can run concurrently. In this type of multitasking, each thread is known as lightweight process. The main advantage of using thread-based multitasking is that each thread of a program shares the same memory space and the context switching time from one thread to another is considerably low in it.

Thread Model

The best part of a multithreaded environment is that each thread functions independent of the other threads of the program. If one thread stops functioning, the functioning of the other threads is not affected. So, the main advantage of using this environment is that the idle time of one thread can be used somewhere else in a program. In a multithreaded environment, each thread can be in one of the following states:

1. **New:** The state when a thread is created but not yet started.

2. **Runnable:** The state when a thread is waiting for the CPU time after invocation of the **start()** method.

3. **Running:** The state when a thread is being executed.

4. **Waiting:** The state when a thread is waiting for another thread to perform a task. In this case, the thread is still alive.

5. **Blocked:** The state when a thread is waiting for a resource being used by another thread.

6. **Terminated:** The state when the execution of a thread is completed.

Thread Priorities

Whenever a thread is created, Java prioritizes it on the basis of its integer value. Priority of a thread in a program represents its importance with respect to other threads in the program. While prioritizing, giving the priority, an integer value ranging from 1 to 10 is assigned to a thread. The highest priority is 10, the lowest priority is 1, and the normal priority is 5. Giving priorities to threads helps in determining the switching time from one currently executed thread to other thread. The process of switching from one thread to another is known as context switching. The following rules are applied for context switching:

1. A thread can voluntarily release control. In such a case, the CPU is provided to the thread with highest priority.

2. A lower-priority thread can be replaced by a higher-priority thread. In such a case, the lower-priority thread is suspended for sometime.

If multiple threads with same priority exist, their executions depend on the operating system being used to run the program. For example, in Windows operating system, a time-slice is set for the execution of threads and the control is transferred to each thread in a round-robin fashion for that particular time-slice.

 Note

The priority determines the order of execution of threads. However, there is no difference between the execution speed of a higher-priority thread and a lower-priority thread.

THE main THREAD

Whenever a Java program starts, one thread starts running immediately. This thread is called as the **main** thread. The **main** thread is treated as parent thread and the rest of threads known as child threads of the program are generated from it. The other important aspect of the **main** thread is that it is the last thread to be executed in a program. When the **main** thread finishes the execution, the program terminates immediately.

Whenever a Java program starts, the **main** thread is created automatically. This thread is available in all Java programs. You can control the execution of a thread by using an object and the member methods of the **Thread** class. To do so, you need to create a reference to the main thread, using the **currentThread( )** method of the **Thread** class, as shown in the following example:

```
Thread obj = Thread.currentThread( );
```

In this example, **obj** is an object of the **Thread** class. Here, the **currentThread( )** method of the **Thread** class return a reference of the current thread in which they are called. Next, that reference is assigned to the **obj** object of the **Thread** class. In the same way, once you get the reference of the **main** thread, you can control its execution.

Example 1

The following example illustrates the concept of the **main** thread. The program will obtain and display the name of the **main** thread. Also, it will change the name of the **main** thread and display it on the screen.

//Write a program to change the name of the **main** thread

```
1   class main_thread_demo
2   {
3       public static void main(String arg[ ])
4       {
5           Thread obj = Thread.currentThread( );
6           System.out.println("Current thread is: " +obj);
7           System.out.println("Name of the current thread is: "
            +obj.getName( ));
8           obj.setName("New Thread");
9           System.out.println("After the change of name, the current
            thread is: " +obj);
10      }
11  }
```

Explanation

Line 5

Thread obj = Thread.currentThread( );

In this line, the **obj** object is created as an object of the **Thread** class. Here, the **currentThread( )** method returns the reference of the **main** thread because it is called inside the **main** thread. Next, the reference of the **main** thread will be assigned to the **obj** object of the **Thread** class.

Line 6

System.out.println("Current thread is: " +obj);

This line will display the following on the screen:

Current thread is: Thread[main,5,main]

In the square brackets given in the above line, the first value, **main**, represents the name of the thread; the second value 5 represents the priority of the main thread; and the third value, **main** represents the name of the group to which the main thread belongs.

Line 7

System.out.println("Name of the current thread is: " +obj.getName( ));

Here, the **getName( )** method of the **Thread** class will return the name of the thread that is referred by the **obj** object. This line will display the following message on the screen:

Name of the current thread is: main

Line 8

obj.setName("New Thread");

In this line, the **setName( )** method of the **Thread** class will change the name of the **main** thread from **main** to **New Thread**.

Line 9

System.out.println("After the change of name, the current thread is: " +obj);

This line will display the following on the screen:

After the change of name, the current thread is: Thread[New Thread,5,main]

The output of Example 1 is displayed in Figure 8-1.

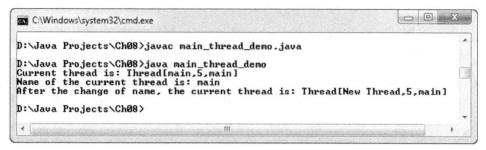

Figure 8-1 The output of Example 1

CREATING A NEW THREAD

In Java, you can create a new thread by using one of the following two ways:

1. By implementing the **Runnable** interface.
2. By extending the **Thread** class.

Implementing the Runnable Interface

To create a new thread by using this method, you first need to declare a class that implements the **Runnable** interface. To implement the **Runnable** interface, it is necessary for the class to implement only one method, the **run( )** method. Inside the **run( )** method, you can specify the code that is executed by the new thread. The syntax for declaring the **run( )** method is given next:

```
public void run( )
{
        //Statements to be executed concurrently
}
```

After the implementation of the interface, you can create an object of the **Thread** class inside the same class by using the **Thread** class constructor. The syntax for creating an object of the **Thread** class is as follows:

```
obj = new Thread(Runnable obj1, name)
```

In this syntax, **obj** is an object of the **Thread** class. The parameter list of the **Thread** constructor contains two parameters: **obj1** and **name**. The **obj1** parameter represents an object of the class that implements the **Runnable** interface and the **name** parameter specifies the name that is assigned to the new thread.

Once the object is created, you need to call the **start( )** method of the **Thread** class on it. The syntax for calling the **start( )** method is as follows:

```
obj.start( );
```

In this syntax, **obj** represents the object of the **Thread** class. Here, the **start( )** method makes a call to the **run( )** method. Now, whenever the execution of the **run( )** method stops, the execution of the thread also stops.

Example 2

The following example illustrates the creation of a thread by using the **Runnable** interface. The program will create a new thread and also display information about the running thread.

//Write a program to create a new thread

```
1    class newthread implements Runnable
2    {
3        Thread obj;
4        newthread( )
5        {
6            obj  = new Thread(this, "New Thread");
7            System.out.println("Starting new thread: " +obj);
8            obj.start( );
9        }
10       public void run( )
11       {
12           try
13           {
14               for(int i=0; i<5; i++)
15               {
16                   System.out.println("Executed new thread");
17                   Thread.sleep(500);
18               }
19           }
20           catch(InterruptedException e)
21           {
22               System.out.println("New thread interrupted");
23           }
24           System.out.println("New thread stopped");
25       }
26       public static void main(String arg[ ])
27       {
28           newthread obj1 = new newthread( );
29           try
30           {
31               for(int i=0; i<5; i++)
32               {
33                   System.out.println("Executed main thread");
34                   Thread.sleep(1000);
35               }
36           }
```

```
37              catch(InterruptedException e)
38              {
39                  System.out.println("Main thread interrupted");
40              }
41              System.out.println("Main thread stopped");
42      }
43  }
```

Explanation
Line 1
class newthread implements Runnable
In this line, the **newthread** class implements the **Runnable** interface by using the **implements** keyword.

Line 3
Thread obj;
In this line, **obj** is declared as an object of the **Thread** class.

Lines 4 to 9
newthread( )
{
        obj = new Thread(this, "New Thread");
        System.out.println("Starting new thread: " +obj);
        obj.start( );
}

These lines define the **newthread( )** constructor. Inside the body, the **obj** object will be created with the constructor of the **Thread** class. Inside the **Thread( )** constructor, the first argument indicates that a call will be made to the **run( )** method on the object that is represented by **this** keyword. The second argument **New Thread** will be assigned to the new thread as its name. Next, the print statement will be executed to display the following message on the screen:

Starting new thread: Thread[New Thread,5,main]

Next, a call will be made to the **start( )** method on the **obj** object. Now, the **start( )** method will execute the new thread from the **run( )** method and the control will be transferred to the **run( )** method.

Line 10
public void run( )
This line represents the declaration of the **run( )** method.

Lines 12 to 19

```
try
{
        for(int i=0; i<5; i++)
        {
                System.out.println("Executed new thread");
                Thread.sleep(500);
        }
}
```

When a call is made to the **run( )** method, the control is transferred inside it and the **try** block is executed. Inside the **try** block, the body of the **for** loop will be executed, which means the new thread will start executing. Inside the **for** loop, the **sleep()** method of the **Thread** class will be called, which will suspend the currently running thread for a specified period of time (here, the time duration is 500 milliseconds). Sometimes, the **sleep()** method can also generate exception of the type **InterruptedException**.

Lines 20 to 23

```
catch(InterruptedException e)
{
        System.out.println("New thread interrupted");
}
```

These lines contain the definition of the **catch** block. This block will be executed only if the **sleep()** method given in the **try** block generates an exception. Otherwise, this block will be skipped.

 Note
*After a call is made to the **start( )** method, the **newthread( )** constructor returns to the **main( )** method and the main thread also starts the execution. Now, both the new and main threads are executed concurrently.*

Line 28

newthread obj1 = new newthread( );
In this line, the **obj1** object of the **newthread** class is created and a call is made to the **newthread( )** constructor. Now, the body of the constructor will execute and a new thread will be created.

Lines 31 to 35

```
for(int i=0; i<5; i++)
{
        System.out.println("Executed main thread");
        Thread.sleep(1000);
}
```

In these lines, the **for** loop comes under the **main** thread. So, when the main thread resumes, the statements given inside the **for** loop will be executed. In this case, the **sleep()** method will suspend the execution of the **for** loop for 1000 milliseconds.

Lines 37 to 40
catch(InterruptedException e)
{

      System.out.println("Main thread interrupted");

}

These lines contain the definition of the **catch** block. This block will execute only if the **sleep()** method given in the **try** block generates an exception. Otherwise, this block will be skipped.

Note

*In the program, the time specified in the **sleep** method of the **main** thread should be greater than the time specified in the **sleep** method of the **new** thread. The reason behind this is that the **main** thread must be the last thread to finish the execution of a program.*

The output of Example 2 is displayed in Figure 8-2.

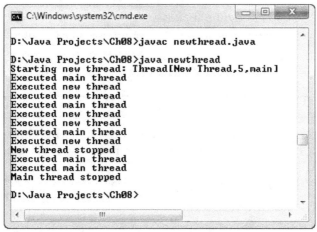

Figure 8-2 The output of Example 2

Note

In multithreading, output may differ due to various factors such as priority, task running on machine, CPU time, sleep time and so on.

Extending the Thread Class

As mentioned earlier, there is another way of creating a new thread. In this method, you need to create a new class that extends the **Thread** class. You already know that the **Thread** class is a part of the default package **java.lang** of Java and it is already included in every Java file. The **Thread** class encapsulates the processing of a package. The **Thread** class also contains methods that can be used to manage threads in a program. Table 8-1 gives the name and description of some of the methods of the **Thread** class.

Table 8-1 *Methods of the class* **Thread**

Method	Description
getName( )	Returns a string that represents the name of a thread.
setName( )	Used to give the name of a thread.
getPriority( )	Returns an integer value ranging from 1 to 10 and represents the priority of the thread. The maximum priority is 10, the minimum priority is 1, and the normal priority is 5.
setPriority( )	Used to set the priority of a thread.
isAlive( )	Returns a boolean type value that indicates whether the thread is running or not.
interrupt( )	Used to interrupt thread.
join( )	Makes a thread wait for another thread to terminate its process.
run( )	Used to define the task that is performed by the thread. This method is executed only after the **start( )** method has been executed.
sleep( )	Used to stop the current executing thread for a specified period of time.
start( )	Used to start the execution of a thread by calling its **run( )** method.

As you already know that to create a new thread by extending the **Thread** class, you need to create a new class that extends the **Thread** class. The syntax for creating a new class that extends the **Thread** class is as follows:

```
class classname extends Thread
```

After creating a class, you need to create an instance of that class. Also, the newly created class should override the **run( )** method of the **Thread** class. Here, the **run( )** method is treated as an entry point of the new thread. You cannot execute the **run( )** method directly, so you need to make a call to the **start( )** method of the **Thread** class.

Example 3

The following example illustrates the method of creating a new thread by extending the **Thread** class. The program will create a new thread and also display information about the running thread.

```
//Write a program to create a new thread
1    class newthread extends Thread
2    {
3        newthread( )
4        {
5            super ("New Thread");
6            System.out.println("Starting new thread: " +this);
7            start( );
8        }
```

```
9        public void run( )
10       {
11           try
12           {
13               for(int i=0;  i<5;  i++)
14               {
15                   System.out.println("Executed new thread");
16                   Thread.sleep(500);
17               }
18           }
19           catch(InterruptedException e)
20           {
21               System.out.println("New thread interrupted");
22           }
23           System.out.println("New thread stopped");
24       }
25       public static void main(String arg[ ])
26       {
27           new newthread( );
28           try
29           {
30               for(int i=0;  i<5;  i++)
31               {
32                   System.out.println("Executed main thread");
33                   Thread.sleep(1000);
34               }
35           }
36           catch(InterruptedException e)
37           {
38                   System.out.println("main thread interrupted");
39           }
40           System.out.println("Main thread stopped");
41       }
42  }
```

Explanation

Line 5

super ("New Thread");

In this line, the **super( )** method represents a constructor of the **Thread** class. Inside the parameter list, the string **New Thread** is passed as an argument that will be assigned to the new thread as its name.

This program will work in the same way as the previous program.

The output of Example 3 is displayed in Figure 8-3.

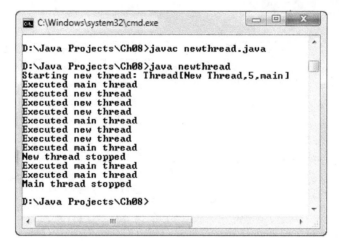

Figure 8-3 *The output of Example 3*

CREATING MULTIPLE THREADS

In the previous sections of this chapter, you have dealt with only two threads: the **main** thread and the new thread. But in this section, you will deal with multiple threads and also learn about the method of creating multiple threads in a program.

Example 4

The following example illustrates the concept of creating multiple threads. The program will create three new threads and also display some information on the screen.

```
//Write a program to create three new threads
1    class Multiple_Thread implements Runnable
2    {
3        String name;
4        Thread obj;
5        Multiple_Thread(String n)
6        {
7            name = n;
8            obj = new Thread(this, name);
9            obj.start( );
10       }
11       public void run( )
12       {
13           try
14           {
15               for(int i=5; i>0; i--)
16               {
17                   System.out.println(name + " is executed");
18                   Thread.sleep(1000);
19               }
20           }
```

```
21          catch(InterruptedException e)
22          {
23              System.out.println(name + " is interrupted");
24          }
25          System.out.println(name + " is stopped");
26      }
27      public static void main(String arg[])
28      {
29          Multiple_Thread first = new Multiple_Thread("First");
30          Multiple_Thread second = new Multiple_Thread("Second");
31          Multiple_Thread third = new Multiple_Thread("Third");
32          String current = new String((Thread.currentThread()).
            getName());
33          try
34          {
35              System.out.println("The "+current+" thread is
                executed");
36              Thread.sleep(10000);
37          }
38          catch(InterruptedException e)
39          {
40              System.out.println("The "+current+ " thread is
                interrupted");
41          }
42          System.out.println("The " +current+ " thread is stopped");
43      }
44  }
```

Explanation

Line 29

Multiple_Thread first = new Multiple_Thread("First");

In this line, **first** is created as an object of the **Multiple_Thread** class. The string **First** will be passed as an argument to the **first** object and it will be assigned to the **String** type variable **n** in line 5. Basically, the string **First** is assigned as name to the first thread.

The working of lines 30 and 31 is the same as line 29.

Line 32

String current = new String((Thread.currentThread( )).getName());

In this line, the name of the current thread will be retrieved to assign it to the **String** type variable **current**.

The output of Example 4 is displayed in Figure 8-4.

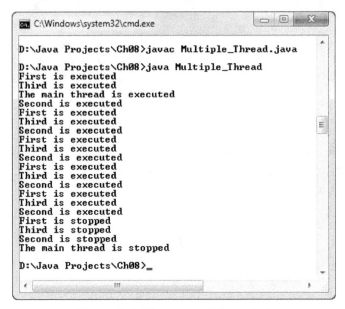

Figure 8-4 *The output of Example 4*

The isAlive( ) and join( ) Methods

In this chapter, you have learned that the **main** thread must be the last thread to finish the program. In all preceding examples of this chapter, this task was accomplished with the help of the **sleep( )** method. In these processes, the **sleep( )** method was defined inside the **main( )** method with the estimated amount of time required by all child threads to complete their processing. However, in these processes, if the estimated time defined by you was not enough to complete the processing of the child threads, one of the child threads would have finished the program. Therefore, the **sleep( )** method is not the best method to ensure that the **main** thread is the last thread to finish the program.

To avoid this problem, Java provides two other methods: **isAlive( )** and **join( )**. These methods ensure that the **main** thread is the last thread to finish the program. These two methods are defined inside the **Thread** class of Java. The **isAlive( )** method checks whether a thread (on which it is called) is still running or not. The return type of this method is of the **boolean** type. If the thread on which it is called is still running on, the method return **true**, otherwise, it will return **false**. The syntax for using the **isAlive( )** method is as follows:

```
final boolean isAlive( )
```

The **join( )** method, which is the most commonly used method, is used to accomplish this task. This method also belongs to the **Thread** class. This method waits until the thread, on which it is called, completes its task. The syntax for using the **join( )** method is as follows:

```
final void join( )
```

You can also use the **join( )** method in another form in the following way:

```
final void join(long time)
```

In this form, the **join( )** method waits for the specified thread to accomplish its task till the specified time.

Example 5

The following example illustrates the use of the **isAlive( )** and **join( )** methods. The program will create multiple threads and also apply the **isAlive( )** and **join( )** methods on them. It will also display some messages on the screen.

/* Write a program to create multiple threads and also illustrate the working of the **isAlive( )** and **join( )** methods */

```
1    class isalive_and_join implements Runnable
2    {
3        String name;
4        Thread obj;
5        isalive_and_join(String threadname)
6        {
7            name = threadname;
8            obj = new Thread (this, name);
9            obj.start();
10       }
11       public void run( )
12       {
13           try
14           {
15               System.out.println("Thread " +name+ " is executed");
16               Thread.sleep(1000);
17           }
18           catch (InterruptedException e )
19           {
20               System.out.println("Thread " +name+ " is interrupted");
21           }
22           System.out.println("Thread " +name+ " is stopped" );
23       }
24       public static void main(String arg[ ])
25       {
26           isalive_and_join thrd1 = new isalive_and_join("First");
27           isalive_and_join thrd2 = new isalive_and_join("Second");
28           System.out.println("Checking the status of each thread:");
29           System.out.println("Thread First: " +thrd1.obj.isAlive( ));
30           System.out.println("Thread Second: "+thrd2.obj.isAlive( ));
31           try
32           {
33               System.out.println("Applying the join( ) method");
34               thrd1.obj.join( );
35               thrd2.obj.join( );
36           }
```

```
37              catch(InterruptedException e)
38              {
39                  System.out.println("Exception occurred in main");
40              }
41          System.out.println("Again checking the status of each thread:");
42          System.out.println("Thread First: " +thrd1.obj.isAlive( ));
43          System.out.println("Thread Second: "+thrd2.obj.isAlive( ));
44          System.out.println("Main thread stopped");
45      }
46  }
```

Explanation

Lines 26 and 27
isalive_and_join thrd1 = new isalive_and_join("First");
isalive_and_join thrd2 = new isalive_and_join("Second");
In these lines, **thrd1** and **thrd2** are created as objects of the **isalive_and_join** class, and **First** and **Second** are the strings that will be assigned as names of the two new threads.

Line 29
System.out.println("Thread First: " +thrd1.obj.isAlive( ));
In this line, the **isAlive( )** method is called on the first thread, which is named as **First**. Here, the **isAlive( )** method will return **true** because the specified thread is currently running.

The working of line 30 is the same as line 29.

Lines 31 to 36
try
{
        System.out.println("Applying the join( ) method");
        thrd1.obj.join( );
        thrd2.obj.join( );
}
These lines contain the definition of the **try** block. Inside the **try** block, the **join( )** method is called on the new threads **First** and **Second**. This method will pause the execution until these threads complete their tasks.

Lines 42 and 43
System.out.println("Thread First: " +thrd1.obj.isAlive( ));
System.out.println("Thread Second: " +thrd2.obj.isAlive( ));
In these lines, the **isAlive( )** method will be called again on both the new threads.

The output of Example 5 is displayed in Figure 8-5.

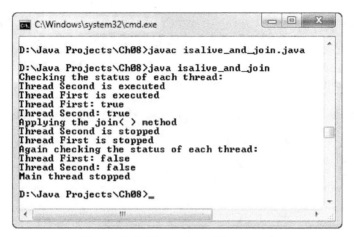

Figure 8-5 *The output of Example 5*

Setting Thread Priorities

You have learned that whenever a new thread is created in a program, the Java environment gives it a priority. Priority of a thread determines when it will be allowed to access the resources such as CPU, processor, and so on.

In Java, a priority is an integer value ranging from 1 to 10. The value 10 is treated as the highest priority, 1 is treated as the lowest priority, and 5 is treated as the normal priority. The normal priority is the default priority, which is assigned to the threads at the time of their creation. A thread with a higher priority utilizes more CPU time than a thread with a lower priority.

You can also set the priority of a thread according to your requirements by using the **setPriority( )** method of the **Thread** class. The syntax for using the **setPriority( )** method is as follows:

```
final void setPriority(int val)
```

In this syntax, the integer variable **val** sets a new priority for the thread, on which the **setPriority( )** method is called. You can assign the priority for a thread using the integer variable **val** in two ways as given next:

1. Assign an integer value from 1 to 10.

2. Assign any one of the three final variables of the **Thread** class. These variables are **MIN_PRIORITY** (equivalent to 1), **MAX_PRIORITY** (equivalent to 10), and **NORM_PRIORITY** (equivalent to 5).

You can also get the current priority of a thread using the **getPriority( )** method of the **Thread** class. The syntax for using the **getPriority( )** method is as follows:

```
final int getPriority( )
```

The **getPriority( )** method returns the current priority (an integer value) of a thread on which it is called.

Example 6

The following example illustrates the use of the **getPriority( )** and **setPriority( )** methods of the **Thread** class. The program will display the current priorities of threads, set their new priorities, and also display some messages on the screen.

```
//Write a program to illustrate the working of the getPriority( ) and setPriority( ) methods
1    class priority implements Runnable
2    {
3        Thread obj;
4        String name;
5        int val;
6        private boolean status = true;
7        priority(int p, String n)
8        {
9            name = n;
10           obj = new Thread(this, name);
11           val = obj.getPriority( );
12           System.out.println("Priority of the thread "+name+" is: "
                 +val);
13           obj.setPriority(p);
14           System.out.println("Thread: " +obj);
15       }
16       public void start( )
17       {
18           obj.start( );
19           System.out.println(obj.getName( ) + " is started");
20       }
21       public void run( )
22       {
23           if(status)
24           System.out.println(obj.getName( ) + " is running");
25       }
26       public void stop( )
27       {
28           status = false;
29           System.out.println(obj.getName( ) + " is stopped");
30       }
31       public static void main(String arg[ ])
32       {
33           priority thrd1 = new priority(3, "First");
34           priority thrd2 = new priority(9, "Second");
35           String current = Thread.currentThread( ).getName( );
36           thrd1.start( );
37           thrd2.start( );
38           try
39           {
40               Thread.sleep(2000);
41           }
```

```
42              catch(InterruptedException e)
43              {
44                  System.out.println("Main thread interrupted");
45              }
46          thrd1.stop( );
47          thrd2.stop( );
48          System.out.println( current+ " is stopped");
49      }
50  }
```

Explanation
Line 3
Thread obj;
In this line, **obj** is declared as an object of the **Thread** class.

Line 6
private boolean status = true;
In this line, **status** is declared as the **boolean** type **private** variable and **true** is assigned as the initial value to it.

Line 7
priority(int p, String n)
This line represents the **priority( )** constructor of the **priority** class. Its parameter list contains two parameters: the **integer** type variable **p** and the **String** type variable **n**. Whenever a call is made to the **priority( )** constructor, the integer value and the character string, which is assigned to **p** and **n** variables respectively, will be passed as arguments to the **priority( )** constructor.

Line 11
val = obj.getPriority( );
In this line, the **getPriority( )** method returns the current priority of the thread, which are represented by the **obj** object. This priority is then assigned to the **integer** type variable **val**.

Line 13
obj.setPriority(p);
In this line, the value of the **p** variable, which is passed during a call to the **priority( )** constructor, is set as the new priority of the thread, represented by the **obj** object.

Lines 16 to 20
public void start( )
{
    obj.start( );
    System.out.println(obj.getName( ) + " is started");
}

These lines contain the definition of the **start( )** method. Inside the body of the method, a call will be made to the **start( )** method on the thread, which is represented by the **obj** object. In the next statement, the **getName( )** method will return the name of the thread.

Lines 21 to 25
public void run( )
{
      if(status)
          System.out.println(obj.getName( ) + " is running");
}

These lines contain the definition of the **run( )** method. Whenever a call is made to the **start( )** method on an object of the **Thread** class, the object, in turn, makes a call to the **start( )** method. Inside the body of the method, the value of the **boolean** type variable **status** will be checked. If this value evaluates to **true**, the next statement will be executed. Otherwise, the **run( )** method will terminate.

Lines 26 to 30
public void stop( )
{
      status = false;
      System.out.println(obj.getName( ) + " is stopped");
}

These lines contain the definition of the **stop( )** method. Inside the body of the method, the value **false** will be assigned to the **boolean** type variable **status**.

Line 33
priority thrd1 = new priority(3, "First");
In this line, **thrd1** is created as an object of the **priority** class. Here, a call will be made to the **priority( )** constructor and the values **3** and **First** will be passed as arguments to it. These values are in turn assigned to the **p** and **n** variables, respectively in the constructor definition. As a result, the priority of the thread, which is **First**, will now be set to **3**.

The working of line 34 is similar to line 33.

Line 35
String current = Thread.currentThread( ).getName( );
In this line, the **currentThread( )** method of the **Thread** class returns the reference of the current object and the **getName( )** method returns the name (main) of the current thread, which is assigned to the **String** type.

Line 36
thrd1.start( );
In this line, a call will be made to the **start( )** method of the **priority** class. Therefore, the control will be transferred to the method definition and the body of the method will be executed. As a result, in this line the thread **First** will start running.

The working of line 37 is similar to line 36.

Line 40
Thread.sleep(2000);
In this line, the **sleep( )** method of the **Thread** class is called to suspend the **main** thread for 2000 milliseconds.

Line 46
thrd1.stop( );
In this line, the **stop( )** method of the **priority** class is called. Now, the control will be transferred to the method definition and the body of the method will be executed. Therefore, in this line the execution of the thread **First** will stop.

The output of Example 6 is displayed in Figure 8-6.

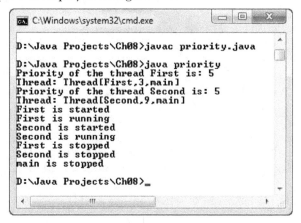

Figure 8-6 *The output of Example 6*

SYNCHRONIZATION

Sometimes, when multiple threads attempt to access the same resource, the concurrency issues are encountered. To overcome these issues, Java offers a solution known as synchronization. Synchronization of threads ensures that only one thread is allowed to access resources at a time. Java uses a mechanism called monitor to support synchronization of threads. This mechanism supports two kinds of thread synchronization.

1. Mutual exclusion
2. Co-operation (Inter-thread communication)

Mutual Exclusion

In mutual exclusion, the monitor acts as mutually exclusive lock which means that only one thread can use monitor on the resource. Once a thread has acquired lock on a resource then no other thread can access the resource or acquire lock on it until the specific lock is released by the first thread. In Java, each object has an implicit monitor associated with it. When a thread acquires a lock, the process is known as **entered the monitor**. When a thread releases a lock, the process is known as **exited the monitor**.

Mutual Exclusion prevents threads from interfering with one another while sharing data. A thread can acquire lock on an object by using the **synchronized** keyword. It can be done by two ways.

1. Synchronized method
2. Synchronized block

When a method or block of code is declared as **synchronized**, it can be used only by a single thread at a time.

Synchronized Method

If you declare any method as synchronized, it is known as synchronized method. When a thread invokes a synchronized method, it automatically acquires the lock for that object and releases it when the thread completes its task. You can synchronize a method using the **synchronized** keyword in the following way:

```
synchronized ret_type method_name
{
    Statements to be executed
}
```

Example 7

The following example illustrates the use of a **synchronized** method. The program will create multiple threads and use synchronized method to synchronize them.

//Write a program to illustrate the use of synchronized method

```
1   class synchro
2   {
3       synchronized void demo(int p, String name)
4       {
5           System.out.println("Priority of thread "+name+" is: "+p);
6           System.out.println("Executing " +name);
7           try
8           {
9               Thread.sleep(1500);
10          }
11          catch(InterruptedException e)
12          {
13              System.out.println("Exception occurred");
14          }
15          System.out.println(name+" is stopped");
16      }
17  }
18  class synchro_demo extends Thread
19  {
20      synchro obj;
21      String current;
22      int priority;
23      synchro_demo(synchro instance, String str)
24      {
25          super(str);
26          current = str;
27          this.obj = instance;
28          priority = this.getPriority( );
29          start( );
30      }
```

```
31      public void run( )
32      {
33          obj.demo(priority, current);
34      }
35  }
36  class synchronized_demo
37  {
38      public static void main(String arg[ ])
39      {
40          synchro obj1 = new synchro( );
41          synchro_demo thrd1 = new synchro_demo(obj1, "First");
42          synchro_demo thrd2 = new synchro_demo(obj1, "Second");
43          synchro_demo thrd3 = new synchro_demo(obj1, "Third");
44          String cur = Thread.currentThread().getName( );
45          try
46          {
47              Thread.sleep(5000);
48          }
49          catch(InterruptedException e)
50          {
51              System.out.println("Exception occurred");
52          }
53          System.out.println(cur+ " is stopped");
54      }
55  }
```

Explanation

Line 3

synchronized void demo(int p, String name)

This line defines the **demo( )** method of the **synchro** class as a synchronized method by using the **synchronized** keyword. The parameter list contains two arguments: an **integer** type variable **p**, which represents the priority of the thread and a **String** type variable **name**, which represents the name of the thread.

Line 23

synchro_demo(synchro instance, String str)

This line represents the definition of the **synchro_demo( )** constructor. In the parameter list, **instance** represents an object of the **synchro** class and **str** is a **String** type variable, which represents the name of the thread.

Line 25

super(str);

In this line, the **super( )** method is called which will invoke the constructor of the **Thread** class and the value of the **str** variable is passed as an argument to it.

Line 27

this.obj = instance;

In this line, the reference of the **instance** object is assigned to the **obj** object.

Line 28

priority = this.getPriority( );

In this line, the **getPriority( )** method of the **Thread** class returns the priority of the current thread and this value of priority is assigned to the integer variable **priority**.

Lines 31 to 34

public void run( )
{
        obj.demo(priority, current);
}

These lines contain the definition of the **run( )** method. Inside the body of the method, a call is made to the synchronized **demo( )** method. The values of the **priority** and **current** variables are passed as arguments to the **demo( )** method. Now, the control will be transferred to the definition of the **demo( )** method.

Line 40

synchro obj1 = new synchro( );

In this line, **obj1** is declared as an object of the **synchro** class.

Line 41

synchro_demo thrd1 = new synchro_demo(obj1, "First");

In this line, **thrd1** is declared as an object of the **synchro_demo** class. Here, a call will be made to the **synchro_demo( )** constructor, and the **obj1** object and the string **First** will be passed as arguments to the constructor. The values given to arguments are assigned to the **instance** object and the **String** type variable **str** in the constructor definition, respectively. The reference of the object, which is passed as an argument, will be assigned to the object of the **Thread** class and **First** will be assigned as the name of the thread.

The working of lines 42 and 43 is similar to line 41.

Line 44

String cur = Thread.currentThread( ).getName( );

In this line, the **getName( )** method returns the name of the current thread, which is assigned to the **String** type variable **cur**.

The output of Example 7 is displayed in Figure 8-7.

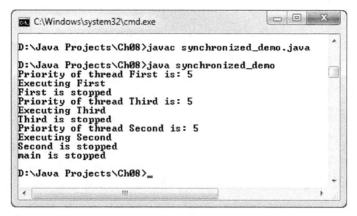

Figure 8-7 *The output of Example 7*

Synchronized Block

A synchronized block can be used to perform synchronization on any specific block of the method. Its scope is smaller than the method. You can synchronize a block of code by using the **synchronized** keyword as given next:

```
synchronized (object)
{
    Statements to be executed
}
```

Here, **object** represents the object being synchronized.

Example 8

The following example (same as previous) illustrates the use of a **synchronized** block. The program will create multiple threads and use synchronized block to synchronize them.

//Write a program to illustrate the use of synchronized block
```
1   class synchro
2   {
3       void demo(int p, String name)
4       {
5           System.out.println("Priority of thread "+name+" is: "+p);
6           System.out.println("Executing " +name);
7           try
8           {
9               Thread.sleep(1500);
10          }
11          catch(InterruptedException e)
12          {
13              System.out.println("Exception occurred");
14          }
15          System.out.println(name+" is stopped");
16      }
17  }
```

```
18  class synchro_demo extends Thread
19  {
20      synchro obj;
21      String current;
22      int priority;
23      synchro_demo(synchro instance, String str)
24      {
25          super(str);
26          current = str;
27          this.obj = instance;
28          priority = this.getPriority( );
29          start( );
30      }
31      public void run( )
32      {
33          synchronized(obj)
34          {
35              obj.demo(priority, current);
36          }
37      }
38  }
39  class synchronized_demo
40  {
41      public static void main(String arg[ ])
42      {
43          synchro obj1 = new synchro( );
44          synchro_demo thrd1 = new synchro_demo(obj1, "First");
45          synchro_demo thrd2 = new synchro_demo(obj1, "Second");
46          synchro_demo thrd3 = new synchro_demo(obj1, "Third");
47          String cur = Thread.currentThread( ).getName( );
48          try
49          {
50              Thread.sleep(5000);
51          }
52          catch(InterruptedException e)
53          {
54              System.out.println("Exception occurred");
55          }
56          System.out.println(cur+ " is stopped");
57      }
58  }
```

Explanation

This program works similar to the previous program, except that in this case, whenever a call will be made to the **run( )** method, the synchronized block of code that is inside the body of the **run()** method will be executed.

The output of this program is also similar to the previous program.

Co-operation (Inter-thread Communication)

Synchronized thread can communicate with each other through co-operation(inter-thread communication). In this process, execution of one thread is paused to allow the execution of another thread. It is implemented by following methods of **Object** class:

1. **wait( )**
2. **notify( )**
3. **notifyAll( )**

The wait() Method

The **wait( )** method notifies a calling thread to give up the monitor and go to sleep mode until some other thread enters the same monitor and call the **notify( )** or **notifyAll( )** method. You can specify the time period till the thread will wait.

The notify( ) Method

The **notify( )** method notifies the waiting thread. If many threads are in waiting, one of them is arbitrarily chosen to notify.

The notifyAll( ) Method

The **notifyAll( )** method notifies all the waiting threads. The highest priority thread will run first.

Example 9

The following example illustrates the use of the **wait( )** and **notify( )** methods. The program will create two threads and apply the **wait( )** and **notify( )** methods on them. It will also display some messages on the screen.

/* Write a program to create two threads and illustrate the working of the **wait( )** and **notify( )** methods */

```
1    class Inter_Thread_demo extends Thread
2    {
3        boolean flag;
4        String name;
5        Inter_Thread_demo(String str)
6        {
7            super(str);
8            name = str;
9            flag = false;
10           start( );
11       }
12       public void run( )
13       {
14           try
15           {
16               for(int i=0; i<=5; i++)
17               {
18                   System.out.println("Executing: " +name);
19                   Thread.sleep(500);
```

```
20                  synchronized(this)
21                  {
22                      while(flag)
23                      {
24                          wait( );
25                      }
26                  }
27              }
28          }
29          catch(InterruptedException e)
30          {
31              System.out.println(name + " is interrupted");
32          }
33          System.out.println("Exiting: " +name);
34      }
35      void wait_new( )
36      {
37          flag = true;
38      }
39      synchronized void notify_new( )
40      {
41          flag = false;
42          notify( );
43      }
44      public static void main(String arg[ ])
45      {
46          Inter_Thread_demo thrd1 = new Inter_Thread_demo("First");
47          Inter_Thread_demo thrd2 = new Inter_Thread_demo("Second");
48          try
49          {
50              Thread.sleep(500);
51              System.out.println("First thread is waiting");
52              thrd1.wait_new( );
53              Thread.sleep(500);
54              System.out.println("First thread is active");
55              thrd1.notify_new( );
56              System.out.println("Second thread is waiting");
57              thrd2.wait_new( );
58              Thread.sleep(500);
59              System.out.println("Second thread is active");
60              thrd2.notify_new( );
61          }
62          catch(InterruptedException e)
63          {
64              System.out.println("The main thread is interrupted");
65          }
66          try
67          {
68              thrd1.join( );
69              thrd2.join( );
70          }
```

```
71          catch(InterruptedException e)
72          {
73              System.out.println("The main thread is interrupted");
74          }
75          System.out.println("Exiting: main");
76      }
77  }
```

Explanation
Line 9
flag = false;
In this line, the **false** value is assigned as an initial value to the **boolean** variable **flag**.

Lines 20 to 26
synchronized(this)
{
    while(flag)
    {
        wait( );
    }
}

These lines represent a synchronized block. Inside the block, the **wait( )** method will be executed until the value of the **flag** variable is **false**.

Lines 35 to 38
void wait_new( )
{
    flag = true;
}

These lines define the **wait_new( )** method. Whenever this method is called, the value of the **boolean** variable **flag** is set to **true**.

Lines 39 to 43
synchronized void notify_new( )
{
    flag = false;
    notify( );
}

These lines define the synchronized **notify_new( )** method. Whenever a call is made to this method, the value of the **boolean** variable **flag** is set to **false** and also a call is made to the **notify( )** method.

The output of Example 9 is displayed in Figure 8-8.

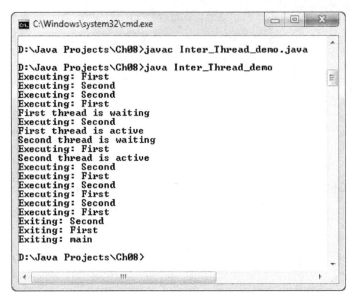

Figure 8-8 *The output of Example 9*

Difference between wait() and sleep() Methods

The difference between the **wait( )** and **sleep( )** methods is given in Table 8-2.

Table 8-2 *Difference between **wait( )** and **sleep( )***

wait()	sleep()
It is the method of object class.	It is the method of Thread class.
It releases the lock	It doesn't release the lock.
It should be notify by **notify( )** and **notifyAll( )** method.	After the specified amount of time, sleep is completed.
It is called from synchronized method or block.	It can be called without synchronized method or block.
It is normally done on condition, Thread wait until a condition is true.	It is just to put your thread on sleep.

DEADLOCK

Deadlock is a situation wherein two threads need resources of one another but neither of them is ready to release their resources. In such a case, both the threads have circular dependency on each other and are blocked forever because no thread can complete its execution due to lack of resources. When a deadlock occurs in a program, the system cannot avoid or rectify it. Therefore, it is the responsibility of the programmer to avoid such situations and ensure that circular dependency never exists between two threads.

Self-Evaluation Test

Answer the following questions and then compare them to those given at the end of this chapter:

1. In _____, multiple threads can run concurrently.

2. In _____ multitasking, multiple programs can run concurrently.

3. The state when a thread waits for the CPU time is known as _____.

4. The normal priority of a thread is _____.

5. The _____ thread must be the last thread to finish the execution of a program.

6. The _____ method of the **Thread** class is used to create reference for the current thread.

7. You can create a new thread by extending the _____ class.

8. The _____ method is used to pause the execution of a thread for a specified period of running time.

9. The _____ method is used to check the thread (on which it is called) whether it is still running or not.

10. The three final variables of the **Thread** class are: _____, _____, and _____.

11. In a program, the execution path of each thread is different. (T/F)

12. You can set the priority of a thread using any one of the **final** variables of the **Thread** class. (T/F)

13. The **run( )** method is executed only after the execution of the **start( )** method. (T/F)

14. The normal priority assigned to each and every thread, is 2. (T/F)

15. The **notify( )** method is used to awake all the threads in the same object. (T/F)

Review Questions

Answer the following questions:

1. Define a thread.

2. Differentiate between the process-based multitasking and the thread-based multitasking.

3. Explain different states of a thread.

4. Explain the **setPriority( )** and **getPriority( )** methods.

5. Explain the **wait( )**, **notify( )**, and **notifyAll( )** methods.

EXERCISE

Exercise 1

Write a program to create two threads and set their names to **Thread1** and **Thread2**, respectively. The program also must display their default priorities and set their new priorities to 10.

Chapter 9

String Handling

Learning Objectives

After completing this chapter, you will be able to:
- *Understand the String class*
- *Understand the methods used for comparing string*
- *Understand the toString( ) method*
- *Understand the methods used for character extraction*
- *Understand the methods used to modify a string*
- *Understand the methods used to change the case of characters*
- *Understand the methods used for searching strings*
- *Understand the concept of valueOf( ) method*
- *Understand the StringBuffer class*
- *Understand the methods of the StringBuffer class*

INTRODUCTION

In most programming languages, a string is implemented as an array of characters. But Java implements a string as an object of the **String** class. The **String** class is a built-in Java class and is defined in the **java.lang** package. The **String** class is declared as **final**, which means it cannot be inherited by any other class. In Java, a string is treated as a single value, not as an array of characters, as done in most of the other programming languages. The **String** class also defines certain methods that can be used to handle or manipulate strings easily.

When an object of the **String** class is created, the string value of that object cannot be changed. This indicates that the objects of the **String** class are immutable. Whenever an existing object of the **String** class is changed, a new object containing the modified string value is created. In such a case, the string value of the original object remains the same.

Java also provides two more classes: **StringBuffer** and **StringBuilder**. These classes are used when you want a string such that it can be modified but it is not immutable. As the **String** class, these classes are also declared as **final** classes and defined in the **java.lang** package.

In this chapter, you will learn in detail about the **String** and **StringBuffer** classes.

STRING

String is a sequence of characters which is treated as object of the **String** class in Java programming language. You can create and manipulate string object by using string literals and concatenation which are discussed next.

String Literals

You can create an object for **String** class by using string literals. A string literal is a group of characters enclosed within double quotes " ". String literals are treated as a single value. You can create an object of the **String** class by using the string literal in the following way:

```
String obj = "Smith";
```

In this example, the **obj** object of the **String** class is created and initialized with the string **Smith**.

This statement is equivalent to the following statements:

```
char arr[ ] = {'S', 'm', 'i', 't', 'h'};
String obj = new String(arr);
```

String Concatenation Using the + Operator

In Java, the **+** operator is used to concatenate two strings and produce a single string.

For example:

```
int val = 500;
String obj = "I earn " +val+ " dollars daily";
```

In this example, the **I earn** string is concatenated with the integer value 500 of the **val** variable with the help of the **+** operator. Here, the integer value of the **val** variable is treated as a string value. Next, the **I earn 500** string is concatenated with the **dollars daily** string and the **I earn 500 dollars daily** string is produced.

THE String CLASS CONSTRUCTORS

The **String** class provides different types of constructors that can be used while creating an object of the **String** type. The description of these constructors is as follows:

String( )

The **String( )** constructor is used to create an object of the **String** class and does not assign any string value to the created object. In other words, the **String( )** constructor is used to create an empty object of the **String** class. This is the default constructor of the **String** class. The syntax for using the **String( )** constructor is as follows:

```
String obj_name = new String( );
```

In this syntax, the object represented by **obj_name** contains no string value.

String(char arr[ ])

The **String(char arr[ ])** is used when you want to assign an initial value to an object of the **String** class. This is the most commonly used constructor. You can use the **String(char arr[ ])** constructor as shown in the following example:

```
char arr[ ] = {'S', 'm', 'i', 't', 'h'};
String obj = new String(arr);
```

In this example, the array **arr** is passed as an argument to the constructor and the "**Smith**" string is assigned as an initial value to the **obj** object of the **String** class.

String(char arr[ ], int start, int length)

The **String(char arr[ ], int start, int length)** constructor is used when you want to assign a string to an array that contains only a subarray of the array, which is passed as an argument to a parameter. In this constructor, the integer variable **start** specifies the beginning of the subarray and the **length** specifies the number of characters included in the subarray. You can use the **String(char arr[ ], int start, int length)** constructor as shown in the following example:

```
char arr[ ] = {'S', 'm', 'i', 't', 'h'};
String obj = new String(arr, 1, 3);
```

In this example, the **mit** string is assigned as an initial value to the **obj** object of the **String** class where m is at the 1st position and t is at the 3rd position.

String(String obj)

The **String(String obj)** constructor is used when you want to assign the same string value, as contained in the **obj** object, to the new **String** object. You can use the **String(String obj)** constructor as shown in the following example:

```
char arr[ ] = {'S', 'm', 'i', 't', 'h'};
String obj = new String(arr);
String obj1 = new String(obj);
```

In this example, the **obj** object contains the **Smith** string. While creating the **obj1** object, the **obj** object is passed as an argument to the constructor. As a result, the same **Smith** string, which is contained in the **obj** object, is assigned to the new **obj1** object. Now, both the **obj** and **obj1** objects contain the same string value.

String(byte asciiarr[ ])

The **String(byte asciiarr[ ])** constructor is used when you want to pass an array of bytes containing ASCII characters to the constructor of the **String** class. In such cases, ASCII characters are decoded to their original values using the ASCII character set. Next, a new string object is initialized with the string that is obtained after decoding the array passed to the constructor. You can use the **String(byte asciiarr[ ])** constructor as shown in the following example:

```
byte arr[ ] = {97, 98, 99, 100, 101};
String obj = new String(arr);
```

In this example, the ASCII values 97 to 101 are decoded into their original values from **a** to **e**, respectively. The array **arr[ ]** contains the **abcde** sequence of characters. Next, the array **arr[ ]** is passed as an argument to the **String( )** constructor and the **obj** object of the **String** class is initialized with the same **abcde** string.

String(byte asciiarr[ ], int start, int length)

The **String(byte asciiarr[ ], int start, int length)** constructor is used when you want to assign a subarray of characters to a new object of the **String** class. The **start** and **length** variables are used in the same way as explained in the **String(char arr[ ], int start, int length)** constructor. You can use the **String(byte asciiarr[ ], int start, int length)** constructor as shown in the following example:

```
byte arr[ ] = {97, 98, 99, 100, 101};
String obj = new String(arr, 1, 3);
```

In this example, the **obj** object of the **String** class is initialized with the **bcd** string where **b**(98) is at the 1st position and **d**(100) is at the 3rd position.

METHODS USED FOR STRING COMPARISON

In Java, the **String** class defines certain methods to compare the contents of two strings. These methods are discussed next.

equals( )

The **equals( )** method of the **String** class is used to check whether two strings are equal or not. The syntax of the **equals( )** method is as follows:

```
boolean equals(String string)
```

In this syntax, **string** represents an object of the **String** class. The return type of this method is **boolean**. If the **string** object contains the same character sequence and is in the same order as represented by the calling object, it will return **true**. Otherwise, it will return **false**.

The comparison by using the **equals( )** method is case-sensitive.

For example:

```
String s1 = "smith";
String s2 = "Smith";
boolean val = s1.equals(s2);
```

In this example, the **s1** object is initialized with the **smith** string and the **s2** object is initialized with the **Smith** string. Here, the **equals( )** method returns **false** because the first character of both the strings has different cases.

equalsIgnoreCase( )

In the above section, you learned that the comparison made with the help of the **equals( )** method is case-sensitive. But sometimes, you need to compare two strings without considering the case differences. In such a case, you can use the **equalsIgnoreCase( )** method of the **String** class. While comparing two strings, the **equalsIgnoreCase( )** method considers both upper case letters (A-Z) and lower case letters (a-z) as same. The syntax for using the **equalsIgnoreCase( )** method is as follows:

```
boolean equalsIgnoreCase(String obj)
```

In this syntax, **obj** represents an object of the **String** class. The return type of this method is **boolean**. This method will return true, if the **string** object contains the same character sequence and in same order as represented by the calling object, it will return **true**. Otherwise, it will return **false**.

For example:

```
String s1 = "smith";
String s2 = "Smith";
boolean val = s1.equalsIgnoreCase(s2);
```

In this example, the **s1** and **s2** objects are initialized with the **smith** and **Smith** string. Here, the **equalsIgnoreCase( )** method returns true because both the strings contain the same character sequence and also in the same order.

Example 1

The following example illustrates the use of the **equals( )** and **equalsIgnoreCase( )** methods of the **String** class. The program will compare strings by using the **equals( )** and **equalsIgnoreCase( )** methods and also display resultant values on the screen.

//Write a program to compare the strings

```
1    class stringcomparedemo
2    {
3        public static void main(String arg[ ])
4        {
5            boolean result;
6            String obj1 = "Your name";
7            String obj2 = "Jack";
8            String obj3 = "YOUR NAME";
9            String obj4 = "Smith";
10           System.out.println("The strings " +obj1+ " and " +obj3+
                 " are equal: " +obj1.equals(obj3));
11           System.out.println("The strings " +obj2+ " and " +obj4+
                 " are equal: " +obj2.equals(obj4));
12           System.out.println("The strings " +obj1+ " and " +obj3+
                 " are equal: " +obj1.equalsIgnoreCase(obj3));
13        }
14    }
```

Explanation
Line 6
String obj1 = "Your name";
In this line, **obj1** is created as an instance of the **String** class and the **Your name** string is assigned as an initial value to the string.

The working of lines 7 to 9 is similar to line 6.

Line 10
System.out.println("The strings " +obj1+ " and " +obj3+ " are equal: " +obj1.equals(obj3));

In this line, the **equals( )** method is used to compare the **Your name** and **YOUR NAME** strings of the **obj1** and **obj3** objects, respectively. Here, the **equals( )** method will return **false**.

The working of lines 11 is similar to line 10.

Line 12
System.out.println("The strings " +obj1+ " and " +obj3+ " are equal: " +obj1.equalsIgnoreCase(obj3));

In this line, the **equalsIgnoreCase()** method is used to compare the **Your name** and **YOUR NAME** strings of the **obj1** and **obj3** objects, respectively. Here, the **equalsIgnoreCase()** method will return **true** because both the strings contain the same character sequence and also in the same order.

The output of Example 1 is displayed in Figure 9-1.

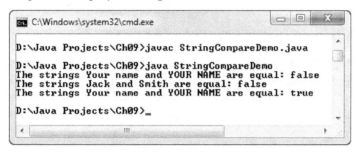

Figure 9-1 *The output of Example 1*

compareTo( )

The **compareTo( )** method is used when you want to sort a list of strings in a predetermined order. This method compares two strings: the string that is passed as an argument to the method and the invoking string, and then checks whether the string passed as an argument is greater than, less than, or equal to another string. The syntax for using the **compareTo( )** method is as follows:

```
int compareTo(String obj);
```

In this syntax, **obj** is declared as an object of the **String** class. Here, the **obj1** string is compared with the string of the invoking object. The **compareTo( )** method returns an integer value that can be any one of the following:

1. If the method returns an integer value that is less than zero, it means that the string of the invoking object is less than the string of the **obj** object (passed as an argument to the method).

2. If the method returns an integer value that is greater than zero, it means that the string of the invoking object is greater than the string of the **obj** object (passed as an argument to the method).

3. If the method returns zero, it means that both the strings, the string of the invoking object as well as the string passed as an argument, are equal.

For example:

```
int result;
String s1 = "Williams";
String s2 = "John";
result = s1.compareTo(s2);
```

In this example, the **Williams** string of the **s1** object is compared with the **John** string of the **s2** object using the **compareTo( )** method. This method returns a value that is greater than zero because the invoking **Williams** string is greater than the **John** string.

Note

*The **compareTo()** method is also case-sensitive like **equals()** method.*

compareToIgnoreCase( )

The **compareToIgnoreCase( )** method is also used to compare two strings, but in this case the comparison will not be case-sensitive. The syntax for using the **compareToIgnoreCase( )** method is as follows:

```
int compareToIgnoreCase(String obj);
```

The **compareToIgnoreCase( )** method also returns an integer value as in the **compareTo( )** method.

The == Operator

The **==** operator is used to compare the memory references of objects of the **String** class. If two objects of the **String** class refer to the same instance in memory, the **==** operator will return **true**. Otherwise, it will return **false**.

Example 2

The following example illustrates the use of the **==** operator. The program will compare the references of the objects of the **String** class by using the **==** operator and display the resultant values on the screen.

//Write a program to compare the references of the objects of the **String** class
```
1   class equaldemo
2   {
3       public static void main(String arg[ ])
4       {
5           String s1 = "Smith";
6           String s2 = "Smith";
7           String s3 = new String(s1);
8           boolean val;
9           val = (s1==s2);
10          System.out.println("The objects s1 and s2 refer to the same
            instance in memory: " +val);
11          val = (s1==s3);
```

```
12          System.out.println("The objects s1 and s3 refer to the same
            instance in memory: " +val);
13    }
14 }
```

Explanation

Line 5
String s1 = "Smith";
In this line, **s1** is created as an instance of the **String** class and the **Smith** string is assigned to it as an initial value.

Line 7
String s3 = new String(s1);
In this line, **s3** is created as an instance of the **String** class and the **Smith** string of the **s1** object is assigned as an initial value to it.

Line 9
val = (s1==s2);
In this line, the **==** operator compares the references of **s1** and **s2** objects of the **String** class. If these objects refer to the same instance in the memory, the operator will return the **boolean** value **true**. Otherwise, it will return the **boolean** value **false**. Next, the resultant value will be assigned to the **boolean** type **val** variable.

The output of Example 2 is displayed in Figure 9-2.

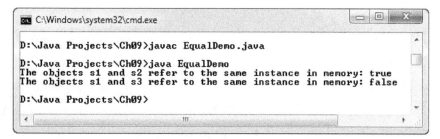

Figure 9-2 The output of Example 2

regionMatches( )

The **regionMatches( )** method of the **String** class is used to match a particular region of one string to a particular region of another string. The syntax for using the **regionMatches( )** method is as follows:

```
boolean regionMatches(int start, String str, int startstr, int number)
```

In this syntax, the integer variable **start** represents the index from where the region of the invoking string object begins. The **str** object of the **String** class represents the second string. The integer variable **startstr** represents the index from where the region of the second string begins. This region will be compared with the region of the invoking string object. The integer variable **number** represents the length of the region or the substring being compared. If a match is found between the specific regions of the invoking string object and the passed string object, the **regionMatches( )** method returns **true**. Otherwise, it returns **false**.

Comparison made using the **regionMatches( )**method is case-sensitive. There is another overloaded version of the **regionMatches( )** method in which the comparison is not case-sensitive. The syntax for using the overloaded version of the **regionMatches( )** method is as follows:

```
boolean regionMatches(boolean ignoreCase, int start, String str, int startstr,
int number)
```

In this syntax, if the value of the **boolean** variable **ignoreCase** is set to **true**, the comparison will be made regardless of the cases of substrings. Otherwise, the comparison will be case-sensitive.

startsWith( )

The **startsWith( )** method is used to compare whether the character sequence of the invoking string starts with the same character sequence as that of the string, which is passed as an argument to the method. The syntax for using the **startsWith( )** method is as follows:

```
boolean startsWith(String str)
```

In this syntax, the **str** object represents the string being matched within the invoking object. If a match is found, the method returns **true**. Otherwise, it returns **false**.

For example:

```
String s1 = "Smith";
String s2 = "Smi";
s1.startsWith(s2);
```

In this example, the **startsWith( )** method returns **true** because the invoking **Smith** string of the **s1** object starts with the same character sequence as does the **Smi** string of the **s2** object.

There is another overloaded version of the **startsWith( )** method, which is as follows:

```
boolean startsWith(String str, int start)
```

In this syntax, the **str** object represents the string being matched with the invoking object. Moreover, the integer variable **start** represents the index within the invoking string, from where the comparison starts.

For example:

```
String s1 = "Smith";
String s2 = "ith";
s1.startsWith(s2, 2);
```

In this example, comparison starts from the second element **i** of the invoking **Smith** string. Here, the method returns **true**.

endsWith( )

The **endsWith( )** method is used to check whether the character sequence of the invoking string ends with the same character sequence as that of the string, which is passed as an argument to the method. If a match is found, the method returns **boolean** value **true**. Otherwise, it returns **false**. The syntax for using the **endsWith( )** method is as follows:

```
boolean endsWith(String str)
```

In this syntax, the **str** object represents the string to be matched within the invoking object. If a match is found, the method returns **true**. Otherwise, it returns **false**.

For example:

```
String s1 = "Smith";
String s2 = "th";
s1.endsWith(s2);
```

In this example, the **endsWith( )** method returns **true** because invoking the **Smith** string of the **s1** object ends with the same character sequence as does the **th** string of the **s2** object.

toString( )

The **toString( )** method is used to represent an object as a string object. It is defined inside the **Object** class. But, you can also overload the **toString( )** method as per your requirements. The syntax for using the **toString( )** method is as follows:

```
String toString( )
```

In this syntax, the **toString( )** method returns an object of the **String** class.

Example 3

The following example illustrates the use of the **toString( )** method of the **Object** class. The program will calculate the square of an integer number and overload the **toString( )** method to display the resultant value on the screen.

```
//Write a program to calculate the square of an integer number
1    class Square
2    {
3        int x, result;
4        Square(int num)
5        {
6            x = num;
7        }
8        void sqr( )
9        {
10           result = x * x;
11       }
```

```
12      public String toString( )
13      {
14          return "the square of " +x+ " is " +result;
15      }
16      public static void main(String arg[])
17      {
18          String str;
19          Square obj = new Square(10);
20          obj.sqr( );
21          str = "After calculation, " + obj;
22          System.out.println(str);
23      }
24 }
```

Explanation

Lines 12 to 15
public String toString( )
{

        return "the square of " +x+ " is " +result;

}

In these lines, the **toString( )** method of the **Object** class has been overloaded. Whenever a call is made to this method, it returns the string that is specified inside the definition of this method with the help of the **return** keyword.

Line 19
Square obj = new Square(10);
In this line, **obj** is declared as an object of the **Square** class and the integer value 10 is passed as an argument to the **Square( )** constructor.

Line 21
str = "After calculation, " + obj;
In this line, the **obj** object of the **Square** class is used in the expression of concatenation. This implicitly makes a call to the overloaded **toString( )** method. After concatenation, the resultant string is assigned to the **str** object of the **String** class.

Line 22
System.out.println(str);
This line will display the following on the screen:

After calculation, the square of 10 is 100

The output of Example 3 is displayed in Figure 9-3.

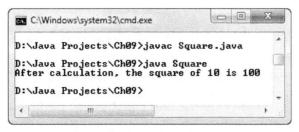

Figure 9-3 *The output of Example 3*

Methods Used for Extracting Characters

As you know that a string is a collection of characters. You can extract these characters from the **String** object using the methods provided by the **String** class. These methods are discussed next.

charAt( )

The **charAt( )** method of the **String** class is used to extract a single character from a string. The syntax for using the **charAt( )** method is as follows:

```
char charAt(int position)
```

In this syntax, the integer variable **position** is treated as an index of the character that you want to extract. The value of the **position** variable should not be negative and must lie within 0 (included) to one less than the length of the string. Otherwise, the method returns an empty string.

For example:

```
String str = "Smith";
char result = str.charAt(2);
```

In this example, first the method **charAt( )** returns the character **i** and then the resultant character **i** is assigned to the character variable **result**.

getChars( )

The **charAt( )** method is used to extract a single character from a string. But if you want to extract more than one character from a string, you can use the **getChars( )** method of the **String** class. The syntax for using the **getChars( )** method is as follows:

```
void getChars(int start, int end, char dest[ ], int deststart)
```

In this syntax, the integer variable **start** specifies the start of the substring that you want to extract from the invoking string. The integer variable **end** specifies the end of the substring. The substring that contains characters from **start** to **end-1** is stored in the character type array **dest[ ]**. The integer variable **deststart** contains an integer value that represents the start offset of the array **dest[ ]**.

> **Note**
> *The size of the character type array should be large enough to accommodate the number of characters of the substring.*

Example 4

The following example illustrates the use of the **getChars( )** method of the **String** class. The following program will extract the specified characters from a string using the **getChars( )** method and also display them on the screen.

//Write a program to extract characters from a string

```
1   class getCharsdemo
2   {
3       public static void main(String arg[])
4       {
5           String str = "Smith has already completed his graduation";
6           int startindex = 6;
7           int endindex = 17;
8           int size = endindex-startindex;
9           char arr[ ] = new char[size];
10          str.getChars(startindex, endindex, arr, 0);
11          System.out.println(arr);
12      }
13  }
```

Explanation
Line 10
str.getChars(startindex, endindex, arr, 0);
In this line, a call will be made to the **getChars( )** method with the **str** string object that contains the string, **Smith has already completed his graduation**. This method will start extracting characters from the 7th character, **h** (included) to the 17th character, **y** (included) of the string, **str**. Now, the resultant substring **has already** will be stored in the character array, **arr**.

Line 12
System.out.println(arr);
This line will display the following on the screen:

has already

The output of Example 4 is displayed in Figure 9-4.

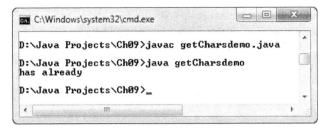

Figure 9-4 The output of Example 4

Methods Used to Modify a String

In Java, all strings are immutable. If you make changes in a string, the modified string will be stored in a new object, but not in the same object of the **String** class. The **String** class provides certain methods to modify a string and create a new copy of the modified string. These methods are given next.

substring( )

The **substring( )** method is used to extract a particular portion or a substring of a string. The syntax for using the **substring( )** method is as follows:

```
String substring(int start)
```

In this syntax, the integer variable **start** represents the index of the specified character in the invoking string from where the substring begins. This method returns a string that starts from the index upto the end of the invoking string.

For example:

```
String str = "How are you?";
String result = str.substring(4);
System.out.println(result);
```

In this example, the **substring( )** method is called on the **str** object of the **String** class. The integer value 4 is passed as an argument, which specifies that the substring begins from the 5th character of the invoking **str** string and contains all remaining characters (upto the end) of the **str** string. The example produces the following output:
are you?

The **substring( )** method is also used in another form as given below:

```
String substring(int start, int end)
```

Here, the integer variable **start** represents the starting index of the substring and the integer variable **end** represents the ending index of the substring. In this form of the **substring( )** method, the character given in the ending index is excluded from the resultant substring.

For example:

```
String str = "How are you?";
String result = str.substring(0, 6);
System.out.println(result);
```

In this example, the substring starts from the character (H) at the 0th position to the character (r) at the 5th position in the invoking **str** string object. Now, the resultant **How ar** substring is assigned to the **result** string object.

concat( )

You already know that the **+** operator is used for the concatenation operation. The **concat( )** method of the **String** class is used to concatenate the invoking string that is passed as an argument to this method. The syntax for using the **concat( )** method is given next:

```
String concat(String str)
```

In this syntax, the **str** object specifies the string being concatenated with the invoking string.

For example:

```
String s1 = "How are you?";
String s2 = " I am fine";
String result = s1.concat(s2);
```

In this example, the **s1** and **s2** string objects contain the **How are you?** and **I am fine** strings, respectively. The **s1** object invokes the **concat( )** method and the **s2** object is passed as an argument to it. The **concat( )** method returns the string after appending the string of the **s2** object at the end of the string of the **s1** object. Now, the resultant **How are you? I am fine** string is assigned to the **result** string object.

Note

*The **concat( )** method always appends a string which is passed as an argument to it, at the end of the invoking string.*

replace( )

The **replace( )** method of the **String** class is used to replace all occurrences of a particular character with another character in a string. The syntax for using the **replace( )** method is as follows:

```
String replace(char exist, char replacement)
```

In this syntax, the character variable **exist** specifies the character to be replaced with the character represented by the character variable **replacement**.

For example:

```
String s1 = "Good Morning";
String result = s1.replace('o', 'w');
```

In this example, all occurrences of the character **o** are replaced with the character **w** in the invoking **s1** string. After replacement, the resultant **Gwwd Mwrning** string is assigned to the **result** string object.

The **replace( )** method is also used in another form where a sequence of characters is replaced with another sequence of characters. The syntax for using the **replace( )** method in this form is as follows:

```
String replace(CharSequence exist, CharSequence replacement)
```

For example:

```
String s1 = "What are you doing?";
String result = s1.replace("doing", "eating");
```

In this example, the occurrence of the character sequence **doing** in the invoking string is replaced with the character sequence **eating**. As a result, the resultant string will be **What are you eating**.

trim( )

The **trim( )** method is used to remove the leading and trailing blank spaces from an invoking string. After removing the blank spaces, a copy of the invoking string is assigned to an object of the **String** class. The syntax for using the **trim( )** method is as follows:

```
String trim( )
```

For example:

```
String s1 = "      How are you?      ".trim( );
```

In this example, the **trim( )** method removes all leading and trailing blank spaces from the invoking **How are you?** string. After removing all blank spaces, the resultant **"How are you?"** string is assigned to the **s1** string object.

Changing the Case of a Character of a String

The **String** class also provides methods to change the case of a character of a string. These methods are discussed next.

toLowerCase( )

The **toLowerCase( )** method converts all uppercase characters of the invoking string into lowercase characters. The syntax for using the **toLowerCase( )** method is as follows:

```
String toLowerCase( )
```

For example:

```
String s1 = "John Smith".toLowerCase( );
```

In this example, the **toLowerCase( )** method converts all uppercase characters (J and S) of the invoking **John Smith** string to lowercase characters (j and s). Now, the resultant **john smith** string is assigned to the **s1** string object.

toUpperCase( )

The **toUpperCase( )** method is used to convert all lowercase characters of the invoking string to uppercase characters. The syntax for using the **toUpperCase( )** method is as follows:

```
String toUpperCase( )
```

For example:

```
String s1 = "John Smith".toUpperCase( );
```

In this example, the **toUpperCase( )** method converts all lowercase characters of the invoking **John Smith** string to uppercase characters. Now, the resultant **JOHN SMITH** string is assigned to the **s1** string object.

Methods Used for Searching Strings

The **String** class provides two methods to search a sequence of characters within another string. These methods are as follows:

indexOf( )

The **indexOf( )** method is used to search the first occurrence of a character or a substring within an invoking string and returns the index position where the match is found. The **indexOf( )** method can be used in the following two ways:

To search for the first occurrence of a character, you can use the **indexOf( )** method in the following way:

```
int indexOf(char ch)
```

In this syntax, the **indexOf( )** method searches for the first occurrence of the character **ch**.

Note
*You can also use the **int** type in place of the **char** type in the parameter list of the **indexOf( )** method.*

To search for the first occurrence of a substring or a sequence of characters, you can use the **indexOf( )** method in the following way:

```
int indexOf(String str)
```

In this syntax, the **indexOf( )** method searches for the first occurrence of the substring that is represented by the **str** string object.

In the **indexOf( )** method, you can also specify the starting point from where the search should start, as shown in the following syntax:

```
int indexOf(String str, int start)
int indexOf(char ch, int start)
```

In these syntaxes, the integer variable **start** specifies the starting point for the search within the invoking string.

lastIndexOf( )

The working of the **lastIndexOf( )** method is same as that of the **indexOf( )** method except that the **lastIndexOf( )** method searches for the last occurrence of a character or a sequence of characters specified as the search item. The **lastIndexOf( )** method is used in the following different forms as given below:

```
int lastIndexOf(char ch)
int lastIndexOf(String str)
int lastIndexOf(String str, int start)
int lastIndexOf(char ch, int start)
```

Example 5

The following example illustrates the use of the **indexOf( )** and **lastIndexOf( )** methods of the **String** class. The program will use different forms of the **indexOf( )** and **lastIndexOf( )** methods to find the first and last occurrences of a character as well as a substring. The program will also display the index positions within the invoking string where the match is found.

//Write a program to find the first and last occurrences of a character and a substring

```
1   class searchdemo
2   {
3       public static void main(String arg[ ])
4       {
5           int index;
6           String s1 = "This is the demo of the methods of the String
7           class that are used for searching strings";
8           System.out.println("------------------------------------");
9           System.out.println("indexof(char ch) and lastIndexOf
            (char ch)");
10          index = s1.indexOf('d');
11          System.out.println("The first occurrence is at: " +index);
12          index = s1.lastIndexOf('d');
13          System.out.println("The last occurrence is at: " +index);
14          System.out.println("------------------------------------");
15          System.out.println("indexof(String str) and lastIndexOf
            (String str)");
16          index = s1.indexOf("the");
17          System.out.println("The first occurrence is at: " +index);
18          index = s1.lastIndexOf("the");
19          System.out.println("The last occurrence is at: " +index);
20          System.out.println("------------------------------------");
21          System.out.println("indexof(String str, int start) and
            lastIndexOf(String str, int start)");
22          index = s1.indexOf('d', 15);
23          System.out.println("The first occurrence is at: " +index);
24          index = s1.lastIndexOf("the", 10);
25          System.out.println("The last occurrence is at: " +index);
26      }
27  }
```

Explanation

Line 10
index = s1.indexOf('d');
In this line, the **indexOf( )** method of the **String** class will search for the first occurrence of the character **d** within the invoking string of the **s1** string object. In this case, the method will find the first occurrence of the character **d** at the index position 12. Next, the method will return 12 as the resultant value and assign it to the **index** variable.

Line 12
index = s1.lastIndexOf('d');
In this line, the **lastIndexOf( )** method of the **String** class will search for the last occurrence of the character **d** within the invoking string of the **s1** string object. In this case, the method will find the last occurrence of the character **d** at the index position 64. Next, the resultant value 64 will be returned by the method and it will be assigned to the **index** variable.

Line 16
index = s1.indexOf("the");
In this line, the **indexOf( )** method will search for the first occurrence of the substring **the** within the invoking string of the **s1** string object. Next, the method will return the index position of the match found within the invoking string.

Line 18
index = s1.lastIndexOf("the");
In this line, the **lastIndexOf( )** method will search for the last occurrence of the substring **the** within the invoking string of the **s1** string object. Next, the method will return the index position of the match found within the invoking string.

Line 22
index = s1.indexOf('d', 15);
In this line, the **indexOf( )** method will search for the first occurrence of the character **d** starting from the 15th index position within the invoking string of the **s1** string object.

Line 24
index = s1.lastindexOf("the", 10);
In this line, the **lastIndexOf( )** method will search for the last occurrence of the substring **the** starting from the 10th index position within the invoking string of the **s1** string object.

The output of Example 5 is displayed in Figure 9-5.

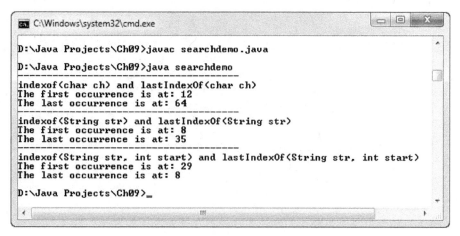

Figure 9-5 *The output of Example 5*

valueOf( )

In the previous section of this chapter, you have learned about the **toString( )** method of the **Object** class. But the main limitation of the **toString( )** method is that you cannot use it to represent the objects of the primitive data types as the **String** object. To solve this problem, Java provides the static **valueOf( )** method. The **valueOf( )** method takes an argument of any primitive data type and converts it into an object for using the **String** class. The syntax for using the **valueOf( )** method is as follows:

```
static String valueOf(type obj)
```

In this syntax, **type** specifies any primitive data type such as **double**, **int**, **boolean**, and so on. Here, the **valueOf( )** method converts the **obj** data type into the **String** object.

For example:

```
boolean i = true;
String s = String.valueOf(i);
```

In this example, the **valueOf( )** method returns the string value **true**, which is assigned to the **s** string object.

Example 6

The following example illustrates the use of the **valueOf( )** method. The program will convert different types of data into strings and also display the resultant values on the screen.

```
//Write a program to convert different types of data into strings
1    class valueOfdemo
2    {
3        public static void main(String arg[ ])
4        {
5            char arr[ ] = {'J', 'o', 'h', 'n', 'S', 'm', 'i', 't', 'h'};
6            int value = 10;
```

```
7            boolean val = true;
8            double dbl = 123.5240;
9            char ch = 'G';
10           System.out.println("String.valueOf(arr) = "
             +String.valueOf(arr));
11           System.out.println("String.valueOf(value) = "
             +String.valueOf(value));
12           System.out.println("String.valueOf(val) = "
             +String.valueOf(val));
13           System.out.println("String.valueOf(dbl) = "
             +String.valueOf(dbl));
14           System.out.println("String.valueOf(ch) = "
             +String.valueOf(ch));
15    }
16 }
```

Explanation

Line 10

System.out.println("String.valueOf(arr) = " +String.valueOf(arr));

In this line, the character type array **arr** is passed as an argument to the **valueOf( )** method. The **valueOf( )** method converts the elements of the character type array **arr** into a single string value **JohnSmith**. Next, the resultant string is returned by this method and it is displayed on the screen as follows:

String.valueOf(arr) = JohnSmith

Similarly, lines 11 to 14, the **valueOf( )** method converts different data types into strings and displays the resultant strings on the screen.

The output of Example 6 is displayed in Figure 9-6.

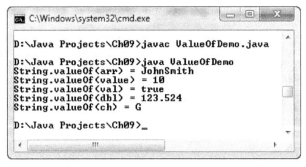

Figure 9-6 The output of Example 6

Finding the Length of a String

You can calculate the length of a string by using the **length( )** method. This method returns an integer value, which specifies the number of characters contained in the string to which it is applied. You can use the **length( )** method as shown in the following example:

```
char arr[ ] = {'S', 'm', 'i', 't', 'h'};
String obj = new String(arr);
int len = obj.length( );
```

In this example, the **length( )** method returns 5, which is the length of the **Smith** string assigned to the **obj** object as its initial value.

THE StringBuffer CLASS

You know that the objects of the **String** class are immutable. This means once the object of this class is created, you cannot make any changes in its content. If you change its content, a new object is created and a modified string is assigned to it. But in Java, you can create and also change contents dynamically with the help of the **StringBuffer** class. The strings assigned to the objects of the **StringBuffer** class are dynamic in nature and can be modified easily. For example, if the number of characters in the **StringBuffer** class is more than the capacity of an object, its capacity will increase automatically to accommodate the increased volume. You can create an object of the **StringBuffer** class in the following way:

```
StringBuffer obj = new StringBuffer( )
```

In this statement, **obj** is created as an object of the **StringBuffer** class. Here, **StringBuffer( )** is the constructor that is used to initialize the **obj** object.

Constructors of the StringBuffer Class

The **StringBuffer** class provides the following three types of constructors:

StringBuffer( )

The **StringBuffer( )** constructor is the default constructor of the **StringBuffer** class. It does not contain any parameter. The **StringBuffer( )** constructor creates an object, initializes it without any character sequence, and reserves an initial capacity of 16 characters. You can use the **StringBuffer( )** constructor as shown in the following example:

```
StringBuffer s1 = new StringBuffer( );
```

In this example, **s1** is created as an object of the **StringBuffer** class. Here, the **s1** object is initialized without any character sequence and reserves an initial capacity of 16 characters.

StringBuffer(int val)

The **StringBuffer(int val)** constructor takes an integer argument. It creates an object, initializes it without any character sequence, and reserves an initial capacity to accommodate the number of characters as is specified by the value of the **val** variable.

For example:

```
StringBuffer s1 = new StringBuffer(20);
```

In this example, **s1** is created as an object of the **StringBuffer** class. Here, the **s1** object is initialized without any character sequence and it reserves an initial capacity of 20 characters (the value 20 is passed as an argument).

StringBuffer(String obj)

The **StringBuffer(String obj)** constructor takes the **String** object as an argument. This constructor creates an object, initializes it with the same character sequence as that of the **obj** string object, and reserves an initial capacity for the total number of characters of the **obj** object, along with the addition of 16 more characters.

For example:

```
StringBuffer s1 = new StringBuffer("Williams");
```

In this example, **s1** is created as an object of the **StringBuffer** class. Here, the **s1** object is initialized with the character sequence **Williams** and reserves an initial capacity of 24 characters (number of characters in the **Williams** string plus 16 more characters).

Methods of the StringBuffer Class

The **StringBuffer** class provides a number of methods to manipulate the objects of this class. These methods are discussed next.

length( )

The **length( )** method of the **StringBuffer** class returns the current number of characters contained in an object. The syntax for using the **length( )** method is as follows:

```
int length( )
```

For example:

```
StringBuffer s1 = new StringBuffer("Good Morning");
int i = s1.length( );
```

In this example, the **Good Morning** string is set as the initial content of the **s1** object. Here, the **length( )** method returns 12 because currently the **s1** object contains 12 characters.

capacity( )

The **capacity( )** method of the **StringBuffer** class returns the number of characters that can be stored in an object without increasing its capacity. The syntax for using the **capacity( )** method is as follows:

```
int capacity( )
```

For example:

```
StringBuffer s1 = new StringBuffer("Good Morning");
int i = s1.capacity( );
```

In this example, the **Good Morning** string is set as the initial string of the **s1** object. Here, the **capacity( )** method returns 28 because the **s1** object contains 12 characters and the memory for 16 characters is already reserved.

ensureCapacity( )

The **ensureCapacity( )** method ensures the minimum capacity that an object of the **StringBuffer** class reserves after its creation. The main function of this method is to ensure the capacity of an object at its creation. The syntax for using the **ensureCapacity( )** method is as follows:

```
void ensureCapacity(int size)
```

In this syntax, the **ensureCapacity( )** method sets the size of the storage area specified by the value of the integer variable **size**.

For example:

```
StringBuffer s1 = new StringBuffer( );
s1.ensureCapacity(85);
```

In this example, the **ensureCapacity( )** method ensures the capacity of the **s1** object to 85.

setLength( )

The **setLength( )** method is used to increase or decrease the length of an object of the **StringBuffer** class. The syntax for using the **setLength( )** method is as follows:

```
void setLength(int length)
```

In this syntax, the integer variable **length** specifies the length of a string.

Note

The value that is passed to the setLength( ) method should always be positive.

If the value passed to the **setLength( )** method is less than the current length of the string, some characters of the current string are lost. If the value passed to the **setLength( )** method is greater than the current length of the string, a huge number of NULL characters are appended to the end of the string.

Example 7

The following example illustrates the use of the **length( )** and **setLength( )** methods. The program will display the current length of a string, set a new length, and also display the string based on the new length.

//Write a program to set a new length of a string

```
1    class setLengthdemo
2    {
3       public static void main(String arg[ ])
4       {
5            int len;
6            StringBuffer s1 = new StringBuffer("Good Morning");
7            len = s1.length( );
8            System.out.println("Current string is: " +s1.toString( ));
9            System.out.println("Length of the current string is: " +len);
10           s1.setLength(8);
11           len = s1.length( );
12           System.out.println("New length is: " +len);
13           System.out.println("Now, the object s1 contains: "
                 +s1.toString( ));
14       }
15   }
```

Explanation

Line 6

StringBuffer s1 = new StringBuffer("Good Morning");

In this line, **s1** is defined as an object of the **StringBuffer** class and the **Good Morning** string is assigned to it as the initial content.

Line 7

len = s1.length( );

In this line, the **length( )** method will return the length (12) of the current **Good Morning** string of the **s1** object. Next, the resultant value will be assigned to the integer variable **len**.

Line 8

System.out.println("Current string is: " +s1.toString( ));

This line will display the following message on the screen:

Current string is: Good Morning

Line 10

s1.setLength(8);

In this line, the **setLength( )** method sets new length 8 of the string contained within the **s1** object.

Line 11

len = s1.length( )

In this line, the **length( )** method returns the new length 8 of the **s1** object. This value is assigned to the integer variable **len**.

The output of Example 7 is displayed in Figure 9-7.

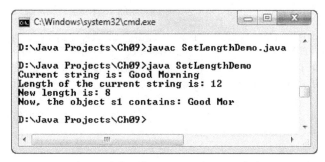

Figure 9-7 *The output of Example 7*

setCharAt( )

The **setCharAt( )** method of the **StringBuffer** class is used to set the value of a particular character within a string. The syntax for using the **setCharAt( )** method is as follows:

```
void setCharAt(int index, char ch)
```

In this syntax, the integer variable **index** specifies the index position of a character whose value is to be set and the character variable **ch** specifies a new value that is assigned to it.

For example:

```
char ch = 'W';
StringBuffer s1 = new StringBuffer("Talk");
s1.setCharAt(0, ch);
```

In this example, the **setCharAt( )** method replaces T with W in the **Talk** string as T is at the 0th position in the string.

reverse( )

The **reverse( )** method is used to reverse the character sequence of the invoking string. The syntax for using the **reverse( )** method is as follows:

```
StringBuffer reverse( )
```

In this syntax, **StringBuffer** is the return type of the **reverse( )** method because after reversing the character sequence of the invoking string, the **reverse( )** method returns an object of the **StringBuffer** class.

For example:

```
StringBuffer s1 = new StringBuffer("Good Morning");
s1.reverse( );
```

In this example, the **reverse( )** method reverses the character sequence of the **Good Morning** string into **gninroM dooG**. Next, the reversed character sequence is returned and assigned to the invoking **s1** object.

append( )

The **append( )** method is used to add values of different type at the end of the string of an object of the **StringBuffer** class. The **StringBuffer** class provides 11 overloaded versions of the **append()** method. You can use these versions to add any type of value at the end of the invoking object. The syntax of 11 versions of the **append( )** method are as follows:

```
StringBuffer append(boolean bool)
StringBuffer append(char ch)
StringBuffer append(String str)
StringBuffer append(int val)
StringBuffer append(Object obj)
StringBuffer append(char[] str)
StringBuffer append(char[] str, int offset, int len)
StringBuffer append(double dbl)
StringBuffer append(float flt)
StringBuffer append(long lng)
StringBuffer append(StringBuffer sb)
```

Example 8

The following example illustrates the use of the **append( )** method. The program will use different versions of the **append( )** method and add different types of data values at the end of a string. Also, the program will display the resultant string on the screen.

```
//Write a program to add different types of data values at the end of a string
1    class AppendDemo
2    {
3        public static void main(String arg[ ])
4        {
5            StringBuffer s1 = new StringBuffer("Good Morning");
6            char arr[] = {'J', 'o', 'h', 'n', 'S', 'm', 'i', 't', 'h'};
7            int value = 10;
8            boolean val = true;
9            double dbl = 123.5240;
10           char ch = 'G';
11           Object refer = "Object Reference";
12           String str = "How are you";
13           s1.append(" ");
14           s1.append(arr);
15           s1.append(" ");
16           s1.append(arr, 0, 4);
17           s1.append(" ");
18           s1.append(value);
19           s1.append(" ");
20           s1.append(val);
21           s1.append(" ");
22           s1.append(dbl);
23           s1.append(" ");
24           s1.append(ch);
25           s1.append(" ");
26           s1.append(refer);
```

```
27          s1.append(" ");
28          s1.append(str);
29          System.out.println("After using append(), s1 contains: "+s1);
30      }
31  }
```

Explanation

Line 5

StringBuffer s1 = new StringBuffer("Good Morning");

In this line, **s1** is defined as an object of the **StringBuffer** class and the **Good Morning** string is assigned to it as its initial content.

Line 13

s1.append(" ");

In this line, a whitespace is added at the end of the **Good Morning** string.

Line 14

s1.append(arr);

In this line, the elements **JohnSmith** of the character type array **arr** will be added at the end of the **Good Morning** string. But, this array will be added after the whitespace that is already added to line 13. Now, the **s1** object will contain the following string:

Good Morning JohnSmith

The working of lines 15 to 28 is similar to that of lines 13 and 14.

Line 29

System.out.println("After using append(), s1 contains: "+s1);

This line will display the following message on the screen:

After using append(), s1 contains: Good Morning JohnSmith John 10 true 123.524 G Object Reference How are you

The output of Example 8 is displayed in Figure 9-8.

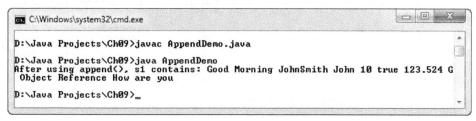

Figure 9-8 *The output of Example 8*

insert( )

The **insert( )** method is used to insert values of different data types within the contents of the invoking string. Using this method, you can insert values at any position in the invoking string. The **StringBuffer** class provides many overloaded versions of different types of data values. The syntax of some of the versions of the **insert( )** method are as follows:

```
StringBuffer insert(int index, int val)
StringBuffer insert(int index, float flt)
StringBuffer insert(int Index, long lng)
StringBuffer insert(int index, boolean bool)
StringBuffer insert(int index, char ch)
StringBuffer insert(int index, char[] str, int offset, int len)
StringBuffer insert(int index, String str)
StringBuffer insert(int index, Object obj)
```

In these syntax, the integer variable **index** specifies the position at which a character, a string, or some other types of data will be inserted into the string of the invoking object.

For example:

```
StringBuffer s1 = new StringBuffer("Very Morning");
s1.insert(5, "Good ");
```

In this example, the **Good** string is inserted after the 5th position within the **Very Morning** string. The **s1** object contains the **Very Good Morning** string.

delete( )

The **delete( )** method is used to delete unwanted characters from the string of an object of the **StringBuffer** class. The syntax for using the **delete( )** method is as follows:

```
StringBuffer delete(int start, int end)
```

In this syntax, the integer variable **start** specifies the index of the first character and the **end** variable specifies the index of the last character. The **delete( )** method deletes the substring that starts from the index position specified by the **start** variable to the index position specified by the **end** variable.

For example:

```
StringBuffer str = new StringBuffer("How are you?");
str.delete(3, 7);
```

In this example, the **delete( )** method deletes the substring from the character at position 3 to the position 7. The example produces the following result:
How you?

deleteCharAt( )

The **deleteCharAt( )** method is used to delete a particular character from a specified index position within the string of an invoking object. The syntax for using the **deleteCharAt( )** method is as follows:

```
StringBuffer deleteCharAt(int location)
```

In this syntax, **location** specifies the index position within the invoking string from where a character has to be deleted.

For example:

```
StringBuffer str = new StringBuffer("How are you?");
str.deleteCharAt(8);
```

In this example, the **deleteCharAt( )** method deletes **y**, which is at the 8th position of the **How are you?** string of the **str** object of the **StringBuffer** class.

replace( )

The **replace( )** method is used to replace a set of characters with another set of characters within the string of an object of the **StringBuffer** class. The syntax for using the **replace( )** method is as follows:

```
StringBuffer replace(int start, int end, String str)
```

In this syntax, the integer variables **start** and **end** specify the start and end of the substring respectively. In this case, this substring is being replaced by another character sequence specified by the **str** object of the **String** class.

For example:

```
StringBuffer s1 = new StringBuffer("Are you mad?");
s1.replace(0, 3, "Were");
```

In this example, the **replace( )** method replaces the character sequence **Are** with the character sequence **Were**. Therefore, the resultant string will be as follows:
Were you mad?

substring( )

The **substring( )** method is used to obtain a substring from the string of the invoking object of the **StringBuffer** class. The syntax for using the **substring( )** method is as follows:

```
String substring(int start)
```

In this syntax, the integer variable **start** specifies the index position from where the substring starts. The string contains all characters upto the end of the invoking string.

For example:

```
StringBuffer s1 = new StringBuffer("Good Morning");
String str = s1.substring(5);
```

In this example, the **substring( )** method obtains a **Morning** substring. This substring starts with the character at the 5th position and contains all characters upto the end of the invoking string.

The **substring( )** method can also be used in a different way, as given below:

```
String substring(int start, int end)
```

In this syntax, **start** and **end** specify the start and end of the substring respectively. This is the substring that is to be obtained from the string of the invoking object.

For example:

```
StringBuffer s1 = new StringBuffer("Good Morning");
String str = s1.substring(5, 10);
```

In this example, the **substring( )** method obtains a **Morni** substring.

Self-Evaluation Test

Answer the following questions and then compare them to those given at the end of this chapter:

1. The **String** class is declared as a _____ class and is defined in the _____ package.

2. The method of the **StringBuffer** class that returns the current number of characters contained in an object is _____.

3. The _____ constructor is used to assign an initial value to an object of the **String** class.

4. The _____ method of the **String** class is used to calculate the length of a string.

5. The _____ operator is used to concatenate two strings.

6. The _____ method of the **String** class is used to check whether two strings are equal or not.

7. The _____ operator is used to compare references of two objects of the **String** class.

8. The _____ method of the **String** class is used to extract a single character from a string.

9. The _____ method is used to remove all leading and trailing blank spaces from an invoking string.

10. The _____ method is used to search for the first occurrence of a character or a substring within an invoking string.

11. The string value of an object of the **String** class can be changed. (T/F)

12. The string value of an object of the **StringBuffer** class cannot be changed. (T/F)

13. The value passed to the **setLength( )** method should always be positive. (T/F)

14. The **append( )** method of the **StringBuffer** class is used to append values of different types at the end of a string. (T/F)

15. The method of the **StringBuffer** class that returns the current number of character is **width( )**. (T/F)

Review Questions

Answer the following questions:

1. Describe different types of constructors of the **String** class.

2. Differentiate between the **equals( )** and **equalsIgnore( )** methods of the **String** class.

3. Differentiate between the objects of the classes **String** and **StringBuffer**.

4. Explain the **ensureCapacity( )** method of the **StringBuffer** class.

5. Explain the **replace( )** method of the **StringBuffer** class.

EXERCISES

Exercise 1

Write a program to illustrate the working of **toLowerCase( )** and **toUpperCase( )** methods of the **String** class.

Exercise 2

Write a program to illustrate the working of the **indexOf( )** and **lastIndexOf( )** methods of the **String** class.

Exercise 3

Write a program to illustrate the working of the **insert( )** method of the **StringBuffer** class.

25

Answers to Self-Evaluation Test

1. final, java.lang, 2. length( ), 3. String(char arr[ ]), 4. length( ), 5. +, 6. equals( ), 7. ==, 8. charAt( ), 9. trim( ), 10. indexOf( ), 11. F, 12. F, 13. T, 14. T, 15. F

Chapter 10

Introduction to Applet and Event Handling

Learning Objectives

After completing this chapter, you will be able to:
- *Understand the Applet class*
- *Understand the life cycle of an applet*
- *Understand the paint() method*
- *Create an applet*
- *Manipulate the color of an applet*
- *Understand the concept of passing parameters to an applet*
- *Understand the getCodeBase( ) and getDocumentBase( ) methods*
- *Understand the event handling*
- *Understand the event delegation mechanism*
- *Understand the event classes*
- *Understand the event sources*
- *Understand the event listener interfaces*

INTRODUCTION

In this chapter, you will learn about some special kind of Java programs that cannot run as stand-alone applications. These programs are known as applets. An applet can only run on a web browser or within an applet viewer. In this chapter, you will also learn about the class **Applet**, and its life cycle. Moreover, you will learn about the creation and execution of various types of **Applet** classes. This chapter will also discuss in detail about manipulating colors of applets, passing parameters to them, and various event handling and event delegation mechanisms that can be applied on applets.

APPLET

Applet is a small Java program that runs on a web browser and is shared over Internet. Its response time is less because it works at client side. Applet is designed to be embedded within an HTML page and needs JVM to view. The JVM can be either a plug-in of the Web browser or a separate runtime environment.

The Applet Class

The **Applet** class defined inside the **java.applet** package is considered as the foundation stone for all Java applets. It provides a number of methods that can be used for creating, manipulating, and executing applets. The **Applet** class is inherited from the **Panel** class, which is inherited from the **Container** class. The **Container** class is in turn inherited from the **Component** class, which is inherited from the **Object** class. All these classes **Object**, **Component**, **Container**, and **Panel** are defined within the package **java.awt** and can be used to create Windows-based graphical user interface as well as to provide support for it. In this way, the **Applet** class also provides support for creating window-based applets. Table 10-1 shows the methods that are defined within the **Applet** class.

Table 10-1 *Methods defined within the **Applet** class*

Method	Description
void init( )	This is the first method to be called when an applet starts execution.
void start( )	This method is called when an applet starts execution.
void stop( )	This method is called by the browser or the applet viewer to stop the execution of an applet.
void destroy( )	This method is called by a web browser or an applet viewer for the cleanup process, just before the termination of applet.
String getAppletInfo( )	This method returns the object **String** that contains description of an applet.
AppletContext getAppletContext( )	This method returns the context of an applet.

Method	Description
AccessibleContext getAccessibleContext( )	This method returns the accessible context of an applet.
AudioClip getAudioClip(URL url)	This method returns the object **AudioClip** that is specified by the argument **url**.
AudioClip getAudioClip(URL url, String name)	This method returns the object **AudioClip** that is specified by the argument **url** and the **String** object **name**.
URL getCodeBase( )	This method returns the URL of the directory that contains an applet.
URL getDocumentBase( )	This method returns the URL of the document in which the applet is embedded.
Image getImage(URL url)	This method returns the object **Image** that contains the image whose location is specified by **url**.
Image getImage(URL url, String name)	This method returns the object **Image** that contains the image whose location is specified by **url** and name is specified by the **String** object **name**.
Locale getLocale( )	This method returns the **Locale** of the applet, if it is set. Otherwise, it returns the default **Locale**.
String getParameter (String name)	This method returns the value of the parameter **name** in the HTML tag. If the specified parameter is not found, it returns **NULL**.
String[ ][ ] getParameterInfo( )	This method returns information about all parameters that are recognized by an applet.
boolean isActive( )	This method returns **true** if the applet is active; otherwise, it returns **false**.
public static final AudioClip new AudioClip(URL url)	This method returns the object **AudioClip** that contains an audio clip received from **url**.
void play(URL url)	This method plays the audio clip whose location is specified by **url**.
void play(URL url, String name)	This method plays the audio clip whose location and name is specified by **url** and **String** object **name**.
void resize(Dimension d)	This method is used to resize the applet according to the dimensions specified by the object **d**.
void showStatus(String s1)	This method is used to display the contents of the object **s1** in the browser or the applet viewer status window.

Method	Description
void resize(int width, int height)	This method is used to resize the width and height of the applet according to the values specified by the integer variables **width** and **height**, respectively.
void paint(Graphics g)	This method is used to draw graphics on an applet.
void update(Graphics g)	**paint()** is not called directly. This is the method that calls **paint()**. You may need to override this method for animation and double buffering graphics.
void setBackground(Color x)	Defines the Background color property.
void setForeground(Color x)	Defines the Foreground color property.
void repaint()	This method is used to redraw the graphics of an applet.

The Life Cycle of an Applet

In Java, each applet has a life cycle during its execution time. The life cycle of an **Applet** undergoes four stages that are discussed next.

init( )

The life cycle of an applet begins from the **init( )** method. This is the first method that is called by the browser or the applet viewer while uploading an applet. Inside the **init( )** method, you should provide the initialization code needed by the applet. The **init( )** method is called only once during the whole life cycle of an applet.

start( )

The **start( )** method is called automatically, immediately after the **init( )** method. This method is used to start the execution of the applet. This method is called whenever an applet resumes the work after the specified time for which it was suspended.

stop( )

The **stop( )** method is called automatically whenever the web browser leaves the control over the web page that contains applet and moves to another web page. With the help of this method, the applet is suspended for some time.

destroy( )

The **destroy( )** method is called when the web browser or the applet viewer, which contains the applet, is completely shut down. This method is called only once during the whole life cycle of an applet.

The paint( ) Method

The **paint( )** method is used to draw graphics on an applet. This method is defined in **java.awt.Component** and contains only one parameter, which is an object of the **Graphics** class.

The syntax for using the **paint( )** method is as follows:

```
public void paint(Graphics g)
```

In this syntax, **g** is an object of the **Graphics** class that contains graphic context in which the applet is running.

Creating an Applet

Before creating an applet, you need to understand the overall frame of an applet, as well as the procedure to save, compile, and run an applet. There are two ways to run an applet. These ways are as follows:

1. By using HTML file.
2. Without using HTML file.

By Using HTML File

To execute the applet using HTML file, create two files: one is the applet file which is saved with *.java* extension and other is the HTML file which is saved with *.html* extension. The following example represents the overall frame of an applet by creating the HTML file:

```
//The following program is for Appletdemo.java
import java.awt.*;
import java.applet.*;
public class Appletdemo extends Applet
{
    public void init()
    {
        //Statements to initialize
    }
    public void start()
    {
        //Statements to start
    }
    public void paint(Graphics g)
    {
        //Statements to display graphics
    }
    public void stop()
    {
        //Statements to stop
    }
    public void destroy()
    {
        //Statements to destroy
    }
}
```

```
//The below program is for Appletdemo.html
<html>
    <applet code= "Appletdemo.class"  width= "500"   height= "100">
    </applet>
</html>
```

In this example, two files are created: one is **Appletdemo.java** and other is **Appletdemo.html**. In **Appletdemo.java**, the first two statements are the **import** statements. These statements are used to import classes such as **Applet**, **Graphics**, and so on into the program. Whenever you create an applet, you must import these two statements. In the next statement, the **Appletdemo** class inherits the **Applet** class by using the **extends** keyword. Inside this class, you can override all methods such as **init( )**, **start( )**, **stop( )**, and so on as per your requirement. In this example, the methods do not contain any definition and as a result the output is an empty applet. However, you can override these methods by adding definition according to your requirement.

To embed the applet code within HTML page, create the **Appletdemo.html** file that contains the **<applet>** tag. Inside the **<applet>** tag, pass the class file of a Java program such as **Appletdemo. class** and also specify the width and height of the applet window.

After saving the files with appropriate extension, compile the program to generate the class file that will be passed to the **<applet>** tag. You can compile the **Appletdemo.java** file with the **javac** command, as shown in the following code line:

```
javac Appletdemo.java
```

Now, you need to execute the applet. You can execute it by using the **appletviewer** command, as given next:

```
appletviewer Appletdemo.html
```

When you execute the applet, an applet window with 500*100 dimensions will be displayed on the screen, as shown in Figure 10-1.

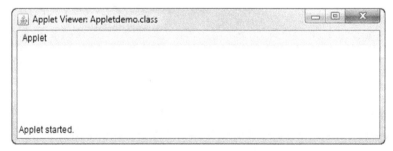

Figure 10-1 *Applet window using HTML file*

Without HTML File

To execute the applet without using HTML file, create an applet that contains applet tag in comment and then compile it. The following example represents the overall frame of an applet without HTML file:

```java
import java.awt.*;
import java.applet.*;
//<applet code= "Appletdemo.class" width= "500"  height= "100"> </applet>
public class Appletdemo extends Applet
{
    public void init()
    {
          //Statements to initialize
    }
    public void start()
    {
          //Statements to start
    }
    public void paint(Graphics g)
    {
          //Statements to display graphics
    }
    public void stop()
    {
          //Statements to stop
    }
    public void destroy()
    {
          //Statements to destroy
    }
}
```

In this example, the first two statements are the **import** statements. These statements are used to import classes such as **Applet**, **Graphics**, and so on into the program. Whenever you create an AWT applet, you must import these two import statements. The next statement contains the HTML **<applet>** tag. Since this tag is not a part of the Java language, it is treated as a comment statement. Inside the **<applet>** tag, you pass the class file of a Java program such as **Appletdemo. class** and also specify the width and height of the applet window. In the next statement, the **Appletdemo** class inherits the **Applet** class by using the **extends** keyword. Inside this class, you can override all methods such as **init( )**, **start( )**, **stop( )**, and so on as per your requirement. In this example, the methods do not contain any definition, so the output will be an empty applet. However, you can override these methods by defining them as per your requirement.

When the coding part is complete, you need to save the file as **Appletdemo.java**. Next, you need to compile the program to generate the class file that will be passed to the **<applet>** tag. You can compile the file **Appletdemo.java** with the **javac** command, as shown in the following code line:

```
javac Appletdemo.java
```

Now, you need to execute the applet. You can execute it by using the **appletviewer** command, as given next:

```
appletviewer Appletdemo.java
```

When you execute the applet, an applet window with 500*100 dimensions will be displayed on the screen, as shown in Figure 10-2.

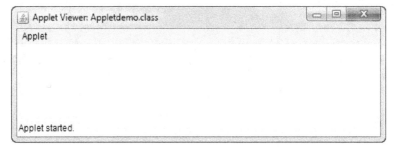

Figure 10-2 *Applet window without using HTML file*

Example 1

The following example illustrates the creation of a simple applet. The program will create an applet that displays a string on the screen.

```
//Write a program to create an applet
1    import java.awt.*;
2    import java.applet.*;
3    //<applet code= "FirstApplet.class" width=300 height=100></applet>
4    public class FirstApplet extends Applet
5    {
6        public void paint(Graphics g)
7        {
8            g.drawString("First applet", 100, 50);
9        }
10   }
```

Explanation
Lines 1 and 2
import java.awt.*;
import java.applet.*;
These lines contain the **import** keyword to import two packages **java.awt.*** and **java.applet.***. All classes defined inside these packages will be included in this program. Now, the **FirstApplet** class can use all classes or methods defined inside these packages.

Line 3
//<applet code="Firstapplet.class" width=300 height=100></applet>
This line contains the HTML **<applet>** tag. Java treats this tag as a comment. Inside the tag, the class file of **FirstApplet** is assigned to the **code** variable. Next, 300 and 100 are the values of the **width** and **height** variables of the applet window, respectively.

Line 4
public class FirstApplet extends Applet
In this line, the **FirstApplet** class is declared as a **public** class. Here, the **FirstApplet** class will inherit all properties of the **Applet** class, which is defined inside the **java.applet.*** package.

Lines 6 to 9
public void paint(Graphics g)
{

       g.drawString("First applet", 100, 50);

}

These lines contain the definition of the **paint( )** method. The parameter list of the **paint( )** method contains the **g** object of the **Graphics** class. This object defines the environment in which the applet will be run. Inside the **paint( )** method, a call will be made to the **draw String( )** method of the **Graphics** class. This method will draw the string **First applet** that begins from the position 100, 50. Here, 100 and 50 are the values of the **x** and **y** coordinates of the applet window, respectively. In Java, the upper-left corner of the applet window has (0,0) coordinates.

The output of Example 1 is displayed in Figure 10-3.

Figure 10-3 *The output of Example 1*

Manipulating the Color of an Applet

You can also set or manipulate the background and foreground colors of an applet. To do so, you can use one of the following two methods:

```
setBackground(Color objColor)
setForeground(Color objColor)
```

These methods are defined by the **Component** class. In these methods, **objColor** specifies the new color, which can take one of the following constant values of the **Color** class:

Color.black
Color.white
Color.orange
Color.blue
Color.cyan
Color.magenta
Color.gray
Color.lightGray
Color.darkGray
Color.red
Color.green
Color.yellow
Color.pink

Example 2

The following example illustrates the use of the **setBackground( )** and **setForeground( )** methods. The program will change the background and foreground colors of an applet.

```
//Write a program to change the background and foreground colors of an applet
1    import java.awt.*;
2    import java.applet.*;
3    //<applet code= "Colorsdemo.class" width=300 height=100></applet>
4    public class Colorsdemo extends Applet
5    {
6        public void init( )
7        {
8            setBackground(Color.cyan);
9            setForeground(Color.blue);
10       }
11       public void paint(Graphics g)
12       {
13           g.drawString("Background color is set to cyan", 65, 30);
14           g.drawString("Foreground color is set to blue", 65, 50);
15       }
16   }
```

Explanation
Lines 6 to 10
public void init( )
{
       setBackground(Color.cyan);
       setForeground(Color.blue);
}

These lines contain the definition of the **init( )** method. The body of this method contains two methods: **setBackground(Color.cyan)** and **setForeground(Color.blue)**. When these methods are executed, they will change the background and foreground colors of the applet to cyan and blue, respectively.

Lines 11 to 15
public void paint(Graphics g)
{
       g.drawString("Background color is set to cyan", 65, 30);
       g.drawString("Foreground color is set to blue", 65, 50);
}

These lines contain the definition of the **paint( )** method. Inside the **paint( )** method, the **drawString( )** method will be called twice to draw two strings: **Background color is set to cyan** and **Foreground color is set to blue**. These strings will be called from the locations that have the coordinates (65, 30) and (65, 50), respectively.

The output of Example 2 is displayed in Figure 10-4.

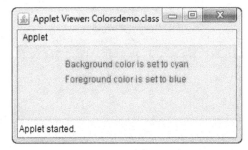

Figure 10-4 *The output of Example 2*

In this example, two methods were used to change the background and foreground colors of an applet. However, if you want to change the current settings of the background and foreground colors of an applet, you can do so by using the following two methods:

    Color getBackground( )
    Color getForeground( )

These methods return an object of the **Color** class, which contains information about the background or foreground color of an applet, depending upon the method used. This means that the **getBackground( )** method will change the background color, whereas the **getForeground( )** method will change the foreground color of an applet.

Passing Parameters to an Applet
The HTML applet tag has an option with which you can pass parameters to an applet. Here, the **getParameter( )** method is used to retrieve a parameter. This method retrieves a value of the specified parameter and returns that value in the form of an **String** object.

Example 3

The following example illustrates the concept of passing parameters to an applet. The program will pass parameters to an applet. It will also retrieve the values of the parameters and display them in the applet window.

//Write a program to pass parameters to an applet
```
1    import java.awt.*;
2    import java.applet.*;
3    /* <applet code= "Parameterdemo.class" width=300 height=100>
4    <param name=studentname value=Williams>
5    <param name=rollnumber value=110>
6    </applet> */
7    public class Parameterdemo extends Applet
8    {
9        String name;
10       String rollnum;
11       public void start( )
12       {
13           name = getParameter("studentname");
14           rollnum = getParameter("rollnumber");
15       }
```

```
16    public void paint(Graphics g)
17    {
18        g.drawString("The name of the student is: " +name, 0,20);
19        g.drawString("The roll number is: " +rollnum, 0,40);
20    }
21 }
```

Explanation

Line 4

<param name=studentname value=Williams>

This line shows a **param** tag. In this tag, **name** specifies the name of the attribute and **value** specifies the value of that attribute. Here, the name of the attribute is **studentname** and its value is **Williams**.

Line 5

<param name=rollnumber value=110>

In this **param** tag, the name of the attribute is **rollnumber** and its value is **110**.

Line 13

name = getParameter("studentname");

In this line, the attribute **studentname** is passed as an argument to the **getParameter( )** method. Now, the **getParameter( )** method will obtain and return the value **Williams** of the attribute **studentname**. Next, the resultant value will be assigned to the **name** string object.

Line 14

rollnum = getParameter("rollnumber");

In this line, the attribute **rollnumber** is passed as an argument to the method **getParameter( )**. Here, the attribute **rollnumber** contains an integer value. The method **getParameter( )** will obtain and return the attribute **rollnumber** as an object of the **String** class. Now, the integer value **110** is treated as the value of the string object. Next, the resultant value will be assigned to the **rollnum** string object.

The output of Example 3 is displayed in Figure 10-5.

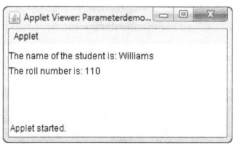

Figure 10-5 The output of Example 3

The getCodeBase( ) and getDocumentBase( ) Methods

In a program, the **getCodeBase( )** method returns the URL of the directory that contains an applet, and the **getDocumentBase( )** method returns the URL of the document in which the applet is embedded. For using these methods, first, you need to import the **java.net** package into the program.

Example 4

The following example illustrates the use of the **getCodeBase( )** and **getDocumentBase( )** methods. The program will obtain the URL of an applet by using the **getCodeBase( )** and **getDocumentBase( )** methods. The program will also display the resultant URL's in the applet window.

```
/* Write a program to illustrate the use of the getCodeBase( ) and methods
getDocumentBase( ) */
1    import java.awt.*;
2    import java.applet.*;
3    import java.net.*;
4    //<applet code= "CodeDocumentBase.class" width=525 height=100>
     </applet>
5    public class CodeDocumentBase extends Applet
6    {
7        String code;
8        URL url;
9        public void paint(Graphics g)
10       {
11           url = getCodeBase( );
12           code = "The getCodeBase( ) returns: " + url.toString( );
13           g.drawString(code, 0, 20);
14           url = getDocumentBase( );
15           code = "The getDocumentBase( ) returns: " +url.toString( );
16           g.drawString(code, 0, 50);
17       }
18   }
```

Explanation
Line 8
URL url;
In this line, **url** is declared as an object of the **URL** class.

Line 11
url = getCodeBase( );
In this line, the **getCodeBase( )** method will return the URL address of directory that contains the applet. Next, the resultant URL will be assigned to the **url** object. The URL that this method will return is as follows:

file:/D:/Java%20Projects/Ch10/

Line 12
code = "The getCodeBase( ) returns: " + url.toString( );
In this line, the **toString( )** method represents the **url** object as a string object. Next, the value of the resultant object will be concatenated to the string **The getCodeBase( ) returns:** and the resultant string will be assigned to the **code** string object.

Line 14

url = getDocumentBase( );

In this line, the **getDocumentBase( )** method will return the URL of the file in which the applet is embedded. Next, the resultant URL will be assigned to the **url** object. The URL that this method will return is as follows:

file:/D://Java%20Projects/Ch10/CodeDocumentBase.java

The output of Example 4 is displayed in Figure 10-6.

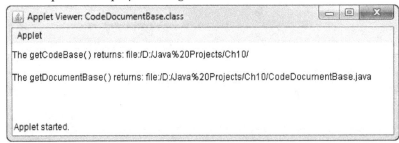

Figure 10-6 *The output of Example 4*

EVENT HANDLING

In the earlier sections of this chapter, you learned about applets and their functions. In this section, you will learn about another important concept called event handling. Java applet is an event-driven program and a graphical user interface used to interact with the end users. When an end user interacts with the GUI in different way, such as by clicking the mouse buttons, moving the mouse, or by entering text into the text field, the applets will generate certain events. To handle these events, certain event handling commands are used inside the program. The **java. awt.event** and **java.util** packages contain the classes that support event handling mechanism.

In this section, you will learn about event handling mechanism, event classes, and constants and methods of event classes.

Event Handling Mechanism

In Java, the latest and simple approach that is used for event handling is known as delegation event model. In this model, the whole process starting from generation to handling events is consistent. The three main components that are used in the delegation event model are as follows:

Event Source

An event source is a GUI component such as button, mouse, keyboard, and so on, with which the end user can interact. Whenever the internal state of the component is changed, one or more events can be generated by the source component.

Event Object

An event object is created when an event occurs. This object encapsulates all information such as the type of event, source of event, and event occurred.

Event Listener

An event listener is an object that is notified by the event source when an event occurs. It notifies the event and processes it accordingly. Each event listener should be registered with a source component.

The following section describes how the delegation event model works and how the three components mentioned before are used in it.

1. First, a listener should be registered with an event source by using the following syntax:

    ```
    public void addTypeListener(TypeListener ref)
    ```

    In this syntax, **Type** is the event name and **ref** is the reference to the event listener. Once the listener is registered with an event source, it waits until an event occurs.

    You will learn more about this method in the next chapter.

2. Second, when an event occurs, an event object is fired to the event listener.

3. Third, when the event object is received by the event listener, the event listener processes the event and performs the specified task.

Event Classes

You know that whenever an event is generated, an event object is created. This object is an instance of one of the event classes. Java provides the following event classes:

1. EventObject
2. AWTEvent
3. ActionEvent
4. ItemEvent
5. AdjustmentEvent
6. TextEvent
7. ComponentEvent
8. InputEvent
9. KeyEvent
10. MouseEvent
11. FocusEvent
12. ContainerEvent
13. WindowEvent

These classes are discussed next.

The EventObject Class

The **EventObject** class is defined inside the **java.util** package. This class lies at the root of hierarchy of the Java event classes and all other event classes are derived from this class. The **EventObject** class defines the following constructor:

```
EventObject(Object source)
```

In this syntax, **source** represents the object (or the GUI component) that generates an event.

The **EventObject** class also contains the following two methods:

getSource( )

The **getSource( )** method returns the object that is the source of the event. The syntax for using the **getSource( )** method is as follows:

```
Object getSource( )
```

toString( )

The **toString( )** method returns the string that represents an event object. The syntax for using the **toString( )** method is as follows:

```
String toString( )
```

The AWTEvent Class

The **AWTEvent** class is defined inside the **java.awt** package. In the hierarchy of the event classes, it comes under the **EventObject** class. Therefore, it is treated as the subclass of the **EventObject** class. But, it is the superclass of all AWT based events.

The ActionEvent Class

When an action is performed on a component such as when a button is pressed, a menu item is selected, and so on, an event object of the **ActionEvent** class is generated. The **ActionEvent** class contains three types of constructors:

```
ActionEvent(Object source, int id, String cmd)
```

In this syntax, **source** represents an object (or a GUI component) that generates an event. The integer variable **id** specifies the type of event and the string object specifies the command of the event.

```
ActionEvent(Object source, int id, String cmd, int modifiers)
```

In this syntax, the first three parameters are the same as defined in the previous constructor. The integer type variable **modifiers** is the fourth parameter and it specifies the modifier keys that were applied while generating an event.

```
ActionEvent(Object source, int id, String cmd, long time, int modifier)
```

In this syntax, the **time** parameter specifies the time period when the event occurred.

The **ActionEvent** class defines four integer constants: **ALT_MASK**, **CTRL_MASK**, **META_MASK**, and **SHIFT_MASK**. These constants are used to identify the modifier keys that were held while generating an event.

The **ActionEvent** class contains the following methods:

getActionCommand( )
The **getActionCommand( )** method returns a command string that is associated with an event. The syntax for using the **getActionCommand( )** method is as follows:

```
String getActionCommand( )
```

getModifiers( )
The **getModifiers( )** method returns an integer value that represents the modifier key applied during the generation of an event. The syntax for using the **getModifiers( )** method is as follows:

```
String getModifiers( )
```

getWhen( )
The **getWhen( )** method returns the time stamp at which the event occurs. The syntax for using the **getWhen( )** method is as follows:

```
long getWhen( )
```

The ItemEvent Class
An event object of the **ItemEvent** class is generated when a check box or list item is selected or deselected. The **ItemEvent** class contains the following integer constants:

1.   DESELECTED
2.   SELECTED
3.   ITEM_STATE_CHANGED

Here, the DESELECTED and SELECTED constants are used for events with two items and the ITEM_STATE_CHANGED constant specifies whether the state of an item is changed or not.

The **ItemEvent** class contains the following constructor:

```
ItemEvent(ItemSelectable source, int id, Object item, int state)
```

In this constructor, the **source** parameter represents an object that generates an event and the integer variable **id** represents the type of event generated. The **item** object specifies the item that is affected by the event. The integer variable **state** represents the current state of the item.

The **ItemEvent** class contains the following methods:

getItem( )
The **getItem( )** method returns the reference to the item that generated an event. The syntax for using the **getItem( )** method is as follows:

```
Object getItem( )
```

getStateChange( )

The **getStateChange( )** method returns an integer value that indicates the state change (selected or deselected) of the event. The syntax for using the **getStateChange( )** method is as follows:

```
int getStateChange( )
```

getItemSelectable( )

The **getItemSelectable( )** method returns the reference of the **ItemSelectable** object that originated the event. The syntax for using the **getItemSelectable( )** method is as follows:

```
ItemSelectable getItemSelectable( )
```

The AdjustmentEvent Class

An event object of the **AdjustmentEvent** class is generated by adjustable objects such as the scroll bar. The **AdjustmentEvent** class defines the integer constants that are as follows:

1. BLOCK_INCREMENT
2. BLOCK_DECREMENT
3. TRACK
4. UNIT_DECREMENT
5. UNIT_INCREMENT
6. ADJUSTMENT_VALUE_CHANGED

The first five mentioned constants are used to identify five types of adjustment events. The last constant **ADJUSTMENT_VALUE_CHANGED** indicates whether the adjustment value is changed or not.

The **AdjustmentEvent** class contains the following constructor:

```
AdjustmentEvent(Adjustable source, int id, int type, int curvalue)
```

In this syntax, the **source** parameter represents the **Adjustable** object that generates an event of the type **AdjustmentEvent**. The integer variables **id**, **type**, and **curvalue** specify the event type, adjustment type, and current value of the adjustment, respectively.

The **AdjustmentEvent** class contains the following methods:

getAdjustable( )

The **getAdjustable( )** method returns the **Adjustable** object that generates an event. The syntax for using the **getAdjustable( )** method is as follows:

```
Adjustable getAdjustable( )
```

getValue( )

The **getValue( )** method returns the amount of adjustment that was made by the adjustment event. The syntax for using the **getValue( )** method is as follows:

```
int getValue( )
```

getAdjustmentType( )

The **getAdjustmentType( )** method returns the type of adjustment that was made during the event. This method returns an integer constant defined by the **AdjustmentEvent** class. The syntax for using the **getAdjustmentType( )** method is as follows:

```
int getAdjustmentType( )
```

The TextEvent Class

An event object of the **TextEvent** class is generated by the text field components such as text box, text area, and so on. This event is generated when an end user enters character values in the text fields. The **TextEvent** class defines an integer constant **TEXT_VALUE_CHANGED**, which shows whether the text in the text fields has changed or not.

The **TextEvent** class contains the following constructor:

```
TextEvent(Object source, int id)
```

In this syntax, **source** represents the object that generates the event. Here, the integer variable **id** identifies the event type.

The ComponentEvent Class

An event object of the **ComponentEvent** class is generated when a component is moved, resized, or whenever its visibility is changed. The **ComponentEvent** class defines four integer constants that are as follows:

1. COMPONENT_HIDDEN
2. COMPONENT_MOVED
3. COMPONENT_RESIZED
4. COMPONENT_SHOWN

All the mentioned integer constants are used to identify four different types of component events that are generated by the **ComponentEvent** class.

The **ComponentEvent** class contains the following constructor:

```
ComponentEvent(Component source, int id)
```

In this syntax, **source** represents the object of the **Component** class that generates the event and the integer variable **id** represents the type of event generated.

The **ComponentEvent** class contains the following method:

getComponent( )

The **getComponent( )** method returns the **Component** object that generated the event. The syntax for using the **getComponent( )** method is as follows:

```
Component getComponent( )
```

The InputEvent Class

The **ComponentEvent** class is the direct superclass of the **InputEvent** class. This class defines certain integer constants that are as follows:

1. ALT_MASK
2. ALT_GRAPH_MASK
3. BUTTON1_MASK
4. BUTTON2_MASK
5. BUTTON3_MASK
6. CTRL_MASK
7. META_MASK
8. SHIFT_MASK

The **InputEvent** class contains the following methods:

getModifiers( )

The **getModifiers( )** method returns all modifier flags. The syntax for using the **getModifiers( )** method is as follows:

```
int getModifiers( )
```

isAltDown( )

The **isAltDown( )** method returns the value **true** or **false** based upon whether or not the ALT modifier was pressed during the event. The syntax for using the **isAltDown( )** method is as follows:

```
boolean isAltDown( )
```

Like the **isAltDown( )** method, there are other methods of the **InputEvent** class as well. These methods return the value **true** or **false** based upon whether their modifiers were pressed or not during the event generation. These methods are given next:

```
boolean isAltGraphDown( )
boolean isControlDown( )
boolean isMetaDown( )
boolean isShiftDown( )
```

The KeyEvent Class

An event object of the **KeyEvent** class is generated when a key is pressed, released, or typed. The **KeyEvent** class defines three integer constants that are as follows:

1. KEY_PRESSED
2. KEY_RELEASED
3. KEY_TYPED

These integer constants are used to identify three different types of key events such as **KEY_PRESSED**, **KEY_RELEASED** and **KEY_TYPED**.

The **KEY_PRESSED** event is generated when a key is pressed and the **KEY_RELEASED** event is generated when a key is released. Whenever a key is pressed, its virtual key code is generated, which identifies that the key is on the keyboard. For example, when the **ALT** key is pressed, its virtual key code **VK_ALT** is generated and the event **KEY_PRESSED** occurs with it. The following list shows some of the virtual key codes the constant **VK** specifies the virtual key code:

1. VK_0 through VK_9   For numeric keys from 0 through 9
2. VK_A through VK_Z   For character keys from A-Z and a-z and their ASCII values
3. VK_ALT   For ALT key
4. VK_CONTROL   For CTRL key
5. VK_DOWN   For down ARROW key
6. VK_UP   For up ARROW key
7. VK_RIGHT   For right ARROW key
8. VK_LEFT   For left ARROW key
9. VK_SHIFT   For SHIFT key

The third event, which is the **KEY_TYPED** event, that is generated when a character is entered in a text field. But in this case, all key presses will not generate characters. For example, when you press the ALT key, it will not generate any character.

The **KeyEvent** class contains the following constructor:

```
KeyEvent(Component source, int id, long time, int modifiers, int code, char
chr)
```

In this syntax, **source** represents the **Component** object that generates an event. The integer variable **id** specifies the type of event and the **long** variable **time** contains the system time when the key was pressed. The integer variable **modifiers** represents the key that was pressed during the event generation. The integer variable **code** represents the virtual key code of the pressed key. But in the **key typed** event, the virtual key code will contain **VK_UNDEFINED**. The character variable **chr** represents the character generated during the event. If the generated character is an invalid unicode character, **CHAR_UNDEFINED** is assigned to the character variable **chr**.

The following are the most commonly used methods of the **KeyEvent** class:

getKeyCode( )

The **getKeyCode( )** method returns the virtual key code that is associated with the key pressed during the event generation. The syntax for using the **getKeyCode( )** is as follows:

```
int getKeyCode( )
```

getKeyChar( )

The **getKeyChar( )** method returns the unicode character that is associated with the key pressed during the event generation. The syntax for using the **getKeyChar( )** is as follows:

```
char getKeyChar( )
```

getKeyText(int keycode)

The **getKeyText(int keycode)** method returns a character string, which defines the parameter **keycode** that is passed to it. The syntax for using the **getKeyText( )** is as follows:

```
String getKeyText(int keycode)
```

The MouseEvent Class

An event object of the **MouseEvent** class is generated when the mouse is moved, dragged, pressed, released, entered, exited, or clicked within a component. The **MouseEvent** class defines the following integer constants:

1. MOUSE_CLICKED
2. MOUSE_DRAGGED
3. MOUSE_ENTERED
4. MOUSE_EXITED
5. MOUSE_MOVED
6. MOUSE_PRESSED
7. MOUSE_RELEASED

All these constants are used to identify mouse events.

The **MouseEvent** class contains the following constructor:

```
MouseEvent(Component source, int id, long time, int modifiers, int x, int y,
int count, boolean popuptrigger)
```

In this syntax, **source** represents the **Component** object that generates an event. The integer variable **id** specifies the type of event and the **long** variable **time** specifies the time when the event is occurred. The integer variable **modifiers** specifies the modifier that was pressed when the mouse event was generated. The integer variables **x** and **y** specify the x and y coordinates of the location of the mouse, and the integer variable **count** specifies the number of mouse clicks. The **boolean** variable **popuptrigger** returns **true**, if the event is generated from a pop-up menu.

The **MouseEvent** class contains the following methods:

getX( )

The **getX( )** method returns the position of the x coordinate of the mouse, relative to the source component when the event was generated. The syntax for using the **getX( )** method is as follows:

```
int getX( )
```

getY( )

The **getY( )** method returns the position of the y coordinate of the mouse, relative to the source component when the event was generated. The syntax for using the **getY( )** method is as follows:

```
int getY( )
```

getPoint( )

The **getPoint( )** method returns an object of the **Point** class. This object contains the positions of the x and y coordinates stored in its instance variables **x** and **y**, respectively. These positions are relative to the source component when the event was generated. The syntax for using the **getPoint( )** method is as follows:

```
Point getPoint( )
```

translatePoint( )

The **translatePoint( )** method is used to change the x and y coordinates of the event by adding to them the values that are passed as arguments to the method. The syntax for using the **translatePoint( )** method is as follows:

```
void translatePoint(int x, int y)
```

In this syntax, the values of **x** and **y** variables are added to the x and y coordinates, respectively.

getClickCount( )

The **getClickCount( )** method returns the number of mouse clicks associated with the event. The syntax for using the **getClickCount( )** method is as follows:

```
int getClickCount( )
```

isPopupTrigger( )

The **isPopupTrigger( )** method returns **true**, if the event is generated from a pop-up menu. Otherwise, it returns **false**. The syntax for using the **isPopupTrigger( )** method is as follows:

```
boolean isPopupTrigger( )
```

getButton( )

The **getButton( )** method returns the changed state of mouse button or the mouse button that generates an event. The syntax for using the **getButton( )** method is as follows:

```
int getButton( )
```

The **getButton( )** method returns one of the following values:

1. NOBUTTON
2. BUTTON1
3. BUTTON2
4. BUTTON3

The FocusEvent Class

An event object of the **FocusEvent** class is generated when a component has gained or lost the focus of input. The **FocusEvent** class defines two integer constants: **FOCUS_GAINED** and **FOCUS_LOST**. These two constants are used to identify two focus events.

The **FocusEvent** class contains the following constructors:

```
FocusEvent(Component source, int id)
```

In this syntax, **source** represents the **Component** object that generates an event and the integer variable **id** represents the type of event generated.

```
FocusEvent(Component source, int id, boolean temporary)
```

In this syntax, **source** represents the **Component** object that generates an event. The integer variable **id** represents the type of event generated. The **boolean** variable **temporary** checks whether the change in focus is temporary or permanent. If the change in focus is temporary, the variable is set to **true**. Otherwise, it is set to **false**.

The **FocusEvent** class contains the following method:

isTemporary( )

The **isTemporary( )** method returns **true**, if the change in focus event is temporary. Otherwise, it returns **false**. The syntax for using the **isTemporary( )** method is as follows:

```
boolean isTemporary( )
```

The ContainerEvent Class

An event object of the **ContainerEvent** class is generated when the contents of a container are changed. In other words, the event object of this class is generated when a component is added or removed from the container. The **ContainerEvent** class defines two integer constants: **COMPONENT_ADDED** and **COMPONENT_REMOVED**. These constants are used to identify container events.

The **ContainerEvent** class contains the following constructor:

```
ContainerEvent(Component source, int id, Component obj)
```

In this syntax, **source** represents the **Component** object that generates an event. In this case, the component is a container. The integer variable **id** represents the type of event generated. The **obj** object represents the component that is added or removed from the container.

The **ContainerEvent** class contains the following methods:

getContainer( )
The **getContainer( )** method returns the **Container** object that generates an event. The syntax for using the **getContainer( )** is as follows:

```
Container getContainer( )
```

getChild( )
The **getChild( )** method returns the **Component** object that was added or removed from the container. The syntax for using the **getChild( )** is as follows:

```
Component getChild( )
```

The WindowEvent Class
An event object of the **WindowEvent** class is generated when a window object is activated, deactivated, iconified, deiconified, opened, closed, gained focus, lost focus, or about to close. To identify these events, the **WindowEvent** class defines the following integer constants:

1. WINDOW_ACTIVATED
2. WINDOW_DEACTIVATED
3. WINDOW_ICONIFIED
4. WINDOW_DEICONIFIED
5. WINDOW_OPENED
6. WINDOW_CLOSED
7. WINDOW_CLOSING
8. WINDOW_GAINED_FOCUS
9. WINDOW_LOST_FOCUS
10. WINDOW_STATE_CHANGED

The **WindowEvent** class contains the following constructors:

```
WindowEvent(Window source, int id)
```

In this syntax, **source** represents the **Window** object that generates an event and the integer variable **id** represents the type of event.

```
WindowEvent(Window source, int id, int previousstate, int newstate)
```

In this syntax, **source** represents the **Window** object that generates an event and the integer variable **id** represents the type of event. In this case, the event type is **WINDOW_STATE_CHANGED**. The integer variables **previousstate** and **newstate** represent the previous window state and the new window state, respectively.

```
WindowEvent(Window source, int id, Window opponent)
```

In this syntax, **source** represents the **Window** object that generates an event. The integer variable **id** represents the type of event. The **opponent** object of the **Window** class represents the other window that is included in the window events.

```
WindowEvent(Window source, int id, Window opponent, int previousstate, int newstate)
```

In this syntax, **source** represents the **Window** object that generates an event. The integer variable **id** represents the type of event. The **opponent** object represents the other window that is included in the window events. The integer variables **previousstate** and **newstate** represent the previous window state and the new window state, respectively.

The **WindowEvent** class contains the following methods:

getWindow( )
The **getWindow( )** method returns the **Window** object that generates an event. The syntax for using the **getWindow( )** method is as follows:

```
Window getWindow( )
```

getOppositeWindow( )
The **getOppositeWindow( )** method returns the opposite window that is included in the window events. The syntax for using the **getOppositeWindow( )** method is as follows:

```
Window getOppositeWindow( )
```

getOldState( )
The **getOldState( )** method returns the previous state of the window. The syntax for using the **getOldState( )** method is as follows:

```
int getOldState( )
```

getNewState( )
The **getNewState( )** method returns the new state of the window. The syntax for using the **getNewState( )** method is as follows:

```
int getNewState( )
```

Event Sources

Event sources are basically Graphical User Interface (GUI) components that generate an event. Some of the major GUI components are as follows:

1. Button
2. TextField
3. TextArea
4. Lists
5. Choice lists
6. Check Boxes
7. Scroll Bars
8. Menu Items

You will learn more about these components and many related concepts in the next chapter.

Creating Event Listener

In the previous section of this chapter, you learned about event listeners. In this section, you will learn how these event listeners are created. You can create event listeners by implementing one or more interfaces that are defined by the **java.awt.event** package.

The ActionListener Interface

The **ActionListener** interface is used to handle only action events such as button clicks. This interface defines the following method:

```
void actionPerformed(ActionEvent eventobj)
```

Whenever an action event occurs, the **actionPerformed( )** method is invoked by the event source and the event object is passed to the method as an argument. The body of the method contains statements, which specify the task that should be performed when an action event occurs.

The ItemListener Interface

The **ItemListener** interface is used to handle only item events such as selecting a check box, selecting an item from a choice list, and so on. This interface defines the following method:

```
void itemStateChanged(ItemEvent eventobj)
```

Whenever an item event occurs, the **itemStateChanged( )** method is invoked by the event source and the event object is passed to the method as an argument.

The AdjustmentListener Interface

The **AdjustmentListener** interface is used to handle only adjustment events such as interacting with a scroll bar. This interface defines the following method:

```
void adjustmentValueChanged(AdjustmentEvent eventobj)
```

Whenever an adjustment event occurs, the **adjustmentValueChanged( )** method is invoked by the event source and the event object is passed to the method as an argument.

The ComponentListener Interface

The **ComponentListener** interface is used to handle only component events such as resizing a component, moving a component, and so on. This interface defines the following four methods:

```
void componentResized(ComponentEvent eventobj)
void componentMoved(ComponentEvent eventobj)
void componentShown(ComponentEvent eventobj)
void componentHidden(ComponentEvent eventobj)
```

Whenever a component is moved, resized, shown, or hidden, a component event occurs. Next, the method corresponding to the component event is called and the event object is passed to the method as an argument.

The ContainerListener Interface

The **ContainerListener** interface is used to handle only container events such as adding component to a container. This interface defines the following two methods:

```
void componentAdded(ContainerEvent eventobj)
void componentRemoved(ContainerEvent eventobj)
```

Whenever a component is added or removed from a container, a container event occurs. Accordingly, one of the mentioned methods is called by the event source and the event object is passed to the method as an argument.

The KeyListener Interface

The **KeyListener** interface is used to handle only key events such as **keyPressed**, **keyReleased**, and **keyTyped**. This interface defines the following three methods:

```
void keyPressed(KeyEvent eventobj)
void keyReleased(KeyEvent eventobj)
void keyTyped(KeyEvent eventobj)
```

Whenever a key event occurs, the methods corresponding to that key event is called and an event object is passed to the method as an argument.

The FocusListener Interface

The **FocusListener** interface is used to handle only focus events such as focus gained and focus lost. This interface defines the following two methods:

```
void focusGained(FocusEvent eventobj)
void focusLost(FocusEvent eventobj)
```

The MouseListener Interface

The **MouseListener** interface is used to handle only mouse events such as mouse clicked, mouse pressed, mouse released, and so on. This interface defines the following five methods:

```
void mouseEntered(MouseEvent eventobj)
void mousePressed(MouseEvent eventobj)
void mouseReleased(MouseEvent eventobj)
void mouseExited(MouseEvent eventobj)
void mouseClicked(MouseEvent eventobj)
```

The MouseMotionListener Interface

The **MouseMotionListener** interface is also used to handle only mouse events such as mouse moved and mouse dragged. This interface defines the following two methods:

```
void mouseMoved(MouseEvent eventobj)
void mouseDragged(MouseEvent eventobj)
```

The WindowListener Interface

The **WindowListener** interface is used to handle only window events such as window activated, window deactivated, window iconified, deiconified, and so on. This interface defines the following seven methods:

```
void windowActivated(WindowEvent eventobj)
void windowDeactivated(WindowEvent eventobj)
void windowIconified(WindowEvent eventobj)
void windowDeiconified(WindowEvent eventobj)
void windowOpened(WindowEvent eventobj)
void windowClosed(WindowEvent eventobj)
void windowClosing(WindowEvent eventobj)
```

The TextListener Interface

The **TextListener** interface is used to handle only text events such as text changed in a text area. This interface defines the following method:

```
void textChanged(TextEvent eventobj)
```

 Note
You will learn more about the implementation of these methods in the next chapter.

Self-Evaluation Test

Answer the following questions and then compare them to those given at the end of this chapter:

1. The program that can run only within a web browser or within an applet viewer is known as an _____.

2. The **Applet** class is defined inside the _____ package.

3. The life cycle of an applet begins from the _____ method.

4. The _____ method is used to draw graphics in an applet.

5. While creating an applet, you must import the _____ and _____ packages into a program.

6. The three main components of the event delegation mechanism are _____, _____, and _____.

7. The _____ class lies at the root in the hierarchy of the Java event classes.

8. The _____ class is the direct superclass of the **InputEvent** class.

9. The integer constants defined by the **FocusEvent** class are _____ and _____.

10. The **destroy( )** method of the **Applet** class is used for the clean up process. (T/F)

11. The **getParameter( )** method returns a value in the form of the string object.

12. The **getCodeBase( )** method returns the URL of the document in which the applet is embedded. (T/F)

13. In the **KeyEvent** class, the constant **VK** specifies the virtual key code. (T/F)

14. The **getWindow( )** method of the **WindowEvent** class returns an object of the **Container** class. (T/F)

Review Questions

Answer the following questions:

1. Define an applet.

2. Explain the life cycle of an applet.

3. Explain the working of the **setBackground( )** and **setForeground( )** methods.

4. Differentiate between the **getCodeBase( )** and **getDocumentBase( )** methods.

5. Explain Different Event classes.

EXERCISES

Exercise 1

Write a program to create an applet that will display the string **Good Morning** at the position 20, 50.

Exercise 2

Write a program to set the background and foreground colors of an applet to dark gray and cyan, respectively.

Answers to Self-Evaluation Test

1. applet, **2. java.applet**, **3. init( )**, **4. paint( )**, **5. java.awt.***, **java.applet.***, **6.** event source, event object, event listener, **7. EventObject**, **8. ComponentEvent**, **9. FOCUS_GAINED**, **FOCUS_LOST**, **10.** T, **11.** T, **12.** F, **13.** T, **14.** F

Chapter 11

Abstract Window Toolkit

Learning Objectives

After completing this chapter, you will be able to:

- *Use AWT windows*
- *Apply AWT graphics*
- *Use AWT controls*
- *Use Layout Managers*

INTRODUCTION

In the previous chapter, you learned about applets, the **Applet** class, and event delegation mechanism. The three main components of the event delegation mechanism are: event source, event object, and event listener. In this chapter, you will learn how an event source generates an event object and how that object is handled by an event listener. Also, you will learn about Abstract Window Toolkit.

AWT WINDOWS

An AWT window is displayed when an applet or a window application is executed. The most common windows used by an AWT are applet window and frame window. An applet window is displayed when an applet program is executed, whereas a frame window is displayed when windows application is executed. The **java.awt.Frame** class supports the frame window. In this section, you will learn in detail about the frame window.

Frame Window

The frame window is the second most commonly used window in the Graphical User Interface. This window is derived from the **Frame** class. It contains the title bar, menu bar, borders, and buttons to resize the window. It can also be used inside the applet windows. You can create a frame window by creating an object of the **Frame** class. In this section, you will learn about constructors of the **Frame** class. You will also learn how to create a frame window and use various methods to apply different settings on frame windows.

Constructors of the Frame Class

The constructors of the **Frame** class are used to create frame windows. The **Frame** class has the following four constructors:

```
Frame ( )
Frame (GraphicsConfiguration gc)
Frame (String title)
Frame (String title, GraphicsConfiguration gc)
```

In these syntaxes, the first constructor **Frame( )** creates a frame window that contains no title in the title bar. The second constructor **Frame(GraphicsConfiguration gc)** creates a frame window that contains GraphicsConfiguration. The third constructor **Frame(String title)** creates a frame window that contains a title specified by the **title** string object in the title bar. The fourth constructor **Frame(String title, GraphicsConfiguration gc)** creates a frame window that contains title and GraphicsConfiguration.

Setting the Size of a Frame Window

You can set the size of a frame window using the **setSize( )** method. The syntaxes for using the **setSize( )** method are as follows:

```
void setSize(int width, int height)
void setSize(Dimension size)
```

In the first syntax, the width and height of the frame window are set as specified by the integer variables **width** and **height**, respectively. In the second syntax, the size of the frame window is set by the **width** and **height** fields as specified by **size**.

You can also get the size of a frame window using the **getSize( )** method. The syntax for using the **getSize( )** method is as follows:

```
Dimension getSize( )
```

In this syntax, the **getSize( )** method returns an object of the **Dimension** class. Here, the **width** and **height** fields of the object contain the current size of the frame window.

Setting the Visibility of a Frame Window

After the creation of a frame window, you can set its visibility using the **setVisible( )** method. The syntax for using this method is as follows:

```
void setVisible(boolean val)
```

In this syntax, if the **setVisible( )** method contains the **boolean** value true, the frame window will be visible. Otherwise, it will not be visible.

Setting the Title of a Frame Window

In the earlier section of this chapter, the constructor of the **Frame** class was used to set the title of the frame window. You can also use the **setTitle( )** method to change the title of a frame window. The syntax for using the **setTitle( )** method is as follows:

```
void setTitle(String title)
```

In this syntax, the **title** string object represents a new title for the frame window.

Closing a Frame Window

To close a frame window, you can use the **WindowClosing( )** method of the **WindowListener** interface. For closing a frame window, you need to write the code in the body of methods. You will learn more about this method later in this chapter.

Creating a Frame Window

In this section, you will learn how to create a frame window.

Example 1

The following example illustrates the procedure of creating a frame window. The program will create a frame window and display a string inside it. Also, the program will display the frame window on the screen.

//Write a program to create a frame window

```
1    import java.awt.*;
2    import java.awt.event.*;
3    class FirstFramedemo extends WindowAdapter
4    {
5       public void windowClosing (WindowEvent event)
6       {
7            System.exit (0);
8       }
9    }
10   class FirstFrame extends Frame
11   {
12      private FirstFramedemo obj1;
13      FirstFrame( )
14      {
15          obj1 = new FirstFramedemo( );
16          setTitle("First Frame");
17          setSize(300, 200);
18          addWindowListener (obj1);
19          setVisible(true);
20      }
21      public void paint(Graphics g)
22      {
23          g.drawString("First Frame Window", 100,110);
24      }
25      public static void main(String arg[ ])
26      {
27          Frame f1;
28          f1 = new FirstFrame( );
29      }
30   }
```

Explanation

Line 3

class FirstFramedemo extends WindowAdapter

In this line, the **FirstFramedemo** class inherits the properties of the **WindowAdapter** class.

Lines 5 to 8

public void windowClosing (WindowEvent event)

{

      System.exit (0);

}

These lines contain the definition of the **windowClosing( )** method of the **WindowListener** interface. The parameter list of this method contains an object **event** of the **WindowEvent** class. Whenever the **close** event will be generated in the program, the event object will be passed to the **event** object. Next, the method will handle the event by executing the **System.exit (0)** statement. This statement will remove the window from the screen.

Line 10
class FirstFrame extends Frame
In this line, the **FirstFrame** class inherits the **Frame** class.

Line 12
private FirstFramedemo obj1;
In this line, **obj1** is declared as an object of the **FirstFramedemo** class. This object will be used to handle window events.

Lines 14 to 21
FirstFrame( )
{

       obj1 = new FirstFramedemo( );
       setTitle("First Frame");
       setSize(300, 200);
       addWindowListener (obj1);
       setVisible(true);

}

These lines contain the definition of the **FirstFrame( )** constructor of the **FirstFrame** class. Inside the body of the constructor, **obj1** is defined as an object of the **FirstFramedemo** class with the help of the **new** operator in the first statement. In the next statement, the **setTitle( )** method will set the **First Frame** string as the title of the frame window. Next, the **setSize( )** method will set the width and height of the frame window to **300** and **200**, respectively. In the next statement, the **obj1** object of the **FirstFramedemo** class will get registered to receive window events. In the last statement, the **setVisible( )** method contains the **boolean** value **true** that will make the frame window visible on the screen.

Lines 21 to 24
public void paint(Graphics g)
{

       g.drawString("First Frame Window", 100,110);

}

These lines contain the definition of the **paint( )** method. Inside the body of this method, the **drawString( )** method is used to draw the **First Frame Window** string at the location 100, 110.

Line 28
Frame f1;
In this line, **f1** is declared as an object of the **Frame** class.

Line 29
f1 = new FirstFrame( );
In this line, the reference of an object of the **FirstFrame** class will be assigned to the **f1** object. Here, a call will be made to the **FirstFrame( )** constructor and the control will be transferred to the definition of the constructor.

The program will be compiled and executed, as shown in the following statements:

> D:\Java Projects\Ch11>javac FirstFrame.java
> D:\Java Projects\Ch11>java FirstFrame

The output of Example 1 is displayed in Figure 11-1.

Figure 11-1 *The output of Example 1*

Creating a Frame Window within an Applet

In the previous example, you observed that the frame window was the top-level window for stand-alone applications. But you can also create a frame window as a child window within an applet.

Example 2

The following example illustrates the procedure of creation of a frame window within an applet. The program will create a frame window within an applet and display a string inside the frame window. Also, the program will display both the applet window and the frame window on the screen.

```
//Write a program to create a frame window within an applet
 1   import java.awt.*;
 2   import java.awt.event.*;
 3   import java.applet.*;
 4   //<applet code="Appletframedemo" width=300 height=100></applet>
 5   class childframe extends Frame
 6   {
 7       childframe( )
 8       {
 9           setTitle("Child Frame");
10           windowadapterdemo adapter = new windowadapterdemo( );
11           addWindowListener(adapter);
12       }
13       public void paint(Graphics g)
14       {
15           g.drawString("Child Frame Window", 10,40);
16       }
17   }
```

```
18  class windowadapterdemo extends WindowAdapter
19  {
20      public void windowClosing (WindowEvent event)
21      {
22          System.exit(0);
23      }
24  }
25  public class Appletframedemo extends Applet
26  {
27      Frame frm;
28      public void init( )
29      {
30          frm = new childframe( );
31          frm.setSize(200, 100);
32          frm.setVisible(true);
33      }
34      public void start( )
35      {
36          frm.setVisible(true);
37      }
38      public void stop( )
39      {
40          frm.setVisible(false);
41      }
42      public void paint(Graphics g)
43      {
44          g.drawString("Applet Window", 10,40);
45      }
46  }
```

Explanation

Line 27
Frame frm;
In this line, **frm** is declared as an object of the **Frame** class.

Lines 28 to 33
public void init( )
{
       frm = new childframe( );
       frm.setSize(200, 100);
       frm.setVisible(true);
}
In these lines, the **init( )** method of the **Applet** class is overridden inside the **AppletFramedemo** class. Inside the **init( )** method, the reference of an object of the **childframe** class will be assigned to the **frm** object of the **Frame** class. Here, a call will be made to the constructor **childframe( )**. Next, the control will be transferred to the body of the **childframe( )** constructor and the title of the frame window will be set to Child Frame in the constructor body. The next statement of the **init( )** method will set the width and height of the frame window to **200** and **100**, respectively. The last statement **frm.setVisible(true)** of this method will make the frame window visible on the screen.

Lines 34 to 37
public void start( )
{
        frm.setVisible(true);
}
In these lines, the **start( )** method of the **Applet** class is overridden inside the **AppletFramedemo** class. Inside the body of the method, **setVisible( )** contains the **boolean** value **true** that will make the frame window visible on the screen. Whenever a call is made to the **start( )** method, an applet and a frame window will be displayed on the screen.

Lines 38 to 41
public void stop( )
{
        frm.setVisible(false);
}
In these lines, the **stop( )** method of the **Applet** class is overridden inside the **AppletFramedemo** class. Inside the body of the method, **setVisible( )** contains the **boolean** value **false** that will hide the frame window from the screen. Whenever a call is made to the **stop( )** method, it will hide both the applet and the frame window from the screen.

Lines 42 to 45
public void paint(Graphics g)
{
        g.drawString("Applet Window", 10,40);
}
These lines contain the definition of the **paint( )** method. The **drawString( )** method inside the body of the **paint( )** method will draw the **Applet Window** string in the applet window at the position 10,40.

The program will be compiled and executed, as shown in the following statements:

    D:\Java Projects\Ch11>javac Appletframedemo.java
    D:\Java Projects\Ch11>appletviewer Appletframedemo.java

The output of Example 2 is displayed in Figure 11-2.

Figure 11-2 *The output of Example 2*

WORKING WITH GRAPHICS

AWT supports a number of methods to work with graphical objects such as lines, rectangles, and so on. In Java, you can draw these graphics inside the windows such as applet, frame, or child frame. In this section, you will learn about how to draw graphics inside a window.

Drawing Lines

You can use the **drawLine( )** method of the **Graphics** class to draw lines inside a window. The syntax for using the **drawLine( )** method is as follows:

```
drawLine(int x, int y, int x1, int y1)
```

In this syntax, the integer variables **x** and **y** represent the start point of the line with respect to the **x** and **y** coordinates of the window. The **x1** and **y1** variables represent the end point of the line with respect to the **x** and **y** coordinates of the window.

Note

Here, the x and y coordinates are represented as pixels.

Example 3

The following example illustrates the use of the **drawLine( )** method. The program will draw certain lines on the specified positions within an applet window and display the applet window on the screen.

//Write a program to draw lines within an applet window
```
1    import java.awt.*;
2    import java.applet.*;
3    //<applet code="DrawLinedemo.class" width=400 height=200></applet>
4    public class DrawLinedemo extends Applet
5    {
6        public void paint(Graphics g)
7        {
8            g.drawLine(200, 0, 200, 200);
9            g.drawLine(0, 100, 400, 100);
10           g.drawLine(0, 0, 400, 200);
11           g.drawLine(400, 0, 0, 200);
12       }
13   }
```

Explanation

Line 8
g.drawLine(200, 0, 200, 200);
In this line, the **drawLine( )** method will draw a line starting from the pixel position 200(x), 0(y) and ending at 200(x1), 200(y1), as shown in Figure 11-3.

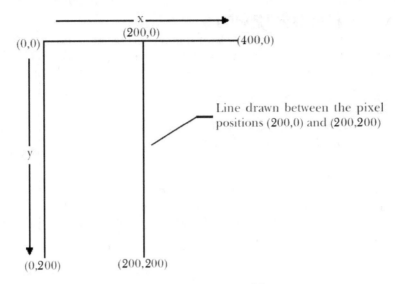

Figure 11-3 Representation of the output

The working of lines 9 to 11 is similar to that of line 8.

The output of Example 3 is displayed in Figure 11-4.

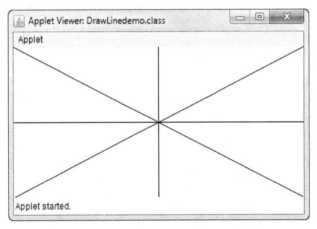

Figure 11-4 The output of Example 3

Drawing Rectangles
You can draw rectangles inside a window using the **drawRect( )** method. The syntax for using the **drawRect( )** method is as follows:

```
drawRect(int x, int y, int wid, int hgt)
```

In this syntax, the integer variables **x** and **y** specify the starting points and **wid** and **hgt** specify the width and height of the rectangle, respectively.

For example:

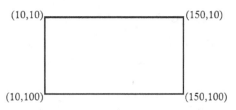

Figure 11-5 *Outline of a rectangle*

```
g.drawRect(10, 10, 150, 100);
```

In this example, the **drawRect( )** method with the specified integer variables creates a rectangle inside a window, as shown in Figure 11-5.

This example shows that the **drawRect( )** method can only draw the outline of a rectangle. But if you want to fill the rectangle, you can do so by using the **fillRect( )** method of the **Graphics** class. The syntax for using the **fillRect( )** method is as follows:

```
fillRect(int x, int y, int wid, int hgt)
```

In this syntax, the integer variables **x** and **y** specify the starting point or the top-left corner of a rectangle. And, the integer variables **wid** and **hgt** specify the width and height of the rectangle, respectively.

For example:

Figure 11-6 *Filled rectangle*

```
g.drawRect(10, 10, 150, 100);
g.fillRect(10, 10, 150, 100);
```

In this example, the **drawRect()** method draws a rectangle with specified dimensions and the **fillRect( )** method fills the rectangle with color (usually black), as shown in Figure 11-6.

You can also draw a rectangle with round corners using the **drawRoundRect( )** method of the **Graphics** class. The syntax for using the **drawRoundRect( )** method is as follows:

```
drawRoundRect(int x, int y, int wid, int hgt, int arcwid, int archgt)
```

In this syntax, the integer variables **x** and **y** specify the starting point (top-left corner) of a rectangle. And, the integer variables **wid** and **hgt** represent the width and height of the rectangle. Moreover, the integer variables **arcwid** and **archgt** specify the horizontal and vertical diameter of the arc, respectively.

You can also fill the round rectangle using the **fillRoundRect( )** method of the **Graphics** class. The syntax for using the **fillRoundRect( )** method is as follows:

```
fillRoundRect(int x, int y, int wid, int hgt, int arcwid, int archgt)
```

In this syntax, the integer variables **x** and **y** specify the starting point (top-left corner) of the rectangle. And, the integer variables **wid** and **hgt** represent the width and height of the rectangle, respectively. Also, the integer variables **arcwid** and **archgt** specify the horizontal and vertical diameters of arc of the rectangle, respectively.

Example 4

The following example illustrates the use of the **drawRect( )**, **fillRect( )**, **drawRoundRect( )**, and **fillRoundRect( )** methods of the **Graphics** class. The program will draw and fill rectangles in an applet window and display the window on the screen.

```
//Write a program to draw and fill rectangles
1    import java.awt.*;
2    import java.applet.*;
3    //<applet code= "RectangleDemo.class" width=275 height=150>
     </applet>
4    public class RectangleDemo extends Applet
5    {
6        public void paint(Graphics g)
7        {
8            g.drawRect(10, 10, 100, 50);
9            g.fillRect(120, 10, 140, 50);
10           g.drawRoundRect(10, 70, 100, 70, 10, 10);
11           g.fillRoundRect(120, 70, 140, 70, 10, 10);
12       }
13   }
```

The working of this program is similar to that of the previous program.

The output of Example 4 is displayed in Figure 11-7.

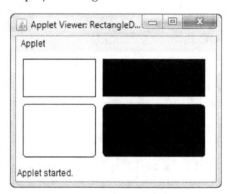

Figure 11-7 *The output of Example 4*

Drawing Circles and Ellipses

You can also draw circles and ellipses inside a window using the **drawOval( )** method of the **Graphics** class. The syntax for using the **drawOval( )** method is as follows:

```
drawOval(int x, int y, int wid, int hgt)
```

The **drawOval( )** method is used to draw an ellipse or a circle within a rectangle or a square whose starting point or the top-left corner is specified by the integer variables **x** and **y**. The width and height of the bounding areas are specified by the integer variables **wid** and **hgt**, respectively.

Like rectangles, you can also fill ellipses or circles using the **fillOval( )** method of the **Graphics** class. The syntax for using the **fillOval( )** method is as follows:

```
fillOval(int x, int y, int wid, int hgt)
```

The description of the **x, y, wid**, and **hgt** variables is the same as the variables of the **drawOval( )** method.

Example 5

The following example illustrates the use of the **drawOval( )** and **fillOval( )** methods. The program will draw and fill ellipses and circles in an applet window and display the window on the screen.

```
//Write a program to draw and fill ellipses and circles
1    import java.awt.*;
2    import java.applet.*;
3    //<applet code= "EllipseCircleDemo.class" width=310 height=300>
     </applet>
4    public class EllipseCircleDemo extends Applet
5    {
6        public void paint(Graphics g)
7        {
8            g.drawOval(10, 10, 100, 100);
9            g.drawOval(150, 10, 100, 70);
10           g.fillOval(10, 130, 140, 140);
11           g.fillOval(150, 90, 150, 100);
12       }
13   }
```

Explanation
Line 8
g.drawOval(10, 10, 100, 100);
In this line, the integer values **10, 10, 100**, and **100** specify the starting point (10,10), width(100) and height(100) of the bounding area of a square. Now, the **drawOval( )** method will draw a circle within this bounding area, as shown in Figure 11-8. Note that in this case, only the circle will be drawn within the applet window, not the bounding area.

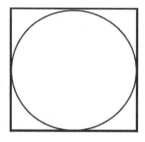

Figure 11-8 A circle within the bounding area

Line 9
g.drawOval(150, 10, 100, 70);
In this line, the integer values **150, 10, 100**, and **70** specify the starting point (150,10), width(100) and height(70) of the bounding area of a rectangle. Now, the **drawOval( )** method will draw an ellipse within that bounding area, as shown in Figure 11-9.

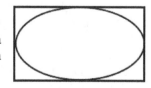

Figure 11-9 An ellipse within the bounding area

Line 10
g.fillOval(10, 130, 140, 140);
In this line, the **fillOval( )** method will fill the circle within the bounding area.

Line 11
g.fillOval(150, 90, 150, 100);
In this line, the **fillOval( )** method will fill the ellipse within the bounding area.

The output of Example 5 is displayed in Figure 11-10.

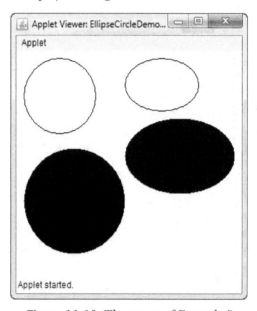

Figure 11-10 The output of Example 5

Drawing Arcs

You can draw circular or elliptical arcs using the **drawArc( )** method of the **Graphics** class. The syntax for using the **drawArc( )** method is as follows:

```
drawArc(int x, int y, int wid, int hgt, int startangle, int arcangle)
```

The **drawArc( )** method draws an arc within a rectangle whose starting point or top-left corner is specified by the integer variables **x** and **y**. The width and height of the rectangle is specified by the integer variables **wid** and **hgt**, respectively. The integer variable **startangle** specifies the beginning angle of an arc and **arcangle** specifies the angular extent of the arc with respect to the starting angle.

Note that you can draw only the outline of an arc using the **drawArc( )** method. To fill the arc, you can use the **fillArc( )** method of the **Graphics** class. The syntax for using the **fillArc( )** method is as follows:

```
fillArc(int x, int y, int wid, int hgt, int startangle, int arcangle)
```

The description of the **x**, **y**, **wid**, **hgt**, **startangle**, and **arcangle** variables is the same as the variables of the **drawArc( )** method.

Example 6

The following example illustrates the use of the **drawArc( )** and **fillArc( )** methods. The program will draw and fill arcs in an applet window and display the window on the screen.

//Write a program to draw and fill arcs
```
1    import java.awt.*;
2    import java.applet.*;
3    //<applet code="arcdemo.class" width=250 height=200></applet>
4    public class arcdemo extends Applet
5    {
6        public void paint(Graphics g)
7        {
8            g.drawArc(10, 10, 50, 40, 0, 105);
9            g.drawArc(70, 10, 100, 100, 0, 180);
10           g.fillArc(10, 70, 50, 80, 0, 105);
11           g.fillArc(70, 100, 100, 110, 0, 180);
12       }
13   }
```

Explanation

Line 8
g.drawArc(10, 10, 50, 40, 0, 105);
In this line, the integer values **10**, **10**, **50**, and **40** specify the starting point (10,10), width(50) and height(40) of the bounding area of a rectangle. Now, the **drawArc( )** method will draw an arc starting from 0-degree angle up to 105-degree angle within that bounding area, as shown in Figure 11-11. Note that here only the arc will be drawn within an applet window, not the bounding area.

Line 9
g.drawArc(70, 10, 100, 100, 0, 180);
In this line, the **drawArc( )** method will draw an arc within the bounding area. Here, the arc starts from 0-degree angle and extends up to 180-degree angle, as shown in Figure 11-12.

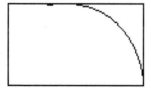

Figure 11-11 An arc of 105 degree angle within the bounding area

Figure 11-12 An arc of 180 degree angle within the bounding area

Line 10
g.fillArc(10, 70, 50, 80, 0, 105);
In this line, the **fillArc( )** method will fill an arc within the bounding area. Here, the arc will start from 0-degree angle and extend up to 105-degree angle, as shown in Figure 11-13.

Line 11
g.fillArc(70, 100, 100, 110, 0, 180);
In this line, the **fillArc( )** method will fill an arc within the bounding area. Here, the arc will start from 0-degree angle and extend up to 180-degree angle, as shown in Figure 11-14.

Figure 11-13 *A filled arc of 105*   *Figure 11-14* *A filled arc of 180*
degree angle within the bounding area   *degree angle within the bounding area*

The output of Example 6 is displayed in Figure 11-15.

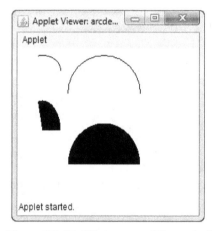

Figure 11-15 *The output of Example 6*

Drawing Polygons

You can draw a polygon with different line segments inside a window using the **drawPolygon( )** method of the **Graphics** class. The syntax for using the **drawPolygon( )** method is given next:

```
drawPolygon(int x[ ], int y[ ], int numberpoints)
```

In this syntax, the integer arrays **x** and **y** contain coordinates that define the endpoints of a polygon. The integer variable **numberpoints** specifies the total number of coordinate pairs that are defined by both the **x** and **y** arrays.

The **drawPolygon( )** method draws only the outline of a closed polygon whose endpoints are defined by **x** and **y** arrays. You can also fill a polygon using the **fillPolygon( )** method. The syntax for using the **fillPolygon( )** method is as follows:

```
fillPolygon(int x[ ], int y[ ], int numberpoints)
```

The description of the integer variables of the **fillPolygon( )** method is the same as the variables of the **drawPolygon( )** method.

Example 7

The following example illustrates the use of the **drawPolygon( )** and **fillPolygon( )** methods. The program will draw and fill polygons in an applet window and display the window on the screen.

//Write a program to draw and fill polygons

```
1    import java.awt.*;
2    import java.applet.*;
3    //<applet code= "polygondemo.class" width=200 height=150></applet>
4    public class polygondemo extends Applet
5    {
6        public void paint(Graphics g)
7        {
8            int x[ ] = {30, 10, 30, 50, 70, 50};
9            int y[ ] = {10, 30, 50, 50, 30, 10};
10           int numberpoints = 6;
11           g.drawPolygon(x, y, numberpoints);
12           int x1[ ] = {100, 80, 100, 120, 140, 120};
13           int y1[ ] = {10, 30, 50, 50, 30, 10};
14           g.fillPolygon(x1, y1, numberpoints);
15       }
16   }
```

Explanation
Line 8
int x[ ] = {30, 10, 30, 50, 70, 50};
In this line, six integer values are assigned to the integer type array **x[ ]** as its coordinates.

Line 9
int y[ ] = {10, 30, 50, 50, 30, 10};
In this line, six integer values are assigned to the integer type array **y[ ]** as its coordinates.

Line 10
int numberpoints = 6;
In this line, the integer value **6** is assigned to the integer variable **numberpoints**. This integer value specifies the total number of endpoints that are defined by the integer arrays **x** and **y**.

Line 11
g.drawPolygon(x, y, numberpoints);
In this line, the integer type arrays **x**, **y**, and the value of the integer variable **numberpoints** will be passed as arguments to the **drawPolygon( )** method. Now, the method will draw a closed polygon on the endpoints ((30, 10), (10, 30), (30, 50), (50, 50), (70, 30), (50, 10)) defined by the arrays **x** and **y**.

Line 14
g.fillPolygon(x1, y1, numberpoints);
In this line, the integer type arrays **x1**, **y1**, and the value of the integer variable **numberpoints** will be passed as arguments to the **fillPolygon( )** method. Now, the method will fill a closed polygon on the endpoints ((100, 10), (80, 30), (100, 50), (120, 50), (140, 30), (120, 10)) defined by the arrays **x1** and **y1**.

The output of Example 7 is displayed in Figure 11-16.

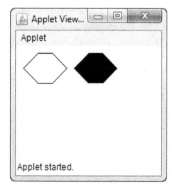

Figure 11-16 *The output of Example 7*

AWT CONTROLS
There are various controls which are used to design GUI using AWT. Most commonly used controls are discussed next.

Label Controls
A **Label** control is an object of the **Label** type and is used to place text in a container. The text of a label is the read-only text that a user cannot modify directly. However, you can modify the text of a label using the application program.

Constructors of the Label Class
The **Label** class provides the following constructors that can be used to create a label object.

```
Label( )
Label(String txt)
Label(String txt, int align)
```

The **Label( )** constructor creates a label object that contains an empty string. This type of label object is also known as blank label. The **Label(String txt)** constructor creates a label object with a string specified by the **txt** string object. Here, the string is left justified. The **Label(String txt, int align)** constructor creates a label object with a string specified by the **txt** string object and the alignment of the string is specified by the integer variable **align**. Here, the integer variable **align** can have one of the following values:

```
Label.LEFT          //Used for left justification
Label.RIGHT         //Used for right justification
Label.CENTER        //Used for center justification
```

Setting the Text of a Label Object

After creating a label object, you can set its text using the **setText( )** method of the **Label** class. The syntax for using the **setText( )** method is as follows:

```
void setText(String txt)
```

In this syntax, the text of a label object is set to string that is specified by the **txt** string object.

You can obtain the text string of a label using the **getText( )** method of the **Label** class. The syntax for using the **getText( )** method is as follows:

```
String getText( )
```

In this syntax, the text string of a label object is returned.

Setting the Alignment of a Text

You can set the alignment of the text of a label using the **setAlignment( )** method of the **Label** class. The syntax for using the **setAlignment( )** method is as follows:

```
void setAlignment(int align)
```

In this syntax, the alignment of text of a label is set to the value of the integer variable **align**. The value of the **align** variable can be one of these three values: **Label.LEFT(0)**, **Label.RIGHT(2)**, and **Label.CENTER(1)**.

You can also obtain the current alignment of the text of a label object using the **getAlignment( )** method of the **Label** class. The syntax for using the **getAlignment( )** method is given next:

```
int getAlignment( )
```

In this syntax, the current alignment of the text string of the label object is returned.

Example 8

The following example illustrates the method to create label objects. Also, in this example, you will use the **setText( )**, **getText( )**, **setAlignment( )**, and **getAlignment( )** methods. The program will create three label objects and add them to applet window.

//Write a program to create three labels

```
1   import java.awt.*;
2   import java.awt.event.*;
3   class close extends WindowAdapter
4   {
5       public void windowClosing (WindowEvent event)
6       {
7           System.exit (0);
8       }
9   }
10  public class LabelDemo extends Frame
11  {
12      public LabelDemo()
13      {
14          close obj = new close( );
15          addWindowListener(obj);
16          Label l1 = new Label("First label left aligned", Label.LEFT);
17          Label l2 = new Label("Second label center aligned", Label.CENTER);
18          Label l3 = new Label("Third Label", Label.LEFT);
19          String text = l3.getText( );
20          int align = l3.getAlignment( );
21          l3.setText("Third label right aligned");
22          l3.setAlignment(Label.RIGHT);
23          add(l1);
24          add(l2);
25          add(l3);
26          System.out.println("Before change, the third label text is "
            +text);
27          System.out.println("Before change, the third label alignment
            is " +align);
28          setTitle("Label Demo");
29          setSize(450, 200);
30          setLayout(new GridLayout(3,1));
31          setVisible(true);
32      }
33      public static void main(String args[ ])
34      {
35          LabelDemo l=new LabelDemo();
36      }
37  }
```

Explanation

Line 16

Label L1 = new Label("First label left aligned", Label.LEFT);

In this line, **L1** is an object of the **Label** type and creates **First label left aligned** text string with **LEFT** alignment.

The working of lines 17 and 18 is similar to that of line 16.

Line 19

String text = L3.getText( );

In this line, a call is made to the **getText( )** method with the label object **L3**. Here, the method returns the current text string which is available in the label object **L3**. Next, the resultant text string will be assigned to the **text** string object.

Line 20

int align = L3.getAlignment( );

In this line, a call is made to the **getAlignment( )** method with the label object **L3**. The method returns the current alignment of the label object **L3**. Here, the method will return 0 because the label is left justified. Next, the resultant integer value will be assigned to the integer variable **align**.

Line 21

L3.setText("Third label right aligned");

In this line, a call is made to the **setText( )** method with the label object **L3**. As a result, method will set the new text string **Third label right aligned** of the label object **L3**. Now, the old text string **Third Label** will be replaced with the new text string **Third label right aligned**.

Line 22

L3.setAlignment(Label.RIGHT);

In this line, a call is made to the **setAlignment( )** method with the label object **L3**. As a result, method will set the new alignment **Label.RIGHT** of the label object **L3**.

Line 23

add(L1);

In this line, the **add( )** method will add the label object **L1**, which is passed as an argument.

The working of lines 24 and 25 is similar to that of line 23.

Line 30

setLayout(new GridLayout(3,1));

In this line, the **setLayout( )** method will set the layout of the window to **GridLayout**. Here, the grid will contain three rows and one column. You will learn more about this method later in this chapter.

The output of Example 8 is displayed in Figure 11-17.

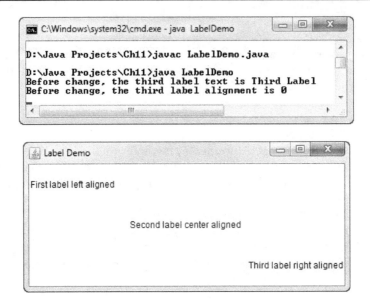

Figure 11-17 *The output of Example 8*

Button Controls

The **Button** controls are the most commonly used components in a GUI application. To create buttons, the **Button** class is used. As these buttons contain labels, they are known as labeled buttons. Whenever a button is pressed, it generates an event and the application performs an action.

Constructors of the Button Class

The **Button** class provides the following constructors to create a button object.

```
Button( )
Button(String text)
```

In these constructors, the first constructor **Button( )** creates a button without a label. Whereas, the second constructor **Button(String text)** creates a button that contains a label, which is specified by the **text** string object.

Setting the Label of a Button

After creating the button, you can set its label by using the **setLabel( )** method of the **Button** class. The syntax for using the **setLabel( )** method is as follows:

```
void setLabel(String txt)
```

In this syntax, the label of a button is set to string that is specified by the **txt** string object.

You can also obtain the current label of a button using the **getLabel( )** method of the **Button** class. The syntax for using the **getLabel( )** method is as follows:

```
String getLabel( )
```

In this syntax, the **getLabel( )** method will return the label of a button.

Example 9

The following example illustrates the method to create buttons and the concept of handling events generated by buttons. The program will create two buttons and add them to an applet window. Also, the program will display the output.

```
//Write a program to create two buttons
1    import java.awt.*;
2    import java.applet.*;
3    import java.awt.event.*;
4    //<applet code= "ButtonDemo.class" width=200 height=100></applet>
5    public class ButtonDemo extends Applet implements ActionListener
6    {
7        Button btn1, btn2;
8        public void init( )
9        {
10           btn1 = new Button("Red");
11           btn2 = new Button("Cyan");
12           add(btn1);
13           add(btn2);
14           btn1.addActionListener(this);
15           btn2.addActionListener(this);
16       }
17       public void actionPerformed(ActionEvent e)
18       {
19           String str = e.getActionCommand( );
20           if(str.equals("Red"))
21           {
22               btn1.setBackground(Color.red);
23           }
24           else if(str.equals("Cyan"))
25           {
26               btn2.setBackground(Color.cyan);
27           }
28       }
29   }
```

Explanation
Line 5
public class ButtonDemo extends Applet implements ActionListener
In this line, the **ButtonDemo** class inherits the **Applet** class and implements the **ActionListener** interface. This interface defines the **actionPerformed( )** method, which is called when an action event is generated by a button.

Line 7
Button btn1, btn2;
In this line, **btn1** and **btn2** are declared as objects of the **Button** type.

Line 10
btn1 = new Button("Red");
In this line, the object **btn1** is created as a button, which contains the **Red** text string as its label.

Line 11
btn2 = new Button("Cyan");
In this line, the object **btn2** is created as a button, which contains the **Cyan** text string as its label.

Line 12
add(btn1);
In this line, the **add( )** method will add the button **btn1** to the applet window, which is passed as an argument to it in the applet window.

Line 13
add(btn2);
In this line, the **add( )** method will add the button **btn2**, which is passed as an argument to it in the applet window.

Line 14
btn1.addActionListener(this);
In this line, the **addActionListener( )** method will add an event listener to the **btn1** button. Now, the listener will receive the action event notification that is generated by the **btn1** button. Here, **this** represents the current listener.

Line 15
btn2.addActionListener(this);
In this line, the **addActionListener( )** method will add an event listener to the **btn2** button. Now, the listener will receive the action event notification that is generated by the **btn2** button.

Lines 18 to 29
```
public void actionPerformed(ActionEvent e)
{
        String str = e.getActionCommand( );
        if(str.equals("Red"))
        {
                btn1.setBackground(Color.red);
        }
        else if(str.equals("Cyan"))
        {
                btn2.setBackground(Color.cyan);
        }
}
```

These lines contain the definition of the **actionPerformed( )** method. A call will be made to this method whenever an event is generated and an object of the **ActionEvent** class is passed as an argument to it. The object of the **ActionEvent** class, passed as an argument to the **actionPerformed( )** method, contains both the reference and the label of the button, which generates the event.

For example, when you click on the **Red** labeled button, an event will be generated and a call will be made to the **actionPerformed( )** method. Next, the object **e** of the **ActionEvent** class contains the **Red** label of the **btn1** button. Inside the body of the method, the **getActionCommand( )** method will return the label of the button, which generates an event, and this label will be assigned to the **str** string object. Next, in the **if** statement, the value of the **str** string object will be compared with the **Red** string with the help of the **equals( )** method. If both strings are equal, the background of the **btn1** button will be set to red. Otherwise, the **else if** statement will be executed and the background of the **btn2** button will be set to cyan.

The output of Example 9 is displayed in Figure 11-18.

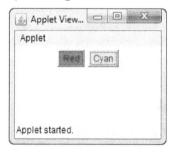

Figure 11-18 *The output of Example 9*

TextField Controls

A text field is a component that provides single-line text area in which a user can enter text. As the text in a text field is editable, a user can directly edit it. The **TextField** class is used to implement a text field.

Constructors of the TextField Class

The **TextField** class provides the following constructors that can be used to create a text field object.

```
TextField( )
TextField(int columns)
TextField(String str)
TextField(String str, int columns)
```

The **TextField( )** constructor creates a text field with default specification. The constructor **TextField(int columns)** creates a text field with maximum width specified by the integer variable **columns**. Here, the maximum width specifies the total number of characters that a user can enter in a text field. The **TextField(String str)** constructor creates a text field that contains a text string specified by the **str** string object. The **TextField(String str, int columns)** constructor creates a text field that contains a text string specified by the **str** string object and the integer variable **columns** to set the maximum width of the text field.

Selecting a Portion of the Text in a Text Field

You can select a particular portion of the text contained in a text field using the **select( )** method.

The syntax for using the **select( )** method is as follows:

```
void select(int start, int end)
```

In this syntax, the sequence of characters which begins from **start** and ends with **end** is selected.

You can also select a particular portion of a text in the text field using the **getSelectedText( )** method. The syntax for using the **getSelectedText( )** method is as follows:

```
String getSelectedText( )
```

In this syntax, the **getSelectedText( )** method will return the selected text string.

Checking the Text in a Text Field

You can check whether the text in a text field is editable or not by using the **isEditable( )** method. The syntax for using the **isEditable( )** method is as follows:

```
boolean isEditable( )
```

In this syntax, if the text in a text field is editable, the **isEditable( )** method returns true. Otherwise, it returns false.

Setting a Special Character in a Text Field

You can set a special character for certain type of confidential text such as passwords using the **setEchoChar( )** method. The syntax for using the **setEchoChar( )** method is as follows:

```
void setEchoChar(char ch)
```

In this syntax, the contents of the text field are displayed in the form of a special character that is specified by the character variable **ch**.

Example 10

The following example illustrates the method to create text fields and also the concept of handling events generated by text fields. The program will create two text fields and add them to an applet window.

//Write a program to create two text fields
```
1    import java.awt.*;
2    import java.applet.*;
3    import java.awt.event.*;
4    //<applet code= "TextFieldDemo.class" width=600 height=150></applet>
5    public class TextFieldDemo extends Applet implements ActionListener
6    {
7        Label login, pass;
8        TextField loginid, password;
9        public void init( )
10       {
```

```
11            login = new Label("Login ID");
12            pass = new Label("Password");
13            loginid = new TextField(20);
14            password = new TextField(20);
15            password.setEchoChar('#');
16            add(login);
17            add(loginid);
18            add(pass);
19            add(password);
20            password.addActionListener(this);
21    }
22    public void actionPerformed(ActionEvent e)
23    {
24        if(e.getSource( )==password)
25        {
26            repaint( );
27            password.setText(loginid.getSelectedText( ));
28        }
29    }
30    public void paint(Graphics g)
31    {
32        g.drawString("The login ID entered by you is: "
             +loginid.getText( ), 10, 100);
33        g.drawString("The password assigned to you is: "
             +password.getText( ), 10, 120);
34    }
33 }
```

Explanation
Line 13
loginid = new TextField(20);
In this line, **loginid** is created as a text field object of the **TextField** type. The maximum width of the text field is set to 20 columns.

The working of line 14 is similar to that of line 13.

Line 15
password.setEchoChar('#');
In this line, the **setEchoChar( )** method will set the text of the text field **password** to a special character **#**. Now, whole text of the text field **password** will be displayed only in **#** characters.

Line 20
password.addActionListener(this);
In this line, an **ActionListener** will be added to the text field **password**. Next, the listener will receive the action event notification generated by the text field **password**. Here, **this** represents the current listener.

Lines 23 to 30
public void actionPerformed(ActionEvent e)
{

      if(e.getSource( )==password)
      {

            repaint( );
            password.setText(loginid.getSelectedText( ));

      }

}

These lines contain the definition of the **actionPerformed( )** method. This method will be called when a particular portion or whole text in the text field **password** is selected. Next, press the ENTER key. When an event is generated, the control will be transferred to this method and the body of this method will be executed. Inside the body of the method, the **if** statement will check the source of the event with the **getSource( )** method. Next, the event source will be compared with the text field **password**. If the comparison returns the **boolean** value true, the body of the **if** statement will be executed. Inside the body of the **if** statement, the **repaint( )** method will again draw the applet window on the screen. Next, the **setText( )** method will set the text, which is selected from the **loginid** and **password** text fields.

The output of the Example 10 is displayed in Figure 11-19.

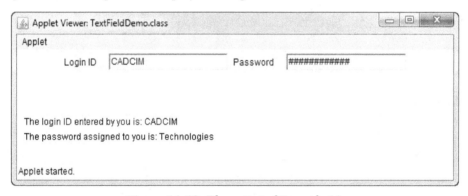

Figure 11-19 The output of Example 10

Check Box Controls

A check box is a graphical component, which has two states: on and off. Each check box contains a label, which describes the option that is represented by the check box. When you select a check box, a check mark is displayed inside the box. This check mark indicates that you have accepted the option that the check box contains. You can create a check box using the **Checkbox** class.

Constructors of the Checkbox Class

The **Checkbox** class provides the following constructors to create a text field object:

```
Checkbox( )
Checkbox(String str)
Checkbox(String str, boolean state)
Checkbox(String str, boolean state, CheckboxGroup grp)
```

In these constructors, the **Checkbox( )** constructor creates a check box that is without a label string. The **Checkbox(String str)** constructor creates a check box with a label string represented by the **str** string object. The **Checkbox(String str, boolean state)** constructor creates a check box with a label string, which is represented by the **str** string object, and the **state** boolean type variable, which represents the initial state of the check box. If the **state** variable contains true, the check box will be initially checked. Otherwise, it will be clear. The **Checkbox(String str, boolean state, CheckboxGroup grp)** constructor creates a check box with a label string, which is represented by the **str** string object, and the **state** boolean type variable which represents the initial state of the check box. Here, the **grp** object of the **CheckboxGroup** class represents the group in which the check box is included. If the check box is not included into the group, the value of the **grp** object will be **null**.

Setting the State of a Check Box

You can set the state of a check box, after you have created it by using the **setState( )** method of the **Checkbox** class. The syntax for using the **setState( )** method is as follows:

```
void setState(boolean state)
```

In this syntax, the state of a check box is set with the new state that is specified by the value of the **boolean** variable **state**.

You can also obtain the current state of a check box using the **getState( )** method of the **Checkbox** class. The syntax for using the **getState( )** method is as follows:

```
boolean getState( )
```

In this syntax, the current state of a check box is returned.

Setting the Label of a Check Box

After creating a check box, you can set its label by using the **setLabel( )** method of the **Checkbox** class. The syntax for using the **setLabel( )** method is as follows:

```
void setLabel(String str)
```

In this syntax, the label of a check box is set with the new label string specified by **str**.

You can also obtain the current label string of a check box using the **getLabel( )** method of the **Checkbox** class. The syntax for using the **getLabel( )** method is as follows:

```
String getLabel( )
```

In this syntax, the **getLabel( )** method will return the current label string of a check box.

Example 11

The following example illustrates the method to create check boxes and also the concept of handling events generated by check boxes. The program will create two check boxes and add them to an applet window. Also, the program will display the output.

//Write a program to create two check boxes

```
1    import java.awt.*;
2    import java.applet.*;
3    import java.awt.event.*;
4    //<applet code="CheckboxDemo.class" width=300 height=150></applet>
5    public class CheckboxDemo extends Applet implements ItemListener
6    {
7        String str = "You have selected: ";
8        String msg = " ";
9        Checkbox cbmusic, cbvideo;
10       public void init( )
11       {
12           cbmusic = new Checkbox("Music");
13           cbvideo = new Checkbox("Video", false);
14           add(cbmusic);
15           add(cbvideo);
16           cbmusic.addItemListener(this);
17           cbvideo.addItemListener(this);
18       }
19       public void itemStateChanged(ItemEvent e)
20       {
21           repaint( );
22       }
23       public void paint(Graphics g)
24       {
25           int x = 10, y =100;
26           if(cbmusic.getState()==false && cbvideo.getState()==false)
27           {
28               g.drawString("No option Selected", x, y);
29           }
30           else
31           {
32               if(cbmusic.getState( ) == true)
33               {
34                   msg = cbmusic.getLabel( );
35                   g.drawString(str+msg, x, y);
36               }
37               if(cbvideo.getState( ) == true)
38               {
39                   msg = cbvideo.getLabel( );
40                   g.drawString(str+msg, x, y+20);
41               }
42           }
43       }
44   }
```

Explanation

Line 5

public class CheckboxDemo extends Applet implements ItemListener

In this line, the **CheckboxDemo** class inherits the **Applet** class and implements the **ItemListener** interface.

Line 9
Checkbox cbmusic, cbvideo;
In this line, **cbmusic** and **cbvideo** are declared as objects of the **Checkbox** class.

Line 12
cbmusic = new Checkbox("Music");
In this line, a new check box is created with the **Music** label. Here, the initial state of the check box is not mentioned in the constructor, so the default state is set to false.

Line 13
cbvideo = new Checkbox("Video", false);
In this line, a new check box is created with the **Video** label and the initial state of this is set to false.

Lines 14 and 15
add(cbmusic);
add(cbvideo);
In these lines, the **cbmusic** and **cbvideo** check boxes are added by the **add( )** method in the applet window.

Line 16
cbmusic.addItemListener(this);
In this line, an event listener is added to the **cbmusic** check box. It handles all the item events that are generated by the **cbmusic** check box.

The working of line 17 is similar to line 16.

Lines 19 to 22
public void itemStateChanged(ItemEvent e)
{
      repaint( );
}
These lines contain the definition of the **itemStateChanged( )** method of the **ItemListener** interface. Whenever an item is selected or deselected by a user, a call is made to this method. Inside the body of the method, a call is made to the **repaint( )** method that redraws the applet window.

Lines 26 to 29
if(cbmusic.getState()==false && cbvideo.getState()==false)
{
      g.drawString("No option Selected", x, y);
}
Here, inside the **if** statement, the **getState( )** method returns the current states of the **cbmusic** and **cbvideo** check boxes. If the current state of both check boxes is false, the **drawString( )** method will draw the **No option Selected** string at the position 10, 100. Otherwise, the statement associated with the **if** statement will be skipped and the control will be transferred to the associated **else** block.

Lines 30 to 42

```
else
{
        if(cbmusic.getState( ) == true)
        {
                msg = cbmusic.getLabel( );
                g.drawString(str+msg, x, y);
        }
        if(cbvideo.getState( ) == true)
        {
                msg = cbvideo.getLabel( );
                g.drawString(str+msg, x, y+20);
        }
}
```

The **else** block will be executed when the condition given in the **if** statement (line 26) evaluates to false. Otherwise, the **else** block will be skipped. Inside the **else** block, the first **if** statement will check whether the state of the **cbmusic** check box is equal to **true** or not. As the condition evaluates to true, the control will be transferred inside the **if** statement where the **getLabel( )** method will return the current **Music** label of the **cbmusic** check box and this label will be assigned to the **msg** string object. In the next statement, the **drawString( )** method will draw the **You have selected: Music** string at the position 10, 100. The working of the second **if** statement is the same as that of the first **if** statement.

The output of Example 11 without any check box selection is displayed in Figure 11-20.

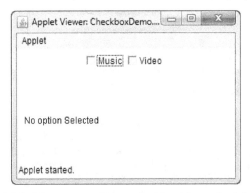

Figure 11-20 The output of Example 11 with no check box selected

In this window, when you select the **Music** labeled check box, an item event is generated and a call is made to the **itemStateChanged( )** method. As a result, applet window gets modified, as shown in Figure 11-21.

In Figure 11-21, only the **Music** check box is selected. Now, when you select the **Video** check box, again an item event is generated and a call is made to the **itemStateChanged( )** method. As a result, the applet window gets modified again, as shown in Figure 11-22.

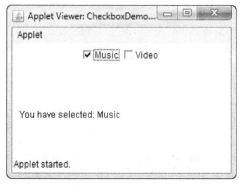
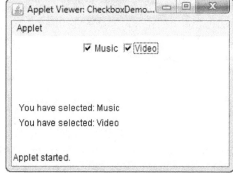

Figure 11-21 *The output of Example 11 after selecting the **Music** check box*

Figure 11-22 *The output of Example 11 after selecting the **Video** check box*

Choice Controls

A choice control is a pop-up menu that contains a list of items. A **Choice** control is created by using the **Choice** class. In this control, a user can select only one item at a time. Whenever a user clicks on the **Choice** control, a pop-up list of items with the item selected by the user as the current title is displayed. In the **Choice** control, each item is represented by a label string.

Constructor of the Choice Class

The **Choice** class provides the following default constructor to create an empty list:

```
Choice( )
```

For example:

```
Choice ch = new Choice( );
```

In this example, **ch** is defined as a new choice control that contains an empty list.

Adding an Item into a Choice Control

You can add an item into a choice control using the **add( )** method of the **Choice** class. The syntax for using the **add( )** method is as follows:

```
void add(String label)
```

In this syntax, the item represented by the **label** string object is added to the **Choice** control.

For example:

```
Choice ch = new Choice( );
ch.add("Item1");
```

In this example, a new choice control **ch** with an empty list is created. In the next line, an item represented by the **Item1** label string is added to the choice control **ch** with the help of the **add( )** method.

Obtaining the Currently Selected Item of a Choice Control

You can obtain the currently selected item of a choice control using the **getSelectedItem( )** or the **getSelectedIndex( )** method. The syntaxes for using the **getSelectedItem( )** and **getSelectedIndex( )** methods are as follows:

```
String getSelectedItem( )
int getSelectedIndex( )
```

In these syntaxes, the **getSelectedItem( )** method returns the label string that represents the currently selected item, whereas the **getSelectedIndex( )** method returns an integer value that represents the index of the currently selected item. In the **Choice** control, the index starts from 0.

Obtaining the Number of Items in a Choice Control

You can also obtain the total number of items contained in a list using the **getItemCount( )** method. The syntax for using the **getItemCount( )** method is as follows:

```
int getItemCount( )
```

In this syntax, the **getItemCount( )** method returns an integer value, which represents the total number of items contained in a list.

Setting an Item as the Currently Selected Item

You can set a particular item as the currently selected item using the **select(String label)** or **select(int index)** methods. The syntaxes for using the **select(String label)** and **select(int index)** methods are as follows:

```
void select(String label)
void select(int index)
```

In these syntaxes, the first form of the **select( )** method sets the item, whose label string is specified by **label** as the currently selected item. The second form of the **select( )** method sets the item, whose index value is specified by the integer variable **index** as the currently selected item.

Obtaining the Label String of a Particular Item from the List

You can also obtain the label string of a particular item from a list using the **getItem( )** method. The syntax for using the **getItem( )** method is as follows:

```
String getItem(int index)
```

In this syntax, the **getItem( )** method returns the label string of an item whose index value is specified by the integer variable **index**.

Example 12

The following example illustrates the method to create a **Choice** control and also the concept of handling events generated by items of the **Choice** control. The program will create a **Choice** control and add it to the applet window. Also, the program will display the output.

//Write a program to create a choice control

```
1    import java.awt.*;
2    import java.applet.*;
3    import java.awt.event.*;
4    //<applet code="ChoicelistDemo" width=300 height=150></applet>
5    public class ChoicelistDemo extends Applet implements ItemListener
6    {
7        Label lblname, lblage;
8        Choice name, age;
9        String str = "The name is: ";
10       String str1 = "The age is: ";
11       public void init( )
12       {
13           lblname = new Label("Name:");
14           lblage = new Label("Age:");
15           name = new Choice( );
16           age = new Choice( );
17           name.add("Williams");
18           name.add("John");
19           name.add("Smith");
20           name.add("Tom");
21           age.add("1-20");
22           age.add("21-40");
23           age.add("41-60");
24           age.add("61-80");
25           age.add("81-100");
26           age.add("> 100");
27           add(lblname);
28           add(name);
29           add(lblage);
30           add(age);
31           name.addItemListener(this);
32           age.addItemListener(this);
33       }
34       public void itemStateChanged(ItemEvent e)
35       {
36           repaint( );
37       }
38       public void paint(Graphics g)
39       {
40           g.drawString(str + name.getSelectedItem( ), 10, 100);
41           g.drawString(str1 + age.getSelectedItem( ), 10, 120);
42       }
43   }
```

Explanation

Lines 15 and 16

name = new Choice( );

age = new Choice( );

In these lines, the **name** and **age** choice controls are created. Here, both the controls contain only empty item lists.

Lines 17 to 20
name.add("Williams");
name.add("John");
name.add("Smith");
name.add("Tom");
In these lines, four items represented by the label strings **Williams**, **John**, **Smith**, and **Tom** are added to the list of the choice control **name**. The label string **Williams**, which is at the index 0, will be displayed by default as the currently selected item from the list.

Lines 21 to 26
age.add("1-20");
age.add("21-40");
age.add("41-60");
age.add("61-80");
age.add("81-100");
age.add("> 100");
In these lines, six items represented by the label strings **1-20**, **21-40**, **41-60**, **61-80**, **81-100**, and **>100** are added to the list of the choice control **age**. The label string **1-20**, which is at the index 0, will be displayed by default as the currently selected item from the list.

Line 28
add(name);
In this line, the **name** choice control is added to the applet window.

Line 30
add(age);
In this line, the **age** choice control is added to the applet window.

Line 31
name.addItemListener(this);
In this line, **ItemListener** is registered by the choice control **name**. Now, whenever an event is generated by an item of the choice control **name**, the event listener will be notified. Next, the listener will perform the specified action to handle the event.

The working of line 32 is similar to line 31.

Lines 34 to 37
public void itemStateChanged(ItemEvent e)
{
      repaint( );
}
In these lines, the **itemStateChanged( )** method of the **ItemListener** interface is overridden to handle the item event that is generated when an item either from the **name** or **age** choice controls is selected. Inside the body of the method, a call is made to the **repaint( )** method that redraws the applet window.

Line 40
g.drawString(str + name.getSelectedItem( ), 10, 100);
In this line, the **getSelectedItem( )** method obtains the currently selected item from the **name** choice control. Next, the resultant string will be drawn at the position 10,100.

The output of Example 12 with default selection is displayed in Figure 11-23.

In Figure 11-23, **Williams** and **1-20** are selected by default because both of them are at the 0th position in index. If you select another item from the **name** choice control such as **John, Smith**, and so on, or from the **age** choice control such as **21-40, 41-60**, and so on, an item event will be generated. Next, a call will be made to the **itemStateChanged( )** method that in turn will make a call to the **repaint( )** method and the applet window will get modified.

The output of Example 12 after selecting another item is displayed in Figure 11-24.

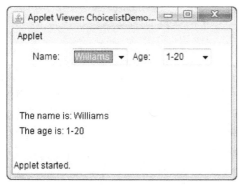

Figure 11-23 *The output of Example 12 with default selection*

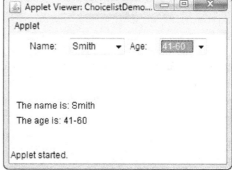

Figure 11-24 *The output of Example 12 after selecting another item*

List Controls
A list control is a scrolling list of text items. A user can select one or more than one item at a time from a list. Therefore, the list control is also known as multiple-choice list. You can create a list control by using an object of the **List** class.

Constructors of the List Class
The **List** class provides the following constructors to create a list control:

```
List( )
List(int total_items)
List(int total_items, boolean multiple_selection)
```

The first constructor **List( )** creates a single-selection list that allows a user to select only one item at a time. By default, only the first four items are displayed in the visible window. In the constructor **List(int total_items)**, the value of the integer variable **total_items** specifies the total number of list items to be displayed in the visible window. In the constructor **List(int total_items, boolean multiple_selection)**, if the value of the **boolean** variable **multiple_selection** is true, then a user can make multiple selections at a time. Otherwise, the list is treated as a single-selection list.

For example:

```
List lstfirst = new List( )
List lstsecond = new List(6)
List lstthird = new List(6, true)
```

In this example, the first statement creates a list control that displays only the first four items in the visible window and the list is treated as a single-selection list. The second statement creates a list control whose first six items are displayed in the visible window. The third statement creates a list control that is treated as a multiple-selection list and the first six items are displayed in the visible window.

Adding an Item into a List Control

You can add an item into a list control using the **add( )** method of the **List** class. This method can be used in the following two ways:

```
add(String label)
add(String label, int position)
```

In these statements, the first statement adds a text item specified by **label** at the end of the list. In the second statement, a text item is added to the index position that is specified by **position**. In a list control, an index begins from 0.

For example:

```
List name = new List( );
name.add("William");
name.add("Smith", 2);
name.add("John", 1);
```

In this example, the list control **name** is created and the text items **William, Smith**, and **John** are added to it. Here, the text items **Smith** and **John** are added to the index positions 2 and 1, respectively.

Setting an Item as the Currently Selected Item in a List Control

You can set a text item as the currently selected item in a scrolling list of text items using the **select( )** method of the **List** class. The syntax for using the **select( )** method is as follows:

```
void select(int position)
```

In this syntax, the text item, whose index position is specified by the integer variable **position** is set as the currently selected item in a list of items.

For example:

```
List name = new List( );
name.add("William");
name.add("Smith");
name.add("John");
name.select(1);
```

In this example, the **select( )** method sets the text item **Smith** (that is at the index position 1) as the currently selected item in the list control **name**.

Obtaining the Currently Selected Item from a List Control

You can obtain the text label or index of the currently selected item from a list control using the **getSelectedItem( )** or **getSelectedIndex( )** method. The syntaxes for using the **getSelectedItem( )** and **getSelectedIndex( )** methods are as follows:

```
String getSelectedItem( )
int getSelectedIndex( )
```

Here, the **getSelectedItem( )** method returns the text label of the currently selected item. For example, when you apply this method in the previous example in which the currently selected item was **Smith**, then this method will return the text label **Smith** as the result. On the other hand, the **getSelectedIndex( )** method returns the index position of the currently selected item. For example, if you apply this method in the previous example in which the currently selected item was **Smith**, you will get the integer value 1 as the result.

The methods discussed above are used only for single-selection lists where a user can select only a single item at a time. But, for multiple-selection lists, you can use the **getSelectedItems( )** and **getSelectedIndexes( )** methods. The syntaxes for using the **getSelectedItems( )** and **getSelectedIndexes( )** methods are as follows:

```
String [ ] getSelectedItems( )
int [ ] getSelectedIndexes( )
```

Here, the **getSelectedItems( )** method returns a string type array that contains text labels of all currently selected items. The **getSelectedIndexes( )** method returns an integer type array that contains index positions of all currently selected items.

Obtaining a Particular Item from a List Control

You can obtain a particular item from a list of items using the **getItem( )** method of the **List** class. The syntax for using the **getItem( )** method is as follows:

```
String getItem(int position)
```

In this syntax, the **getItem( )** method returns the text label of the item whose index position is specified by the integer variable **position**.

For example:

```
List name = new List( );
name.add("William");
name.add("Smith");
name.add("John");
----------;
----------;
String str = name.getItem(2);
```

In this example, the **getItem( )** method returns the label **John** (that is at the index position 2) and is assigned to the **str** string object.

Obtaining the Total Number of Items in a List

You can obtain the total number of items contained in a list using the **getItemCount( )** method of the **List** class. The syntax for using the **getItemCount( )** method is given next:

```
int getItemCount( )
```

In this syntax, the **int getItemCount( )** method returns an integer value that specifies the total number of items contained in a list.

For example:

```
List name = new List( );
name.add("William");
name.add("Smith");
name.add("John");
int total = name.getItemCount( );
```

In this example, the **getItemCount( )** method returns the integer value 3 because the list **name** contains three text items.

Example 13

The following example illustrates the method to create a list control and also the concept of handling events generated by the items of the control. The program will create a list control and add it to an applet window. Also, the program will display the output.

```
//Write a program to create a list control
1    import java.awt.*;
2    import java.applet.*;
3    import java.awt.event.*;
4    //<applet code= "ListDemo.class" width=300 height=150></applet>
5    public class ListDemo extends Applet implements ActionListener
6    {
7       List colors;
8       int i;
9       public void init( )
10      {
```

```
11          colors = new List ( );
12          colors.add("Red");
13          colors.add("Dark Green");
14          colors.add("Blue");
15          colors.add("Dark Gray");
16          colors.add("Magenta");
17          add(colors);
18          colors.addActionListener(this);
19      }
20      public void actionPerformed(ActionEvent e)
21      {
22          repaint( );
23      }
24      public void paint(Graphics g)
25      {
26          int i = colors.getSelectedIndex( );
27          String str = colors.getSelectedItem( );
28          switch(i)
29          {
30            case 0:
31            {
32                colors.setForeground(Color.red);
33                setForeground(Color.red);
34                g.drawString("You have selected: " +str,10,100);
35                break;
36            }
37            case 1:
38            {
39                colors.setForeground(Color.green);
40                setForeground(Color.green);
41                g.drawString("You have selected: " +str,10,100);
42                break;
43            }
44            case 2:
45            {
46                colors.setForeground(Color.blue);
47                setForeground(Color.blue);
48                g.drawString("You have selected: " +str,10,100);
49                break;
50            }
51            case 3:
52            {
53                colors.setForeground(Color.gray);
54                setForeground(Color.gray);
55                g.drawString("You have selected: " +str,10,100);
56                break;
57            }
58            case 4:
59            {
60                colors.setForeground(Color.magenta);
61                setForeground(Color.magenta);
62                g.drawString("You have selected: " +str,10,100);
63                break;
```

```
64                    }
65               default:
66               {
67                    colors.setForeground(Color.cyan);
68                    setForeground(Color.cyan);
69                    g.drawString("Please select an item from the list",
                          10,100);
70               }
71          }
72     }
73 }
```

Explanation

Line 11

colors = new List ( );

In this line, **colors** is created as a single-selection control **List** from which the end user can select only one item at a time. By default, the **colors** list control displays only the first four items in the visible window.

Lines 12 to 16

colors.add("Red");
colors.add("Dark Green");
colors.add("Blue");
colors.add("Dark Gray");
colors.add("Magenta");

In these lines, the text items **Red, Dark Green, Blue, Dark Gray,** and **Magenta** are added to the **colors** list control with the help of the **add( )** method.

Line 17

add(colors);

In this line, the **colors** list control is added to the applet window with the help of the **add( )** method.

Line 18

colors.addActionListener(this);

In this line, **ActionListener** is registered with the **colors** list control. The listener will notify and perform the required action each time when an event is generated by text items of the **colors** list control. Whenever a text item of the **colors** list control is double-clicked by the end user, an action event will be generated. After the event is generated, the listener will make a call to the **actionPerformed( )** method which is used to handle all types of action events.

Lines 20 to 23

public void actionPerformed(ActionEvent e)
{
        repaint( );
}

These lines contain the definition of the **actionPerformed( )** method. Whenever an event is generated, a call is made to this method to handle the event. Inside the body of the method, a call will be made to the **repaint( )** method, which is used to redraw the applet window on the screen.

Line 26
int i = colors.getSelectedIndex( );
In this line, the **getSelectedIndex( )** method returns the index value of the currently selected item in the **colors** list control. Next, the resultant value will be assigned to the integer variable **i**.

Line 27
String str = colors.getSelectedItem( );
In this line, the **getSelectedItem( )** method returns the label string of the currently selected item in the **colors** list control. Next, the resultant string will be assigned to the **str** string object.

Line 28
switch(i)
In this line, the **switch** statement is used and the integer variable **i** (that contains the index value of the currently selected item) is treated as a control variable. Here, the value of the integer variable **i** will be matched with different cases given inside the **switch** block. If the match is found, statements associated with that particular case will be executed and the remaining cases will be skipped. If no match is found, statements associated with the **default** case will be executed.

Lines 30 to 36
case 0:
{

       colors.setForeground(Color.red);
       setForeground(Color.red);
       g.drawString("You have selected: " +str,10,100);
       break;

}
In these lines, the statements associated with **case** will be executed, if the value of the **i** variable is equal to 0. Inside the block, the first statement will set the foreground color of the **colors** control list and the applet window to red. Now, the entire text in the applet window will be displayed in red color. In the next statement, the **drawString( )** method will display the following statement at the position 10, 100:

You have selected: Red

In the next line, the **break** statement will transfer the control outside the **switch** block and all remaining cases will be skipped.

The working of all remaining cases starting from case 1 to case 4 is similar that of case 0.

Lines 65 to 70
default:
{

       colors.setForeground(Color.cyan);
       setForeground(Color.cyan);
       g.drawString("Please select an item from the list",10,100);

}

These lines, which represent the **default** case, will be executed when no particular match is found in all the given cases. When the applet window is displayed for the first time, the **default** case will be executed because no item from the **colors** list control is selected. The working of the **default** case will be same as that of the case 0.

The output of Example 13 with default foreground color is displayed in Figure 11-25. In the applet window, no text item is selected from the **colors** list control. Therefore, the **default** case will be executed and the foreground color in the applet window will be set to cyan. When a user selects **Red** from the list control by double-clicking, an event will be generated. Next, a call will be made to the **actionPerformed( )** method that, in turn, will make a call to the **repaint( )** method. The **repaint( )** method in turn will make a call to the **paint( )** method. Inside the **paint( )** method, the **getSelectedIndex( )** method returns the index value 0 that will be assigned to the **i** variable. Here, the value of the **i** variable will be matched with the case 0 and the statements associated with it will be executed. As a result, the applet window will be redrawn, as shown in Figure 11-26.

Similarly, if you double click on any other text item from the **List** control, an event will be generated and the applet window will be redrawn and displayed on the screen.

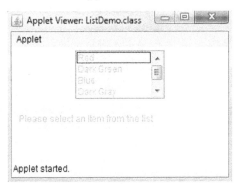

Figure 11-25 *The output of Example 13 with default foreground color*

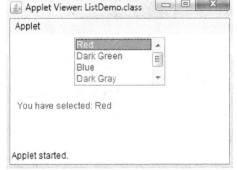

Figure 11-26 *The output of Example 13 after double-clicking on **Red** from the list*

Scroll Bar Controls

A scroll bar control is used when the information to be viewed extends beyond the visible area of a window. The scroll bar, which appears at the bottom of the window is known as horizontal scroll bar and the scroll bar that appears on the right of the window is known as the vertical scroll bar. Each scroll bar contains a slider and scroll arrows. You can create a scroll bar control by using an object of the **Scrollbar** class.

Constructors of the Scrollbar Class

The **Scrollbar** class provides the following constructors to create a scroll bar control:

```
Scrollbar( )
Scrollbar(int orientation)
Scrollbar(int orientation, int val, int size, int min, int max)
```

In these constructors, the first constructor **Scrollbar( )** creates a vertical scroll bar. The second constructor **Scrollbar(int orientation)** creates a scroll bar based on the value of the integer variable **orientation**. For example, if the value of the integer variable **orientation** is **Scrollbar.HORIZONTAL**, a horizontal scroll bar will be created. Whereas, if the value is **Scrollbar.VERTICAL**, a vertical scroll bar will be created. The third constructor creates a scroll bar whose orientation is specified by the integer variable **orientation**. In this constructor, the integer variable **val** specifies the initial values of the scroll bar; **min** and **max** specify the minimum and maximum values of the **val** variable; and the integer variable **size** specifies the size of the visible area of the scroll bar.

Example 14

The following example illustrates the method to create a horizontal scroll bar and also the concept of handling events generated while moving the slider or clicking on the scroll bar arrows. The program will create a horizontal scroll bar and add it to an applet window. Also, the program will display the output.

```
//Write a program to create a horizontal scroll bar
1    import java.applet.*;
2    import java.awt.*;
3    import java.awt.event.*;
4    //<applet code= "ScrollbarDemo" width=400 height=100></applet>
5    public class ScrollbarDemo extends Applet implements
     AdjustmentListener
6    {
7        Scrollbar hori;
8        public void init( )
9        {
10           hori = new  Scrollbar(Scrollbar.HORIZONTAL, 1, 1, 1, 100);
11           hori.addAdjustmentListener(this);
12           add(hori);
13           setLayout(new GridLayout(4,2));
14       }
15       public void adjustmentValueChanged(AdjustmentEvent e)
16       {
17           repaint( );
18       }
19       public void paint(Graphics g)
20       {
21           int val = hori.getValue( );
22           g.drawString("Slider is moved to position: " +val, 10, 75);
23       }
24   }
```

Explanation
Line 5
public class scrollbardemo extends Applet implements AdjustmentListener
In this line, the **scrolldemo** class inherits the **Applet** class and implements **AdjustmentListener** using the **implements** keyword.

Line 10
hori = new Scrollbar(Scrollbar.HORIZONTAL, 1, 1, 1, 100);
In this line, a horizontal scroll bar **hori** is created whose initial value is 1, size of the visible area is 1, minimum size is 1, and the maximum size is 100.

Line 11
hori.addAdjustmentListener(this);
In this line, **AdjustmentListener** will be registered with the **Scrollbar** object **hori**. This listener will be notified each time an event is generated by the scroll bar. This listener will perform the required action to handle the event.

Line 12
add(hori);
In this line, the horizontal scroll bar **hori** will be added to the applet window using the **add( )** method.

Lines 15 to 18
public void adjustmentValueChanged(AdjustmentEvent e)
{
        repaint( );
}
These lines contain the definition of the **adjustmentValueChanged( )** method. Whenever the slider of the scroll bar is moved or an arrow is clicked, an event will be generated and the listener will make a call to this method. This method will, in turn, make a call to the **repaint( )** method, which will make a call to the **paint( )** method and the applet window will be redrawn.

Lines 19 to 23
public void paint(Graphics g)
{
        int val = hori.getValue( );
        g.drawString("Slider is at position: " +val, 10, 100);
}
Inside the body of the **paint( )** method, the **getValue( )** method will return an integer value that specifies the current position of the slider. Next, the resultant value will be assigned to the **val** variable.

The output of Example 14 with initial position of slider is displayed in Figure 11-27.

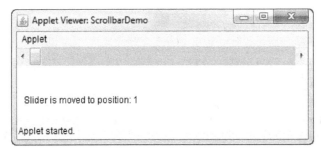

Figure 11-27 *The output of Example 14 with slider at initial position*

In Figure 11-27, the slider is at its initial position 1. Now, when you move the slider directly or when you click on an arrow using the mouse, an event will be generated and the applet window will be redrawn, as given in Figure 11-28.

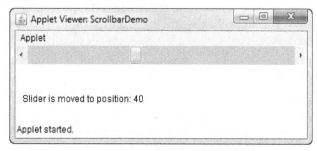

Figure 11-28 *The output of Example 14 after moving the slider*

TextArea Controls

As you learned earlier that a text field contains a single line of text, but in certain cases, a single line of text is not enough to enter complete text. For entering multi-line text, Java provides another AWT control, the **TextArea** control. A text area is a multi-line region in which you can enter or edit multiline text. You can use an object of the **TextArea** class to create a text area control.

Constructors of the TextArea Class

The **TextArea** class provides the following constructors to create a text area control:

```
TextArea( )
TextArea(String str)
TextArea(int rows, int columns)
TextArea(String str, int rows, int columns)
TextArea(String str, int rows, int columns, int scrollbar)
```

In these constructors, the first constructor creates an empty text area. The second constructor creates a new text area with a text string specified by **str**. The third constructor creates a new text area with the number of rows and columns specified by the **rows** and **columns** variables, respectively. The fourth constructor creates a new text area. This constructor specifies the text string that the text area will contain, and the **rows** and **columns** variables specify the number of rows and columns that the text area will contain. The last constructor creates a new text area with the specified text string, number of rows and columns, and the scroll bar that is specified by the integer variable **scrollbar**. Here, the **scrollbar** variable can contain any one value from the following four constants:

```
SCROLLBARS_BOTH or 0
SCROLLBARS_VERTICAL_ONLY or 1
SCROLLBARS_HORIZONTAL_ONLY or 2
SCROLLBARS_NONE or 3
```

Example 15

The following example illustrates the method to create a text area. The program will create a text area of 10 rows and 50 columns with the text string **Hello**. Also, the text area will contain both the horizontal and vertical scroll bars, add the text area into an applet window, and display the output on the screen.

```
//Write a program to create a text area
1    import java.awt.*;
2    import java.applet.*;
3    //<applet code= "TextAreaDemo.class" width=500 height=200>
     </applet>
4    public class TextAreaDemo extends Applet
5    {
6        TextArea ar;
7        public void init( )
8        {
9            ar = new TextArea("Hello", 10, 50, 0);
10           add(ar);
11       }
12   }
```

Explanation
Line 10
ar = new TextArea("Hello", 10, 50, 0);
In this line, a new text area **ar** is created. This text area contains 10 rows, 50 columns, both horizontal and vertical scroll bars, and the **Hello** text string.

Line 11
add(ar);
In this line, the text area **ar** will be added to the applet window using the **add( )** method.

The output of Example 15 is displayed in Figure 11-29.

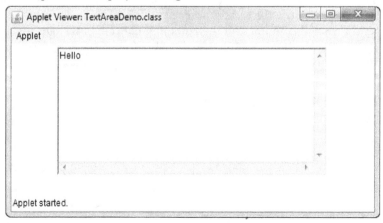

Figure 11-29 The output of Example 15

LAYOUT MANAGERS

In Java, the layout managers define how various components such as buttons, text fields, and so on can be added to a container such as applet, frame, and so on. A layout manager is an object of a class that implements the **LayoutManager** interface. A layout manager controls the position and size of components that are added into a container. Whenever a container is used, the default layout is used to position the components in it. But, if the container's default layout is not as per your requirement, you can easily set another layout manager for it. The AWT provides the following layout managers:

```
FlowLayout
BorderLayout
GridLayout
CardLayout
GridBagLayout
```

In these layout managers, the **FlowLayout**, **BorderLayout**, and **GridLayout** are the most commonly used layout managers. You will learn about these three layout managers in this section. The **CardLayout** and **GridBagLayout** layout managers are beyond the scope of this book.

FlowLayout

FlowLayout is the default layout manager for applets. This layout manager positions the components from left-to-right in a container just like the words are positioned in a text editor. In this layout, the components are placed in separate rows starting from the top-left corner of the container. When a row is filled with components, the layout moves to the next line and starts placing the remaining components. By default, this layout leaves an empty space of 5 pixels between any two consecutive components. In this layout, each row is center aligned by default. You can understand the placing of components in this type of layout easily by resizing, widening or narrowing the container. On doing so, the components move from one row to another according to the width of the container.

Constructors of the FlowLayout

The **java.awt.FlowLayout** provides the following constructors to create a new layout:

```
FlowLayout( )
FlowLayout(int align)
FlowLayout(int align, int hori, int vert)
```

In these constructors, the first constructor creates a layout with default specifications such as the rows are center aligned, space between the two components is 5 pixels in both horizontal and vertical directions, and so on. The second constructor creates a layout with the alignment specified by the integer variable **align**. This variable can have one of the following values:

1. FlowLayout.LEFT
2. FlowLayout.RIGHT
3. FlowLayout.CENTER
4. FlowLayout.LEADING
5. FlowLayout.TRAILING

This constructor also provides 5 pixels empty space between two components in both horizontal and vertical directions. The third constructor creates a layout with the alignment specified by the integer variable **align**; and the horizontal and vertical spaces between components are specified by the integer variables **hori** and **vert**, respectively.

Example 16

The following example illustrates the use of the **FlowLayout** layout manager. The program will set the layout of a frame window to **FlowLayout**, set the alignment of the layout to left, and display the container on the screen.

//Write a program to set the layout of a frame window to flow layout

```
1   import java.awt.*;
2   import java.awt.event.*;
3   class layoutdemo extends WindowAdapter
4   {
5      public void windowClosing (WindowEvent event)
6      {
7          System.exit (0);
8      }
9   }
10  class flowlayoutdemo extends Frame
11  {
12     Button btn1, btn2, btn3, btn4, btn5;
13     flowlayoutdemo ( )
14     {
15         setLayout(new FlowLayout(FlowLayout.LEFT));
16         layoutdemo obj = new layoutdemo ( );
17         addWindowListener(obj);
18         setTitle("Flow Layout Demo");
19         btn1 = new Button("Button 1");
20         btn2 = new Button("Button 2");
21         btn3 = new Button("Button 3");
22         btn4 = new Button("Button 4");
23         btn5 = new Button("Button 5");
24         setSize(250,200);
25         add(btn1);
26         add(btn2);
27         add(btn3);
28         add(btn4);
29         add(btn5);
30         setVisible(true);
31     }
32     public static void main(String arg[])
33     {
34         flowlayoutdemo obj1 = new flowlayoutdemo ( );
35     }
36  }
```

Explanation

Line 15

setLayout(new FlowLayout(FlowLayout.LEFT));

In this line, the **setLayout( )** method will set the layout of the frame window to **FlowLayout** and set the alignment of the layout to left. Now, all components that will be added into this frame window will be left aligned.

The output of Example 16 is displayed in Figure 11-30.

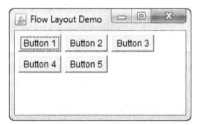

Figure 11-30 *The output of Example 16*

In this frame window, the buttons are placed in two rows because of the width of the frame window. Now, when you resize (widen) the window, the buttons placed in the second row will move to the first row, as shown in Figure 11-31.

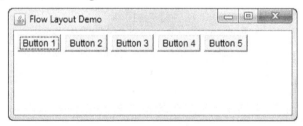

Figure 11-31 *The output of Example 16 after resizing the window*

BorderLayout

BorderLayout is the default layout manager of the frame or window. The border layout provides five regions, north, south, east, west, and center. In a regions, you can place only one component at a time. The components of north and south region are placed horizontally, whereas the components of east and west regions are placed vertically in the container window. The remaining empty space (between the horizontal and vertical areas) is filled by the component of the center region. The **BorderLayout** manager provides the following constants that can be used to select a particular region in a container window:

1.   BorderLayout.NORTH
2.   BorderLayout.SOUTH
3.   BorderLayout.EAST
4.   BorderLayout.WEST
5.   BorderLayout.CENTER

Adding a Component in a Region

You can add a component in one of the five regions given above using the **add( )** method. The syntax for using the **add( )** method to add component in a region is as follows:

```
add(Component obj, Object region)
```

In this syntax, the object **obj** of the **Component** class represents a component such as a button, text field, and so on. And, the **region** specifies a particular region in which the component **obj** will be placed.

Example 17

The following example illustrates the use of the **BorderLayout** layout manager. The program will set the layout of an applet to **BorderLayout**, add five buttons to different regions in it, and display the resultant applet window on the screen.

```
//Write a program to set the layout of an applet to border layout
1    import java.awt.*;
2    import java.applet.*;
3    //<applet code= "BorderLayoutDemo" width=300 height=150></applet>
4    public class BorderLayoutDemo extends Applet
5    {
6        Button btn1, btn2, btn3, btn4, btn5;
7        public void init( )
8        {
9            setLayout(new BorderLayout( ));
10           btn1 = new Button("Button 1");
11           btn2 = new Button("Button 2");
12           btn3 = new Button("Button 3");
13           btn4 = new Button("Button 4");
14           btn5 = new Button("Button 5");
15           add(btn1, BorderLayout.NORTH);
16           add(btn2, BorderLayout.SOUTH);
17           add(btn3, BorderLayout.EAST);
18           add(btn4, BorderLayout.WEST);
19           add(btn5, BorderLayout.CENTER);
20       }
21   }
```

Explanation

Line 9
setLayout(new BorderLayout( ));
In this line, the **setLayout( )** method will set the layout of the applet window to **BorderLayout**.

Line 10
btn1 = new Button("Button 1");
In this line, a new button control named **btn1** will be created with the label **Button 1**.

The working of lines from 11 to 14 is similar to line 10.

Line 15
add(btn1, BorderLayout.NORTH);
In this line, the **add( )** method will place the button **btn1** in the north region, which is specified by the constant **BorderLayout.NORTH** of the applet window.

The working of lines 16 to 19 is similar to that of line 15.

The output of Example 17 is displayed in Figure 11-32.

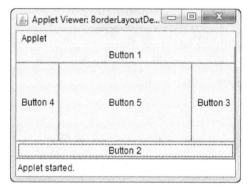

Figure 11-32 *The output of Example 17*

GridLayout

The **GridLayout** layout manager divides a container into a grid and places all components in it. A grid is just like a two-dimensional array containing rows and columns. In a grid, the height and width of all placed components are equal.

Constructors of the GridLayout

The **java.awt.BorderLayout** provides the following constructors to create a **GridLayout**:

```
GridLayout( )
GridLayout(int rows, int columns)
GridLayout(int rows, int columns, int horspace, int vertspace)
```

In these constructors, the first constructor creates a grid layout with default specifications and the grid contains only a single column. The second constructor creates a grid with number of rows and columns specified by the **rows** and **columns** variables, respectively. The third constructor creates a grid with specified number of rows and columns. In this constructor, the integer variables **horspace** and **vertspace** specify the horizontal and vertical space.

Example 18

The following example illustrates the use of the **GridLayout** layout manager. The program will set the layout of an applet to **GridLayout**, add five buttons to different regions in it, and display the resultant applet window on the screen.

//Write a program to set the layout of an applet to grid layout

```
1    import java.awt.*;
2    import java.applet.*;
3    //<applet code= "GridLayoutDemo" width=300 height=150></applet>
4    public class GridLayoutDemo extends Applet
5    {
6        Button btn1, btn2, btn3, btn4, btn5;
7        public void init( )
8        {
9            setLayout(new GridLayout(3, 2));
10           btn1 = new Button("Button 1");
11           btn2 = new Button("Button 2");
12           btn3 = new Button("Button 3");
13           btn4 = new Button("Button 4");
14           btn5 = new Button("Button 5");
15           add(btn1);
16           add(btn2);
17           add(btn3);
18           add(btn4);
19           add(btn5);
20       }
21   }
```

Explanation
Line 9
setLayout(new GridLayout(3, 2));
In this line, the **setLayout( )** method will set the layout of the applet window to **GridLayout**. Here, the grid will contain three rows and two columns.

Line 10
btn1 = new Button("Button 1");
In this line, a new button control **btn1** will be created with the label **Button 1**.

The working of lines from 11 to 14 is similar to line 10.

Line 15
add(btn1);
In this line, the **add( )** method will place the button **btn1** in the top-left cell.

The working of lines 16 to 19 is similar to that of line 15.

The output of Example 18 is displayed in Figure 11-33.

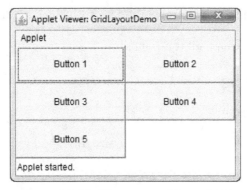

Figure 11-33 *The output of Example 18*

Self-Evaluation Test

Answer the following questions and then compare them to those given at the end of this chapter:

1. The _____ method is used to set the size of a frame window.

2. The _____ method of the **Graphics** class is used to draw a line inside a window.

3. The text of a label control is only a _____ text.

4. The _____ method is used to set the alignment of the text of a label control.

5. Three constants of the **Label** class are _____, _____, and _____.

6. Whenever a button is pressed, the _____ event is generated.

7. The _____ interface is implemented by a class to handle an action event.

8. A _____ control provides a single-line text area in which a user can enter text.

9. A _____ is a graphical component that has two states, _____ and _____.

10. A _____ control is a pop-up menu that contains a list of items.

11. The **drawLine( )** method of the **Graphics** class contains five parameters in its parameters list. (T/F)

12. The **Label** control does not generate any event. (T/F)

13. The **TextField** control generates an item event. (T/F)

14. The default layout manager of a frame window is **BorderLayout**. (T/F)

15. In the **GridLayout** manager, all components in a container are of same size. (T/F)

Review Questions

Answer the following questions:

1. Explain the methods that are used to set the size, title, and visibility of a frame window.

2. Explain the methods that are used to create and fill a rectangle.

3. Explain the methods that are used to set the text and alignment of text of a label.

4. Explain how to create a **Choice** control. Give an example as well.

5. Define a layout manager.

EXERCISES

Exercise 1

Write a program to create an applet window such that it accepts a value from the user whenever the **Click** button is pressed, and also displays the value on the screen.

Exercise 2

Write a program to create an applet window that contains a grid with nine buttons in three rows and three columns. The buttons should be labeled from 1 to 9.

Answers to Self-Evaluation Test
1. setSize( ), **2. drawLine( )**, **3.** read-only, **4. setAlignment( )**, **5. Label.LEFT**, **Label.RIGHT**,
Label.CENTER, **6.** action, **7. ActionListener**, **8. TextField**, **9.** check box, on, off, **10. choice**
11. F, **12.** T, **13.** F, **14.** T, **15.** T

Chapter 12

The Java I/O System

Learning Objectives

After completing this chapter, you will be able to:

- *Understand the Stream Class*
- *Understand the Byte Stream Classes*
- *Understand the Character Stream Classes*
- *Understand the Reader Stream Classes*
- *Understand the Writer Stream Classes*
- *Understand the File Class*
- *Understand the Random Access Files*

INTRODUCTION

In this chapter, you will learn about the Input/Output(I/O) files in Java. You will also learn about I/O operation in Java and the classes used for file handling. The chapter discusses in detail about the serialization process that helps an object to write data into the streams and read it back again. It also covers some file system operations, including random access files. Most of the classes covered in this chapter are from the **java.io** package or the **java.util** package. These packages are home to most of the classes that you will use in this chapter for performing input and output operations.

STREAM CLASSES

In Java terminology, **stream** means flow of data. A stream should always have a source and a destination. A stream is a sequence of information (bytes) of undetermined length that either brings in or takes out information to/from a source/destination. The Java stream classes either move information from an external source such as text file to Java or from Java to the external source/destination.

Most of the stream classes are part of the **java.io** package. There are various I/O Stream classes that can be used for handling I/O operation in Java. These classes can be grouped into two categories, as given below:

1.   The Byte Stream classes
2.   The Character Stream classes

The Byte Stream Classes

The byte stream classes perform I/O operations on bytes. You can use the byte stream classes for reading and writing bytes in streams and files. One of the limitations of these classes is that they can transmit data only in one direction. This means that flow of data using these classes are uni-directional. The byte stream classes contain the following two classes:

1.   The InputStream class
2.   The OutputStream class

The InputStream Class

The **InputStream** class is used to read bytes from the stream. Also, this class is used to read bytes or an array of bytes from an input source. The input source can be a file, a string, or a location that contains data to read. When you create an input stream, it is automatically opened. After reading, you do not need to close the input stream explicitly because if the object finds nothing in the data source, it closes implicitly. However, you can close an input stream explicitly by calling the **close()** method of the **InputStream** class.

The **InputStream** class can read the following sources:

1.   An array of bytes
2.   A file
3.   A pipe

The **InputStream** class supports a number of subclasses for various input related functions. Figure 12-1 shows various subclasses of the **InputStream** class.

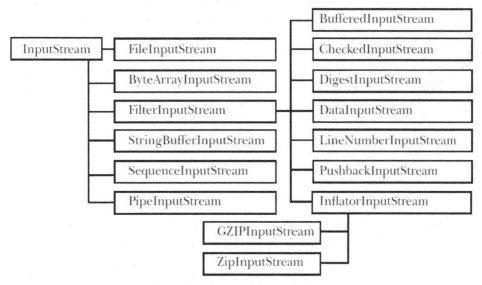

Figure 12-1 *Subclasses of the **InputStream** class*

The classes inherited from the **InputStream** class provided by the **java.io** package are used for various purposes, refer to Figure 12-1.

The **InputStream** class defines some methods that can be used for reading bytes or arrays of bytes, skipping bytes of input, resetting the current position of bytes within the stream, marking locations in the stream, and finding out the number of bytes available for reading. These methods are discussed next.

The available() Method
This method returns the number of bytes that can be read or skipped from the input stream without blocking the next call of the method for input stream.

The close() Method
This method is used to close the input stream and release the resources associated with it.

The mark() Method
This method is used to mark the current position of the input stream. The syntax for using the **mark()** method is as follows:

```
mark(int read_limit)
```

In this syntax, the **read_limit** parameter is an integer value. It indicates the maximum number of bytes that can be read before the mark position becomes invalidate.

The marksupported() Method

This method is used to test whether the input stream supports the **mark()** and **reset()** methods of the **InputStream** class. This method returns **True** when the stream instance supports the **mark()** and **reset()** methods. Otherwise, it returns **False**.

The read() Method

This method is used to read bytes next to the input stream. It returns the number of bytes as an integer value ranging from 0 to 255. It returns -1, when no byte is available to read or the stream reaches at the end of the file.

The read(byte[] byt) Method

This method reads some of the bytes from the input stream and stores these bytes into the **byt** buffer array. It returns the integer value that is equivalent to the number of bytes it reads. It returns -1, when no byte is available to read or the stream reaches at the end of the file. If **byt** is null, a **NullPointerException** is thrown. It returns zero, when the length of **byt** is zero.

The read(byte[] byt, int start, int len) Method

This method reads the **len** bytes of the data from input stream into the **byt** buffer array. It returns the integer value that is equivalent to the number of bytes it reads. It returns -1, when no byte is available to read or when the stream reaches at the end of the file. If **byt** is null, a **NullPointerException** is thrown. This method returns zero, if the length of **byt** is zero. If **start** or **len** is negative, or if the sum of the values of **start** and **len** is greater than the length of the buffer array **byt**, it will throw **IndexOutOfBoundsException**.

The reset() Method

This method is used to reposition the pointer input stream to the position where the **mark()** method was called last.

The skip() Method

This method is used to skip over or discard the bytes of data from the input stream. The **skip()** method returns the actual number of bytes skipped.

The syntax for using the **skip()** method is as follows:

```
skip(long n)
```

In this syntax, **n** is the number of bytes to be skipped. If **n** is negative, no bytes will be skipped.

The OutputStream Class

The **OutputStream** class is used to write bytes in the memory location. This class is used to write a byte or an array of bytes to an output source. The output sources can be a file, a string, or any memory location that contains data. When you create an output stream, it is automatically opened. After writing, you do not need to close the output stream explicitly because if the object finds nothing in the data source, it closes implicitly. However, you can close it explicitly by calling the **close()** method of the **OutputStream** class.

The **OutputStream** class can write bytes in three different sources, which are as follows:

1. An array of bytes
2. A file
3. A pipe

The **OutputStream** class supports a number of subclasses for various output related functions, which are shown in Figure 12-2.

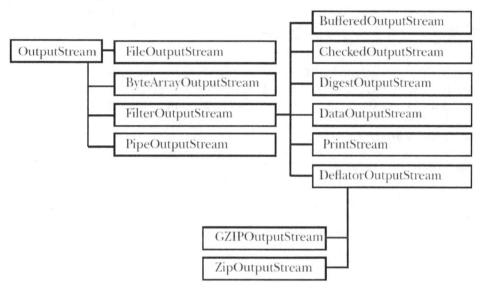

*Figure 12-2 Subclasses of the **OutputStream** class*

The classes inherited from the **OutputStream** class provided by the **java.io** package are used for different purposes.

The **OutputStream** class defines the methods of writing bytes or arrays of bytes to the stream and flushing out the stream. An output stream is automatically opened when you create it. You can explicitly close an output stream using the **close()** method or let it be closed implicitly when the object finds nothing in the data source. The methods provided by the **OutputStream** class are discussed next.

The write(int b) Method
This method writes the specified byte to the output stream. Generally, the functioning of this method is to write one (1) to the output stream.

The write(byte[] b) Method
This method writes the **b** bytes from the specified location or the byte array to the output stream. Here, **b** is the buffer array, which stores data to write.

The write(byte[] byt, int start, int len) Method

In this method, **byt** is the data in bytes, which you want to write into the source stream. The **start** is the integer value that indicates the position in the buffer array **byt**, where you want to write data, and **len** is the number of bytes to write.

The **write()** method of the **OutputStream** class writes the **len** bytes from the specified byte array, starting from the **start** position of the output stream. The general functioning of **write(byt, start, len)** is that some of the bytes in the array **byt** are written to the output stream. The order of writing bytes in the output stream is that the first byte is written as **byt[start]**, second as **byt[start+1]**, and this process continues till the last byte, which is written as **byt[start + len - 1]**.

If **byt** is null, the exception **NullPointerException** is thrown. The **read()** method returns zero, when the length of **byt** is zero. If **start** or **len** is negative or both **start** and **len** are greater than the length of the buffer array **byt**, it will throw the exception **IndexOutOfBoundsException**.

The flush() Method

The **flush()** method forces the buffered bytes to be written to the output stream. Calling the **flush()** method indicates that the previously written bytes have been buffered by the output stream and such bytes must be written immediately to their destination.

The close() Method

This method of the **OutputStream** class is used to close the output stream and release the system resources used by it.

Note

It is important to close the output files because sometimes the buffer does not get flushed out completely.

The Character Stream Classes

The character stream classes are used to read and write 16-bit Unicode characters. The functionality of these classes is similar to those of the byte stream classes. The advantage of using the character stream classes is that they do not follow a specific character, so they are not character dependent. Like the byte stream classes, the character stream classes also possess the following two types of classes:

1. The Reader Stream classes
2. The Writer Stream classes

Reader Stream Classes

The reader stream classes are used to read characters from files. The classes belonging to the reader stream classes are very similar to the **InputStream** class with the only difference that the **InputStream** class use bytes, whereas the reader stream classes use characters. In fact, both the classes use the same methods.

The hierarchy of the reader stream classes is given in Figure 12-3.

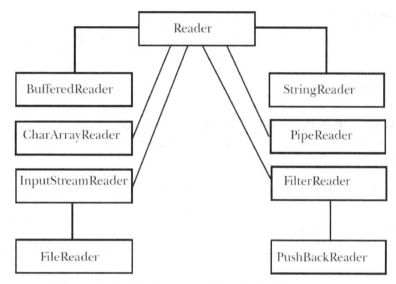

Figure 12-3 *The hierarchy of the Reader Stream classes*

Writer Stream Classes

The writer stream classes are used to write characters to files. The writer stream classes are similar to the **OutputStream** class with the only difference that the **OutputStream** class use bytes, whereas the writer stream classes use characters. Infact, both the classes use the same methods.

The hierarchy of the writer stream classes is given in Figure 12-4.

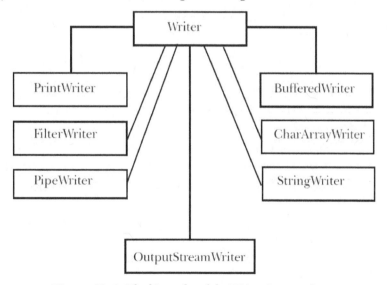

Figure 12-4 *The hierarchy of the Writer Stream classes*

THE FILE CLASS

The **File** class is used to create files and directories in Java. It belongs to the **java.io** package. This class performs various operations related to file handling. The **File** class can be used for creating, opening, closing, and deleting a file. You can also get the name and size of a file with the help of the **File** class.

Naming Conventions for Creating a File

There are some naming conventions that must be followed while creating a file. These conventions are as follows:

1. The name of file should be unique and of string type.

2. The name of file can be divided in two parts. For example, test.text and test.dat.

3. Before using any file, you should know its purpose, whether it is meant for writing, reading, or both.

4. Data type of the file operation, whether it will be in bytes or characters.

Example 1

The following example illustrates how to create a file in Java with the help of the **java.io** package. The program will create a text file on the current directory of a project.

//Write a program to create a file in Java

```
1    import java.io.*;
2    public class NewFile
3    {
4        public static void main(String[] args) throws IOException
5        {
6            File nf;
7            nf=new File("NewFile.txt");
8            if(!nf.exists())
9            {
10               nf.createNewFile();
11               System.out.println("A file with the name \"NewFile.txt\" is
                 created in your current directory");
12           }
13           else
14           System.out.println("The file with the name \"NewFile.txt\"
                 already exists");
15       }
16   }
```

Explanation

Line 6
File nf;
This line declares the **nf** object of the **File** class.

Line 7
nf=new File("NewFile.txt");
This line creates the **nf** object, and a file with the name *NewFile.txt* is passed as a string argument to the **File** class.

Lines 8 to 14
if(!nf.exists())
{
      nf.createNewFile();
      System.out.println("A file with the name \"NewFile.txt\" is created in your current directory");
}
else
System.out.println("The file with the name \"NewFile.txt\" already exists");

These block of lines indicate that if the file with the name *NewFile.txt* does not exist in the current directory of the project, it will be created in the current directory. In case, the *NewFile.txt* already exists, the control will pass to line 15 and the message **The file with the name "NewFile.txt" already exists** will be displayed. The property **exists()** checks whether the file *NewFile.txt* exists or not in the current directory. Whereas, the **createNewFile()** method creates a new file.

The output of Example 1 is displayed in Figure 12-5.

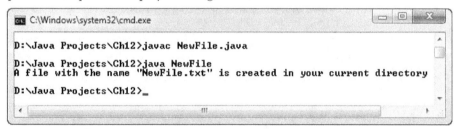

Figure 12-5 The output of Example 1

Reading and Writing a Character File
There are basically two classes that are used to read and write character files, the **FileReader** and **FileWriter** classes. Go through the next example to understand the concept of reading and writing files with characters.

Example 2

The following example illustrates the concept of reading and writing a file with character using the **FileReader** and **FileWriter** classes. The program will open an existing file, read it, and create another file with the same content as the existing file.

/* Write a program to open an existing file, read it, and create another file with the same content as the existing file */

```
1   import java.io.*;
2   class Characters
3   {
4       public static void main(String args[ ])
5       {
6           File OldFile=new File("OldFile.txt");
7           File NewFile=new File("NewFile.txt");
8           FileReader OldF=null;
9           FileWriter NewF=null;
10          try
11          {
12              OldF=new FileReader(OldFile);
13              NewF=new FileWriter(NewFile);
14              int ch;
15              while((ch=OldF.read())!=-1)
16              {
17                  NewF.write(ch);
18              }
19              System.out.println("A file with the name \"NewFile.txt\" is
                    created and written from the file \"OldFile.txt\" in your
                    current directory.");
20          }
21          catch(IOException e)
22          {
23              System.out.println(e);
24              System.exit(-1);
25          }
26          finally
27          {
28              try
29              {
30                  OldF.close();
31                  NewF.close();
32              }
33              catch(IOException e) {}
34          }
35      }
36  }
```

Before running this program, rename the existing file *NewFile.txt* to *OldFile.txt* in your current project directory. Also, write some contents in the file.

Explanation
Line 6
File OldFile=new File("OldFile.txt");
This line indicates that the **OldFile** object of the **File** class has been created and the existing file with the name *OldFile.txt* is passed as a string argument to the **File** class.

Line 7
File NewFile=new File("NewFile.txt");
This line indicates that another **NewFile** object of the **File** class has been created and a new file, which has to be created with the name *NewFile.txt*, is passed as a string argument to the **File** class.

Line 8
FileReader OldF=null;
This line indicates that an object with the name **OldF** of the **FileReader** class has been declared and initialized with the null value.

Line 9
FileWriter NewF=null;
This line indicates that an object with the name **NewF** of the **FileWriter** class has been declared and initialized with the null value.

Line 12
OldF=new FileReader(OldFile);
This line indicates that the **OldF** object has been created and the **OldFile** object is passed as an argument to the **FileReader** class.

Line 13
NewF=new FileWriter(NewFile);
This line indicates that the **NewF** object has been created and the **NewFile** object is passed as an argument to the **FileWriter** class.

Lines 15 to 18
while((ch=OldF.read())!=-1)
{
        NewF.write(ch);
}
These lines indicate that first the existing file *OldFile.txt* will be read and then the contents of this file will be written in the *NewFile.txt* file. The process of reading and writing the file will be on the basis of the characters and it will be continued till the control reaches to the end of the file.

Line 21
catch(IOException e)
This line indicates that an I/O exception will be raised, if any error is found in the I/O handling of the file.

Line 30
OldF.close();
This line will close the file **OldF** object for reading.

Line 31
NewF.close();
This line will close the file **NewF** object for writing.

The output of Example 2 is displayed in Figure 12-6.

```
C:\Windows\system32\cmd.exe

D:\Java Projects\Ch12>javac Characters.java

D:\Java Projects\Ch12>java Characters
A file with the name "NewFile.txt" is created and written from the file "OldFile
.txt" in your current directory.

D:\Java Projects\Ch12>_
```

Figure 12-6 The output of Example 2

Reading and Writing a File with Bytes

There are two classes that can be used for reading and writing a byte file. These classes are **FileInputStream** and **FileOutputStream**.

Example 3

The following example illustrates the concept of reading and writing a file with bytes using the **FileInputStream** and **FileOutputStream** classes. The program will create a new file and write some byte contents in it.

//Write a program that will create a new file and write some byte contents in it.

```
1   import java.io.*;
2   class Bytes
3   {
4      public static void main(String args[])
5      {
6         byte states []={'C','A','L','I','F','O','R','N','I','A','\t',
          'F','L','O','R','I','D','A'};
7         FileOutputStream NewFile=null;
8         try
9         {
10           NewFile=new FileOutputStream("states.txt");
11           NewFile.write(states);
12           System.out.println("The byte file with the name \"states.txt\"
             has been created in your current directory");
13           NewFile.close();
14        }
15        catch(IOException e)
16        {
17           System.out.println(e);
18           System.exit(-1);
19        }
20     }
21  }
```

Explanation

Line 6

byte states []={'C','A','L','I','F','O','R','N','I','A','\t','F','L','O','R','I','D','A'};

This line indicates that an array **states** of the byte data type has been declared and initialized with some letters.

Line 7
FileOutputStream NewFile=null;
This line indicates that an object named **NewFile** of the **FileOutputStream** class has been declared and initialized with the **null** value.

Line 10
NewFile=new FileOutputStream("states.txt");
This line indicates that the **NewFile** object has been created and the file *states.txt* is passed as an argument to the constructor of the **FileOutputStream** class.

Line 11
NewFile.write(states);
This line will write the contents of the **states** variable to the **NewFile** object with the help of the **write()** method.

Line 13
NewFile.close();
This line will close the **NewFile** object for writing.

Line 15
catch(IOException e)
This line indicates that an I/O exception will be raised, if any error is found in I/O handling of the file.

The output of Example 3 is displayed in Figure 12-7.

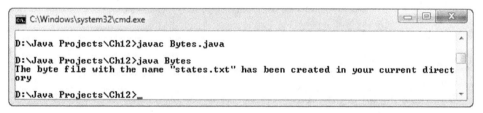

Figure 12-7 *The output of Example 3*

RANDOM ACCESS FILES

Random access means ability to access any location within a file and then read or write the data to that location in the file. The **java.io** package provides the **RandomAccessFile** class that can be used to read and write the text, bytes, or primitive Java data types of the file at any location. It treats class as a collection of records.

The **RandomAccessFile** class provides a pointer to a file that behaves like an index and indicates the location from where the read or write operation will start. This class implements both the interfaces **DataInput** and **DataOutput** to read and write the data into files.

The following code of Java is used to create an instance of the **RandomAccessFile** class to read and write the file:

```
RandomAccessFile Ran_File = new RandomAccessFile(File_name, "r");
```

This code creates an instance of the **RandomAccessFile** class. The **RandomAccessFile()** constructor takes two arguments: First is the file name that is used to read and write the data, and second is the operation mode that can be read (r) or read-write (rw) mode. The above code is used to open the file in the read mode (r).

The following code is used to open the file in the read-write mode:

```
RandomAccessFile Ran_File = new RandomAccessFile(File_name, "rw");
```

The **RandomAccessFile** constructor checks the existence of the file that you passed as an argument. If the file does not exist, it will throw an **IOException**. Also, if an attempt is made to read the end of the file, the **read()** method will throw the exception **EOFException** (which is a part of the **IOException**).

The **RandomAccessFile** class provides various methods for different operations. These methods are as follows:

      Close()
      getChannel()
      getFD()
      getFilePointer()
      length()
      read()
      read(byte [] b))
      read(byte [] b, int off, int len)
      write(byte [] b))
      write(byte [] b, int off, int len)
      write(int b)
      seek(long pos)
      setLength(long newLength)
      skipBytes()

Example 4

The following example illustrates the concept of writing a file using the **RandomAccessFile** class and its methods. The program will illustrate the concept of writing a file using the **RandomAccessFile** class.

/* Write a program that will open the existing file in the read-write mode and write bytes in it */

```
1    import java.io.*;
2    public class RandomAccessFileDemo
3    {
4        public static void main(String[] args)
5        {
6            try
7            {
8                BufferedReader inF = new BufferedReader(new
                 InputStreamReader(System.in));
9                System.out.print("Enter File name : ");
10               String str = inF.readLine();
11               File file = new File(str);
12               if(!file.exists())
13               {
14                   System.out.println("File does not exist.");
15                   System.exit(0);
16               }
17               RandomAccessFile rndFile = new RandomAccessFile(file,"rw");
18               rndFile.seek(file.length());
19               rndFile.writeBytes("www.cadcim.com");
20               rndFile.writeBytes("The random access means to go any
                 location within the file.");
21               rndFile.close();
22               System.out.println("Write Successfully");
23           }
24           catch(IOException e)
25           {
26               System.out.println(e.getMessage());
27           }
28       }
29   }
```

Explanation
Line 8
BufferedReader inF = new BufferedReader(new InputStreamReader(System.in));
This line indicates that an **inF** object of the **BufferedReader** class been created and the instance of the **InputStreamReader** class is passed as an argument. The argument **System.in** of the constructor of the **InputStreamReader** class is used to read the user's input.

Line 9
System.out.print("Enter File name : ");
This line will prompt a message **Enter File name**.

Line 10
String str = in.readLine();
This line declares the **str** variable as **String** and assigns the value entered by the user (file name) to it.

Line 11

File file = new File(str);

This line indicates that an **file** object of the **File** class has been created and initialized by passing the file name as string (**str**) to the constructor of the **File** class.

Lines 12 to 16

if(!file.exists())

{

   System.out.println("File does not exist.");

   System.exit(0);

}

These lines check the existence of the specified file. If the file does not exist, they will print a message **File does not exist.**, and the program will exit without executing the rest of the codes.

Line 17

RandomAccessFile rndFile = new RandomAccessFile(file, "rw");

This line indicates that an **rndFile** object of the **RandomAccessFile** class has been created and it is initialized by passing the **file** object and the mode **rw** as String (**r** for read and **rw** for read-write) to the constructor of the **RandomAccessFile** class.

Line 18

rndFile.seek(file.length());

This line will set the file-pointer to the end of the file. Here, the **file.length()** function will return the length of the file, which is passed as an argument to the **seek()** method. The **seek()** method sets the file-pointer to the position indicated by the value returned by **file.length()**.

Lines 19 to 22

rndFile.writeBytes("www.cadcim.com");

rndFile.writeBytes("The random access means to go any location within the file.");

rndFile.close();

System.out.println("Write Successfully");

These lines will write bytes to the file. The **writeBytes()** method of the **RandomAccessFile** class takes string as an argument and writes it to the file. Make sure the file is opened in the write mode. The **close()** method of the **RandomAccessFile** class will close the random access file stream and set the resources used by the program free.

Lines 24 to 27

catch(IOException e)

{

System.out.println(e.getMessage());

}

These lines will handle the error, which will occur due to the I/O operation. Here, the function **e.getMessage()** returns the text message regarding the error.

The output of Example 4 is displayed in Figure 12-8.

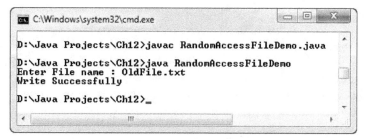

Figure 12-8 *The output of Example 4*

Example 5

The following example illustrates the concept of reading a file using the **RandomAccessFile** class and its methods. The program will read an existing file and write bytes in it.

```
//Write a program that will open the existing file in the read mode and write bytes in it.
1    import java.io.*;
2    public class File_read
3    {
4        public static void main(String[] args)
5        {
6            try
7            {
8                BufferedReader inF = new BufferedReader(new
                     InputStreamReader(System.in));
9                System.out.print("Enter File name : ");
10               String strFile = inF.readLine();
11               File file = new File(strFile);
12               if(!file.exists())
13               {
14                   System.out.println("File does not exist.");
15                   System.exit(0);
16               }
17               RandomAccessFile rndFile = new RandomAccessFile(file,"r");
18               int ctrl=(int)rndFile.length();
19               System.out.println("Length: " + ctrl);
20               rndFile.seek(0);
21               for(int ct = 0; ct < ctrl; ct++)
22               {
23                   byte b = rndFile.readByte();
24                   System.out.print((char)b);
25               }
26               rndFile.close();
27           }
28           catch(IOException e)
29           {
30               System.out.println(e.getMessage());
31           }
32       }
33   }
```

Explanation

Line 8
BufferedReader inF = new BufferedReader(new InputStreamReader(System.in));
This line indicates that an **inF** object of the **BufferedReader** class been created and the instance of the **InputStreamReader** class is passed as an argument. The argument **System.in** of the constructor of the **InputStreamReader** class is used to read the user's input.

Line 9
System.out.print("Enter File name : ");
This line will prompt a message **Enter File name**.

Line 10
String strFile = inF.readLine();
This line declares the **strFile** variable as **String** and assigns the value entered by the user (file name) to it.

Line 11
File file = new File(strFile);
This line indicates that an **file** object of the **File** class has been created and it is initialized by passing the file name as string (**strFile**) to the constructor of the **File** class.

Lines 12 to 16
if(!file.exists())
{
**   System.out.println("File does not exist.");**
**   System.exit(0);**
}
These lines check the existence of the file. If the file does not exist, it will print a message **File does not exist.** and the program will exit without executing the rest of the codes.

Line 17
RandomAccessFile rndFile = new RandomAccessFile(file,"r");
This line indicates that an **rndFile** object of the **RandomAccessFile** class has been created and it is initialized by passing the **file** object and mode **r** as string(**r** for read and **rw** for read-write) to the constructor of the **RandomAccessFile** class.

Lines 18
int ctrl=(int)rndFile.length();
These lines indicate that the **ctrl** variable is declared as **int**. Also, the **ctrl** variable has been assigned with a value returned by **rndFile.length()**. Here, **rndFile.length()** returns the length of the file that you assign at the declaration of the **rndFile** object (line 17).

Line 19
System.out.println("Length: " + ctrl);
This line will print **Length:** and the value of **ctrl**.

Line 20
rndFile.seek(0);
In this line, the **seek()** method of the **RandomAccessFile** class sets the file-pointer to the beginning of the file, at which the next read or write event occurs.

Lines 21 to 25
for(int ct = 0; ct < ctrl; ct++)
{

  byte b = rndFile.readByte();
  System.out.print((char)b);

}
These lines will read bytes from the file. The **rndFile.readByte()** method will read bytes from the existing file, which is passed as an argument (in line 17). The **for** loop will be executed till **rndFile.readByte()** reads bytes from the file, and **(char)b** will convert bytes to character.

Lines 28 to 31
catch(IOException e)
{

  System.out.println(e.getMessage());

}
These lines will handle the error, which occurs during to the I/O operation. Here, the **e.getMessage()** method will return the text message regarding the error.

The output of Example 5 is displayed in Figure 12-9.

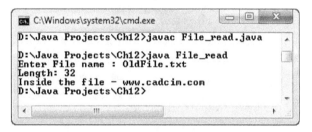

Figure 12-9 *The output of Example 5*

Self-Evaluation Test

Answer the following questions and then compare them to those given at the end of this chapter:

1. The term **stream** indicates the _____ of data.

2. The byte stream classes perform the input/output operations on _____.

3. The names of the classes that are used for reading and writing byte files are _____ and _____.

4. The **InputStream** class is used to read bytes from the _____.

5. The **OutputStream** class is used to write the bytes to the _____ location.

6. The Reader Stream classes are used to read _____ from files.

7. The _____ method is used to mark the current position in the input stream.

8. The _____ class extends the **FilterInputStream** class.

9. The **Character Stream** classes contain two types of classes: _____ and _____.

10. There are basically two class for reading and writing character files,_____ and _____ classes.

Review Questions

Answer the following questions:

1. List different types of the stream classes.

2. Write different sources that can be read by the **InputStream** class.

3. What is the **reset()** method? Explain.

4. Define the **OutputStream** class.

5. Create a file with the help of the **File** class.

EXERCISES
Exercise 1

Write a program to read the bytes from existing file.

Exercise 2

Write a program to append the bytes in the existing file using the **RandomAccessFile** class.

Answers to Self-Evaluation Test
1. flow, **2.** bytes, **3. FileInputStream, FileOutputStream, 4.** stream, **5.** memory, **6.** characters,
7. mark(), 8. DataInputStream, 9. Reader Stream, Writer Stream, **10. FileReader, FileWriter**

Index

This page intentionally left blank

Other Publications by CADCIM Technologies

The following is the list of some of the publications by CADCIM Technologies. Please visit *www.cadcim.com* for the complete listing.

CINEMA 4D Textbooks
- MAXON CINEMA 4D Studio R18: A Tutorial Approach, 5th Edition
- MAXON CINEMA 4D Studio R17: A Tutorial Approach, 4th Edition
- MAXON CINEMA 4D Studio R16: A Tutorial Approach, 3rd Edition
- MAXON CINEMA 4D Studio R15: A Tutorial Approach

Autodesk 3ds Max Design Textbooks
- Autodesk 3ds Max Design 2015: A Tutorial Approach, 15th Edition
- Autodesk 3ds Max Design 2014: A Tutorial Approach
- Autodesk 3ds Max Design 2013: A Tutorial Approach
- Autodesk 3ds Max Design 2012: A Tutorial Approach
- Autodesk 3ds Max Design 2011: A Tutorial Approach

Autodesk 3ds Max Textbooks
- Autodesk 3ds Max 2017 for Beginners: A Tutorial Approach, 17th Edition
- Autodesk 3ds Max 2016 for Beginners: A Tutorial Approach, 16th Edition
- Autodesk 3ds Max 2017: A Comprehensive Guide, 17th Edition
- Autodesk 3ds Max 2016: A Comprehensive Guide, 16th Edition
- Autodesk 3ds Max 2015: A Comprehensive Guide, 15th Edition
- Autodesk 3ds Max 2014: A Comprehensive Guide
- Autodesk 3ds Max 2013: A Comprehensive Guide
- Autodesk 3ds Max 2012: A Comprehensive Guide

Autodesk Maya Textbooks
- Autodesk Maya 2017: A Comprehensive Guide, 9th Edition
- Autodesk Maya 2016: A Comprehensive Guide, 8th Edition
- Autodesk Maya 2015: A Comprehensive Guide, 7th Edition
- Autodesk Maya 2014: A Comprehensive Guide
- Autodesk Maya 2013: A Comprehensive Guide
- Autodesk Maya 2012 A Comprehensive Guide

Digital Modeling Textbook
- Exploring Digital Modeling using 3ds Max and Maya 2015

Fusion Textbooks
- Blackmagic Design Fusion 7 Studio: A Tutorial Approach, 3rd Edition
- The eyeon Fusion 6.3: A Tutorial Approach

Flash Textbooks
- Adobe Flash Professional CC 2015: A Tutorial Approach, 3rd Edition
- Adobe Flash Professional CC: A Tutorial Approach
- Adobe Flash Professional CS6: A Tutorial Approach

ZBrush Textbooks
- Pixologic ZBrush 4R7: A Comprehensive Guide, 3rd Edition
- Pixologic ZBrush 4R6: A Comprehensive Guide

Premiere Textbooks
- Adobe Premiere Pro CC: A Tutorial Approach
- Adobe Premiere Pro CS6: A Tutorial Approach
- Adobe Premiere Pro CS5.5: A Tutorial Approach

Nuke Textbook
- The Foundry NukeX 7 for Compositors

Autodesk Softimage Textbooks
- Autodesk Softimage 2014: A Tutorial Approach
- Autodesk Softimage 2013: A Tutorial Approach

AutoCAD Electrical Textbooks
- AutoCAD Electrical 2017 for Electrical Control Designers, 8th Edition
- AutoCAD Electrical 2016 for Electrical Control Designers, 7th Edition
- AutoCAD Electrical 2015 for Electrical Control Designers, 6th Edition
- AutoCAD Electrical 2014 for Electrical Control Designers, 5th Edition
- AutoCAD Electrical 2013 for Electrical Control Designers
- AutoCAD Electrical 2012 for Electrical Control Designers

AutoCAD Textbooks
- AutoCAD 2017: A Problem-Solving Approach, Basic and Intermediate, 23rd Edition
- AutoCAD 2017: A Problem-Solving Approach, 3D and Advanced, 23rd Edition

SOLIDWORKS Textbooks
- SOLIDWORKS 2017 for Designers, 15th Edition
- SOLIDWORKS 2016 for Designers, 14th Edition
- SOLIDWORKS 2015 for Designers, 13th Edition
- SolidWorks 2014 for Designers, 12th Edition

Autodesk Inventor Textbooks
- Autodesk Inventor 2017 for Designers, 17th Edition
- Autodesk Inventor 2016 for Designers, 16th Edition
- Autodesk Inventor 2015 for Designers, 15th Edition
- Autodesk Inventor 2014 for Designers

CATIA Textbooks
- CATIA V5-6R2016 for Designers, 14th Edition
- CATIA V5-6R2015 for Designers, 13th Edition
- CATIA V5-6R2014 for Designers, 12th Edition
- CATIA V5-6R2013 for Designers, 11th Edition
- CATIA V-5R21 for Designers

Autodesk Revit Architecture Textbooks
- Exploring Autodesk Revit 2017 for Architecture, 13th Edition
- Autodesk Revit Architecture 2016 for Architects and Designers, 12th Edition
- Autodesk Revit Architecture 2015 for Architects and Designers, 11th Edition

Autodesk Revit Structure Textbooks
- Exploring Autodesk Revit 2017 for Structure, 7th Edition
- Exploring Autodesk Revit Structure 2016, 6th Edition
- Exploring Autodesk Revit Structure 2015, 5th Edition

Computer Programming Textbooks
- Learning Oracle 12c: A PL/SQL Approach, 2nd Edition
- Introduction to C++ Programming, 2nd Edition
- Learning ASP.NET AJAX

Textbooks Authored by CADCIM Technologies and Published by Other Publishers

3D Studio MAX and VIZ Textbooks
- Learning 3DS Max: A Tutorial Approach, Release 4
  Goodheart-Wilcox Publishers (USA)
- Learning 3D Studio VIZ: A Tutorial Approach
  Goodheart-Wilcox Publishers (USA)

CADCIM Technologies Textbooks Translated in Other Languages

SolidWorks Textbooks
- SolidWorks 2008 for Designers (Serbian Edition)
  Mikro Knjiga Publishing Company, Serbia
- SolidWorks 2006 for Designers (Russian Edition)
  Piter Publishing Press, Russia
- SolidWorks 2006 for Designers (Serbian Edition)
  Mikro Knjiga Publishing Company, Serbia

NX Textbooks
- NX 6 for Designers (Korean Edition)
  Onsolutions, South Korea
- NX 5 for Designers (Korean Edition)
  Onsolutions, South Korea

Pro/ENGINEER Textbooks
- Pro/ENGINEER Wildfire 4.0 for Designers (Korean Edition)
  HongReung Science Publishing Company, South Korea
- Pro/ENGINEER Wildfire 3.0 for Designers (Korean Edition)
  HongReung Science Publishing Company, South Korea

Autodesk 3ds Max Textbook
- 3ds Max 2008: A Comprehensive Guide (Serbian Edition)
  Mikro Knjiga Publishing Company, Serbia

AutoCAD Textbooks
- AutoCAD 2006 (Russian Edition)
  Piter Publishing Press, Russia
- AutoCAD 2005 (Russian Edition)
  Piter Publishing Press, Russia

Coming Soon from CADCIM Technologies
- Exploring ETABS
- Exploring ArcGIS
- Mold Design using NX 11.0: A Tutorial Approach
- Autodesk Fusion 360: A Tutorial Approach
- Introducing PHP/MySQL
- Blender 2.77 for Digital Artists
- Modo 10.0 for Digital Artists

Online Training Program Offered by CADCIM Technologies

CADCIM Technologies provides effective and affordable virtual online training on various software packages including computer programming languages, Computer Aided Design and , Manufacturing, and Engineering (CAD/CAM/CAE), animation, architecture, and GIS. The training will be delivered 'live' via Internet at any time, any place, and at any pace to individuals as well as the students of colleges, universities, and CAD/CAM/CAE training centers. For more information, please visit the following link: *www.cadcim.com*